Understanding
the Sociology of Health

Understanding
the Sociology of Health

3rd edition

Anne-Marie **Barry** and Chris **Yuill**

SAGE

Los Angeles | London | New Delhi
Singapore | Washington DC

First edition published 2002, reprinted 2003.
Second edition published 2008, reprinted twice in 2010, 2011
This edition published 2012

SAGE Publications Ltd
1 Oliver's Yard
55 City Road
London EC1Y 1SP

SAGE Publications Inc.
2455 Teller Road
Thousand Oaks, California 91320

SAGE Publications India Pvt Ltd
B 1/I 1 Mohan Cooperative Industrial Area
Mathura Road
New Delhi 110 044

SAGE Publications Asia-Pacific Pte Ltd
3 Church Street
#10-04 Samsung Hub
Singapore 049483

Library of Congress Control Number: 2011930328

British Library Cataloguing in Publication data

A catalogue record for this book is available from the British Library

ISBN 978-1-4462-0187–9
ISBN 978-1-4462-0188–6 (pbk)

Typeset by C&M Digitals (P) Ltd, Chennai, India
Printed by MPG Books Group, Bodmin, Cornwall
Printed on paper from sustainable resources

Brief Contents

Table of Contents

About the authors

Anne-Marie Barry is a research consultant in Edinburgh and former lecturer in health sociology at Robert Gordon University, Aberdeen. Her research interests primarily focus on social inequalities and health and wellbeing and have also included alcohol and drug use, sexual health, mental health and bereavement.

Chris Yuill is a lecturer at Robert Gordon University, Aberdeen. In addition to *Understanding the Sociology of Health* he has co-authored other textbooks on health and on sociology with Sage, including *Key Concepts in Health Studies* (with Iain Crinson and Eilidh Duncan) and *Sociology for Social Work* (with Alastair Gibson), both published in 2010. Chris has additionally published a variety of journal articles exploring the relationships between alienation and health, and aspects of urban experience. He is also a member of the British Sociological Association and until recently has sat as a member of both its national council and national executive, where he held responsibility for the publishing activities of the association.

Acknowledgements

We would like to thank Joyce Lishman for being such a wonderful head of school and creating an academic culture that encouraged both the pursuit of new knowledge and the conveying of what is all ready known in a manner that is clear, concise but still challenging.

Special mention must go to Emma Milman at Sage, who kept the project on track with her timely reminders and endless enthusiasm. We also deeply appreciate the input and words of advice from the various anonymous referees who commented on various drafts of the chapters.

Chris would also like to thank Ruth, Sophie and Jo for allowing him to type just a little bit too noisely in the evenings!

Finally, a mention for the Old East Stand and for everyone who enjoyed it's less than splendid decor and general decrepitude, and drunk the too hot coffee, downed the fantastic pies and pizzas at half-time, but more importantly *stood* and watched a game of football there.

Every effort has been made to trace all copyright holders for, but if any have been inadvertently overlooked the publishers will be pleased to make the necessary arrangement at the first opportunity.

Companion website

Visit the companion website at www.sagepub.co.uk/barryandyuill3e to find a range of teaching and learning material for lecturers and students including the following.

For lecturers:

- Tutors' notes: This useful resource sets out seminar plans to correspond to each chapter of the book. Each seminar plan relates to the main points in the chapter and includes further reading and discussion questions.
- PowerPoint slides: Each chapter has its own dedicated PowerPoint slide show. These can be used as they are or adapted to meet a lecturers' particular needs.

For students:

- Online readings: A range of free, in-depth, scholarly articles are available to complement each chapter of the book.
- Web links: These websites will help you to further explore the issues you have learned about in each chapter of the book.
- Glossary: Sociology can often present new concepts and ideas that can be a little daunting to grasp at first. This glossary is an accessible collection of key concepts and terms.
- Podcasts: The authors have created podcasts which are directly related to the material in the book.

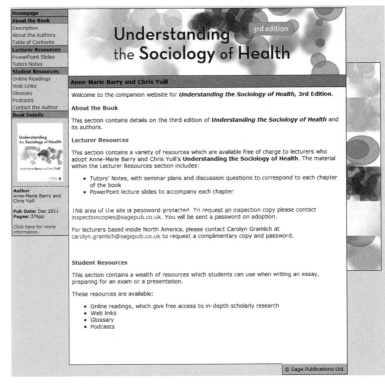

Introduction

The book you are now reading should not be regarded as being as all there is to *Understanding the Sociology of Health*. It is just one part of an overall package that offers web-based material, links to further reading and other learning materials (such as podcasts). All of the additional material just mentioned can be found on the companion website and all you have to do in order into access that material is complete the online registration. We also hope to regularly add new material on the companion website in order to keep the resources there as current as possible. There is also an option available on the companion website that allows you the reader to contact us the authors. We would be happy to hear from readers about their experiences of using the textbook and suggestions for additional material or resources that could be added to the companion website.

It will be this book, however, that will be the main resource for most readers. As with all introductory texts one has to be selective in the material that is covered. There are so many fascinating and stimulating ideas, concepts, theories and pieces of research out there being produced by medical sociologists and other social scientists that it is impossible to cover everything. What we have chosen to do instead is to try and cover what we would consider to be the essential starting points for understanding the sociology of health (for example, how class, gender and ethnicity interweave with health), plus some of the more advanced debates (for example on income inequality) that are reshaping our understanding of health and that have a resonance beyond academia. We have also chosen to keep the style as straightforward as possible but without losing sight that ideas and learning should also be challenging and stimulating. So, hopefully, we have avoided being too conversational or lapsing into the obscure phrases of complex academic jargon. If you do wish to pursue topics in greater depth then each chapter ends with suggestions for further reading, and more in-depth readings written by leading academics on particular topics can be downloaded from the companion website.

Throughout the book you will see various features that we hope will you assist in the understanding and learning of the sociology of health. These features are found embedded in the text and in the introductions and conclusions of each chapter. The features include:

- An opening summary of the main points, issues and concepts that are covered in a chapter.
- A list of keywords that indicate the main content of a chapter.
- *Definitions*, which provide clear and concise definitions of key concepts and terms.
- *Questions*, which allow the reader to reflect on issues and topics raised in the text.
- *Links*, which indicate where related information in other chapters can be found.
- And finally, each chapter ends with a summary of the main points that were discussed in the chapter and a case study that allows the reader to apply the *knowledge* they have gained of a particular subject within the sociology of health to a particular situation.

The book unfolds in the following three sections. The first section 'Theories, Perspectives and Concepts' (Chapters 1–5) provides an overview of sociological perspectives on health and how we can scientifically and objectively research and understand society. This perspective begins in Chapter 1 by exploring and defining the remit of sociology as a discipline, the various types of sociological theory and how developing a sociological imagination can open new insights into health. We then move on, in Chapters 2–4, to interrogate medicine as the dominant mode of understanding health. The discussion of which involves tracing the historical roots of medicine in The Enlightenment. Attention then turns in Chapter 5 to how sociology attempts to understand health and the variety of approaches and methods that socioogists use in their research.

The second section 'Key Themes' (Chapters 6–12) focuses on several important issues within the sociology of health. We discuss, for example, some of the main forms of inequality in society relating to class, gender, ethnicity and sexuality and how those social processes shape and condition health. The chapter on class has been extensively revised to include a fuller discussion of Wilkinson and Pickett's (2009) work on income inequality as outlined in *The Spirit Level*, while we have a new chapter on sexnalities and health that examines how prevailing social prejudices impact on the health of lesbian, gay, bisexual and tansgendered people. This section also outlines sociological approaches to mental health, as well as offering sociological perspectives on ageing and the lifecourse.

The third section, 'Contexts' (13–17) also introduces new chapters that explore and discnss health in relation to sport, death and dying, and the history of health and healing. The sport chapter examines how sport is interwoven into wider social dynamics and is not necessarily all about health. The death and dying chapter centers on contemporary debates about whether or not modem society seeks to deny or accept the existence of death. While the final new chapter in this publication outlines the history of health and healing and provides a more thorough account of the historical aspects of health than are available elsewhere in this book.

The two original chapters that cover places of care, in particular the differences between communities and institutions, and health policy remain.

Overall, we trust that this book is enjoyable to read and will provide you with helpful and useful resources for the study of the sociology of health.

SECTION 1

Theories, Perspectives and Concepts

1

Sociological theory: explaining and theorising

Main points

● Sociology is a scientific approach to understanding people in society.
● Social structures can often exert more influence over our behaviour than we would expect.
● Sociological perspectives on health emphasise that it is vital to understand the social in order to fully understand health and illness.
● The sociological imagination invites us to think beyond our own subjective perceptions.
● Sociological theories are useful in moving away from common-sense under-standings of society.

Key concepts

The sociological imagination   structure   agency   theory   discourse functionalism symbolic interactionism   Marxism   feminism   discourse   postmodernism.

Introduction

The aim of this chapter is to introduce the discipline of **sociology** and to focus, in particular, on the significance of the sociological study of health, illness and medicine for health-related professions. In order to do so it is necessary to begin by establishing the scope and remit of sociology as a subject area *and* as an explanatory method.

Sociology is concerned with the study of **society**, and specifically with key issues such as explaining change and the distribution of power between different social groups. The discipline of sociology also offers its students specific methods of investigation and explanation. For example, this chapter introduces you to the concept of the **sociological imagination**, asking you to adopt a critical and questioning approach to even the most mundane aspects of social life. Sociological knowledge is based on a 'scientific' approach built upon evidence to support theoretical perspectives. This chapter offers an introduction to a range of sociological perspectives.

Sociology: a method of enquiry and explanation

The raw material of sociology is human society, the development of groups, and the ways in which social groups are organised and change over time. Sociology is, therefore, the study of society. Such a statement, however, tells us very little about sociology and does nothing to draw out what is distinctive about the discipline in relation, for example, to psychology or simply to our own observations of society and social groups. Sociology is concerned with the study of human society (Giddens 1994: 7) in terms of the interaction between individuals and groups and the interaction between groups. It is not individuals *per se* who draw our attention, but how they interact with the social environment. Giddens uses the term 'society' to refer to 'a cluster, or system of institutionalised modes of conduct' (1986: 8). Sociologists refer to society as a 'system' and our own behaviour as 'institutionalised' to draw attention to what is external to the individual, that is 'society' itself. 'Society' refers to the structural or external factors that influence our beliefs and behaviour and that establish some predictability and regularity in our lives.

Sociology is the study of the interaction between groups and individuals in human society. The term society refers to a range of external factors that influence our beliefs and behaviours.

What troubles many new students of sociology is the suggestion that something referred to as 'society' shapes or determines our behaviour. Such an explanation seems to take away what is individual about us and suggests that our behaviour and our beliefs are not unique but may be determined by an external force and replicated by many other individuals. On reflection, however, this process of shaping and influencing is evident in all that we do. **Socialisation** into the norms and values of a particular society enables us to predict and make sense of the behaviour of others and ourselves. 'Society' provides us with the cultural resources to live in the social world because patterns of behaviour, responses and ways of behaving are not invented anew each day but exist outside any one individual. In most human

Socialisation refers to the process whereby we become aware of the values and beliefs of society.

encounters within a specific society, there are roles to be played out, responses to be predicted and cues to be acted upon.

Questions

Pause for a moment and ask yourself how many of our own actions and responses are automatic in the sense that we 'know' how to act in that given situation.

Rosenhan's study 'On being sane in insane places' (1973) is an excellent illustration of the potential for our identities to be imposed on us by others. Rosenhan's experiment involved eight researchers posing as 'insane' who presented themselves to mental health professionals, claiming to hear voices. Apart from the supposed symptoms, the researchers told the truth about their circumstances and background. All eight researchers were admitted to hospital. Except for the initial alleged symptoms, the researchers acted normally and upon admittance stated that they no longer had any symptoms. According to Rosenhan, it is therefore problematic to say that we 'know' what insanity is. The medical professionals in this case responded to certain cues (alleged symptoms) and interpreted the researchers' behaviour and histories in the light of their assumed insanity. This experiment is important in so far as it illustrates the way in which others can impose identities upon us. The behaviour of the researchers was interpreted in the light of a set of shared symbols and meanings. In this case, the shared symbols and meanings referred to the diagnostic categories developed and used by the medical profession. The diagnosis of insanity only had meaning in the light of these categories. This particular experience begs the question of whether patients actually present 'real' symptoms or whether the symptoms are in the minds of the people who make the diagnosis.

A further example of the way and extent to which the group influences individual behaviour can be illustrated with reference to the work of Festinger et al. (1956). In this case, the group was a cult that was prophesying the end of the world by a very specific date and time. When the prophecy was proven false, the beliefs of the group members were *not* fundamentally altered. A message from God, relayed by the group leader, indicated that the end of the world was not to happen at this point after all, since the group manifested such goodness that the world would be saved from destruction. Festinger then asks why beliefs persist even in the light of contradictory evidence. The explanation lies within the group itself and its ability to reinforce the original belief. The power to do so is greater when the group consists of a close network without any dissenters. Festinger notes that, in this case, people who had been part of the group but who had not gathered in one place prior to the alleged catastrophe did not show the same adherence to the original prophecy.

Links

Chapter 6 provides an example of the complex relationship between structural factors and personal choice in relation to health inequalities.

The relationship between society and individuals

Thus far this discussion has been concerned to demonstrate what sociology 'is' by examining the subject matter or what has been referred to as the 'raw material' of study, namely society. However, the discussion has developed further in terms of suggesting a specific and distinct relationship between individuals and the society or **structure** in which they live. A helpful example of the way in which structure (society) influences the actions and experiences of individuals is provided by Giddens. He uses the analogy of language to illustrate the relationship that individuals have with the wider social structure. None of us has invented the language that we use, but without it social activity would be impossible because it is our shared meanings that sustain 'society'. However, as Giddens (1994) also points out, each of us is capable of using that language in a creative, distinct and individual way, and yet no one person creates language. In the same way human behaviour is not determined in a mechanical way by the structure we call society. Later chapters discuss the significance of social class in determining levels of morbidity and mortality and yet not every person in each social class category will have identical experiences. There will, however, be enough similarities in patterns of health within each social class for us to justifiably place people in these specific groupings. Similarities in people's experiences can be seen in terms of income levels, of availability of local resources such as GPs, of geographical location, and of their physical environment and patterns of expenditure. The relationship and interplay between society and the individual is explained in terms of **structure** and **agency**. The latter is a concept used to refer to a cluster of ideas about the potential for individuals to determine their lives, to change their environment and, ultimately, to influence the wider structure. The concept of agency, therefore, allows us to appreciate the way in which we are shaped by society, and in turn shape society.

The term structure is similar to that of 'society' in so far as it draws our attention to those factors that help determine our experiences through the establishment of expected ways of behaving. In contrast, the concept of agency reminds us that individuals do not simply act out predetermined roles but 'interpret' those roles in a way unique to them.

If the subject matter of sociology is human society, and behaviour is explained primarily in terms of 'structure', then this logically denotes specific factors in the explanatory framework of the discipline. Sociological explanations of what determines our state of health will necessarily differ from, for example, biological explanations. Clearly disease is a biological and physical entity experienced through the medium of the body. The causes of disease, while biological, can also be considered in terms of social and structural factors. The immediate cause of a disease may be infection but the factors that lead to this may be many and varied. If we reflect upon patterns of morbidity and mortality over the last two centuries, then it is possible to observe a significant shift away from infectious diseases to chronic conditions. Commentators such as Doyal (1979) argue that improved standards of living, better hygiene and the availability of medicine via the NHS have caused this change. In other words, when we consider the factors that influence a person's state of health, the risk of infection, an ability to fight infection and genetic predisposition are greatly important but, within sociology, these are not our main focus. Social and environmental factors such as age, social class and gender are as, if not more, important.

Questions

Gender is a good example of how structures shape our lives and how we make individual choices about how we live. As a man or a woman, what experiences do you share in common with your gender? In what do you consider yourself 'unique' and different from all other women or men?

It is possible to define what we mean by 'sociology' by sketching out the discipline's remit in terms of the study of human society. From this it is logical to conclude that the study of sociology is relevant to understanding and explaining health in so far as health and its determinants need to be explained within a social context. Within nurse education, for example, the emphasis placed on 'holistic' care can also be used to justify the study of sociology in that it provides information that places an individual within a social context. To conclude that this is all that the discipline of sociology can offer in terms of studying health, illness and medicine is mistaken and unnecessarily limiting. What sociology offers is a questioning and critical way of thinking and a distinct method of explanation. To fully appreciate this element of sociology it is helpful to understand how, why and when the discipline came into being.

A sociological understanding of health considers structural and social factors, rather than simply biological explanations of health and disease.

In historical terms, modern is a term used to refer to the time period from the late nineteenth century to the mid twentieth century.

The historical origins of sociology

The discipline of sociology is fundamentally a **modern** one, bound up with attempts to explain, anticipate and alter a rapidly changing world. According to Giddens (1986), the focus of sociology at its inception was the structures and relationships that derived from industrialisation (1986). An examination of the works of the founding fathers of sociology (Comte, Durkheim, Weber and Marx) suggests a preoccupation with attempts to understand a rapidly changing world and to do so in a way that was 'scientific', objective and rational. Auguste Comte, for example, believed that the development of any society was ultimately positive and progressive, and identified three different phases: the religious, the metaphysical and the scientific. Each of these phases represented a mode of thought and explanation: the religious period represented a supernatural interpretation of the world; the metaphysical one replaced religion with a belief in forces such as nature; and the final, scientific, stage represented the most positive and rational phase of human development (Craib 1997: 23). Understanding this new and complex society meant adherence to rational, scientific and empirical methods. The underlying motivation of the discipline was to reveal the reality of social relationships. For Karl Marx, this meant making plain the 'real' relationships of power and exploitation behind social class. For Emile Durkheim, getting to the heart of the reality meant the observation and recording of 'facts' to provide a picture of the world as it is, rather than to anticipate how the world should be.

> Sociology strives to be scientific in the sense that it seeks to evidence its findings and to ensure that explanations are consistent. A fundamental difference between the social and natural sciences is that the subject matter of the social sciences, unlike that of the natural sciences, is human beings and their behaviour.

Can sociology be 'scientific'?

To the extent that sociological explanations attempt to be rational and empirical they share certain features with scientific disciplines. According to Bruce (1999), scientific explanations are consistent (that is to say they cannot contradict themselves) and must accord with the evidence; and when evidence is found to refute an explanation, the explanation itself must be changed (1999: 3). A fundamental issue for sociologists is whether sociology is a science in the same sense as the physical sciences. Bruce suggests that one crucial difference is in the methods employed to uncover evidence. Natural sciences are able to make full use of the experimental method because of the relative simplicity of their subject matter. As Bruce points out, we can explain why, how and when water boils but because the water 'has not *decided* to boil we do not need to refer to the consciousness of the water' (1999: 12). However, any explanation of human society and human behaviour has to take into account the consciousness of the subject, because actions have meanings which derive from consciousness. For these reasons the experimental method is impractical for sociologists.

This does not mean, however, that evidence need not be sought when sociologists generate and test theories. Despite apparent difficulties in establishing the 'truth', Bruce (1999: 17) argues, it is still possible to arrive at an accurate account of people's lives. He draws an analogy between sociological evidence and evidence in a court of law: in both cases, he suggests, it is possible to establish the truth from what appear to be contradictory accounts.

Questions

Summarise the main differences between sociological methods of enquiry and those associated with the natural sciences.

The 'sociological imagination'

There is little doubt that sociology is one of the most controversial of all academic subjects, often giving rise to hostile reactions. Sociology has been associated with a radical and left-wing perspective, and despite the fact that sociologists such as Comte and Durkheim conceived of the subject in terms of describing and analysing what actually exists as opposed to speculating on what ought to exist, sociology has always been strongly associated with critiques of existing societies and speculation about the possibility of change. Zygmunt Bauman recognises that this questioning approach can invoke hostility: 'In an encounter with that familiar world ruled by habits … sociology acts as a meddlesome and often irritating stranger' (cited in Kirby et al. 2000: 43).

What critics might see as most questionable about the discipline of sociology, its practitioners see as its main strength. Anthony Giddens, for example, writes that the study of sociology is essentially liberating because 'it teaches appreciation of cultural variety and allows us an insight into the workings of social institutions' (cited in Kirby et al. 2000: 3). To 'do' sociology requires one to think in a specific way; fundamentally, it requires what C. Wright Mills describes as the **sociological imagination**. C. Wright Mills urges us to think outside our own experiences and look at what appears to us as 'mundane' in a new light. Using the sociological imagination means departing from what are referred to as common-sense explanations: this implies an explanation of phenomena based on limited observations of human behaviour and our own, again limited, experiences of the social world. C. Wright Mills (1970) states that the sociological imagination enables three fundamental questions to be asked: (1) What is the structure of this particular society? (2) Where does this society stand in human history? (3) What varieties of men and women now

> The concept of the sociological imagination refers to a specific way of thinking about the world, characterised by a willingness to think beyond our own experiences and to challenge common-sense or obvious explanations of human society and human behaviour.

prevail in this society and this period? What is important here is the questioning attitude to what is given, what is seen. Asking and answering all three questions ensures that no assumptions are made about what is being studied and that the context, both cultural and historical, is taken into account when considering any explanation of what is observed.

We seek to argue that without this critical and questioning edge, 'doing' sociology ceases to have any real purpose other than to describe, to provide background detail and a social context. Such an approach does not require one to ask the critical questions posed by C. Wright Mills, and neither, crucially, does it ask us to think about why social situations are as they are. One of the fundamental concerns of sociology is the distribution of power in society and its consequences. When, later in this book, you analyse inequalities in health you will see that social class is one of the main factors influencing levels of morbidity and mortality. What Chapter 6 will describe and analyse are not simply differences but inequalities in people's chances of good health and longevity. Inequality in terms of health is, literally, a matter of life and death. Social classes don't exist in isolation from one another, they form part of a social relationship; social disadvantage has another side, and that is social advantage. An understanding of theories of power is therefore essential to 'doing' sociology successfully.

The sociological imagination is crucial to 'doing' sociology as it provides a critical and questioning edge, without which the discipline would be limited to simply describing social phenomena.

This chapter has drawn out what is unique about the discipline of sociology in terms of its subject matter, the nature of sociological evidence, methods of explanation and the mindset described as the sociological imagination. The next section seeks to expand upon these themes by presenting an explanation of how sociologists explain social phenomena in terms of different theoretical perspectives.

An introduction to sociological theory

In this section we seek to explain and illustrate how sociologists explain the social world. To do this we will examine various competing theoretical approaches. To begin, however, it is necessary to think about what is meant by the term **theory** as a method of explanation. In common-sense terms a theory refers to a set of ideas or propositions used to explain and predict social phenomena. Our explanations derive ultimately from a particular perspective or worldview. Comte, for example, as we have already seen, divided human history into three phases, each characterised by a particular mode of thought (religious, metaphysical and scientific). Each of these modes of thought permits only certain kinds of explanation. The rational and

Within the discipline of sociology, theory refers to attempts to provide systematic and consistent explanations of social phenomena. The term paradigm refers to a systematic way of thinking.

scientific phase does not tolerate explanations that cannot be evidenced. Similarly, Seale and Pattison (1994), in their study of the history of medicine, identify 'paradigms' or world-views that characterised different stages in the development of medicine. Scientific medical knowledge is just one example of a medical **paradigm** and is based on what Seale and Pattison refer to as 'systematic investigation of all aspects of human biology … and includes experimental manipulation of body functions and testing of treatments under scientifically controlled conditions' (1994: 28).

Sociological theory and common-sense theory

Bruce (1999: 3) argues that sociological explanations should share characteristics with scientific explanations in so far as they should be consistent, must accord with the evidence and must change if evidence can be found to refute them. To the extent that this is true, it seems that sociological explanations differ from more common-sense explanations. It is possible to argue that the latter do not have to be supported by evidence, and when evidence *is* produced there is little or no attempt to scrutinise its validity. Common-sense theories tend to be more in the nature of opinion than of fact. So far, then, this discussion has succeeded in establishing that sociological theory is characterised by the need to be consistent and evidenced. What also distinguishes sociological theory from common-sense theories is its ability to provide an 'account of the world which goes beyond what we can see and measure' (Marshall 1998: 666). 'Doing' and using sociological theory, therefore, enables us to explain phenomena of which we have no direct experience. Such a definition highlights what is unique and exciting about the discipline of sociology: its ability to inform us of differences and to think beyond our own experiences. Understanding the nature of sociological theory is a reminder of the importance of using the 'sociological imagination' as described by C. Wright Mills. Sociology is characterised by a range of different theoretical approaches, each providing a very different way of understanding social phenomena. The purpose of what follows is to provide you with an overview and an introduction to these differing perspectives.

> Doing and using sociological theory enables us to explain phenomena of which we do not have direct experience.

Functionalism

The first approach to be examined is **functionalism**. This theoretical approach is based on an analogy between society and a biological organism. Just as the body is made up of different but interrelated and interdependent parts, so society is made up of a number of different systems and subsystems. These different parts achieve unity in so far as they function to sustain the whole, in this example the wider social structure. Therefore, functionalism is less concerned

Functionalism offers an explanation of human society as a collection of interrelated substructures, the purpose of which is to sustain the overarching structure of society. As such, functionalism provides a 'consensual' representation of society based, first, on an agreement to sustain society as it is and, second, on shared norms and beliefs.

with the individual, and his or her aims, beliefs and consciousness, than with how our actions and beliefs function to maintain the system as a whole. An essential element in ensuring that the system is maintained is the cultural subsystem which ensures that individual motivations are in line with the values of the system as a whole. Without this central value system society would cease to function, because its cohesiveness could not be ensured. Each person has a certain role or function to fulfil, bounded by a certain set of expectations about how they will behave and how others should respond. These social expectations are referred to as role relationships, each of which carries with it a specific set of rights and obligations. The fulfilment of these roles and relationships ensures order and continuity in society.

When a person takes on the 'sick role', they are excused from their normal roles and responsibilities. The medical profession determines who is legitimately 'sick'. This regulatory role ensures that not too many people are unable to fulfil their normal roles – otherwise illness would have a detrimental effect on the society as a whole.

In relation to the study of health and illness, for example, the functionalist perspective is usefully illuminated by Talcott Parsons' concept of the **sick role**. First, the concept is used to analyse sickness as a social role, not merely as a biological phenomenon and physical experience. For any society to function smoothly, 'sickness' needs to be managed in such a way that the majority of people maintain their normal social roles and obligations. This perspective is based on the assumption that if too many people were to describe themselves as 'sick' and in need of being excused from their normal range of social obligations, this would be 'dysfunctional' in the sense of being disruptive for society as a whole. Those individuals who are judged by the medical profession as genuinely ill are only temporarily excused from normal obligations, and then only if they comply with the rules of the sick role. Those people taking on the sick role do so only if they agree to comply with the regime given by the medical practitioner and if they are committed to getting well as soon as possible.

Links

Chapter 3 provides an illustration of the functionalist explanation of the doctor/patient relationship.

The functionalist perspective is a consensual approach to understanding society, which also assumes that the latent or hidden functions of everyday activities have significance for maintaining the system as a whole. In relation to something as simple as eating, Lupton (1996) argues that the 'function' of food can be seen in broader terms than just as nutritional intake. A functionalist perspective serves to highlight the way in which 'food practices serve to support co-operative behaviour or structures of kinship in small groups' (1996: 8). Lupton has also argued that the meal is a way of illustrating the culture of a specific society in terms of the order in which food is served (savoury then sweet) and the mixing of food types and temperatures.

> Symbolic interactionism explains social phenomena from the perspective of its participants. An essential element of this theoretical perspective is the unique nature of the social world as made up of the actions of participants motivated by human consciousness. The meaning of human action cannot, therefore, be observed or assumed, but must be interpreted by studying the meanings that people attach to their behaviour.

However, the functionalist perspective has been subject to much criticism. In relation to the sick role, for example, it has been suggested that Parsons overlooked the potential for conflict between the patient and the practitioner and that he misguidedly assumed that the practitioner would always act in the best interests of the patient. However, the main criticism is that it is an unproven assumption that situations have a fixed, obvious and shared meaning.

Symbolic interactionism

In contrast, **symbolic interactionism** is based on the premise that there is a fundamental difference between the subject matter of sociology and that of the natural sciences. While the study of the natural world deals with physical, inanimate objects, the subject matter of sociology consists of people whose actions are motivated by human consciousness. Symbolic interactionism is, therefore, concerned with how people see and understand the social world. This theoretical approach is concerned less with the larger social system or structure than with interpreting human behaviour. As with the 'sociological imagination', the emphasis here is on looking again at the most common-sense and commonplace aspects of our culture and questioning what we assume to be 'natural' and 'normal'.

The significance of this approach can be seen in relation to understanding health behaviour that appears to be irrational. Graham (1993) examined patterns of cigarette smoking among mothers on low incomes. What was revealed were relatively high levels of spending on cigarettes in low-income households. In terms of what can be observed or assumed, this behaviour might well indicate a degree of irrationality in that it contradicts dominant health messages about the dangers of smoking, and diverts limited financial resources from the family. Graham, however, favours a theoretical approach dependent upon the symbolic interactionism tradition of interpreting human behaviour in the context of people's own beliefs and meanings. This alternative interpretation associates cigarette smoking with the

In the context of this discussion, micro refers to the
small-scale aspects of human
behaviour, for example why
individuals embark on criminal activities. Macro refers to
the larger, structural aspects
of society. In terms of criminal
activities, this might involve
analysis of the economic circumstances of criminals, of
law making and law enforcement, and of the role of
the state in regulating such
behaviour.

maintenance of normal, caring routines in that smoking creates a
'space' between the mothers and their children, providing 'time
out' from the demanding routines of caring. 'Viewed within the
context of mothers' daily lives, cigarette smoking appears to be
a way of coping with the constant and unremitting demands of
caring: a way of temporarily escaping without leaving the room'
(1993: 93).

What the interactionist tradition presents us with is insight
into two important aspects of social phenomena. First, in terms
of the emphasis placed on the disputed nature of meaning, we
are clearly reminded of what is central to the discipline itself,
namely the questioning of the taken-for-granted. Second, the
focus is on what are referred to as the **micro** elements of society, that is, the small-scale interactions between individuals and
between individuals and groups. An overview of the research
based on this approach indicates both the strengths and the
weaknesses of symbolic interactionism. Becker's (1974) analysis of deviance is an excellent
illustration of the symbolic interactionist perspective. The definition of deviance that Becker
offers does not assume that what is described as deviant is fixed for all time, or that different
cultures have the same definition of what counts as deviant. Becker's analysis focuses instead
on the understanding of the meaning of deviance and the way in which that definition may
be considered fluid rather than static. Becker defines deviance as any act that is perceived as
such. Deviance is a label attached to the behaviour of an individual, rather than a quality of
their behaviour. His own research tended to concentrate on certain types of 'deviant' behaviour such as illicit drug use and prostitution, the process that led to an individual taking on
a deviant career, the factors that sustained him or her in that deviant career, and the processes whereby deviant behaviour became labelled as such. Becker's research concentrated
less on the structural factors that might help explain crime and deviance, such as poverty,
and placed little emphasis on the source of power of those agencies, such as criminal justice
agencies, who label some people deviant. Becker talked of 'moral entrepreneurs' as influential
shapers of public morals but made little or no attempt to place these individuals and groups
within the social context of society. In other words, the **macro** elements of the social structure were given much less emphasis.

Marxism

Strictly speaking Marx did not set out to be a sociologist, and it was mainly with the political radicalisation of the 1960s that his ideas became part of the sociological mainstream. His
ideas, however, do provide powerful insights into the structure of society, suggesting that it is
the economic structure of any society that determines the social relations contained within

that structure. It is the distribution of the ownership of the means of production that gives rise to specific patterns of class relations, which, crucially, in all societies are characterised by inequalities of power. Marx described modern societies in the west as capitalist, that is to say divided between those who privately own the means of production (a minority) and those who are dependent on selling their labour power to make a living (the majority). This classic division provides a description of the two main classes, the bourgeoisie and the proletariat. The relationship between the two is unequal, primarily in that the relations of production result in the exploitation of the latter in a way that is systematic and oppressive.

Marxist theory is used to question the 'naturalness' of capitalist relations and to unmask the reality of what is fundamentally an exploitative relationship. This theoretical approach is representative of the structural analysis of society – less concerned with the micro elements and more concerned with the larger picture, the underlying factors that explain social, economic and political relationships. Marxist theory, therefore, is a distinct sociological perspective, a tool for our analysis of the social structure. It would be a mistake to assume that all that this theoretical perspective can offer us is an appreciation of the significance of economic factors on, for example, health chances. Such an approach would lose sight of what Marxist theory can provide us with in terms of a critique of existing social, economic and political relationships. Vicente Navarro's

> Marxism explains social phenomena as primarily determined by the economic structure of society. Social change, it is argued, is the product of changes in economic relationships. In the context of the modern period the advent of capitalism and industrialisation produced social divisions based on the ownership or non-ownership of property. The economic inequalities that result from ownership or non-ownership of property are the starting point for understanding why there are inequalities in health between the middle and the working classes.

analysis (1976, 2002) of the causes of ill health and the relationship between the state and the medical profession is based on such insights. What Navarro provides us with is an explanation both of the causes of inequalities of health between different social classes and of why this situation continues and is, as he argues, maintained by the medical profession (Moon and Gillespie 1995:73).

The key to this situation is, Navarro suggests, to be found in the alliance of interests between the ruling classes and the medical profession; each, for different reasons, derives power from the continuation of these conditions of inequality. For the ruling classes, health inequalities are an indication of the difference in life chances that exist between themselves and the working classes in particular. The provision of health care through a system such as the National Health Service is largely about maintaining a reasonable level of health among the working classes, sufficient to ensure that people are able to work and be returned to work following illness. Navarro in part explains the medical profession's alliance with the ruling classes in terms of their shared willingness to perpetuate the belief that the principal causes of ill health are personal and physical rather than social. Such a situation in turn strengthens the position of the medical profession in explaining illness to the lay population but also, significantly, fosters a dependency on medicine to cure illness and disease. To admit that patterns of disease and illness are largely determined by economic and social factors would be to rob the medical profession of ideological dominance, which is founded on the claim that it is medical advances and medical technology that have produced the most startling improvements in the health of the nation. Therefore, the alliance between the ruling classes and the medical profession serves the interests of both by maintaining the professional dominance of the latter and by sustaining a reasonably healthy working population for the former.

Feminism

Marxist theory has been criticised in particular for its almost exclusive emphasis on the economic determinants of social relationships and for the resulting primacy of social class in any analysis of inequality. **Feminist theory** from the 1960s onwards sought to challenge what was seen as the invisibility of gender in sociological theory. Giddens suggests that sociology has as its main focus 'the study of the social institutions brought into being by the industrial transformations of the past two or three centuries' (1986: 9). Feminist critics argued that the founding fathers of sociology were concerned with a narrow range of topics such as social class, the division of labour in industrial society and the role of the state.

> Feminism is a broad concept that explains social structures as fundamentally based on inequalities between women and men. In general, feminist sociologists have challenged the traditional preoccupation of the discipline with the effects of industrialisation and the world of paid work and institutional politics. Such an approach, it is argued, has ignored significant elements of society such as the family and gender relationships.

It is possible to argue that two essential elements of this social transformation were largely overlooked. The first relates to the way in which industrialisation impacted specifically upon women, compared to men. According to Ramazanaglu (1989) one of the most significant changes for women related to the shift of work for remuneration from the home (or near the home) to a separate and distinct space, such as the factory. Such a split set up for the first time the dilemma of how to combine 'work' and childcare. The second element illuminates the practical changes in women's lives as well as conceptual shifts in explanations of social phenomena. The modern era is associated with a perceived split between the 'public' and the 'private' spheres. It was assumed that the natural area of study for sociology was the 'public' world of paid work, politics and the state. Since these were also the areas where men were dominant, it was this aspect of the social world that came to be associated with them. Women, on the other hand, remained within the 'private' sphere of the home, family and unpaid work. The former sphere was clearly seen as open to change, while the latter was assumed to be unchanging and 'natural'. The result of this conceptual split was an unquestioning acceptance of women and men as fundamentally different from one another and an assumption that these 'natural' differences could not be altered.

Links

Chapter 4 includes a discussion of the male dominance of medicine in relation to reproductive technology.

As a challenge to these assumptions, feminist theory can make a substantial contribution to our understanding of the social world in general and to the study of health and illness in particular. Feminist theory provides, for example, an analysis of gender relations on the basis of the way in which female inequality has been structured and maintained in society. One rather controversial concept used to explain this inequality is that of **patriarchy**, literally meaning the rule of men over women and of older men over younger men. In terms of uncovering what is distinct about women's lives as compared to men's, the concept of patriarchy provides a unique insight into many aspects of women's lives. Writers such as Oakley (1984) have argued that women's lives have been subject to far greater control and regulation by the medical profession than have men's. Particular examples can be seen in relation to pregnancy and childbirth, where what was previously seen as a 'natural' event attended by women rapidly became the focus of medical intervention, and now principally takes place in hospital, with the profession of obstetrics being dominated by men.

Postmodernism

The final theoretical approach to be discussed in this chapter is less a school of thought than part of a recent critical and challenging questioning of traditional sociological theory. **Postmodernism** refers to the present historical period characterised by the globalisation of the economy and culture, and by a fragmentation of individual identity such that old certainties of class, national and gender identity are called into question. The term 'postmodern' also refers to a particular paradigm or worldview. In this case, what is being challenged is the certainty of our knowledge about the world, the ability of sociological theory to uncover the 'truth' about the social world, and the desirability of this. Thus, the emphasis of this particular approach is less on producing an all-embracing theory which explains all aspects of the social structure, and more on enquiring into the nature of knowledge itself.

Postmodernist theories veer away from all-embracing theories such as those described above that attempt to explain all social phenomena. Instead, the emphasis is on the impossibility of uncovering the 'truth' about society. Postmodernism draws our attention to how our knowledge of the social world is constructed, and offers a critical and questioning approach to understanding the world around us. Medical knowledge is an example of an established body of thought that is challenged by postmodernism as just one interpretation of reality. In other words, the 'truth' of medical knowledge is challenged.

Michel Foucault argued that in order to understand science and medicine we have to think about them as 'discourses' about the body, health and the natural world, rather than accepting these disciplines as objective descriptions of reality. The concept of **discourse** is an important one within contemporary sociology and represents a distinct way of thinking, seeing and conversing about particular phenomena, all of which create a virtual 'arena', ruling some ways of thinking as legitimate and others as not. Medicine is often described as a dominant discourse in relation to the study of health, disease and the body because western biomedicine has become the accepted, and therefore legitimate, way of thinking, talking about and seeing these aspects of human experience. Medicine represents one discourse on health, disease and the body and Foucault draws our attention to previous, non-scientific explanations of disease and perceptions of the body. Postmodernist theory makes two main contributions to the study of health and disease. First, we are offered a way of challenging the dominance of medicine and questioning what appears to be scientific, true and objective. Second, we can appreciate the way in which knowledge discourses can be used to discipline us. According to Bilton et al., medicine cannot be seen, then, as merely and actively associated with clinical healing: 'the medicalisation of the body … has to be understood as a process of social control' (1996: 424). We have seen from the earlier example of feminist theory and the critique of the regulation of pregnancy and childbirth that the application of medical techniques and knowledge often results in the control and regulation of patients.

> Discourse refers to a specific way of thinking about and conceptualising a particular subject. The essence of a discourse is the language used to express thoughts. Science is an example of a discourse that rules out some kinds of explanations (for example, spiritual) and only allows for others (for example, rational and evidenced 'facts').

Conclusion

This chapter has sought to establish the nature of the discipline of sociology by detailing what is distinctive about its subject matter and method of enquiry. You have also been introduced to various theoretical explanations of social phenomena. Only by having such theoretical perspectives are we able to glimpse what is beneath the common-sense surface perceptions. In the rest of the book you will see how this distinctive way of looking at the world helps to bring about an understanding of health in its fullest and widest sense. What will emerge is that health is clearly bound up with the social world, with some of the main inequalities and patterns of health and illness only explainable by reference to sociology.

Summary points

- Sociology is concerned with the study of society and specifically with key issues such as inequalities in life chances.
- Sociology offers what Bruce (1999) terms a 'scientific' method of enquiry characterised by the search for valid evidence.
- The study of sociology requires us to think outside our own experiences and to employ the 'sociological imagination'.
- Sociological theory can be distinguished from 'everyday theory' by its requirement to resort to reasoned, evidenced and coherent explanations of social phenomena.

Taking your studies further

This chapter will have helped you understand many of the key terms, concepts, theories and debates relating to sociological theory. Listed below are books that will provide deeper and more detailed discussions of the points raised in this chapter. You will also find what is available on the companion website. This offers downloads of relevant material, plus links to useful websites in addition to podcasts and other features.

Recommended reading

Benton, T. and Craib, I. (2001) *Philosophy of Social Science: The Philosophical Foundations of Social Thought*. Basingstoke: Palgrave.

Bruce, S. (1999) *Sociology: A Very Short Introduction*. Oxford: Oxford University Press.

Craib, I. (2004) *Classical Social Theory: An Introduction to the Thought of Marx, Weber, Durkheim and Simmel*. Oxford: Oxford University Press.

Scambler, G. (2002) *Health and Social Change: A Critical Theory*. Buckingham: Open University Press.

On the companion website

Scott, J.P. (2004) *Social Theory: Central Issues in Sociology*. London: Sage. Chapter 1.

2

Concepts of health and medicine

Main points

- Modern medicine emerges out of the Enlightenment, a critical historical period when society became secular and scientific; this replaced religious explanations of the natural world.
- The medical model of health stresses a mechanistic view of the body and a reliance on biological causation to explain illness.
- The social model provides a holistic approach, stressing that health and illness can only be explained by analysing the social.
- Foucault's concept of the clinical gaze draws our attention to how medicine observes and treats the body as a physical entity devoid of reference to the person.

Key concepts

The Enlightenment ● science ● rationality ● paradigm ● social model ● medical model ● bedside medicine ● clinical medicine ● laboratory medicine ● the clinical gaze.

Introduction

The aims of this chapter are twofold: to provide a historical account of the development of modern medicine, and to examine the social construction of medical knowledge. We employ the concept of the **sociological imagination** to stress the necessity of a historical and questioning approach to the study of medicine and the development of the medical profession.

Medicine represents a specific type of knowledge about the human body that is applied to either care for or cure of the recipient of medical treatment. In order to understand the practice of medicine at the present time, it is necessary to know how it developed historically. This chapter seeks to explain two main elements of medical knowledge: first, its historical origins and, second, the type of knowledge underpinning the practice of medicine.

> The Enlightenment refers to a body of thought, first developed in the eighteenth century, which challenged explanations of the world based on religious or superstitious explanations. Enlightenment thought was based on a commitment to rational, secular and scientific explanations.

The development of modern medicine: science, rationality and the legacy of the Enlightenment

Before we begin to examine medical perspectives on the body, it would be helpful to ascertain the origins of these ideas. According to Stacey (1988) various cultural, social and economic factors, all of which have their origins in the eighteenth-century Enlightenment, help explain the development of modern medicine. The term **the Enlightenment** refers to a body of thought rather than to a specific period in European history. Underpinning this intellectual movement was a strong emphasis on reason rather than belief, superstition or even religious thought. The Enlightenment is traditionally associated with rationality and the search for evidence. It was anticipated that, on the basis of rational, reasoned and evidenced thought, traditional institutions and ideas could be replaced with 'modern' practices. This element of the Enlightenment paved the way for a secular understanding of society and of people's place within it. The application of reason to human life, it was argued, opened up the possibility of the advancement of the human race by uncovering the massive potential of *science* and reason. Stacey (1988: 47) argues that the developments that took place laid the basis from which biomedicine developed, led to its domination over all alternative healing systems and established a division of health labour that its practitioners also dominated.

In the first instance, the growing **secularisation** of society opened the way for alternative, scientific explanations for disease. 'Medical' labels and 'scientific' explanations could be used to understand the origins of disease and their potential cures. Chapter 9, which examines mental health, will illustrate these arguments in detail. Explanations of 'madness' in spiritual terms or in terms of 'possession' gave way to explanations drawn from the examination of the body and brain based on empirical observation and the recording of the underlying physical, organic cause. This drive to uncover the specific

> The concept of science is associated with the study of the natural and physical world, characterised by observation, measurement, experimentation and objectivity. Secularisation refers to the acceptance of non-religious explanations of the world.

aetiology of a disease by examining the human body is exemplified in the desire to explore the bodies of the dead as well as the living. The search for knowledge about the body encouraged early medical practitioners to act unlawfully by taking possession of cadavers procured illicitly. This illegal trade thrived despite the fact that practitioners already enjoyed access to the bodies of the poor and destitute who had died in workhouses and other institutions.

Questions

How important for the medical profession is the continuing use of bodies for research and teaching? What is the connection between the decline in religious belief and the greater use of bodies for research and teaching?

Edinburgh was notorious for its 'body snatchers' or 'Resurrectionists', principally because of its strong tradition of medical education. The best-known practitioners of this trade were Burke and Hare who, in the early part of the nineteenth century, also murdered to provide corpses. When captured, the latter turned king's evidence. Burke was hanged in front of a crowd of 20,000 and his own body later dissected in the same way as those he had procured. A wallet made from Burke's skin can still be seen within the Medical School at Edinburgh University.

> Visitors to older Edinburgh graveyards must have noticed their strange resemblance to zoological gardens, the rows of iron cages suggesting rather the dens of wild animals than the quiet resting places of the dead. And, in fact, these barred and grated cells were designed as a protection against human wolves who nightly prowled about such places in quest of prey, and furnish very real testimony to the fears by which our forebears were beset respecting the security of the sepulchres ... It is obvious that the lawful supply of subjects was wholly inadequate to meet the growing needs of the new [medical] school ... the surgeons and barbers' apprentices had been in use diligently to till the soil and reap the harvest of what had been finely called 'Death's mailing' ... At first zealous apprentices were the only body snatchers, but owing to the popularity of the Edinburgh medical school and the great increase of students, there arose a class of men who, adopting as a business the raising of the dead, became known as the Resurrectionists. (Roughhead 2000 [1921]: 152)

The Enlightenment underpinned the development of specific *methods* of investigation in relation to medicine, namely scientific methods. The superiority of scientific thought was said to lie in the fact that evidence and theories were derived not from belief but from observation, and were confirmed through a process of experimentation. Evidence developed in this way was seen as unbiased, *rational* and purely descriptive of the natural world. Scientific facts could not be disputed except by employing the same methods to question or disprove an assertion. In Chapter 4 we will examine **alternative medicine** and see that the same assumed superiority of scientific methods is still used to question the validity of practices such as homoeopathy.

The ability of science to provide rational explanations continues to be one of its main strengths. Rational means adherence to a logical and tenable process of explanation.

Medical perspectives on the body, health and illness

Biomedicine is the principal way of understanding health and illness in western culture, being widely accepted not just by the medical profession but also by the lay (non-professional) population. There is general agreement among contributors to debates in medical sociology that the *medical model* of explanation has a number of defining characteristics. Nettleton (1995: 5), for example, describes five features:

1 *Mind–body dualism.* This refers to an acceptance that when one is treating disease the mind and the body can be considered as two separate entities. The physical body rather than the more problematic 'mind' is *the* subject of medicine. Medicine's appropriation of the body is such that, until recently, there was very little written by sociologists about the body; this was the domain of the medical profession.

2 *Mechanical metaphor.* Nettleton uses this concept to draw our attention to the way in which medicine is said to view the body as a machine, the functioning of which is determined by biological and scientific laws. Having knowledge of how the body functions allows medical practitioners to 'repair' any dysfunction.

3 *Technological imperative.* This refers to the significance attached to medical methods of intervention, whether pharmacological or surgical, in treating the body. As we shall see, there is often a tendency to overemphasise the curative element of biomedicine and underplay the beneficial contributions made by, for example, changes in diet or environment. While the development of medical technology brings with it considerable benefits, these developments also have a cost, for instance in terms of the harmful consequences either of medicines or of medical intervention.

4 *Reductionist tendency.* Biomedicine is described by Nettleton as 'reductionist' in that there is a tendency to reduce all explanations to the physical workings of the body. There is an echo of this reductionist tendency in the dualistic nature of medicine as well as in the significance attached to the 'technological imperative' in the primary role attached to all things physical. One of the major criticisms of the medical model stems from its apparent unwillingness to acknowledge that both social and psychological factors influence health.

5 *Doctrine of specific aetiology.* This refers to the belief that all disease originates from specific and knowable causes.

The medical model is a specific way of thinking about
and explaining disease based
on biological factors.

Such a description of the medical model may well strike you as rather rigid, and as a far more accurate account of medicine and medical practice in the past rather than today. We would argue, however, that central elements of medical knowledge remain but that medicine is a dynamic body of thought, capable of changing and adapting in the light of new discoveries. The fluid nature of medical knowledge means that some elements of the medical model may be more or less important now than they were in the past.

Links

A more detailed discussion of the body and chronic illness is provided in Chapter 11.

It is perhaps easier to see the relevance of such a model in the past, when infectious diseases were the main cause of morbidity and mortality. The major killers of the twentieth and twenty-first centuries are long-term, chronic illnesses. What distinguishes these conditions from diseases of the past is that their causes are 'social'. Heart disease is the main cause of death in Scotland and some cities like Glasgow, for example, have particularly high rates. While some causes of heart disease can be traced back to a specific dysfunction of the organ, the principal cause is an unhealthy lifestyle. It may be difficult to defend the medical model as outlined by Nettleton when public awareness campaigns attach such a degree of significance to individuals changing their lifestyles rather than to the medical profession repairing what appears simply to be a faulty machine. Pharmaceuticals such as lipids may be able to reduce the harmful effects of heart disease and hypertension but they cannot eradicate the disease.

Authors such as Lupton (1994) have urged us to consider the way in which the medical model has developed and reinvented itself to the point where it can embrace social as well as psychological factors. It is, therefore, not always appropriate to contrast the medical model of medicine with the **social model** of medicine. The social dimensions of heart disease are a topical example of this, as is the recent acknowledgement by the British Medical Association that diseases such as ME have both a physical and a psychological dimension. It would be a mistake to accept the medical model as a static representation of medical thought and practice. Medicine and medical practice are no longer solely concerned with the biological and the physical but, because of the changing nature of disease, are able to place disease and the diseased body in a social context. Medicine goes beyond simply treating disease and is now actively engaged in a moral crusade to change the way in which people live, and to influence the choices that they make. Turner suggests that the growth in the influence of medicine over our lives, coupled with the demise of religious influence, has resulted in a new moral order: 'the doctor has replaced the priest as the custodian of social values' (1994: 37). This 'moralistic' element of medicine cannot be adequately accounted for in terms of the five characteristics identified above. In order to embrace the modern dimensions of medicine and medical practice we have to be prepared to extend the traditional medical model to a more complex body of thought that can and does embrace social and psychological aspects of health and disease.

'Medical paradigms': the social construction of medical knowledge

Thus far, this chapter has explored the intellectual and cultural origins of medicine and provided an account of the main characteristics of the medical model. The significance of this discussion, and that of other chapters that follow, is that it allows the student of sociology to place the development of medicine within a historical context, and thus fulfils one of the essential criteria of the request to employ the 'sociological imagination'. The second objective of this chapter is to explain the social construction of medical knowledge.

Social constructionism is characterised by an emphasis on the extent to which 'society' is actively and creatively produced by human beings. The world is portrayed as made or invented – rather than as given or taken for granted. 'Social worlds are interpretive nets woven by individuals and groups' (Marshall 1998: 609). The extent to which medical knowledge can also be said to be socially constructed, that is, the degree to which medical knowledge is a product of those engaged in its practice, can be illustrated by Jewson's (1976) concept of *paradigms* of medical knowledge. The term **paradigm** (introduced in Chapter 1) refers to a model or mode of thought, a particular way of seeing the world, that sets boundaries to *what* we see, *how* we might measure and record that information, and *which* factors are significant and which are not.

Paradigms of knowledge shift and change over time, as illustrated by the earlier discussion of the medical model, and, therefore, offer us a way of conceptualising the fluid and dynamic nature of medical knowledge.

TABLE 2.1   Jewson's three paradigms of medical knowledge

Bedside medicine	Clinical medicine	Laboratory medicine
• Disease as a total 'psychosomatic' experience • Lay and 'medical' practitioners	• Specific aetiology of diseases • Specialist practitioners in possession of specialist knowledge about the body	• Disease as a 'biochemical disturbance' • Specialist practitioners, knowledge of cellular construction of the body
• Place of treatment: home	• Place of treatment: hospital	• Place of treatment: laboratory

Source: Seale and Pattison (1994)

Table 2.1 represents a simplification of the three paradigms. It is a useful starting point in the **analysis** of the social construction of medical knowledge and raises the following significant points:

- Medical knowledge has changed and developed over time. What was once held as a reasonable explanation may later be disputed and cast aside. Early medical theories of hysteria, for example, maintained that the womb of 'hysterical' women moved around the body.
- Medical knowledge and, more generally, knowledge about health and disease has become increasingly specialised, first focusing on the 'whole' person, then examining specific parts of the body, and finally analysing the construction of cells. Theoretical knowledge of the body, learned knowledge, has taken precedence over experiential knowledge. Medicine and medical practice have increasingly become the preserve of those educated and trained by current practitioners and registered with their professional bodies. Lay practitioners, such as lay midwives, were systematically excluded from the practice of medicine.
- Each paradigm shift in thought has entailed a shift in the nature of the relationship between the practitioner and the patient. The 'bedside manner' paradigm suggests that, at least in the case of the wealthy, practitioners were 'patronised' by clients. Clients paid directly for the service and those providing it were often considered their social inferiors; power lay with the patient. If you compare and contrast this with the quality of, and the balance of power in, the contemporary relationship between practitioner and patient, a very different picture emerges. Despite the clear benefits which derive from the provision of a National Health Service, the position of general practitioners as 'independent contractors' within the service means that payment is gained not directly from the patient but via the health service itself. It could be argued that because of this the service provided is organised around the needs of the practitioners rather than of the patients. Appointment times might be one example. Most appointments are offered within the confines of the working day and, with the exception of emergencies, only on Monday to Friday. Given this, for many people in work it is hard to find a suitable time to see a GP without taking time off paid work.

The paradigm that accords best with our experiences of medicine in contemporary terms is that of clinical or hospital medicine. The following discussion provides a more detailed consideration of this aspect of medical knowledge and practice.

Foucault and the clinical gaze

The concept of the **clinical gaze** is associated with Foucault and refers to a specific way of conceptualising the body, rather than simply describing the physical location of the examination.

This new conceptualisation of the body stemmed from a number of developments, some of which have been mentioned in the discussion above. For example, the Enlightenment gave rise to the dominance of scientific and rational thought, an essential element of which was the opportunity to see the physical body as part of the 'natural' world. Part of this way of conceptualising the body is based on the idea of the mind–body split, enabling us to perceive the body as a physical object outside, external to and separate from ourselves as represented by the mind.

The concept of the clinical gaze is part of a specific discourse on the body in which the body is perceived as a physical object capable of being observed, measured and treated with little or no reference to the person.

Links

Chapter 11 explains the central role of medicine in interpreting the human body. The contested nature of knowledge is explored in Chapter 1 in a general discussion of postmodernism.

The ability to conceive of the body as an object in part stemmed from the increasing trend towards its physical dissection. The corpse became the source of knowledge about the body and that knowledge was the domain of medical science. The concept of the clinical gaze was used by Foucault (1973) to describe a specific and distinct method of examination and understanding, made possible by the physical examination of the internal workings of the body. Foucault's analysis contains the possibility of extending our knowledge of the socially constructed nature of reality. What may appear to us as real – for example, the physical make-up of the body – is actually the outcome of a specific kind of knowledge. To interpret the body and its workings requires a 'guide' because the body and its functions are not self-evident. Our representations of the body, whether through models or through diagrams, are the product of how we understand it. Without some training in what to look for and some general acceptance of the functions of the different parts of the anatomy, it is argued, we would not be able to interpret what we see. A map of a geographical area is a representation of it, full of complex signs and symbols that help us interpret what we see. The map is not an accurate representation of what we actually see as we walk about a city, but it is a guide that helps us interpret what we see. In the same way, medical knowledge provides a guide by which to read the body.

That medical science does not represent 'reality' can be illustrated with reference to explanations once held as 'true' but since revised in the light of new knowledge. The example of medical understanding of the blood is a useful illustration. As late as 1750 the nature and function of blood were interpreted in a very different way from today. It is worth remembering that this belief dominated despite the discovery of the circulation of the blood by the English physician William Harvey in 1628.

> Working with the understanding that there are two independent systems of blood vessels, the arteries and the veins, Galen [Greek physician, second century AD] believed that some almost immaterial vivifying substance (that is to say a substance endowing life), *pneuma*, was brought in from the air when we breathe, taken to the lungs and from there to the left chamber of the heart, where it was mixed with ordinary blood and was then drawn into the arteries. Its life possessing and life giving properties were evident to the senses when it was compared with the blood in the veins; arterial blood was bright, frothy, it spurted when the artery was cut, it needed the strong walls of the arteries to contain its natural tendency to expansion, and it had the pulse of life. Venous blood, by contrast was slow moving, and the thinner walls of its vessels showed no pulse. (Cunningham 1994: 62)

The physical examination of the body provided the opportunity to distinguish between normal and abnormal functions. On this basis, it is hardly surprising that the dominant definition of 'health' is as the absence of disease, and that medicine is so closely associated with the treatment of dysfunction rather than the promotion of health. The physical setting of the clinic or the hospital provided practitioners with the opportunity to examine bodies in large numbers and establish concepts of normality and abnormality. The benefits of such a distinction are clear. Practitioners are able to distinguish between a working kidney and one that is malfunctioning. We know that it is normal for babies to be born with a fontanelle, but in cases where this gap has prematurely closed surgery is necessary to allow the brain to develop normally. The question of normality and abnormality seems unproblematic in cases such as these. Sociologists of health and illness are concerned, however, that such judgements extend further to embrace human behaviour and lifestyles, for example in relation to mental health and well-being. What begins to emerge from this analysis is a picture of medicine and medical practice as both caring and potentially controlling, suggesting as it does what is normal and abnormal. The next chapter examines these issues in detail.

Conclusion

This chapter has explored the development of modern medicine by providing a historical account of the belief systems that gave rise to the practices that are still with us today. Medicine as a distinct scientific body of knowledge did not just come into being 'by itself' or by chance. Certain social and historical circumstances were necessary for its development. This occurred in the eighteenth century during the Enlightenment, a period when religious explanations and understandings of the natural world gave way to secular and scientific understandings. At this point it became increasingly legitimate to seek explanations of disease and illness with reference to the biological workings of the body as opposed to explanations which made reference to divine sanctions or superstitious causes.

This initial focus on the body shaped the future development of medicine. Biological systems, and particularly their failures, became the dominant perspective of medicine over more holistic accounts of the causes and cures of illness. This has seen medicine favouring a mechanical metaphor of the body, with technology and science as being the best (if not the only) ways to treat illness. As the rest of this book discusses, health and illness cannot be explained solely by reference to the internal workings of the biological body. What happens with the body is only one aspect of the whole 'story' of health.

Summary points

- This chapter has explained the development of modern medicine as a specific form of knowledge about the human body.
- The development of medical knowledge is strongly associated with science, rationality and the Enlightenment.
- Scientific medical knowledge represents a specific way of seeing and understanding the functions of the body. One example of this is the traditional idea of the mind–body split.
- Medical knowledge is dynamic and evolving.
- The possession of specialist medical knowledge leads to an increasing tendency to engage with the disease rather than with the patient.
- Medical knowledge is a form of power, with the potential to control and influence the lives of its recipients.

Case study

Imagine that you are being asked to publicly debate the use of embryos in medical research. Embryonic materials can be used to grow stem cells that in turn can be used to develop replacement organs for those that have failed and thus, ultimately, to save and prolong human lives. You are encountering strong resistance from the opposing side, made up of religious groups who disagree with the use of embryos in medical research.

1 On what grounds might religious groups protest about the use of embryos to grow stem cells?
2 What arguments could you produce to allow this kind of research to continue?
3 On a personal level, reflect upon your own feelings about this kind of research.

Taking your studies further

This chapter will have helped you understand many of the key terms, concepts, theories and debates relating to health and medicine. Listed below are journal articles and books that will provide deeper and more detailed discussions of the points raised in this chapter. You will also find what is available on the companion website. This offers downloads of relevant material, plus links to useful websites in addition to podcasts and other features.

Recommended reading

Calnan, M., Wainwright, D., O'Neill, C., Winterbottom, A. and Watkins, C. (2007) 'Illness action rediscovered: a case study of upper limb pain', *Sociology of Health and Illness*, 29 (3): 321–46.

Foucault, M. (1973) *The Birth of the Clinic: An Archaeology of Medical Perception*. London: Random House.

Lupton, D. (2003) *Medicine as Culture: Illness, Disease and the Body in Western Societies*, 2nd edn. London: Sage.

Stacey, M. (1988) *The Sociology of Health and Healing*. London: Routledge.

On the companion website

Tausing, M., Subedi, S. and Subedi, J. (2007) 'The bioethics of medical research in very poor countries', *Health*, 11 (4): 145–61.

3

Medical power and knowledge

Main points

- The medical profession exerts a great deal of power in society, though current social policy developments seek to limit clinical autonomy.
- Some medical decisions can create and lead to illness.
- Public health measures can lead to surveillance and control of people's lives beyond their health.

Key concepts

Power • clinical autonomy • the clinical method • surveillance.

Introduction

The purpose of this chapter is to consider the implications of the **power** of the medical profession. The nature and extent of this power can be understood in a positive sense (caring for) in terms of improving our quality of life and extending our span of life. However, a sociological **analysis** of medical power must take cognisance of the way in which this same ability can also be used as a means of controlling and regulating human lives. Like Bob the Builder, the medical profession, in most cases, can answer the question 'Can we fix it?' with an emphatic 'Yes we can!' The power of medicine is

The meaning of the concept of power is the subject of much debate within sociology. In the context of this discussion, however, the concept refers to (a) the ability to ensure that a particular point of view prevails in a disputed situation, (b) the capacity to ensure that someone acts in a certain way, and (c) the ability to stifle opposition to a particular perspective.

beyond doubt, but simply saying we can do something does not imply that we should. To say, for example, we can clone animals is not the same thing as saying that we should. Developments within modern medicine have meant that what in the past may have been purely clinical decisions are now ethical decisions. For example, the age at which premature babies can survive has steadily decreased, raising the question of at what stage of pregnancy terminations should be permitted. Medical staff have increasingly found themselves, on the one hand, trying to maintain the life of a child and, on the other, aborting a foetus of the same age.

'Clinical autonomy': doctor knows best

The concept of **clinical autonomy** is best understood as the freedom of clinicians to make decisions on the basis of their professional judgement and specialist knowledge. Doctors are not unique in claiming this level of autonomy; most professions make similar claims on the basis of the possession of an exclusive body of knowledge and a specialist education. Doctors, dentists, lawyers, nurses and even dieticians have their claim to specialist knowledge and judgement supported by the state in the form of state registration. Only those who have fulfilled the necessary training and experience are allowed to practise.

Clinical autonomy therefore suggests freedom to both diagnose and treat patients with appropriate means. As Seale and Pattison comment, the **clinical method** itself is premised on 'an overriding orientation towards action' (1994: 100) (see Figure 3.1).

The concept of clinical autonomy refers to the freedom of clinicians to make decisions on the basis of their professional judgement and specialist knowledge. This definition implies the downgrading of other assessments of the same situation.

Challenges to this degree of clinical freedom have come from a variety of sources. Patients are generally better informed about their condition than in the past, and those with chronic long-term conditions can accumulate an impressive level of knowledge and understanding of their illness. Cultural and political developments have encouraged us to see ourselves as consumers of health care, with resulting rights to adequate treatment

Diagnosis – take a history – define symptoms – examination – signs – prognosis

FIGURE 3.1   The clinical method (Seale and Pattison 1994)

and recourse if we feel that the treatment has not been appropriate. A second challenge has come from alternative practitioners who have raised serious questions about the effectiveness of conventional treatments and their potentially damaging long-term effects.

Health managers' attempts to curb the power of clinicians

A third challenge to clinical autonomy has come from within the National Health Service itself in terms of various reforms that have sought to enhance the power of managers to control the activities of clinicians. Proposals made in the 1989 White Paper *Working for Patients* (DH 1989) and later enacted in the NHS and Community Care Act 1990, aimed at curtailing the power of clinicians. Any attempt to control and regulate expenditure in the NHS, it was argued, must encompass the activities of clinicians. Decisions made by virtue of clinical autonomy can also be translated into expenditure figures, so in effect clinicians make not just medical decisions but also financial ones. Hunter comments: 'Getting a grip on the freedom enjoyed by clinicians and holding them to account for the expenditure they incur is seen as the last unmanaged frontier of the NHS' (1994: 6). Significantly, Hunter adds that attempts to manage doctors' activities may not be successful unless time and effort are devoted to 'developing a managerial consciousness' among doctors, and unless there is 'an understanding of the doctor's world and culture' (1994: 12).

Essential elements of 'the doctor's world and culture' can be gleaned from the previous chapter in terms of the ideas, influences and conditions that gave rise to modern medicine. As Chapter 2 makes clear, a significant part of the medical model is the technological imperative – the ability and the requirement to intervene to produce a positive change in the body. The development of modern medicine is also crucially linked to ideas that emerged during **the Enlightenment**, and this adherence to the principle of improving human welfare, combined with the Hippocratic oath, means that a doctor's first commitment has always been to the patient, or so it is argued. It is hardly surprising, then, that attempts to influence the behaviour of clinicians have been resisted. An analysis of the response of doctors to the introduction of the NHS in 1948 is evidence of this resistance. Doctors were willing to become employees of the NHS but also wanted to retain their right to carry out work in the **private sector**. To this day general practitioners remain independent contractors who do work on behalf of the NHS but do not formally work *for* the NHS. Some attempts are being made to introduce salaried general practitioners – partly to ensure the availability of services in particularly deprived areas, but also to gain some influence over the activities of doctors.

It is important to note that restrictions on the activities of doctors have largely been intended to get to grips with the cost implications of their decision making, rather than to place restrictions on their professional autonomy. However, two regulatory bodies have been established in the UK in recent years – the National Institute for Clinical Excellence (NICE) in England and Wales, and NHS Quality Improvement Scotland (NHS QIS) – both of which rule on which drugs should be prescribed by the NHS. The roles of these organisations are principally to end what has been described as 'postcode prescribing', where local health boards (health authorities in England and Wales) make independent decisions about whether or not a specific drug can be prescribed within their area. NICE, for example, recommended the prescribing of Aricept, a drug for the treatment of Alzheimer's disease. The decision was made on the basis of clinical effectiveness rather than purely on cost-effectiveness. The prescribing practices, however, of health authorities and health boards vary to such a degree that some patients will not have access to Aricept.

> The clinical method refers to the process that begins with diagnosis and leads to a prognosis and subsequent treatment.

The **clinical method**, the process that takes us from diagnosis to prognosis and treatment, remains very much intact. This should neither surprise nor, for the most part, alarm us, for the vast majority of clinical judgements are reasonable and bring about positive changes in the patient. However, some decisions can lead to negative effects on the patient; some are based on assumptions rather than on medical 'fact', while others are made without clear evidence to support them.

Medical harm: iatrogenesis

The first basis on which we can question the power of clinical freedom is in terms of its iatrogenic effects. The concept of **iatrogenesis**, associated with Illich, refers to an illness caused by a doctor; that is to say, harm would not have been caused *without* the medical intervention. Illich argues that the 'damage done by medicine to the health of the individuals and populations is very significant' (1993). This is referred to as 'clinical' iatrogenesis and Illich cites drug therapies, doctors or hospitals as the cause of harm. A second aspect is 'cultural' iatrogenesis, which denotes a dependence on medicine to cure and to care for people. Illich argues that cultural iatrogenesis means that people no longer take responsibility for their own health problems and the diagnosis of their symptoms. Illich asserts that 'medical practice sponsors sickness ... reinforcing a morbid society that encourages people to become consumers of curative, preventative, industrial and environmental medicine' (1993: 158). The result of this dependency is a situation of 'medical nemesis', where the harm caused by medicine is difficult to eliminate except by recourse to further medical intervention, which in itself results in further harm. Illich paints a picture of an inevitable decline into an increasingly unhealthy world, where the provision of health care ultimately has a negative effect on our well-being.

> Iatrogenesis literally means harm caused by doctors. In its most literal sense it refers to the harmful consequences of medical intervention. Illich also uses the concept to draw our attention to our cultural dependence on medicine and medical practitioners, such that we do not seek alternative explanations or alternative remedies for ill health.

> ## Questions
>
> What examples can you give of instances where medical intervention has had negative effects?

A balanced account of the harm resulting from health care would also, clearly, have to take into account positive developments in medicine. Hardley (1998) characterised the 1950s and 1960s as a period of great optimism about the potential of medicine to cure and care for people, and evidences this with reference to mass vaccination programmes that eradicated diseases such as polio and smallpox. At one end of the spectrum medicine can save and prolong life through radical interventions such as organ transplants, while at the more mundane end of the spectrum the symptoms of minor ailments such as headaches and menstrual pain can be eliminated by readily available pain relief. It is hardly surprising, therefore, that lay people may have a sense of dependency on medicine. Compared to people's experiences of health in the past, our own ill health may well seem trivial. Giddens comments that a glance at those experiences 'provides graphic evidence of the level to which illness and the prospect of an early death haunted the lives of individuals in the eighteenth century. Infectious diseases were rampant and the ordinary person suffered from a range of chronic complaints which many of us in modern social conditions would find intolerable' (1997: 47–8).

> In the eighteenth century in particular, deadly fevers – contemporaries called them 'spotted', 'miliary', 'hectic', 'malignant', etc. – struck down hundreds of thousands, young and old alike, while the so called 'new' diseases gained ground – some crippling such as rickets; some fatal, such as tuberculosis. Today's minor nuisance, like flu, was yesterday's killer. 'The Hooping Cough is yet with us', wrote George Crabbe in 1829, 'and many children die of it.' And all this against a backdrop of endemic maladies, such as malaria and infantile diarrhoea, and a Pandora's box of other infections (dysentery, scarlatina, measles, etc.) that commonly proved fatal, above all to infants, to say nothing of the 101 other pains, eruptions, swellings, ulcers, scrofula and wasting conditions, not least the agonizing stone and the proverbial gout, which threatened livings and livelihoods, and all too often life itself. (Porter and Porter 1985, reprinted in Giddens 2001:116)

Fact or fiction? The making of medical decisions

The above discussion illustrates one strand of thinking which is critical of clinical autonomy on the basis of the harm resulting from medical intervention. The second level on which one can question the dominance of clinical autonomy is that clinical decisions are sometimes made on the basis of assumptions and beliefs rather than on scientific, objective grounds.

Links

Chapter 2 provides a detailed account of the 'scientific' basis of the practice of medicine.

The previous chapter highlighted the extent to which the medical model is based on a commitment to scientific methods and empirical evidence, both of which suggest a high degree of objectivity. Critics of the medical model, however, have suggested that medicine is also the product of its social and cultural environments and, as such, is bound to reflect values dominant in society. Historically, the treatment of female patients provides a useful illustration of the extent to which medical categories reflect broader social and cultural values. Medicine does more than simply describe sets of symptoms; it may also create certain types of behaviour by applying a label to describe and categorise. According to Lupton,

Hysteria is the name of a 'disease' once associated with the movement of the womb around the body but later described as a disease of the nervous system. The symptoms of hysteria were described as weeping, fainting and a general malaise (James 1994).

medicine can be seen as a 'moral exercise … used to define normality, punish deviance and maintain social order' (1996: 57). A historical example of such a 'moral exercise' is **hysteria**.

James (1994) provides a detailed account of hysteria, its symptoms and its remedies, from Greek theories of the womb's tendency to move around the body, to eighteenth-century theories of hysteria as a demonstration of the greater delicacy of women, particularly celibate women. Such theories clearly resonated with ideas dominant at the time about women's essential differences from men. According to Turner (1994), descriptions of hysteria were linked to ideas about the subordination of women in so far as women were seen as 'naturally' frail and emotional. It had frequently been noted that the women who were most likely to experience hysteria (James 1994: 80) were unmarried and, therefore, seen as either sexually inactive or sexually active but in an inappropriate manner. Neither celibacy nor unlicensed sexual activity was seen as conducive to good physical or mental health. The remedy for hysterical behaviour was, therefore, marriage and reproduction. It is important to remember that the eighteenth and nineteenth centuries are associated with the beginnings of the modern women's movement, with its demand, for example, for equal access to education. Coincidentally, hysteria just happened to be diagnosed among women whose sexuality was not expressed 'normally', according to the prevailing values of the time, through marriage and child-bearing, and among women who attempted to pursue their education and careers. Turner writes that it was 'the absence of normal sexual activity designed to bring about reproduction which was associated in medical discourse with the prominence of hysteria' (1994: 84). The diagnosis of hysteria was linked not just with maintaining women's health but also with maintaining a specific pattern of gendered social relationships.

This chapter has established the ways in which medical power and knowledge can be used both positively and negatively. The concept of clinical autonomy suggests that 'doctor knows best'. The preceding discussion has sought to highlight the specific nature of this professional dominance with examples such as the NHS reforms of the late 1980s and early 1990s when government attempted to rein in the power of the clinician. Two further examples, the concept of iatrogenesis and hysteria, were discussed to illustrate that clinical autonomy can be used to further ends other than to enhance the well-being of the patient. However, it might be argued that these are rather extreme examples, and that for the most part medicine does enhance health and well-being. Underpinning this line of argument is a strong belief that medicine is essentially a benign practice and that its ultimate function is to care for rather than to control. The following discussion challenges this idea by examining further the degree to which medicine is a disciplinary practice as much as a caring one.

Public health: the morality of everyday life

Links

The moralistic element of medicine was introduced in Chapter 2.

The previous discussion of the **medical model of health** draws our attention to the ways in which that model embraces issues relating to lifestyles and choice. 'Public health' refers to those areas of health and disease shared by the population in general and which are seen to be amenable to preventative intervention. Strategies to tackle public health cover more than simply medical techniques and have included measures to address housing problems, for example, and to ensure the supply of clean water and adequate sanitation. Contemporary definitions of public health have tended to take as their object the environment, including social, psychological and physical elements (Peterson 1997: 192–3).

There are four significant points that arise from these public health initiatives. First, the at-risk category embraces most people. Health and the practice of medicine, therefore, no longer embrace only those who are diseased but now encompass even those who are well. Second, public health appears to be concerned with the regulation and control of individual bodies. Lupton (1994: 30) argues that controlling and preventing the spread of disease has largely involved confining bodies and controlling their movements. Third, over and above the control and regulation of individuals is the regulation of the social body. Many of the facts and figures presented throughout this book are themselves a product of the public health movement and, in particular, of attempts to

Surveillance refers to a form of scrutiny and observation but one that does not necessarily depend directly on the physical proximity of the watcher and the watched. Instead, subtle forms of surveillance are said to characterise modern society, typified by the tendency of individuals to act in ways that they think they 'ought' to.

'map' the spread of disease and its distribution within the population. Epidemiology involves the recording of information, 'constant record-taking, measuring and reporting back to a system of government agencies' (1994: 31). Increasingly our risk of disease becomes understood in terms of statistical probability calculated for us by experts. Finally, what emerges from an analysis of public health initiatives is a sense of what is pathological (diseased) and what is normal health and behaviour. 'Normal' is often understood as what is statistically average. Seale points to this tendency and highlights its implications in terms of the association of normality with what *ought* to be the case (1998: 105).

Links

Chapter 11 provides a discussion of the body as a site of control and regulation, not only for health professionals but for individuals as well.

The control and regulation of disease

The act of collecting information, analysing that information and calculating 'risk' suggests that knowledge is being used as a form of power and influence. At one end of the spectrum, this form of power could be described as 'disciplinary' (for example, confining infected bodies to their homes), or at the very least as 'directional' (for example, directing us towards healthy eating practices). The work of Foucault leads us to the conclusion that the modern period is associated with subtle forms of power, control and regulation. The best illustration of this form of power is the panopticon – a construction containing a central observation tower around which other buildings are placed and into which the occupant of the central tower can see. The occupants of the outlying buildings are not afforded the same opportunity and do not know when or if they are being watched. The aim of this system of **surveillance** is to ensure that this state of uncertainty is transformed into self-surveillance. Such a system is in stark contrast to sovereign forms of power, exemplified by sixteenth- and seventeenth-century monarchs. Under their regimes, Seale argues, power was manifest in rather more obvious and brutal forms, principally through 'physical coercion and public punishment for wrongdoing' (1998: 105). Public acts of punishment were a reminder of the power of the monarch and it was the act of punishment that marked an individual as an 'out law'. In contrast, disciplinary power 'operated by constructing and promoting, with the aid of statistical information, particular definitions of normality. From being coerced to follow the will of the king, citizens learned to survey themselves as bearers of normality' (1998: 105).

Questions

Can you identify any incidents in your own life where you have been assessed for 'normal functioning'?

A specific example of surveillance and self-surveillance can be found in the case of screening for cervical cancer. Research carried out by McKie suggests that in this instance 'screening is both creating and reinforcing a surveillance of women's sexual lives and health' (1995: 441). As the above discussion describes, screening involves not only uncovering infection but also identifying groups at risk. In the case of cervical cancer, treatment is not confined to women with cervical cancer but includes those women identified as having pre-cancerous cells that might develop into cervical cancer at a later stage. An additional complication with this form of screening is that there are difficulties in establishing the causes of cervical cancer and thus there is a further difficulty in differentiating between those women who might consider themselves normal and those who might be most at risk. For this reason the at-risk category essentially embraces all women. Failure to recognise your own at-risk status is viewed in negative terms: 'Women are encouraged to attend on a regular basis and those who do not are often considered by health care workers to be irresponsible, feckless and non-compliers' (1995: 445).

McKie highlights the extent to which much of the surveillance carried out by the medical profession on behalf of the state is of behaviours that are believed to lead to the spread of the disease. Despite the causes of cervical cancer being unclear, many researchers maintain that the human papilloma virus HPV, which can be transmitted through sexual intercourse, is to be found in the majority of cancers. As McKie points out, this in itself raises the question of the causes of HPV, and a number of factors are said to place women at greater risk. These include age, heterosexual intercourse, lower age at first intercourse and smoking status. It is, therefore, not just the cervix itself that is subject to surveillance but types of behaviour, many of which – such as sexual intercourse at an early age and sexual promiscuity – have negative connotations. To receive a positive result for a cervical cancer may stigmatise the woman as someone who 'sleeps around' (1995: 449). In this instance it is possible to argue that screening does not simply describe what is the case (the number of women with cervical cancer) but has implications for what ought to be by suggesting a link between stigmatised behaviours and the causes of the disease. Screening for cervical cancer, therefore, carries with it certain normative assumptions about how women ought to behave, and this extends to the assumption that all women are heterosexual. This assumption is especially significant since many practitioners use the 'smear' as an opportunity to talk to women about other health issues, principally contraception and sexual health, again based on the same assumption of exclusively heterosexual experiences.

The preceding discussion raises the issue of medicine as a moral discourse regulating various aspects of our lives. An important aspect of this regulation is surveillance of our own behaviour, convinced as we are of the morality of what we are required to do when, for example, submitting ourselves to screening for diseases. Surveillance is a form of power that does not physically constrain or persecute people but apparently gives people the freedom of taking responsibility for their own health and well-being. As Seale comments, concepts of normality become internalised 'so that under disciplinary power, people constantly monitor themselves for signs of pathology. Thus people draw upon a widespread knowledge of what it is to be sane, healthy and good, and of their opposites, madness, disease and criminality' (1998: 106).

One conclusion that can be drawn is that the power of clinicians resides not so much in the person as in the profession. Such conclusions are well recorded within the sociology of health. Parsons' concept of the **sick role** is a clear example of a model that not only accepts that there is inequality in the clinician/patient relationship, but maintains that this actually benefits both parties. The following discussion examines the continuing power of the medical profession.

The latter-day 'resurrectionists': the continuing power of the medical profession

Parsons' functionalist account of the sick role lays out the roles, responsibilities and rights of patients and practitioners based on an assumption of a consensus between the two parties, ultimately beneficial to both (see Table 3.1).

Links

A description of the functionalist approach is available in Chapter 1.

TABLE 3.1 Parsons' concept of the sick role

1 Legitimises withdrawal from a range of 'normal' obligations, such as paid work
2 A person cannot get well without the intervention of a medical professional
3 People have a social obligation to get well as soon as possible; this is the only basis upon which legitimate access to the 'sick role' is granted
4 Care has to be provided by a competent medical practitioner
5 The doctor/patient relationship is characterised by neutrality
6 In return for compliance with the 'sick role', the patient is provided with medical care
7 Doctors have the right to diagnose, examine and treat patients

Source: adapted from Turner (1994: 46)

A number of criticisms of the concept of the sick role are particularly relevant to this discussion about the power of the medical profession. According to Turner, one major area of criticism has been Parsons' assumption that the doctor/patient relationship is 'complementary and functional' (1994: 46). Not only does sociological research suggest that patients may be well informed and, therefore, questioning of the treatment provided, but it also suggests that the power of the practitioner is not always used for the benefit of the patient. Certainly, arguments such as these have been used to justify the practice of clinical autonomy. The NHS reforms of the 1980s and 1990s challenged the undisputed power of clinicians with the introduction of the principle of general management. It was not difficult for critics of the reforms to argue that it could only be practitioners who had the best interests of the patients at heart since it was practitioners, not managers, who had direct contact with them. Counter-arguments centred on questioning whether practitioners could also use clinical autonomy to safeguard their own professional interests. Resources might be used to research a particular disease, for example, with ultimate benefit to the patient. However, resources for research might also further an individual clinician's career in so far as it enabled someone to pursue a particular interest and add to their reputation and knowledge.

A contemporary example of the tendency of the population to contest the power of the medical profession is the current resistance to the MMR triple vaccine. Despite reassurances by the medical profession that the triple vaccine is safe, large sections of the general public remain sceptical.

Links

The concept of the sociological imagination is detailed in Chapter 1. Chapter 2 provides a detailed discussion of the clinical gaze.

To fully understand the nature of the relationship between the practitioner and the patient it is necessary to employ the **sociological imagination** to uncover what lies behind the obvious. Within sociology, there is a long tradition of acknowledging that the possession of knowledge is a form of power. Such an approach is evident in the work of Foucault and the concept of the **clinical gaze**. The 'gaze' not only reveals a specific way of 'seeing' the body (or the insides of the body); with it comes a whole vocabulary by which to know and interpret the body. This specialist knowledge has the effect of excluding other, alternative explanations of the body and disease. The work of Becker (1974) and the labelling tradition also allows us to explore how knowledge is used as a form of social control. A central tenet of labelling theory is the acceptance of the social construction of knowledge. In other words, meanings are not fixed but are the outcome of a process of definition, a process in which some groups and individuals have considerably more say than others. Within the labelling tradition, deviance has 'no consistent unitary content or essence' (Turner 1994: 73). It is possible to interpret medical knowledge as a form of labelling in so far as diagnostic categories are ways of describing and categorising behaviour. It is useful to reflect on an example of research used in the opening chapter. There we outlined Rosenhan's work 'On being sane in insane places' (1973), which concluded that diagnostic categories were social constructs with which it was possible to both describe and create 'madness'.

The making of life-and-death decisions

The ability to diagnose, recommend and carry out treatment represents a distinctive form of power. Simple examples of this power are found in relation to pregnancy and death. Pregnancy may be evident to the mother-to-be and those around her, but it awaits 'official' confirmation by the medical profession. Again, it may be clear to others that death has taken place but it is not for them to confirm that. Illich argues that the degree of control exercised by the medical professional is extensive: it 'starts with the monthly prenatal check-up when he decides if and how the foetus shall be born; it ends with his decision to abandon further resuscitation' (1976, cited in Harvey 1997: 719).

Reproductive technology involves new techniques of surveillance and examination, such as ultrasound and foetal monitoring, that make the woman and the unborn child 'visible' in a way that turns them both into objects and subjects of medical, legal and state intervention. Doyal (1994) calls the foetus the 'newly discovered second patient' and describes situations where doctors seek court orders to protect the best interests of their 'new' patients.

The legal and medical professions, it is argued, are the 'managers' of death. Harvey asserts that the medical dominance of death is reflected in the mirroring of medical images of death in the popular consciousness. She argues that 'the "straight green line" on the oscilloscope has become a compelling late-twentieth-century image of death, while the electronic alarm signal has replaced the (organic) death rattle in popular consciousness' (1997: 725). Harvey suggests that in situations where therapeutic intervention has reached its limits and there is no improvement in the patient's condition, clinicians may consider 'withdrawal of active support' (1997: 724). Such support is reduced on a gradual basis, Harvey's research suggests, in order to mimic a natural, gradual death. There are said to be specific benefits to this approach. In the first instance, it allows relatives of the patient to come to terms with the imminent death of a loved one. Second, death is less dramatic, less like pointing a gun at someone, as one of the interviewed consultants suggested.

> ## Questions
>
> Prior to the rise of the medical profession, who would have been actively involved in the diagnosis of death?

The making of 'end-of-life decisions' is clearly fraught with medical, technological, legal and ethical considerations. With the power to save and prolong life comes the onerous power to end it. Wade (2001), a consultant and professor in neurological disability, explores the specific example of patients in a permanent vegetative state (PVS). This state is characterised by Wade using the following criteria (2001: 352):

1 The patient shows no behavioural evidence of awareness of self or environment.
2 There is brain damage, usually of known cause, consistent with the diagnosis.
3 There are no reversible causes present.
4 At least six (usually 12) months have passed since the onset of PVS.

A number of ethical issues are raised not just by the decision to end a life but, Wade suggests, by the diagnosis itself. He suggests that the diagnosis is not certain and there is no standard test to assess levels of awareness. The actual decision to withdraw feeding is loaded with legal and ethical issues. For example, treating a patient who may be regarded as 'non-sentient' raises questions about how to maintain that person's dignity and privacy. Committing resources to the care of people in a permanent vegetative state raises issues about the rationing of scarce health resources: 'is it equitable to allocate substantial scarce resources to someone who is unaware of their situation and will not recover awareness?'(2001: 352). Wade recognises that the issue raises questions outside the remit of individual clinicians, and argues that one solution might be to take into consideration the interests of other parties 'and to use a full ethical accounting procedure' (2001: 352) (Table 3.2). The suggestions are interesting, if only because they seek to share out the responsibility for decision making in relation to the ending of life.

Decision making relating to the ending of life is complex and demonstrates both the actual and the potential power that clinicians have to make decisions. In the light of technological advancement they are increasingly being faced with decisions that might appear to be purely clinical but are also ethical and legal. While the death of a patient might be seen as a failure in terms of the medical profession's ability to maintain life, death itself provides important information and 'resources' that can save other lives and advance medical knowledge. One of the key factors that allowed the development of clinical medicine was the ability to examine the corpse and to learn from this. Thus pathology plays an important part in developing medical knowledge. Clinicians no

TABLE 3.2 Permanent vegetative state: interested parties and their interests

Patient	Relatives (and friends)
May have pre-existing statement of wishes	May have a financial interest (will or settlement)
May have wished to donate organs	May have other legal interests
May have had strong beliefs (religious or otherwise)	May have emotional or other stressful experiences
May or may not be experiencing emotions	May be ignoring children or others
May have strong beliefs	
Ward staff	**Organisation giving care**
May have emotional interests in patient or family	May have financial interests (positive or negative)
May have strong beliefs	May have political or public relationship interests
Organisation funding care	**Society**
May wish to allocate resources differently	May wish to preserve sanctity of life
	May wish to avoid 'slippery slope'
	May support different allocation of resources

Source: Wade (2001)

longer have to rely upon 'Resurrectionists' to supply them with bodies, since social and cultural taboos about the use of dead bodies have largely been eroded. It is a legal requirement in the case of sudden or violent death for a post-mortem to take place and for tissue to be retained as evidence. Many thousands of people carry organ donor cards and the medical profession talks openly about the 'harvesting' of organs for the purpose of transplants.

Despite a general acceptance of the use of dead bodies for teaching and research purposes and the desirability of 'harvesting' organs in order to prolong the life of others, revelations about the extent and nature of the retention of such material has caused national outrage. When it emerged in 1999 that various organs from children treated at the Alder Hey Hospital in Liverpool had been removed and retained without the knowledge or consent of parents, there were calls for government to ensure that this would not happen again. While there was widespread condemnation of these practices by other clinicians, the case, nevertheless, represented a dilemma for the medical profession. It was important to be seen to act ethically and with the consent of relatives, but at the same time there was a necessity to secure an adequate supply of human tissue to continue research.

> Professor Gordon McVie, director general of the Cancer Research Campaign, told the *BMJ* [*British Medical Journal*] that, although researchers remained 'extremely sensitive to the issue of patient consent', it was unreasonable to expect scientists to list every use a tissue sample might be put to.

'It's impossible to predict everything you are going to do. There are 3,000 genes linked to breast cancer. Are you going to list them all on a consent form?'

Professor McVie expressed concern that plans to create banks of excised tumour tissue to aid cancer research could be put at risk if all collection of tissue was restricted. (Hunter 2001: 322)

Liam Donaldson, Chief Medical Officer in England and Wales, advised that informed consent should be sought rather than simple 'lack of objection' and that consent forms should contain 'details of the tissue and organs to be retained, the uses to which they might be put, and the agreed length of time for retention' (Hunter 2001: 322). Confusion had arisen in particular about the ambiguous use of the word 'tissue', which to lay people suggested small, insignificant parts of organs or blood vessels. In contrast, clinicians used the term as a catch-all category to include substantial body parts such as the heart. The characteristics of the medical model outlined in the first chapter are a reminder of the 'mechanical' metaphor for the workings and parts which make up the human body. It is possible to argue on the basis of the Alder Hey scandal that the medical model and the clinical gaze have the effect of dehumanising the body and obscuring the ability of those involved to appreciate the significance of the 'whole' body for family and friends.

Links

Chapter 2 provides an overview of the significance of the autopsy and post-mortem in the 'opening up' of human bodies for the development of medical knowledge.

Conclusion

This chapter has examined the extent and nature of the power of the medical profession in relation to clinical autonomy, public health and contemporary examples of decisions made about ending life and retaining human organs for research. Much of the apparent power of clinicians rests on the possession of a specialist body of knowledge that provides a justification for the exclusion of others from the process of decision making. This conclusion does not deny the obvious benefits of medical intervention but seeks to draw attention to the implications of the use of power.

Public health programmes such as mass screening have played a central role in the elimination of diseases such as polio, but it is also clear from the examples discussed above that such programmes are underpinned by a strong sense of what people 'ought' to do.

It is possible, therefore, to conclude that public health is at least directional, if not a form of disciplinary power. Contemporary examples of the practice of medicine, such as the Alder Hey scandal, underline the fact that medicine is open to criticism. The next chapter considers the basis upon which such criticisms have been made and looks at possible alternatives to current orthodox medical knowledge and practice.

Summary points

- Medicine's power is based on a specialist knowledge base and clinical autonomy.
- Medical decisions are not always based on evidence.
- Critics, such as Illich, point to how medicine can cause harm.
- Public health programmes can also act as a form of social control.

Case study

Callum has been in a permanent vegetative state for three months, following a car crash. There are no signs to indicate that he will ever gain consciousness again, leaving his parents in a state of confusion and misery. His body appears unmarked and undamaged, but there is no hope of recovery. At the age of 18 he was a fit and healthy young man, but now it appears that his life is over. His parents are reluctant to do anything that will end his life. As long as he stays this way he is at least not lost to them, and yet there can be no more engagement with him.

Drawing on the various criteria outlined by Wade in his 'interested parties' concept (Table 3.2), analyse this situation and reflect upon how ending Callum's life would impact on all the people involved, both family and care providers.

Taking your studies further

This chapter will have helped you understand many of the key terms, concepts, theories and debates relating to medical power and knowledge. Listed below are journal articles and books that will provide deeper and more detailed discussions of the points raised in this chapter. You will also find what is available on the companion website. This offers downloads of relevant material, plus links to useful websites in addition to podcasts and other features.

Recommended reading

Harvey, J. (1997) 'The technological regulation of death: with reference to the technological regulation of birth', *Sociology*, 31 (4): 719–35.

Petersen, A.R. and Lupton, D. (2000) *The New Public Health: Discourses, Knowledges, Strategies*. London: Sage.

Seymour, J.E. (1999) 'Revisiting medicalisation and "natural" death', *Social Science and Medicine*, 49 (5): 691–704.

Seymour, J.E. (2000) 'Negotiating natural death in intensive care', *Social Science and Medicine*, 51 (8): 1241–52.

On the companion website

Lee-Treweek, G. (2001) '"I'm not ill, it's just this back": osteopathic treatment, responsibility and back problems', *Health*, 5 (1): 31–49.

4

Challenging medical dominance

Main points

- Medicine has encroached upon many aspects of life that were once considered normal or 'natural'. This is termed 'medicalisation'.
- One example of medicalisation is pregnancy and childbirth. Doctors and medical technology can challenge women's control and experiences of fertility.
- Alternative, or complementary, medicine is becoming increasingly popular, due to increased individualism, disengagement with community and dissatisfaction with mainstream medicine.

Key concepts

Complementary medicine • alternative medicine • reproductive technology • medicalisation.

Introduction

The previous chapter gave specific examples of medical power by exploring the concept of **clinical autonomy**, the morality implicit in public health messages, and medicine's continuing access to and control over the body. This chapter seeks to analyse the basis upon which critics have challenged that dominance. There are two major themes to be explored here. The first is that of the medical control and regulation of women's lives in the context of reproduction and **reproductive technology**. Feminist critiques of medicine are concerned not only with the numerical dominance of men in the profession in general as well as in specific areas such as acute services, but with challenging the values, beliefs and ideology associated with the theory and practice of medicine. The second theme to be examined is that of alternative or complementary therapies. Like the feminist critique of medicine, alternative perspectives represent a radical challenge to the most basic concepts and practices of western biomedicine.

Reproductive technology embraces a range of medical interventions (pharmaceutical and invasive), the purpose of which is either to promote or to prevent pregnancy. The concept of medicalisation is used to describe a tendency to explain behaviour and experiences in medical terms.

Links

See Chapter 3 for a related discussion of the concept of clinical autonomy.

'The miracle of life': the medical colonisation of reproduction

Feminist critiques of medicine challenge the way in which women's lives, principally in relation to reproduction, have been subject to the control of the medical profession, with women themselves seen as passive objects. The phrase **reproductive technology** refers not only to pregnancy and birth but also to the use of contraception and to assisted conception in the form of IVF, for example. Oakley suggests that reproduction embraces both the 'promotion of pregnancy' and the 'preventing of pregnancy' (1987: 40). This type of control and regulation is representative of the degree to which women's lives are subject to **medicalisation**. Previous chapters have already made reference to the manner in which medical knowledge can be used as a form of power, and the extent to which the practice of medicine can be based on moral judgements rather than on scientific evidence. In relation to this discussion of reproduction it is particularly helpful to think about medicalisation as the way in which specific 'behaviours or conditions are given medical meanings and thus medical practice becomes the appropriate vehicle for their elimination or control' (Levinson 1998: 75). In this way, the apparently 'natural' process of reproduction is defined as a medical condition requiring 'expert' knowledge, treatment and intervention.

A significant aspect of the concept of medicalisation is the extent to which natural experiences are transformed into medical ones. Oakley provides historical evidence of how the experiences of pregnancy and childbirth were significantly changed by medical intervention. Prior to the widespread dominance of biomedicine, Oakley argues, the main healers in society were lay women: 'Childbirth occurred at home. There was no systematic medical care during pregnancy. Institutions grouping pregnant and labouring women as "patients" along with the sick did not exist' (1987: 37). It was not until the eighteenth century that childbirth became increasingly technical and appropriated by male medical practitioners. The opportunity to study pregnancy and childbirth was facilitated by the use of hospitals to care for women.

Links

The medicalisation of death is dealt with in Chapter 3.

Similar themes emerge from Reissman's (1992) account of the medicalisation of childbirth in mid-nineteenth-century America. Like Oakley, Reissman argues that childbirth increasingly came to be seen as a technical problem, thus requiring the expert intervention of the medical profession within a suitable physical location, namely the hospital rather than the home. She suggests that this process of medicalisation resulted in a fundamental change to the nature of childbirth: 'the meaning of childbirth for women was transformed from a human experience to a medical technical problem' (1992: 127). The emerging profession of obstetrics reached a position of dominance for a variety of social and medical reasons. Obstetricians were male, mainly white and middle class, enjoying social and class dominance over the female, lower-class, and mainly immigrant midwives. Of particular importance, argues Reissman, was the ability of the emerging profession to convince both colleagues and the public that pregnancy required medical and technical intervention in order to reach a successful conclusion. Most significantly of all, mothers were seen as passive objects, knowing less about their own pregnancy than the medical expert.

Oakley (1987: 39) suggests that this shift towards the definition of women as 'mindless mothers' emerged at the same time as the technological dominance of pregnancy. The notion of women as 'walking wombs' is clearly illustrated by the following conversation recorded by Oakley (1987: 46):

Patient:	It's the tightening I worry about.
Doctor:	It's normal in pregnancy. Your womb is supposed to tighten.
Patient:	I didn't have it with the other three.
Doctor:	Every pregnancy is different. Let's see you in one week. [Reading notes] You do seem to have put on a bit of weight.
Patient:	What does that mean?
Doctor:	It doesn't necessarily mean anything but you must take things easy.
Patient:	That's what my husband says. It's easy for men to say that.
Doctor:	You shouldn't blame us.
Patient:	I'm not blaming you. It's not your fault.
Doctor:	It's your set-up at home. You should have organised things better.
Patient:	Well, I've got three kids to look after.
Doctor:	Yes.

Oakley's analysis of the conversation is intended to illustrate the power dynamics implicit in the doctor/patient relationship. She argues that first the doctor dismisses the patient's understanding of her condition, and the authority of his own knowledge is reaffirmed. Second, the conversation reveals the power the doctor possesses in terms of withholding information. The patient's weight is commented upon but the doctor does not reveal the significance of this fact. The conversation also reveals a general acceptance on the part of both the patient and the doctor of women's responsibility for childcare and housework. The patient herself is seen as being responsible for not taking things easy. Oakley concludes that the doctor is concerned primarily with the technical management of the pregnancy rather than with the real person coping with both her pregnancy and her domestic responsibilities. 'The problem of pregnancy management as he has defined it discounts the importance of the whole person' (1987: 47).

Feminist critics have questioned the reasoning behind the accepted ways of treating pregnancy and delivering babies. Doyal (1994) talks about potentially demeaning practices such as the shaving of pubic hair and the giving of enemas. Other commentators have questioned the need for the majority of births to take place in hospitals, suggesting that most labours are 'uneventful' and as such could take place in the woman's own home (Lupton 1994: 148). Removing pregnant women to the hospital environment suggests that pregnancy is an illness, and has the added disadvantage of placing women in an environment unknown to them at a time when they are particularly vulnerable. Responses to such criticisms have come in two main forms: the development of a natural childbirth movement, and a change in the attitudes and practices of the medical profession itself. Natural childbirth is defined as childbirth with 'as little drug intervention as possible' (1994: 148). The degree to which the medical profession has embraced a more 'natural' model of childbirth is subject to debate, but there is a growing recognition of the need to allow women to make informed choices about how and where they deliver.

Feminist critique can suggest that medicine and medical practitioners see women as objects and mindless mothers who play no part in deciding what kind of medical care they receive. What is perhaps lacking from this analysis is an appreciation that women have at times welcomed technological interventions and even benefited from them. Reissman argues that women 'participated in the medicalisation of childbirth for a complex set of reasons' (1992: 128). The principal reason was a desire to find relief from the pain and frequency of childbirth. The desire for pain relief was, Reissman comments, part of a change in social attitudes towards pregnancy, with childbirth no longer seen as 'a condition to be endured with fatalism and passivity' (1992: 129). An overall reduction in fertility rates, especially marked among the middle and upper classes, meant that the experience of birth was changing. The fact that women had fewer children resulted in increased anxiety about childbirth and a greater desire for the delivery to take place safely. In the broader context of medicalisation generally, Lupton (1994: 98) reminds us that patients and doctors might well collude, effectively enhancing the medical dominance of the latter. While medical power can be seen as 'disciplining' and controlling people's lives, it may well be true that people give themselves over to medical power voluntarily because of the apparent benefits that accrue.

Questions

In terms of pregnancy and childbirth, what are the benefits of medical intervention?

Part of Oakley's critique of the medicalisation of pregnancy and childbirth is the failure of the medical profession to take into consideration the whole person. Instead, she argues, women are seen as 'mindless mothers' whose own experiences and knowledge of pregnancy are often ignored. An essential element of the concept of medicalisation can thus be understood as the transformation of human experiences into medical and technical ones. According to Oakley, the personal and social implications of medical treatment are rarely considered:

> It took some twenty years for the practitioners of obstetric ultrasound to wake up to the fact that seeing her foetus on the screen might change the way a woman felt about it. This elementary piece of wisdom has translated into technical paediatric language and the notion of prenatal mother–child bonding was born. (1987: 52)

Links

Chapter 3 examines the ability of the medical profession to place the body, even in its inner workings, under surveillance.

In a similar vein, Lupton (1994) has considered how the procedure of genetic testing involves a new discourse of the body. It is impossible, Lupton suggests, to separate the technical aspects of genetic screening from its social and emotional implications. Part of the basis upon which people are persuaded of the necessity of undergoing such tests is an appeal to their emotions and anxieties about being a 'good' and responsible parent. Genetic screening provides a very different way of understanding the body; it becomes a collection of codes, like a machine-based system, that can only be interpreted by 'experts'. Lupton suggests that this particular discourse on the body has little meaning to lay people. Being told of your risk of passing on a genetically inherited disease in purely statistical terms can appear overly abstract and difficult to translate into the decision to carry on with or terminate the pregnancy. Lupton contrasts the 'abstract language of biomedicine' with the 'individualised narratives' provided by the parents themselves (1994: 152).

Assisted conception

The medicalisation of pregnancy and childbirth has a relatively long history, but medical dominance is increasingly interpreted in terms of the ability to create life in the various forms of assisted conception. The following discussion has two main strands: first, an examination of the social, ethical and cultural implications of assisted conception; and second, a consideration of the implications of the medical dominance of women's lives. The preceding chapter outlined the scope and power of medicine in relation to its ability to prolong and enhance life. It was noted that while science provides the means to transform our lives, it does not answer the question of whether or not such interventions should take place. Ethical debates about the use of biomedicine are nowhere more acute than around the use and potential of assisted conception. Debates about assisted conception necessarily go beyond helping those people who are unable to conceive naturally, and embrace complex arguments about its use (and potential misuse), such as the storing of human embryos.

The use of assisted conception brings into sharp relief the question of who is the parent of the child, and under what circumstances. In normal circumstances, the parentage of a child seems a simple matter. This is true in the case of the mother (there can be little dispute about who has given birth) but is slightly more problematic in the case of the father who, it can be argued, does not know beyond doubt that he is the father of the child, without the aid of blood tests. Parentage, however, is more than simply providing the genetic material to produce a child: it also involves the social roles and responsibilities associated with raising that child. As Smart (1996) has commented, 'motherhood' is more than a biological relationship; simply giving birth does not result in 'motherhood' or 'mothering'. However, with assisted conception it is possible to extend the notion of 'mother'. Lupton (1994) comments that we can refer to someone as 'egg mother', 'birth mother', 'surrogate mother', 'legal mother' or 'adoptive mother'. Similarly, sperm donation raises the question of whether the donor could enjoy the status of 'father' (1994: 156). The Human Fertilisation and Embryology Act of 1990 attempts to circumvent this complex debate by providing what Franklin describes as a technical definition of 'mother'. The Act describes a mother as 'the woman who is carrying or has carried a child as a result of the placing in her of an embryo or of sperm and eggs' (Franklin 1997: 226).

Links

For a related discussion on the ability of the medical profession to make life-or-death decisions, see Chapter 3.

The use of assisted conception raises a further complex question about who should have access to those techniques and enjoy the experience and status of a parent. Debates about access are only partly about the resources to fund such techniques; perhaps more importantly these debates also centre upon a person's (usually a couple's) desire and suitability to parent. According to Franklin (1997), the desire to parent is seen as a 'natural' impulse. The Warnock Report (1985), set up to debate ethical issues arising from techniques of assisted conception, argued that for many childless couples the social pressures to parent were very significant. Being childless is often seen as a 'failure' to fulfil convention (Franklin 1997: 91). Franklin cites the authors of *The Fertility Handbook* who argue that there is a biological impulse to reproduce: 'Call it a cosmic spark or spiritual fulfilment, biological need or human destiny – the desire for a family rises unbidden from our genetic souls' (Bellina and Wilson 1986: xv, cited in Franklin 1997: 91). It is equally clear, however, that this desire to have a child has to be understood within a social and cultural context, and in the case of many western countries this is within the framework of the family, most commonly understood as a heterosexual (married) couple. Such a definition excludes both single women and lesbians who, presumably, are not thought to possess the same biological desire to reproduce. Patrick Steptoe, one of the pioneers of assisted conception techniques, argued that such women should be excluded on the basis that for them to have children would be unnatural and morally wrong (Franklin 1997: 92).

Questions

There are many restrictions placed on who may parent via assisted conception. What would your reaction be if similar restrictions were placed on parents who can conceive without medical intervention?

Access to techniques of assisted conception is, therefore, restricted on social and moral grounds. Doyal (1994) argues that access to reproductive technology is thus only possible with what she refers to as the tacit or explicit agreement of the medical profession.

For Castells, as for many commentators, the advent of reproductive technologies such as assisted conception represents women's 'growing control over the timing and frequency of child bearing' (1997: 135). For others, such as Porter (1990), this optimism is misguided, as access to such techniques, she argues, is only achieved via the gatekeepers of services, namely the medical profession. Porter highlights the extent to which developments in assisted conception have meant the medicalisation of conception as well as of contraception and childbirth. The end result is the imposition of controls over 'means of reproduction – access to procedures, technology, information and so on – and thereby controls over women's bodies and ultimately their lives' (1990: 185).

Porter's research indicated that medical professionals worked with 'ideal types' in relation to the provision of specific methods of contraception. The ideal patient for sterilisation was 'a woman in her early thirties, happily married with two or three children. The ideal type Depo-Provera patient was a woman in her early thirties with a large number of unwanted pregnancies, not in a stable relationship and living in local authority housing in a poor part of the city' (1990: 195). The significance of these ideal types lies in the way in which doctors were reluctant to offer alternative forms of contraception to women who did not fit their ideal type.

Oakley (1987) has noted that in relation to pregnancy and childbirth women largely appear as passive objects and recipients of care. A similar tendency to describe women in passive terms – here as recipients of embryos – is noticeable in relation to assisted conception. Lupton highlights a contrast: 'male scientists and doctors are commonly portrayed as active, expert and rational, the "producers" and "fathers" of "test-tube babies", while women are represented as desperate for children, passive, reacting emotionally to their chance to experience the joys of desired motherhood' (1994: 157). According to Franklin (1997: 103), descriptions of IVF treatment tend to underplay the role of would-be parents, in particular that of the mother, and to emphasise the creative power of medical technology. An unquestioning commitment on the part of the hopeful parents to the technological processes involved is ensured by seeking to portray the medical profession as simply lending a helping hand in an otherwise completely 'natural' process (1997: 103). Franklin describes initial accounts of IVF as oversimplified – omitting, for example, to provide an accurate representation of the failure rate. The only agency referred to is that of the 'invisible hand of technology' which facilitates conception (1997: 104). Medicine itself has brought forth the 'miracle of life'.

The preceding discussion has sought to illustrate both the dominance of the medical profession and the challenges made to this position by feminist critics. In the following discussion, a further dimension of the challenge to biomedicine is introduced in the form of alternative therapies.

Challenging the dominance of the biomedical model: alternative therapies

Alternative, or complementary, therapies embrace many philosophies and methods but collectively represent a challenge to the concepts of health and disease articulated in the medical model. This part of the discussion begins by defining what is meant by 'alternative' practices and provides specific examples.

In their broadest sense, the terms **alternative medicine** and **complementary medicine** can be used to describe any practices that fall outside the boundaries of conventional medicine. West (1993) acknowledges that it is problematic to try and define such a diverse body of practices but offers the possibility of categorising different types. The main categories are identified as physical, psychological and paranormal.

Alternative medicine embraces any medical practice that falls outside the boundaries of conventional medicine. Some commentators use the term complementary medicine to imply that non-conventional medicine can be used in conjunction with western bio-medicine rather than as a radical alternative.

She suggests a further distinction between practices that demand a high level of training and those she describes as virtually 'do-it-yourself'. For others the principal distinction between 'alternative' and biomedicine is the former's 'holistic' emphasis. Saks suggests that in 'orthodox' medicine, the overwhelming emphasis is on the physical, with the mind and the spirit 'still typically regarded as relatively peripheral to health care' (1998: 198). In contrast and despite their apparent diversity, most alternative therapies deal 'with the unity of the mind, body and spirit' (1998: 198). The following are examples of two alternative approaches to understanding health and illness.

Two examples of alternative practices

Homoeopathy is an effective and scientific system of healing which assists the natural tendency of the body to heal itself. It assumes that all symptoms of ill health are expressions of disharmony within the whole person and that it is the patient who needs treatment not the disease.

Source: www.apothecary.co.uk

Acupuncture is medical treatment that can relieve symptoms of some physical and psychological conditions and may encourage the patient's body to heal and repair itself, if it is able to do so. Acupuncture stimulates the nerves in skin and muscle, and can produce a variety of effects. We know that it increases the body's release of natural painkillers – endorphin and serotonin – in the pain pathways of both the spinal cord and the brain. This modifies the way pain signals are received.

But acupuncture does much more than reduce pain, and has a beneficial effect on health. Patients often notice an improved sense of well-being after treatment. Modern research shows that acupuncture can affect most of the body's systems – the nervous system, muscle tone, hormone outputs, circulation, antibody production and allergic responses, as well as the respiratory, digestive, urinary and reproductive systems.

Source: www.medical-acupuncture.co.uk

The professional marginalisation of alternative medicine

An important element of alternative medicine's status as 'other' and different from orthodox medicine rests on the different conceptualisations of the relationship between the mind, body and spirit. A second and equally important element of the status of alternative practices is their institutional and professional marginalisation in relation to orthodox medicine. Chapter 3 examined the extent of the professional dominance of biomedicine, a dominance powerfully signalled by the illegality of other occupational groups carrying out tasks for which medical practitioners alone are state registered. Surgical procedures, for example, are the exclusive province of doctors. Other professionals, such as nurses, may observe and assist but not carry out the procedure itself. Saks (1994) argues that this professional dominance was enhanced by the establishment of the NHS in 1948 because the only form of health care accessible, 'free at the point of delivery', and available to all was orthodox medicine. He describes the state-sponsored NHS as being dominated by 'the drug treatment and surgical interventions of orthodox medicine', thus relegating alternative therapies to the private health care market (1994: 86).

Orthodox medicine occupies a position of power and dominance over alternative medicine, as illustrated by the definitions of alternative practices offered by professional organisations such as the British Medical Association. The BMA draws a distinction between complementary therapies and alternative practices: the former are defined as treating patients while they are receiving drug therapy from a registered doctor, and the latter as treating patients *in place of* a registered doctor. The BMA offers a definition of orthodox medicine based principally on *who* delivers the treatment, in this case a 'registered medical practitioner' (1993: 7). In a similar vein the definition of 'non-conventional' medicine centres around *what it is not*, that is orthodox, rather than considering *what it is* in terms of the concepts of health and disease underpinning alternative practices. Non-conventional medicine is defined as 'those forms of treatment which are not widely used by orthodox health care professions, and the skills of which are not taught as part of the undergraduate curriculum of orthodox medical and paramedical health care courses' (1993: 7). Saks (1994) argues that orthodox medicine has conducted a 'strong campaign' against its alternative competitors and draws on evidence from a report by the BMA published in 1986. This report, he suggests, 'extolled the scientific aspects of modern biomedicine, whilst at the same time generally depicting alternative medicine as superstitious dogma' (1994: 88). Supporters of orthodox medicine are keen to point out the importance of the patient having 'faith' in alternative practitioners and argue that this reinforces the message that the therapy will work. In contrast, it is suggested that orthodox medicine does not depend on this element of faith but stands on its proven ability to eradicate disease.

Alternative concepts of health

The following discussion requires you to draw on the examples of specific practices outlined above. The central elements of alternative medicine are detailed in Table 4.1.

Attempts to describe particular alternative practices and to detail what is specific about the concepts of health underpinning this approach reveal the essential differences between alternative medicine and the biomedical model. The discussion has sought to draw your attention to differing conceptions of health, disease and the relationship

TABLE 4.1   Alternative medicine: concepts of health (Aakster 1993)

Alternative medicine	Biomedicine
Health as a balance of opposing forces within the body	Health as the absence of disease
Disease understood as indicating the presence of negative, disruptive forces within the body. Symptoms are the product of the body's attempts to rid it of toxic substances	Disease as defined in relation to a specific part of the body. Essentially, disease is understood as a deviation from normal functioning
'Reading' the body, examining dietary habits, lifestyles and constitution types to achieve diagnosis	Diagnosis achieved by examining the form and structure of specific organisms and the degree to which the presence of a disease indicates a deviation from normal functioning
Therapy is based on an attempt to strengthen vitalising, positive forces within the body	Therapy consists of attempts to destroy or suppress disease

Source: Aakster (1993)

between mind, body and spirit. Biomedicine has sought to emphasise a further distinction between itself and alternative practices by asserting the supremacy of science over superstition. Previous discussions of biomedicine have dealt with its commitment to scientific methods free from social or political bias (BMA, cited in Saks 1992). The scientific observation of natural phenomena allows for the development of laws governing such phenomena and, perhaps most significantly, such laws and the resulting 'facts' can be said to be valid because the results can be reproduced repeatedly, proving their validity. This reproducibility of results, it is argued, cannot be matched by alternative medicine.

Questions

Go back to the descriptions of homoeopathy and acupuncture and contrast and compare them with the concepts of health as outlined in Table 4.1.

Links

See Chapter 3 for a detailed discussion of medicine as a dominant discourse.

The juxtaposition of 'scientific' medicine and 'unscientific' alternative practices leaves little scope for debate, as both sides appear to base their arguments on criteria not accepted by the other. It is biomedicine, however, that enjoys the dominant position as *the* established form of medicine. An essential element of this dominance can be traced back to a wide acceptance of the validity of science and scientific methods during **the Enlightenment**. The practice and philosophy of alternative medicine are, arguably, at a distinct disadvantage because science has reached the status of 'truth'. In the opening chapter, you were introduced to some of the basic elements of a postmodern critique of society and knowledge. Postmodernism is critical and sceptical of attempts to offer single, monolithic explanations of any phenomenon and so the whole basis of rational scientific knowledge has been questioned. Saks (1998: 204) argues that this critique of 'science, reason and enlightenment' provides a useful tool with which to reappraise the philosophical basis of alternative medical practices. Since postmodernism is characterised by 'the acceptance of multiple realities and coexisting narratives' (1998: 204) it is possible to appraise the relative merits of alternative medicine and biomedicine in such a way that both are accepted as different but equally valid conceptions of the body, health and disease. Interestingly, the British Holistic Medical Association also draws attention to changes in modes of thinking and in particular to an acceptance of the non-scientific in terms of recognising the significance of human spirit and conscience. It argues that medicine in the twenty-first century will increasingly come to recognise the significance of the relationships between the mind, body and spirit and the human capacity to alter both the internal and the external environment (www.bhma.org).

Choosing to use alternative medicine

Alternative medicine clearly demonstrates the possibility of a philosophical challenge to the dominance of orthodox medicine. It should also be evident from the critique of medicine presented in the preceding chapter that the practice of orthodox medicine is also ripe for criticism. Looking at the reasons for increasing use of alternative and complementary health care, McQuaide (2005) points to several trends in wider society. These indicate a growing individualism and dissociation from civic society and mainstream medicine. This ties in with Putnam's (2000) ideas on the decline of civic society in the US. Contemporary Americans are less likely to direct their efforts towards communal goals and activities and instead seek private solutions to their problems. Alternative health care fits this trend, as often the individual seeks out an alternative therapy for themselves as opposed to engaging with something like the NHS, with its communal orientation to health.

In relation to mainstream medicine, McQuaide makes the point that it is the unequal power relationship that puts people off using such services. More equal and participatory relationships are sought in alternative therapies and that appears to be one of their main attractions. Earlier work by Sharma (1992) found that in general people used alternative medicine because they placed a high value on what they found to be the more equal and informed relationship between practitioners and patients and because of the importance attached to the consideration of the personal circumstances of their illness. Further to this point, Coward (1993) argues that biomedicine not only has medicalised many aspects of human existence but has done so in an inhumane way. The examples of iatrogenic practices discussed in Chapter 3 included a consideration of the harmful side-effects of drugs as well as examples of medical interventions, such as surgery, that have resulted in harm to the patient. The later discussion of mental health will also illustrate that the practice of medicine, as well as specific forms of treatment, has been uncaring and inhumane. The supposed neutrality of biomedicine, its ability to see disease as a purely biological entity, may not always be perceived as beneficial. As Coward comments, a purely rational explanation of disease as arbitrary does not, perhaps, satisfy a more fundamental need to understand why our own life has been affected in this way.

In addition to these individualistic currents, McQuaide also notes the influence of the baby boomer generation (those born between 1945 and 1960). As a generation they grew up with counter-cultural ideas strongly influenced by the 'hippie' idealism of the 1960s where nature and all things natural enjoyed a strong profile. Alternative health care, with its associations of being natural, neatly mirrors the culture that this generation were part of in their youth. This preference for all things natural, coupled with a desire to maintain health by purchasing that health care, has opened up a considerable market for alternative health care. This has to be tempered by acknowledging that it is only really a viable option for those with a disposable income. Other reasons for the popularity of alternative medicine are identified in Table 4.2.

We have highlighted the assumed advantages of alternative practices over ortho-dox medicine. However, these practices themselves have been subject to critical scrutiny. Commentators such as Coward have emphasised the individualistic assessment of health underpinning many alternative practices. Such an approach can be contrasted with the **social model of health** which draws our attention to the social, economic and cultural determinants of health. Chapter 6, examining class inequalities in health, seeks to place pat-terns of morbidity and mortality in a social context. There is widespread acceptance within the discipline of sociology that economic and social factors have a significant impact upon health outcomes. Sociologists of health do not deny the importance of **agency** (that is to say, the capacity of individuals to act rather than be acted upon) but maintain that agency has its limitations. In contrast, Coward argues, alternative medicine stresses the extent to which individuals can determine their health status and an explanation that leads almost inevitably to the conclusion that individuals are responsible for their own health regardless of their social circumstances.

TABLE 4.2 Explaining why people use alternative medicine

The limits of biomedicine
Biomedicine is unable to 'cure' certain conditions
Biomedicine does not place enough emphasis on the causes of illness and is preoccupied with relieving symptoms
The side-effects of biomedical treatment are potentially harmful
Biomedical treatment is often too drastic and too invasive

The benefits of alternative medicine
Provides an explanation of the causes of ill health and disease in the context of a person's individual lifestyle
Provides a more egalitarian relationship between patient and practitioner
Offers an alternative to 'high-tech' medicine
Treats the whole person
Encourages individuals to take greater responsibility for their health

The use of alternative medicine as an expression of postmodern society
Expresses a greater desire for self-determination and choice
Challenges the cultural dominance of biomedicine
Reflects a more general trend for maintaining the body through the purchase of consumer goods and services

Sources: Sharma (1992), Coward (1993), Lupton (1994)

Links

A detailed discussion of the regulated body is provided in Chapter 11.

This appeal to the individual is, Coward suggests, part of a cultural obsession with the performance and appearance of the body. It is important to note, however, that a central theme in the world of the 'worried well' is an obsession with appearance in terms of the body as a project, something owned by the individual and open to change and development by them. The widespread popularity, for example, of diets to lose weight, fitness to tone the body, and cosmetic surgery to alter it, is evidence of the new significance attached to the body. Working on the body to alter or enhance its appearance is represented as a matter of choice and self-determination. Good health and poor health, therefore, become matters of personal responsibility and, as Lupton reminds us, contain strong moral overtones of how we ought to care for the body.

Coward argues that part of the attraction of alternative medicine is its association with the natural world and the healing power of nature (cited in Lupton 1994: 126). Like the concept of 'science' with its association with the values of rationality, objectivity and progress, 'nature' is closely linked to ideas of virtue, goodness and purity (1994: 127). Such an association suggests that nature and natural remedies are implicitly good for you and inevitably prefer-able to artificial substances such as pharmacological drugs. Lupton argues that it is impos-sible to support such a clear-cut distinction between natural and artificial substances since 'many naturally occurring substances can be toxic, and many chemicals are derived from naturally occurring substances' (1994: 126). Many freely available herbal remedies carry the potential to be harmful when not taken in an appropriate manner. One such exam-ple, for the treatment of depression, would be the use of St John's wort, available over the counter and capable of being used even when a diagnosis of depression has not been made. It is perhaps ironic to note that, at a time when the use and efficacy of drugs are subject to more stringent regulation (through, for example, NHS Quality Improvement Scotland and the National Institute for Clinical Excellence in England and Wales) and when there is a requirement for pharmaceutical manufacturers to provide detailed patient information, natural remedies are not subject to the same degree of regulation. Most herbal remedies are in fact not classified as medicine and, therefore, are not subject to the same requirement for testing and regulation as artificial substances.

Conclusion

This chapter has described and analysed two challenges to the dominance of biomedicine – by feminist critiques and by alternative medicine.

Following on from some points made earlier, we discussed here how medicine encroaches on many aspects of life that were traditionally outside its reach. Pregnancy and childbirth are good examples of this impulse of medicine not just to take control but also to redefine a natural state of being (in this case, for women) as being closer to illness than to health. Control is exercised in two ways: first, by locating the place of delivery away from the home and into the hospital and therefore into medicine's 'home turf'; and second, by attaching less status and importance to women's experiences and their interpretations of pregnancy and childbirth. This can be done overtly by overriding their concerns, or more subtly by fram-ing pregnancy and childbirth as a time of risk and danger and thereby raising fears that the pregnancy is more likely to go wrong as opposed to right.

One should be careful not to see it all as 'one-way traffic', where people meekly submit to medical control. The growth of alternative or complementary medicine provides an example where disenchantment with mainstream medicine is visible and where people make active choices to seek other forms of health care. Alternative medicine offers the promise of the indi-vidualistic and holistic care that is supposedly absent in mainstream medicine. It also reflects other processes apparent in late modernity, such as a focus on individualistic, as opposed to collective, solutions and a belief that natural remedies are superior to (and safer than) scientific or technological remedies. This may appear to be a more propitious state of affairs for people seeking a cure for an illness or to improve their health, but alternative medicine has one feature in common with its mainstream counterpart: there is little emphasis on the deeper structural or social aspects of health and illness. In Section 2 we shall explore how structures (such as class, ethnicity and gender) are incredibly powerful in affecting and influencing health and illness.

Summary points

- The process of medicalisation has transformed natural experiences into medical ones. This is particularly true of pregnancy and childbirth.
- Medicine acts as a gatekeeper to reproductive technology. Decisions about access to reproductive technology are made not on the basis of medical and objective evidence but on the basis of prevailing social and cultural values.
- Authors such as Oakley argue that medicalisation has resulted in women patients being seen as passive recipients of care.
- Alternative medicine represents a fundamental challenge to the belief system underpinning biomedicine, as illustrated by two specific examples, homoeopathy and acupuncture.
- For an increasing number of people, alternative medicine represents a positive alternative to biomedicine.

Case study

Kathy was recently treated in hospital for a grade A streptococcal infection that led to cellulitis, septicaemia and pneumonia. During her period of illness, she was given large doses of antibiotics and strong painkillers. The former placed a huge strain on her kidneys, while the latter made her drowsy and 'spaced out'. Kathy never questioned the treatment she received even though she did not fully understand everything that she was told by the doctors and nurses.

Kathy is also a regular user of alternative medicine for the treatment of migraine. She has taken on board what she has been told by her homoeopathic practitioner and altered her diet and tried to deal positively with stressful situations.

1 How can Kathy be a user of both orthodox medicine and alternative medicine?
2 Given that Kathy actively sought out a second opinion on her migraine and attempted to address the underlying causes of the condition through non-medical means, do you find it odd that she simply accepted what happened to her in hospital?
3 Talk to friends and colleagues and try and find out who uses or has used alternative medicine. Have they visited a practitioner or have they treated themselves by purchasing herbal medicines? For which conditions were people more likely to use alternative medicine?

Taking your studies further

This chapter will have helped you understand many of the key terms, concepts, theories and debates relating to medical dominance. Listed below are journal articles and books that will provide deeper and more detailed discussions of the points raised in this chapter. You will also find what is available on the companion website. This offers you downloads of relevant material, plus links to useful websites in addition to podcasts and other features.

Recommended reading

Jackson, S. and Scambler, G. (2007) 'Perceptions of evidence-based medicine: traditional acupuncturists in the UK and resistance to biomedical modes of evaluation', *Sociology of Health and Illness*, 29 (3): 412–29.

McQuaide, M.M. (2005) 'The rise of alternative health care: a sociological account', *Social Theory and Health*, 3 (4): 286–301.

Oakley, A. (2005) *The Ann Oakley Reader: Gender, Women and Social Science*. London: Policy.

Teijlingen, E. van, Lowis, G., McCaffery, P. and Porter, M. (eds) (2004) *Midwifery and the Medicalization of Childbirth: Comparative Perspectives*. New York: Nova.

Turner, B.S., Tovey, P., Easthope, G. and Adams, J. (2003) *Mainstreaming Complementary and Alternative Medicine: Studies in Social Context*. London: Routledge.

On the companion website

Stevenson, F. (2004) 'Images of nature in relation to mood modifying medicines: a user perspective', *Health*, 8 (4): 241–62.

5

Evidence and enquiry: an overview of sociological research

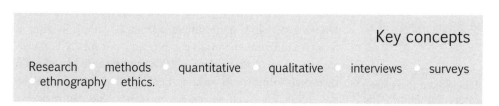

Main points

- Research is integral to sociology, as it both provides evidence for existing claims about society and prompts new ways of thinking and theorising about society.
- Research is a practical activity, which needs careful planning and coordination to realise its aims.
- There are two main methodological traditions: quantitative and qualitative.
- Quantitative methods focus mainly on statistical relationships, as gathered through surveys.
- Qualitative methods focus mainly on experiences, as gathered through interviews or focus groups.
- Research has to be ethically sound in order to prevent distress or harm for the people who participate in the research.

Key concepts

Research • methods • quantitative • qualitative • interviews • surveys • ethnography • ethics.

Introduction

Research is integral to sociology and it is vital for the following two reasons. First, without research many of the insights and observations that sociologists put forward about society would have no validity or evidence to support the claim being made.

So, for example, sociologists make claims that health is distributed unevenly across society, according to class, gender and ethnicity. If you turn to the various chapters on those social structures in Section 2, then you will find summaries of some of the evidence that sociologists use to give credence to those statements. Second, research makes sociologists think about society in new ways, with the result either of challenging existing ways of thinking about something or of raising questions that have never been posed before. A useful example here is Bury's (1991) work on chronic illness. Following his interviews with young people with rheumatoid arthritis, Bury drew attention to the social aspects of chronic illness. His research helped to generate the concept of 'disrupted biography', which enables sociologists to gain insights and explain the challenges that chronic illness can present to people with conditions such as multiple sclerosis or Parkinson's disease.

In this chapter, we will be exploring some of the main issues concerning the focus of sociological research and the various methods that are involved in trying to find out about society. We will begin by considering whether or not sociology is a science, before moving on to some of the nuts and bolts of going about developing a research project. Attention will then turn to reflecting on types of research methods and how they reveal different aspects of society and how people experience society. Finally, a review of ethical issues will examine why it is important to provide safeguards for the people who participate in a research project and some of the steps necessary to do so.

Sociology as a science

Research question refers to the aspect of the social world that is to be investigated.

Literature review refers to a systematic analysis of all published material that is of interest or relevant to the research.

Method refers to the way in which the actual data are gathered.

Analysis means making sense of the data and deriving conclusions that inform the research question.

Dissemination refers to making the results and conclusions of the research known to a wider audience.

As discussed in Chapter 1, sociology shares many of the characteristics of other sciences. These characteristics include using rigorous and systematic methods during research and developing from that research logical and theoretically informed discussions and conclusions. To that extent sociology is a science, but it does have one quite notable difference in contrast to the natural sciences. That difference is in what sociologists study. Sociologists have as their object of study *people* in a *society*. Studying people is quite different from, let us say, looking at how two different chemicals combine in a test tube. Chemicals are not aware of themselves, nor are they capable of acting on their own volition and making their own decisions. People, on the contrary, are self-aware, are conscious, and can make up their own minds and purposefully act accordingly. Therefore, we have to be alert not just to recording and observing what transpires when people interact and engage in activities but also *why* they interact and the motives and thinking behind their engagement with certain activities. So, for example, in Chapter 4 we looked at the increasing uptake of alternative therapies. Much of the research in that area explores why people are opting for such therapies and the motives and reasons that lie behind their actions. What it reveals is that many people opt for alternative therapies because of disillusionment with mainstream medicine and a desire to be treated in an individual and holistic manner.

Links

See Chapter 1 for more information on sociology as science.

Doing research

Engaging in research requires a great deal of planning and prior thought. Getting the planning right (or as right as possible) before any actual fieldwork is carried out can make a decisive difference to the success of the final project. There is a great deal to organise and think about. Building the research project on a firm foundation is essential if the research is to be able to answer the questions that it sets out to examine. Research is very much a practical activity shaped by a variety of constraints and considerations, where the researcher has to be aware of and attuned to what they can deliver rather than what they might wish to do. Let us now look at what the planning stage involves.

Research question

First of all, it is crucial to work out what the **research question** is, and to be absolutely clear about what the research is trying to find out. A research question is what the research seeks to do, and what aspects of the social world need to be understood. What initially prompts a research question is quite varied. Sometimes the research question is posed by theoretical concerns to prove or disprove an existing **theory**, sometimes by a knowledge gap that is noted in the literature, or sometimes because a funding body (for example a local authority or a charity) needs information on some aspect of its service.

Once the research question has been formulated, you have to be aware of the practical limitations of what you are seeking to do. Research is very much the 'art of the possible' – understanding what resources one has to put into play and how much time is available to do the research. A potential trap in all research is that the initial ambition of a research project is too big and to realise the aims would require excessive amounts of time, funding and people. Often, planning research involves honing the research question down to a very tight set of aims that can actually be answered and can be practically pursued.

So, for example, you might wish to research how having a chronic illness has impacted on all of the sufferers' sense of self, changed the dynamics of family and personal relationships, and so on. This would involve perhaps interviewing everyone in the UK about what differences and experiences they have encountered in their lives since the onset of, let us say, multiple sclerosis, HIV/AIDS, or Parkinson's disease. Undoubtedly, if this could be done, it would be a very valuable piece of research; however, given the numbers of people to be interviewed (potentially tens of thousands), the time (months, if not years) needed to do it, and the army of research assistants and interviewers necessary to carry out the interviews, plus the no doubt astronomical cost, it simply could not happen. Instead, it would be much more practical to select just one chronic illness, for example multiple sclerosis (MS). Again, one would not be able to interview everyone with MS, for the same reasons as before, given the numbers of people with the condition and the time and financial implications. This in turn means reducing the intended number of people that could be asked to participate in the research. The main point is that one always has to be practical in what can be achieved and to make sure that the research question can be addressed in a relevant and meaningful way.

Literature review

The next stage involves going through the literature that already exists on the subject. It is highly unlikely that any piece of research is entirely novel or unique. A great deal (if not all!) of research follows on from and is informed by other pieces of research. It is therefore essential to consult and read all the other existing relevant material. Doing so will aid the researcher in many ways. It will provide an awareness of the main findings and issues that have been put forward so far and how new research can contribute to this body of knowledge. Sometimes this contribution will illuminate gaps in the previous research or offer different or critical counterpoints to what other researchers have found and discussed.

Choosing an appropriate research method

Once the research question has been posed and the literature reviewed, attention turns to how to actually do the research. This requires the selection of an appropriate **method** to answer the research question. In some respects, this will involve choosing between quantitative and qualitative methods. The differences between the two approaches will be explored later in this chapter, but essentially quantitative methods tell us about 'how many' and 'how much', while the qualitative methods answer questions of 'what', 'how' and 'why' (Green and Thorogood 2004: 5).

Analysing the data

Data unfortunately do not 'speak' for themselves and they require further work to produce meaningful information. The actual type of data collected determines the type of analysis that is required. For statistical data, one of the most common approaches is to use some form of software package such as SPSS. This allows the researcher to model any relationships and variables that the research set out to find. Qualitative data, on the other hand, require a different approach; they are the spoken words of the research participants. They have to be fully transcribed (typed out) before themes can be identified in the various participants' responses.

Disseminating research findings

Gathering, analysing and interpreting data and reaching a conclusion or raising important issues as a result of research is not the end of the process. Of equal importance is what one does with the research when it is complete and how results are conveyed to the wider world. In terms of reaching a wider audience, Burawoy (2004) has made an appeal for what he terms 'public sociology', arguing that sociologists should strive to make their research and ideas relevant and understandable to the wider society. It is not only academics who are interested in what research has to say; other people, such as user groups, those involved in the study, policy makers and indeed the public at large, are also concerned.

Quantitative and qualitative methods

As outlined above, it is important to select the correct method to help you answer your research question. Within sociological research it can be useful to distinguish between two broad methodological approaches. These are **quantitative research** and **qualitative research**. Within these approaches, each method has its own orientation to the ways in which we can investigate society. On a very simple level, quantitative research methods place an emphasis on statistics and on measuring the differences between, relationships among and extent of various social phenomena, while qualitative research methods place an emphasis on how people experience and make sense of the society in which they live.

We shall look at specific examples of qualitative methods shortly, but first it is useful to look at some of the debates that have surrounded both approaches as they can help us to understand their relative advantages and disadvantages. Much of

Quantitative research refers to mainly statistics-based research that is useful for answering research questions that focus on measuring the extent and range of particular phenomena.

Qualitative research refers mainly to interview-based research that seeks to find out the meanings that people attach to their experiences and actions.

the debate over the years concerning methods has centred on which approach is the more 'effective' and the more 'scientific'. Qualitative research has often been criticised for being unscientific in that it is closer to a form of journalism, given its emphasis on interviews as opposed to, for example, the randomised control sampling and statistical techniques prevalent in certain quantitative research. Other criticisms are that qualitative researchers lack the impartiality and the objectivity that is supposedly part of quantitative research.

Quantitative research, on the other hand, has been taken to task on many grounds. Even though quantitative methods can tell us a great deal of useful information and are ideal for establishing predictive information, various problems and drawbacks have been identified. For example, much of the survey work on class and health inequalities clearly indicates that one can predict that people found in the lower social classes will have a greater chance of increased morbidity and early mortality. While this is very valuable, this form of research only tells us about one level of social reality. What is missing are insights into how people experience and construct their worlds. The reliance that quantitative methods have on statistical modelling can also be problematic. In compiling and cross-referencing statistics some of the important features of the social world are lost, such as context and the power relationships between people.

Even though there are strong arguments for and against both methods, they should be thought of as complementary. It is the strengths of each that should be appreciated and those strengths in turn should be matched with the research question in hand. So, for example, if the purpose of the research is to investigate the frequency of consultations on a certain condition (for example, depression) by social class in a certain area, then a quantitative method, such as a survey, would be useful. If, on the other hand, the research seeks to explore what it means to be a working-class person with depression then a qualitative method, such as an in-depth interview, would be the preferred option.

The discussion above has presented the choice of quantitative and qualitative methods as being an either/or option, where one has to be selected rather than the other. Increasingly we are seeing the use of mixed methods, where both methods are used in the same piece of research.

Quantitative method: surveys

If a very large population is to be researched then a survey can be a useful way to do this. Surveys can take a variety of forms. Traditionally, they have involved the distribution of postal questionnaires or the conducting of structured interviews (either in person or by telephone), though with current technology surveys can be completed using websites or other online media. A defining characteristic of the survey approach is the way in which questions are asked. Questions are tightly *structured*, involving a specific set of questions, asked in a designated order, usually with a limited range of answers. The purpose of such a fixed set of questions and answers is to allow information to be collated and compared across a distinct population. Variables (for example, age, class, ethnicity and gender) can therefore be identified and various associations can be made.

Survey questions: examples

- Please circle which of the following responses is closest to what you thought overall of the Middlefield Wellman Project.

Very satisfied   Satisfied   Happy   Dissatisfied   Very dissatisfied

- How often did you attend the Middlefield Wellman Project? Circle as appropriate.

On one occasion   Two or three occasions   On four or more occasions

Qualitative methods: interviews

One very common research approach in the sociology of health and illness is the in-depth interview. Typically, this is carried out on a one-to-one basis where highly detailed information and data are elicited by talking with someone who meets the criteria of the research project. Most interviews last between one and two hours and are usually recorded using a tape or digital recorder. This recording is then transcribed so that the interview can be analysed.

In many respects, one can think of an interview as a purposeful conversation where the actual data collected are in the form of what someone says (Green and Thorogood 2004). It is up to the interviewer to guide or facilitate the conversation. This can be done in two ways. There is a *structured* approach (as in the survey approach outlined above) but more commonly in interviews one follows a *semi-structured* approach. This is very much a 'looser' and more open technique. The interviewer will have certain topics she will wish to explore, with the emphasis being on allowing the interviewees to express and communicate what they feel or have experienced about what is being researched. So, instead of having a fixed agenda of questions the interviewer will have an outline of areas or issues to be addressed and will raise those areas or issues as and when appropriate during the interview. This can mean being flexible and not rigidly adhering to a preset order or question format or style.

Conducting a semi-structured interview requires certain skills, techniques and styles of approaches. One should remember that someone is giving up their time to discuss what can be quite intimate and personal details of their life, and due respect should be accorded. It also entails behaving and acting in certain ways before, during and after the interview. Before the interview takes place it is important to identify and create a non-threatening and relaxed atmosphere for the interviewee. This can involve identifying a venue that is familiar to the person who is being interviewed; this could include many different places, such as their home or place of work, so long as they are comfortable there. During the interview the interviewer should be attentive to what the interviewee is discussing and always appear interested. This can be achieved in a variety of ways. Often, the most effective are quite subtle actions such as nodding one's head or briefly commenting on how useful or important something is that the interviewee has said. Engaging with someone in this way also makes it more likely that the interview will elicit the information that the research requires. Questions should always be open (that is, not questions that have yes or no responses) and allow the interviewee room to explore issues they regard as being important.

Semi-structured questions: examples

- How did you feel about having physiotherapists and occupational therapists coming into your home?
- Could you tell me more about what you felt when you heard the diagnosis from the specialist?

Importantly, the interview is not about obtaining some form of universal 'truth', nor should it necessarily match an 'objective reality'. This is one possible objection to the interview approach: that it may not be able to gather accurate data, and therefore any conclusions reached may be invalid. This could be because the interviewee is unable to recall specific events, or has a particular view (or bias) about the research topic. However, it is how the person sees *their* world that is sought in an interview, and not whether or not this matches some other view of the world (for example the researcher's or that of a powerful social group, such as the medical profession).

Focus groups

Another highly popular method is the focus group approach. This involves a small interactive group of people discussing and commenting on issues and questions prompted by the researcher. As with interviews, a focus group will also be recorded and then transcribed for subsequent analysis and, as with in-depth interviews, the group session can last anywhere between one and two hours. Who actually populates the focus group is dependent on the research questions and aims. Sometimes this can be a wide range of people if the researcher wishes to explore, let us say, how take-up and perception of alternative therapies differ by social class. Other times it can be people who share a particular characteristic, for example depression, if the research is investigating the day-to-day experiences of people with mental health problems.

Focus groups can be very useful research tools in a number of ways. First, unlike interviews, where there is a one-to-one conversation between the interviewer and the interviewee, talking with a group of people is much closer to how people interact in the rest of their lives and therefore creates a more 'natural' and 'commonplace' environment, hopefully making it easier for people to contribute what they want. For the researcher this natural aspect of the focus group also allows insights into group dynamics and the ways in which people express their ideas and relate to others. Second, the views and experiences of a number of people can be accessed in a relatively short period. Given the time and financial considerations that affect most research, this can be a very appealing option.

There can be some problems with a focus group, and these relate to the very fact that it is a group. As in any social situation, where a group of people are gathered together to discuss a particular subject, some people will be more vocal than others, while some people may feel too nervous to contribute. It can be difficult to keep everyone on track and it is usually necessary to set ground rules, such as asking group members not to interrupt someone who is making a contribution. The points made about successful interviewing also apply here in that the interviewer needs to be attentive and interested throughout, while creating a relaxed and participative atmosphere.

Ethnography and participant observation

Wogan (2004) playfully refers to ethnography as 'deep hanging out'. This remark is not as flippant as it sounds, since ethnography is about spending a great deal of time with a group of people in order to discover how they see the world, while observing, sharing and participating in their everyday experiences. Sometimes this can involve just witnessing what is going on or perhaps (though this can be problematic) going 'under cover' and attempting to become one of the group which is being studied.

One of the best-known examples of ethnography in sociology is Goffman's *Asylums* (1961). In this study, Goffman adopted the role of assistant to an athletic director (similar to what we would call a physiotherapist today) and spent as much time as possible talking to and interacting with patients in St Elizabeth's, a hospital for people with mental illnesses. The aim of the research was to investigate the effects that institutional life had on the identities and experiences of those patients. Famously, he identified the processes that lead to institutionalisation, a state of being where an individual's own identity is replaced by an identity that suits the requirements of an institution. Reflecting on the usefulness of ethnography after he had completed the research, Goffman noted:

> It was then and still is my belief that any group of persons – prisoners, primitives, pilots or patients – develop a life of their own that becomes meaningful, reasonable, and normal once you get close to it, and that a good way to learn about any of those worlds is to submit oneself in the company of the members to the daily round of petty contingencies to which they are subject. (1961: 8)

What Goffman is putting forward here is that only by being with a group of people for a length of time can one come close to understanding the contours and rhythms of their lives.

This is unlike the other methods that were discussed above, as they only capture a snapshot – albeit what can be a fairly detailed snapshot – of the lives and experiences of certain groups of people. Ethnography can help to get into the nitty-gritty of social life and reveal how people construct and produce their day-to-day lives.

One issue that all researchers face before embarking on ethnographic research is how much information to divulge about themselves to the group or **community** they are going to be studying. This is an issue because there are two approaches that one can adopt during an ethnographic research: covert or overt. A covert approach entails a certain level of concealment and deception. This could mean pretending that you are one of the group or someone who would normally be associated with the group. For some research projects this may be entirely appropriate, but can be challenging for a number of reasons. Let us take a slightly exaggerated example to illustrate what a covert ethnography might entail. If one was to do an ethnographic study of the stresses and strains facing junior doctors one could pretend to be a junior doctor. This would allow the researcher first-hand observations of the actual experiences of junior doctors as they work through their various shifts. One would be able to witness the rhythms and con-tours of what causes the most stress and the various coping strategies junior doctors may employ. On one level this would appear to be an excellent method of gathering some very detailed and accurate information. There are, however, certain drawbacks associated with this covert approach: most importantly, would the researcher have the necessary skills to pass himself off as a doctor? This is highly unlikely, given the number of years required to amass such specialised knowledge, and most sociologists simply would not have time to do that. There are also ethical issues (of which more later in this chapter). If you were pretending to be a junior doctor then this would inevitably require the treating of patients, which is where such an approach would run into severe problems, as it would be utterly irresponsible to do this.

An overt approach, on the other hand, requires the researcher to disclose their identity as a researcher and be up-front as to what they are doing. This may avoid some of the ethical issues outlined above but it can lead to other problems, the main one being that the naturalistic flow of events is disrupted. Having someone observing (or 'hanging out') and recording what is happening is highly unusual (unless they are a medical student, for example) and this can make people reflect on what they are doing and interact in unchar-acteristic ways.

An important feature of ethnography is to keep a detailed account of what one observes and encounters. As Crang and Cook (2007) point out, keeping a thorough detailed notebook (though this could include all sorts of digital media) is an essential part of the ethnography. It is where observations, thoughts and conversations are recorded for future analysis. In effect, the notebook *is* the data and what is recorded in the notebook becomes the basis for the conclusions or conjectures that are advanced from the research.

Analysing qualitative data

As we discussed earlier, one of the defining attributes of qualitative research is the collection of the spoken word during an interview or focus group. This forms the data of the research. Analysing such data requires a distinctive approach in that the researcher is not applying mathematical formulae or models to the data, as is usual with quantitative data. Rather, one of the most common approaches is for the researcher to identify themes within the data. This involves going through the transcripts from the interviews and 'coding' what is said. Unlike slotting numbers into a software package or into equations, this is not always a 'neat' task. It often means scribbling notes and annotations on transcripts, cutting up those transcripts or attaching stick-on notes, and keeping memos. Crang and Cook capture this part of the research project well:

> It is a process that involves doing nitty-gritty things with paper, pens, scissors, computers and software. It's about chopping up, (re)ordering, (re)contextualising and (re)assembling the data we have so diligently constructed. It's about translating a messy process into a neat product. (2007: 133)

Let us now turn more closely to this 'messy process'. If we follow what is referred to as a 'grounded theory' approach (one of the most commonly used in health research) we begin with what Strauss (1987) calls 'open coding'. Here the researcher reads though the transcript and begins to note down what she or he deems to be significant or what crops up several times. There is a certain amount of 'trial and error' in doing this. Some codes will work and emerge throughout the transcripts while others will not. The codes one attaches could be those that the researcher sees emerging in the transcripts or could be *in vivo* codes: these are the ways that the participants involved in the research see the world in which they live and how they think about their own experiences. There is a cyclical process at play here, with the researcher going back through the transcripts continually refining and 'neatening up' the codes that have been previously identified. This cyclical process stops either when no new concepts emerge out of the data or when the existing concepts cannot be refined any further.

Once no new codes can be generated or further honed from existing codes, the next stage involves trying to make sense of all the different codes and seeking out ways of making them meaningful by looking for connections and relationships. This is referred to as *axial coding*.

After all the relationships have been worked out and identified, attention can turn to the final stage. This is where you try to work out the one central or *core category* that helps to explain what all the other codes and themes mean. Essentially, this entails taking an overview of those codes and themes and seeing what commonality runs through all of them. This may involve a more theoretical or abstract code than the other themes that have been discussed so far.

TABLE 5.1   Example of coding themes on a transcript of an interview

Line	Interview	Themes
101	*Int:* So, what really gets you down at work?	
102	*Steve:* Gets me down? Aye, heaps of things!	
103	Mainly, it's that they're always looking at you,	Surveillance
104	you know, always got their nose in what you're	
105	doing. It's like, you know, they dinnae trust you.	Trust
106	Hate that!	Anger
107	*Int:* Anything else?	
108	*Steve:* As I said – heaps! The other thing is that	
109	you are not allowed to make your own	Lack of autonomy
110	decisions. If it does not fit their perceived little	
111	wee plans, then ye cannae just go ahead and do	
112	it. Everything is controlled, and worked out to	
113	so minute a degree. And you've got to stick to it,	
114	even if it doesnae work or takes longer, know	
115	what I mean? They just don't trust you with	Trust
116	anything!	
117	*Int:* How does that make you feel?	
118	*Steve:* Well, angry again, but pretty depressed as	Anger/depression
119	well. It's all day with your heid against the	
120	same brick wall.	Lack of job fulfilment

In the example given in Table 5.1, we can see how this might take place. This is a transcript of research on the psycho-social health of workers in a Scottish call centre. The research sought to investigate the link between how the requirements of performing emotional labour all day to people down a telephone line created certain emotional states that in turn had possible health consequences.

Ethics

Invariably, with research into health, sociologists encounter ethical issues. This applies especially when the research is investigating issues that are quite personal and intimate for the subjects of the study, or potentially involves accessing confidential medical and clinical information. Sociologists often have to seek ethical approval for their research due to the very real possibility of causing either distress or upset. This can include, for example, unintentionally making information public concerning diagnosis of chronic illness, or revealing someone's sexuality or their views on other people in a user group. All of this could cause

Ethics refers to guiding principles and considerations concerning the conduct of the researcher in ensuring that no harm is done to the physical and emotional wellbeing of those who participate in the research.

embarrassment but could also seriously damage and hinder relationships or future courses of treatment and care for the subject.

To avoid causing problems, the researcher is required to follow two courses of action. The first is to adhere to a code of **ethics**. In the UK all sociologists should consult and follow the British Sociological Association's (BSA) code of ethics, which outlines the considerations that sociologists should follow when engaging in research activity. Part of the guidelines, on relationships with participants in this instance, is shown below. A neat summary of the code, as well as good all-round advice when engaging in research with people, is 'to do no harm'.

Relationships with research participants

- Sociologists have a responsibility to ensure that the physical, social and psychological well-being of research participants is not adversely affected by the research. They should strive to protect the rights of those they study, their interests, sensitivities and privacy, while recognising the difficulty of balancing potentially conflicting interests.

- Because sociologists study the relatively powerless as well as those more powerful than themselves, research relationships are frequently characterised by disparities of power and status. Despite this, research relationships should be characterised, whenever possible, by trust and integrity.

- In some cases, where the public interest dictates otherwise and particularly where power is being abused, obligations of trust and protection may weigh less heavily. Nevertheless, these obligations should not be discarded lightly.

- As far as possible participation in sociological research should be based on the freely given informed consent of those studied. This implies a responsibility on the sociologist to explain in appropriate detail, and in terms meaningful to participants, what the research is about, who is undertaking and financing it, why it is being undertaken, and how it is to be disseminated and used.

- Research participants should be made aware of their right to refuse participation whenever and for whatever reason they wish.

www.britsoc.co.uk/ (search for equality and ethics)

Some ethics codes

The Economics, Social and Research Council:
   www.esrc.ac.uk/ (search for framework for research ethics)
The College of Occupational Therapists:
   http://www.cot.org.uk/ (search for ethics)
The Chartered Society of Physiotherapy:
   http://www.csp.org.uk/ (search for research ethics)

Many other bodies have their own ethical codes and they too are worth consulting. Overall, these ethical codes share similar concerns about maintaining professional standards in terms of behaviour and not exposing participants in research to any harm or distress.

The second course of action involves submitting a proposal to an **ethics committee**. This could be an internal body, such as a university ethics committee, or an external body, such as the local NHS ethics committee. Due to heightened – and very real – concerns about people's rights, these have become increasingly common and, in some ways, increasingly demanding. In the proposal the researcher will outline what the study is about, what the possible risks to the people involved in the subject are, and what measures will be taken to avoid creating or encountering ethical problems. This can be quite complex and the ethical considerations and safeguards of the NHS in particular can be very demanding and thorough. Once clearance has been obtained from the committee, or the researcher has acted on their recommendations to enhance the protection of the people in the study, then the research can go ahead.

One very common ethical consideration, and something of vital importance when involving people in research, is that the researcher must obtain informed consent from those taking part in the research. This will involve providing them with an outline of what the research is about, what they will be asked to do in the research, and how the information they provide will be handled, stored, and disseminated. Consent is usually sought by asking those who are taking part to sign a form that lays out the points just made. It is vital that at all times communication is understandable to the respondent. When the research involves people who may not be able to understand what is being required of them, such as children, then some form of proxy consent is required.

Conclusion

Research is an essential part of the sociological project and provides both questions and answers in our attempts to understand society. The focus of sociological research though differs from that of the natural sciences. Sociologists are faced with the dynamic flow of an ever-changing world animated by the actions of thinking and purposeful human beings. Understanding their motives, interpretations and experiences therefore forms a great deal of what sociologists do. This in turn affects and influences the research methods that are used in the pursuit of knowledge. In addition to the statistical profiles of the more familiar quantitative approaches, sociologists employ qualitative approaches, which seek to access and bring forward the motives and narratives of people in everyday life.

Summary points

- Research is a vital part of sociology.
- Sociological research is scientific like the natural sciences, but deals with purposeful self-aware people as opposed to inanimate objects.
- Research is a very practical activity and requires the researcher to be realistic in what they can do in order to meet their research question.
- Quantitative methods include surveys and mass questionnaires and are useful for establishing the size and extent of particular social phenomena.
- Qualitative methods include focus groups, in-depth interviews and ethnography and are useful for understanding the experiences and motives of people.
- Interviewing people requires certain skills so as to create an environment in which research participants feel at ease, where they can discuss and comment on their experiences.
- Ethical considerations are an important aspect of research. Care must be taken not to physically, psychologically or emotionally harm people who participate in the research.

Case study

The following tasks could be useful for you to consider in relation to the points raised above. Read the tasks and then reflect on the questions below.

Task A

Students are often young people who, when they move away from home for the first time, have to adapt quickly to being independent. Often universities find that the first year is very stressful for students. As is discussed in this book, stress can be a cause of ill health. How would you research the issues that students face at this stage in their college and university careers and the effects these issues have on their health?

Task B

Most universities have a range of students on a variety of courses. Intuitively one would think that students on health-related courses would have better or wider knowledge of health and have a healthier lifestyle than students on non-health-related courses. How would you research this comparison between different cohorts of students?

(Continued)

(Continued)

For each task, think about the following

1   What would a suitable research question be?
2   Where would you look for previous literature on student experiences away from home?
3   What method would you use – quantitative or qualitative?
4   What problems might you encounter in doing the research?
5   What ethical issues would you have to be aware of? What permissions and consents would have to be obtained?

Taking your studies further

This chapter will have helped you understand many of the key terms, concepts, theories and debates relating to sociological research. Listed below are books that will provide deeper and more detailed discussions of the points raised in this chapter. You will also find what is available on the companion website. This offers downloads of relevant material, plus links to useful websites in addition to podcasts and other features.

Recommended reading

Bryman, A. (2001) *Social Research Methods*. Oxford: Oxford University Press.
Crang, M. and Cook, I. (2007) *Doing Ethnographies*. London: Sage.
Green, J. and Thorogood, N. (2004) *Qualitative Methods for Health Research*. London: Sage.
Hugman, R. (2005) *New Approaches in Ethics for the Caring Professions*. London: Palgrave Macmillan.
Mason, J. (2002) *Qualitative Researching*. London: Sage.
Richards, L. (2005) *Handling Qualitative Data: A Practical Guide*. London: Sage.
Seale, C. (1999) *The Quality of Qualitative Research*. London: Sage.
Silverman, D. (2001) *Interpreting Qualitative Data*, 2nd edn. London: Sage.
Strauss, A.L. and Corbin, J. (eds) (1997) *Grounded Theory in Practice*. Thousand Oaks, CA: Sage.
Strauss, A.L. and Corbin, J. (1998) *Basics of Qualitative Research: Techniques and Procedures for Developing Grounded Theory*. Thousand Oaks, CA: Sage.

On the companion website

You will find a selection of research-based articles that provide examples of the various research methods outlined in this chapter.

SECTION 2

Key Themes

6

Class and health

Main points

- There are enduring differences between social classes in relation to health.
- In terms of early mortality, morbidity and a range of other health indicators, disadvantaged groups have considerably poorer outcomes than advantaged groups.
- Substantial relative poverty is prevalent in the UK, with high levels of child poverty in many areas.
- Two current, and in many ways rival, theories attempt to explain class and health inequalities: the psycho-social and the neo-material.
- The psycho-social perspective highlights how societies lacking in social cohesion have poor health, while the neo-material perspective emphasises access to resources.

Key concepts

Class inequality poverty psycho-social explanations neo-material explanations place.

Parts of this chapter have already been published in the following article and have been reproduced by kind permission of Inderscience Publishers:

Yuill, C. (2010) '"The Spirit Level", health inequalities and economic democracy', *International Journal of Management Concepts and Philosophy*, 4(2): 177–193

Introduction

Health inequality is a recurrent feature of British society. Writing in the mid-1800s the young Engels, before he collaborated with Marx, claimed that the high levels of poor health in the newly industrialising towns of Manchester, Liverpool and Glasgow and the sheer scale of early morbidity were a form of 'social murder' committed by the ruling classes of the day. Even though British society has considerably changed since then, the differences in health between social classes in Britain still obstinately remain. A variety of reports over time all point in the same direction: that morbidity and mortality are intimately linked to class. Following the Registrar General's classification scheme, men from social class VI, for example will currently live on average 7.5 years less than men from social class I (ONS 2004) (Figure 6.1). That statistic is a useful national average but more notable, and potentially troubling, localised examples of health inequality can be identified. Men in the deprived area of Calton in Glasgow have a life expectancy of just 54 years, in comparison

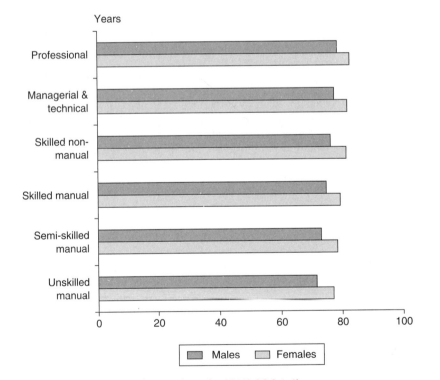

FIGURE 6.1 Life expectancy by class and gender (ONS 2004: 6)

Source: National Statistics website: www.statistics.gov.uk. © Crown copyright

with the 82 years expected by men in the more affluent suburb of Lenzie, just a few miles up the A803 roadway (CSDH 2008). In Sheffield the average life expectancy gap between the worst-off and best-off neighbourhoods is 17.9 years (Thomas et al. 2009). Explanations for health inequalities which do not point to social class have come and gone. Artefact effects, genetic causation and social drift, amongst others, have all been dismissed (for a useful summary see Macintyre 1997). So too should the so-called 'risk factors' (smoking, poor diet and lack of exercise) be treated with caution (see Bartley 2003). They tend to be symptomatic of particular social relations and not an explanation in themselves of why so many health inequalities persist over time.

The only remaining credible explanation is that health inequalities are something to do with how we as embodied beings experience features, aspects or the structure of the society in which we live and work – and that is the focus for the rest of this chapter. With that purpose in mind, this chapter begins with a discussion of class, attempting to define class and exploring how class is represented in statistics. The following section turns to the extent of health inequalities in Britain today. The focus then moves to income inequality and poverty, with an overview of what poverty is and levels of poverty in Britain today. The final section outlines the current two leading explanations for health inequalities: the psycho-social approach, as popularised in Wilkinson and Pickett's book *The Spirit Level* (2009), and the neo-material perspective.

What is class?

British readers of this book may have a certain idea of what class is – consisting of titled wealthy individuals in top hats on the one hand, and tracksuit wearing 'chavs' on the other hand. There may be something in these cultural differences in people's appearance; however, class is a complex and dynamic power relationship between people and not just how people speak or dress. Class societies are also distinctive from other societies that are also stratified into some form of hierarchy of power. For example, in feudal society distinctions between people were rigid, immobile and seen to be religiously ordained. The reason why you were a lord or a peasant was because God willed it that way and there was no way to change it. In contemporary capitalist societies, one can be more socially mobile and move between classes. This is because, in many ways, you *achieve* your class position and it is not fixed by your birth. Nevertheless, most people tend to stay within or near the class they were born into.

Class refers to a complex stratification of society based on access to and control of power, status and economic resources.

Class is also, as mentioned above, more than just how people dress and speak. In fact, those forms of distinction are becomingly increasingly eroded in contemporary society. No longer do all stockbrokers and bank managers in the City of London wear bowler hats, for instance. More importantly, it is the very real and dramatic differences between people both economically and in terms of power of which we must be aware. It is those differences that lead to class differences. Later in this chapter we look at economic differences between different classes. What we will identify there is that considerable wealth is owned by a very small percentage while a sizeable percentage lives on or near the poverty line. In terms of power, people in the higher social class have greater control over a whole range of resources. So, for example, people in higher social classes generally have more control over how they organise their work, with less intervention from supervisors and managers. Indeed, they may be a manager, meaning that they can control the working conditions of others. Also, by having greater income people in higher social classes will have greater control and power over their day-to-day lives: for example, being able to afford foreign travel, eat organic food, or have more frequent leisure time.

Measuring class

Defining and measuring class can be very difficult. In the UK, official statistics until 2001 used the Registrar-General's Social Class (RGSC) scheme, a system that had been in use since 1911. This was a descriptive, not a theoretical, approach that ranked six classes in order of what was commonly held to be occupational advantage. In 2001 the RGSC was replaced by the National Statistics Socio-economic Classification (NS-SEC). It is hoped that the new approach more accurately reflects current perceptions of both occupations and occupational advantage. Even though it is 10 years or so on since the change, you are quite likely to encounter both systems both in this book and in the wider literature. What the titles and numbers mean are laid out in Tables 6.1 and 6.2, and this should make it easier to read the various tables and graphs included in this chapter. It is, however, worth pointing out that both approaches have their good and bad points, but both provide much useful information.

Questions

Which of the two ways of trying to classify class do you find the more convincing? Where do you think you would be classified as a student? Where do you think you will be classified when you graduate?

Health inequalities

We will now look a little more closely at the shape and extent of class and health inequalities. In the introduction we noted, and saw in Figure 6.1, that there was a great deal of difference

TABLE 6.1 Eight-class grouping of the National Statistics Socio-economic Classification

Classification title	Examples of occupation
1 Higher managerial and professional occupations	Doctors, lawyers, dentists, professors, professional engineers
2 Lower managerial and professional occupations	School teachers, nurses, journalists, actors, police sergeants
3 Intermediate occupations	Airline cabin crew, secretaries
4 Small employers and own account workers	Non-professionals with fewer than 25 employees, e.g.: self-employed builders, hairdressers or fishermen, shopkeepers with own shop
5 Lower supervisory and technical occupations	Train drivers, employed plumbers or electricians, foremen, supervisors
6 Semi-routine occupations	Shop assistants, postmen, security guards, call centre workers, care assistants
7 Routine occupations	Bus drivers, waitresses, cleaners, car park attendants, refuse collectors
8 Never worked and long-termed unemployed	People who have either never worked or are long-term unemployed and therefore cannot be classified

Source: National Statistics website: www.statistics.gov.uk. © Crown copyright

TABLE 6.2 Registrar General's Social Class

		Examples of occupation
Non-manual		
I	Professional	Doctors, lawyers, chartered accountants, professionally qualified engineers
II	Intermediate	Managers, school teachers, journalists
IIIN	Skilled non-manual	Clerks, cashiers, retail staff
Manual		
IIIM	Skilled manual	Supervisors of manual workers, plumbers, electricians, bus drivers
IV	Partly skilled	Warehousemen, security guards, machine tool operators, care assistants
V	Unskilled	Labourers, cleaners, messengers

Source: National Statistics website: www.statistics. gov.uk. © Crown copyright

between people's life expectancies depending on the class to which they belong. In fact, this difference for men has increased over the years. Between 1972 and 1976 a man from class I could expect to live 5.5 years longer than a man from class V. By 1997 to 1999, however, a class I man could expect to live nearly 7.5 years longer than a man from class V. In the same period the same difference for women increased from 5.3 years to 5.7 years (ONS 2004: 79).

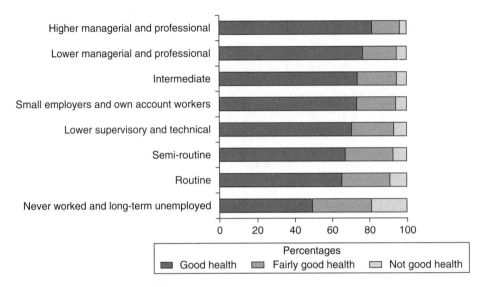

FIGURE 6.2 Self-reported health by NS-SEC (ONS 2001)

Source: National Statistics website: www.statistics.gov.uk. © Crown copyright

There are many other ways in which the health, morbidity and mortality of those in the most disadvantaged groups in society is worse than of those in the most advantaged groups. Another example of this can be found in self-reported health; this is where you ask people to assess how they themselves would rate their health. Again, we find a sharp difference between the classes (see Figure 6.2), with nearly four times the number of men and women who are long-term unemployed or have never worked rating their health as poor in comparison to men and women in the managerial and professional classification.

Questions

How would you assess your health: (a) good (b) fairly good, or (c) not good? How does your assessment of health relate to the statistics mentioned above?

One of the clearest ways in which class and health inequalities can be seen is in death rates (see Figure 6.3). Over the last few years the death rate for all classes has dropped but there still remains a distinct class gradient. The gradient tends to be clearer for men but a little more irregular for women. Gender differences in health will be explored in more depth in Chapter 8.

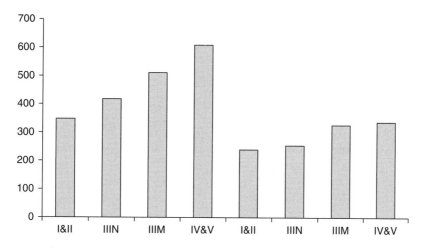

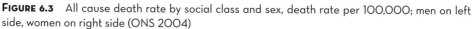

FIGURE 6.3 All cause death rate by social class and sex, death rate per 100,000; men on left side, women on right side (ONS 2004)

© Crown copyright

Links

Chapter 8 discusses gender and health in more detail.

This pattern of what is known as the 'class and health gradient' is also visible when we look at specific conditions. In just about every case there is greater mortality as we move across the class scale. Figure 6.4 indicates this trend using selected causes of death as examples.

It is not just in physical health that people from classes IV and V exhibit a greater burden of ill health. We can also see it with mental health (see Figure 6.5 on page 91). There is higher prevalence of many forms of mental ill health among people from classes IIIN, IV and V.

Links

Chapter 9 discusses mental health in more detail.

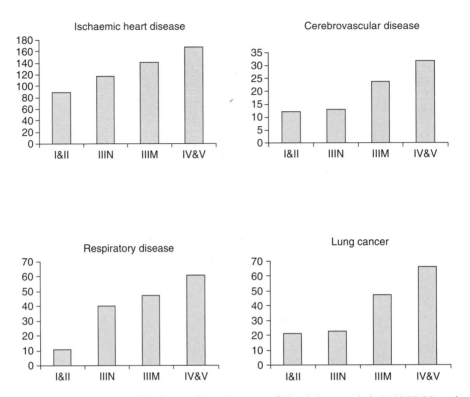

FIGURE 6.4 Trends in mortality from selected causes of death by social class, 1997-99, males aged 35-64, directly age-standardised death rates (DSRs) per 100,000 per year (ONS 2003)

Source: National Statistics website: www.statistics.gov.uk. © Crown copyright

Work by Shaw et al. (1999) and Dorling et al. (2000) at the turn of the century has drawn our attention to how there appears to be some form of relationship between health and place. Poor health will be mainly found in areas of poverty and deprivation, though other factors such as environment (how clean the streets are, levels of crime and vandalism, and so on) and access to facilities can also contribute to the poor health of certain areas. Shaw et al. (1999), in a survey of postal code districts of Britain, found that the worst areas for health in Britain were mainly in inner-city Glasgow, Scotland. For example, Shettleston, Springburn, Maryhill and Pollok all exhibited high standardised mortality ratios (SMRs) that were around twice the average. Shettleston emerged as the worst health place in Britain in this particular survey, with 71 per cent of deaths in that area being avoidable had those people not lived in poverty. These statistics contrast with the best health places in Britain. Many were leafy suburban districts in the south of England, such as Woodspring and Romsey;

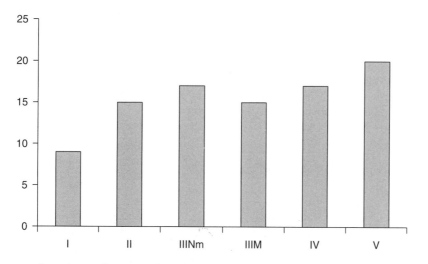

FIGURE 6.5 Prevalence of neurotic disorders by social class, 2000, Great Britain, percentages (ONS 2004: 78)

Source: National Statistics website: www.statistics.gov.uk. © Crown copyright

Wokingham, situated to the west of London, came out top with an SMR nearly half the average and no avoidable deaths.

It is always worthwhile to reflect on what lies behind these rather cold and stark statistics. What we see here is that there are people living in different parts of the same country, but leading quite different lives in terms of quantity and quality of life. The numbers of unnecessary deaths can be placed at 10,887 (Smith et al. 2000). Another study into health inequalities and excess mortality (Mitchell et al. 2000) also pointed to a substantial number of lives that could be saved each year if certain changes in social policy were made. The potential numbers of lives that could be saved and the policy changes that could bring that about are summarised in Table 6.3.

TABLE 6.3 Lives saved by various changes in social policy

No of lives saved per year	Policy change
7,597 among people under 65	If wealth inequalities were reduced to their 1983 level
2,504 among people under 65	If there was full employment
1,407 among those under 15	If child poverty was eradicated
11,508 total (after rounding)	If all three measures were implemented

Source: Mitchell et al. (2000). Reproduced by kind permission of The Policy Press

Questions

Shaw et al. (1999) draw our attention to the effect of place. Look at the photographs in Figure 6.6 of an area associated with deprivation. What do you think it would be like living in this area? In what ways could your health be affected? In addition to the material effects of poverty, what about stress?

FIGURE 6.6   Images of deprivation

The above information may give the impression that there is a 'north–south' divide in Britain, with the south being affluent and healthy while the north is poor and unhealthy. One must take care here, as the picture is a little more complex. Poverty and deprivation may be disguised and camouflaged in what, on first glance, appear to be relatively affluent areas. A closer analysis of the data and research reveals that there exist pockets of poverty in the south-east where conditions are similar to those found in places such as Glasgow Shettleston. Social geographer Danny Dorling has identified a north–south divide in relation to health and other inequalities. There is, however, no neat boundary line, and the terms 'north' and 'south' referring to different and unequal levels of health and poverty are possibly more metaphorical than actual. What Dorling notes is that as the economic and social recession following the banking crisis of 2009 unfolds, the levels of poverty and inequality we associate with the north of Britain, and with Wales and Scotland, move outwards. There are also quite considerable areas of poverty and inequality in the south of England, too.'This situation is illustrated in a report by Dorling et al. (2000) into poverty and health inequality in London. Drawing on Charles Booth's classic study of poverty in London in 1896 (Booth 1902), they found that not much had changed in the last 100 years. Booth's study involved a painstaking house-by-house, street-by-street analysis of poverty and wealth in London. He then produced a colour-coded map of London indicating the poorest areas in black and the most affluent areas in light yellow. What Dorling found was that Booth's map still held up as a very powerful indicator of where to find both poverty and ill health. This indicates, first, that even in a relatively prosperous area such as the south-east of England there exist dense pockets of poverty; and second, that 100 years of apparent social progress and social policy have produced little change in parts of the UK. '

Income inequalities and poverty

One feature of contemporary British society is that there are clear and enduring inequalities, whether in health (as seen earlier), income or wealth. This section will explore those inequalities further and outline that Britain today is still a very divided and unequal place to live. We shall, in particular, explore differences in wealth and income and the associated social problems of poverty.

Income and wealth inequality

A clear and persistent trend over the last 30 years or so has been the location of vast amounts of wealth (the money found in shares, savings, artwork, jewellery, land) in the hands of a small percentage of people (see Table 6.4). In fact the wealthiest 1 per cent owns as much wealth as the poorest 50 per cent – a very sizeable inequality!

Inequality is also apparent in income. The highest paid in British society earn 10 times as much as the lowest paid in terms of average gross weekly pay, as Table 6.5 indicates.

TABLE 6.4 Distribution of wealth

	1976	1986	1991	1996	2001
Most wealthy 1%	21	18	17	20	23
Most wealthy 2%	71	73	71	74	75
Most wealthy 3%	92	90	92	93	95

Source: National Statistics website: www.statistics.gov.uk. © Crown copyright

TABLE 6.5 Top ten highest and lowest average gross weekly incomes

		Average gross weekly pay (£)
Highest paid		
1	Directors and chief executives of major organisations	2301.2
2	Medical practitioners	1186.4
3	Financial managers and chartered secretaries	1124.2
4	Solicitors and lawyers, judges and coroners	925.8
5	Marketing and sales managers	888.6
6	Information and communication technology managers	872.4
7	Management consultants, actuaries, economists and statisticians	863.1
8	Police officers (inspectors and above)	863.1
9	IT strategy and planning professionals	844.4
10	Financial and accounting technicians	838.1
Lowest paid		
1	Retail cashiers and checkout operators	207.6
2	Launderers, dry cleaners, pressers	217.6
3	Bar staff	217.9
4	Waiters, waitresses	218.2
5	Kitchen and catering assistants	228.4
6	Hotel porters	229.9
7	Hairdressers, barbers	231.8
8	Animal care occupations (not elsewhere classified)	232.3
9	Sewing machinists	239.8
10	Shelf fillers	241.5

Source: National Statistics website: www.statistics.gov.uk. © Crown copyright

Poverty remains a pressing issue in today's society in the UK, with just under 13 million people living below the poverty line. There are two forms of poverty: **absolute poverty**, that is the complete absence of clothing, food and shelter, typically seen in developing countries; and **relative poverty**, where people have a standard of living that is lower than an acceptable standard of living in a given society. Relative poverty is the main type that is found in Europe. The European Community offers the following definition of relative poverty:

> Persons, families and groups of persons whose resources (material, cultural and social) are so limited as to exclude them from the minimum acceptable way of life in the Member State to which they belong. (SPIU 1997: 1)

There is a considerable debate as to how and why poverty is defined in certain ways, and this has consequences for government policy and action. The Conservative government during the 1980s made the point that there was no poverty in the UK; it was simply that some people had less than others, a feature of any advanced industrial country. This contrasts with Tony Blair's Labour government which sought during the late 1990s and early in the new century to reduce levels of poverty and inequality. There are indications that they have achieved some, albeit limited, success in this regard.

Absolute poverty refers to having such restricted access to food, shelter and clothing that life is threatened.

The debates that rage around defining and subsequently measuring poverty are interesting and challenging. It is not within the scope of this section to pursue them in any great depth, though a brief consideration will be given below.

Relative poverty refers to having the minimum requirements of a particular society in relation to other people in that society.

Households below average income

One of the most frequently used measures of poverty relies upon using 50 per cent mean and/or 60 per cent median of average income for a particular household (Figure 6.7). The figures such a measure produces are of income *before* or *after* housing costs. However, after-housing-costs figures are mainly used because, for poorer people, housing costs are inescapable fixed costs and using after-housing-costs figures provides a more accurate reflection of disposable income. The poverty line for certain types of household using this particular measure is shown in Table 6.6. Using this measure of poverty we can chart the growth of poverty since 1979, as Figure 6.7 indicates.

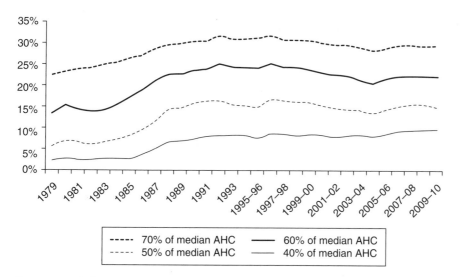

FIGURE 6.7   Relative poverty: percentage of individuals in households with incomes below various fractions of median income, after housing costs (Institute of Fiscal Studies 2011: 38)

TABLE 6.6   UK poverty line for a range of households based on 60 per cent of the median UK income after housing costs have been paid, 2008-9

Household type	Poverty line: household income (£ per week)
Single person	£119
Couple	£206
Lone parent with two children (aged 5 and 14)	£247
Couple with two children (aged 5 and 14)	£333

Source: Child Poverty Action Group

Structural explanations

Poverty here is seen as the result of government policy and the booms and busts of the global economic system. During the 1980s in the UK the then Conservative government introduced free-market policies that led to a major readjustment of the UK industrial landscape. Many traditional heavy industries, such as coal mining and steel production, went into terminal decline. This resulted in the economic blight of many areas, particularly south Wales and northern England. It should be borne in mind that, when a major employer in an area ceases production, not only do the workers lose their jobs but the whole local economy suffers. Shock waves are sent through the local community, resulting in difficulties for the local service sector and small businesses.

Structural explanations of poverty highlight failures of government policy and fluctuations in global economics as the root causes of poverty. However, in the 1980s it was not just changes to industrial policy that led to an increase in poverty. Changes in taxation and policies concerned with the redistribution of wealth also had a major impact on poverty levels, according to this perspective. Again, during the 1980s, we see a dramatic shift taking place in policy direction. The Conservatives pursued policies that saw a move of wealth up the class scale, as opposed to across it.

Individual explanations

Individual explanations of poverty highlight individual weakness and individuals taking advantage of state benefits. This view of poverty gained prominence during the 1980s and 1990s, championed by commentators such as David Marsland in the UK and Charles Murray in the US. It attributes poverty either to individual weakness or fecklessness, or to people misusing welfare services. Murray developed the notion of an underclass consisting of people who have voluntarily absented themselves from the working world and who instead live on over-generous state benefits. Many adherents of this view called for the introduction of workfare-style policies, whereby eligibility for benefits is dependent on the completion of some form of training or work. Marsland (1996) points to the welfare state as being responsible for creating a 'dependency culture', where there is little incentive to work.

Questions

Which of the two different explanations of poverty – structural or individual – do you find the more convincing, and why?

Explaining class and health inequalities

So far, we have examined a great deal of material about the disparities that exist in health and income/wealth across different groups. These statistics provide a great deal of information and strongly indicate that class and health inequalities exist. Statistics alone, however, are never enough for the sociological imagination and we must turn to theories that can explain those statistics. Essentially, we must ask why and how these differences come into existence. What we shall see is that it is more complicated than just that poor people eat unhealthy food options or that the rich have access to private health care.

This focus on the more complex causes of health inequality forms the main purpose of this section: to explore beneath the surface and see what causes so many people to have the length of their lives reduced and to experience greater ill health than others. To do so we will begin by briefly looking at the Black Report, a highly influential piece of work published in 1980 which drew attention to many forms of health inequality in British society.

Attention will then turn to the current debate between two, in many ways rival and competing, theories that seek to explain class and health inequalities: the psycho-social and the neo-material. These theories emphasise different reasons why class and health inequalities exist. The *psycho-social* focuses on the negative emotional experiences, the stresses and strains, of living in an unequal society. The *neo-material* favours an explanation that concentrates on the distribution of various resources such as good housing and education.

The Black Report

Published back in 1980, the Black Report (Black et al. 1980) has, in many respects, set the agenda for research into all manner of health inequalities in the UK. Mainly drawn from epidemiological research, the report identified that there were clear and distinct differences in health between men and women, between ethnic minority groups and between classes. In terms of class, the Black Report put forward four different possible explanations of why class has such a strong bearing on health: artefact, social selection, cultural and material. Over the years these explanations of why class and health inequalities exist have been challenged, modified or developed. However, given the importance of the Black Report at the time, it is useful to have an awareness of both the reasons it suggested for health inequalities and what the subsequent research has found. All of this is summarised in Table 6.7.

TABLE 6.7   Summary of Black Report and lessons from subsequent research

Suggested reasons for health inequalities	Subsequent research
Artefact explanation The existence of health inequalities is due to the way in which the statistics are collected and the way in which we construct the concept of 'class' in surveys and statistical research	If anything, the statistics under-report the extent of class and health inequalities
Social selection explanation It is poor health that assigns people to lower-class groups rather than any of the effects of belonging to a lower-class group. Thus it is the other way around: health affects our class, rather than class affecting our health	There may be some evidence of social selection at younger ages but the overall effect over a lifetime is very minor
Behavioural/cultural explanations Ill health is due to people's choices and decisions; working-class people tend to make the wrong choices to smoke, drink too much and eat the wrong foods	Even among people who follow 'healthy lifestyles' we find similar patterns of ill-health. Lifestyle choices may only account for a quarter of social class inequalities
Structural/material explanations Poor conditions, such as bad housing and low incomes, make it virtually impossible for working-class people to lead a healthy lifestyle	This perspective will be explored in greater depth in the rest of this chapter

Psycho-social or neo-material explanations

We will now discuss the psycho-social and neo-material explanations that attempt to explain the existence of class and health inequalities. To do so, we shall summarise Richard Wilkinson and Kate Pickett's book *The Spirit Level* (2009), as it best encapsulates the psycho-social position, before turning to the neo-material critiques of the general psycho-social perspective.

A convenient metaphor for explaining the differences between the two approaches is provided by Lynch et al. (2000). Society is like a passenger plane. There are a few roomy comfortable business-class seats at the front while the rest of the plane consists of less spacious economy-class seats. From the psycho-social perspective the poor health of the economy-class passengers is due to them feeling stressed at seeing the comfort of the business-class passengers. From the neo-material perspective the health inequality is due to the cramped conditions of their seating.

The Spirit Level

The Spirit Level by Wilkinson and Pickett (2009) advances a serious, well-constructed and evidenced understanding and explanation of health inequalities and other social maladies in contemporary high-income ('rich') societies. Their central message is that once a society has gone beyond a certain material threshold then it is not the *absolute* levels of income that animate social problems but rather *relative* income. Critically, they also add, the larger the income inequality existing between the richest and poorest sections of a society, the greater the social problems facing that society. A substantial array of data drawn from a variety of sources is marshalled into a series of thought-provoking graphs to support and outline their thesis. Each graph in turn consistently plots the same relationship between inequality and a number of social problems, such as health inequality, drug misuse, high rates of teenage pregnancy and increases in the number of people experiencing some form of mental distress. The United Kingdom, the United States of America, and Singapore prominently figure as the worst examples of the relationship between high inequality and social problems. In contrast, the Nordic countries and Japan consistently do well, exhibiting both high levels of equality and low levels of the examples of problems just listed.

Wilkinson and Pickett's emphasis on relative income differences and inequality may, at first, seem counterintuitive. A wealthy society should, after all, be more than able to meet the basics of the good life that its members require. It should be in a position to provide sound housing, an adequate diet and reasonable education – the accepted building blocks of 'well-being'. The evidence Wilkinson and Pickett presents strongly overturns such an otherwise reasonable observation. Wealthy societies can be quite incapable of eradicating health inequalities if they exhibit high levels of inequality. America, the world's richest nation-state, for example, demonstrates some of the worst health differences between the richest and the poorest sections of its society despite its substantial wealth.

So what matters, time and again, is the presence of inequality. How that inequality translates into health inequality is explained by reference to **psycho-social** considerations and how they translate into a variety of biological systems within the human body. In an earlier work Wilkinson neatly sums up why it is important to focus on psycho-social processes as opposed to purely psychological or sociological processes:

> Psychological literature, concentrating as it does on the individual, too often ignores our susceptibility to the powerful sociological processes that drive social differentiation and discrimination against those lower down the social hierarchy. On the other hand, the sociological literature that addresses issues of social class stratification usually ignores its interaction with individual psychology. (2005: 33)

The focus on psycho-social factors allows Wilkinson to go beyond (but not necessarily completely dismiss) material factors (such as poor housing or bad diet) and to explain how people's experiences of inequality can have such a devastating effect on their health and on wider society. In part, the reasons for health inequality are to do with stress (albeit stress of a chronic and persistent nature) connected by having low control over one's life, for example. The reasons for health inequality are, however, Wilkinson argues, more to do with what we have inherited from our evolutionary past. Humans have evolved to be aware of status and rank, and are sensitised to experiencing and perceiving hierarchy. The experience and perception of status and rank trigger various internal biological systems that, in turn, create a variety of harmful states that negatively impact on our health.

Wilkinson rallies a variety of non-human primate studies to provide empirical proof for the relationship between psycho-social factors and biology. In *Unhealthy Societies: The Afflictions of Inequality* (1996) he draws on the work of primatologist Sapolsky. Researching wild baboons in the Serengeti, Sapolsky (1992) identified how social hierarchies and social dominance within those hierarchies lead to deleterious physiological effects on these primates. Key to harm occurring is the release of glucocorticoids triggered by social stressors. The long-term presence of these biochemicals increases the chances of cardiovascular disease and high blood pressure.

Other researchers working with humans have similarly noted the negative effects of certain physiological systems being 'switched on' for too long. McEwen's (2000) work on stress in humans, for example, identifies the highly damaging effects of having one's stress system permanently active. A variety of biochemicals, in particular the corticoids, that are adaptive for short-term stressors become highly maladaptive when produced over extended periods, especially when one's body permanently adjusts to being stressed.

In addition to the biological reactions outlined above, Wilkinson and Pickett (2009) claim highly unequal societies generate particular forms of harmful social interactions, divisive cultures and damaged individual subjectivities. Chief amongst damaged subjectivities, for example, is the increase of a self-promoting, insecure egotism. Easily mistaken for having high self-esteem, those with insecure egos who exhibit self-promoting behaviours (think of the time people spend on Facebook or Bebo, and what they say about themselves) can experience high evaluation anxiety and increased cortisol levels when others perceive them as failures. Self-value means little while peer evaluation seems to mean all. Inequality also exerts negative pressures on society in terms of corroding bonds of trust between people, ultimately leading to a retreat from community into more private, but more troubled, spheres of life. As a result of this more inward lifestyle, people look to protecting themselves and creating cultures that place symbolic and actual barriers between themselves and others. Wilkinson points to the uptake of aggressively if not militaristically named sport utility vehicles (SUVs), as if everyday life in New York or London is somehow as dangerous as everyday life in Baghdad.

Urban researcher Anna Minton (2009) highlights a similar dynamic in her work. She notes the increasing privatisation of formerly public space and the parcelling up of the urban landscape into supposedly secure, but ultimately isolated, gated communities. Fear of an imagined other, then, appears to be part and parcel of an unequal society. Inequality also breeds harsh disrespect for those lower in the social hierarchy and obsequiousness towards those above. Adorno's bicycling metaphor is employed by Wilkinson and Pickett (2009) to illustrate this situation. This metaphor projects the image of someone holding the handlebars of their bikes as if bowing to someone above them, while at the same time kicking down on those below as they pedal away.

The neo-materialist critics

While welcomed by many for attempting to develop a deeper theoretical perspective on health inequalities, Wilkinson's work has nevertheless generated much critique and criticism. The debate surrounding his main contention – that income inequality is the main cause of health inequalities – has at times become quite heated, if not intractable. A substantial literature now exists where claim and counter-claim are voiced, or objections advanced and then repudiated (Navarro 2002). Space forbids a detailed exploration of these exchanges. Instead, the main themes are highlighted in order to provide a 'balance sheet' of where the debate takes us.

The majority of objections to Wilkinson's thesis are voiced by a group of scholars commonly referred to as the neo-materialists. Their points of criticism can be briefly summarised as follows. Wilkinson provides no insights in his thesis as to how inequalities arise in the first place, nor does he provide an analysis of the processes and social forces that maintain and perpetuate income inequalities. In particular, he is silent on the logics of capitalism, the modes of domination and exploitation, and the conditioning influences of political ideologies. Therefore, for example, in *The Spirit Level* the increasing trend of inequality in the United States and United Kingdom is noted and framed as being a negative development, but the reasons for the increase in inequality go unexplained (Wilkinson and Pickett 2009: 234–6). What Wilkinson may have identified by focusing on income inequality as an indicator and cause of health inequality is, in critical realist parlance, more likely to be at the level of actualisation of deeper causal generative mechanisms rather than the causes themselves (Lawson 1997: 22; Scambler 2001).

An overly subjective understanding of health provides another basis of criticism. Muntaner (2004) critically reflects that Wilkinson commits the philosophical error of Cartesian mind–body dualism. The psychological processes are stripped away from their material contexts. The effects of poverty, inadequate housing and health care provision are therefore excluded from view, and some form of 'change of mind' or mass therapy is all that is required to reduce health inequalities. There is, again, much validity in this observation. Wilkinson's critics, however, make the opposite error and conversely slip into an over-determination of structure. Subjectivity and the lived experiences of working-class people are mentioned in their critiques (see Lynch 2005) but never adequately explored or theorised (Crinson and Yuill 2008). What we have here is a rerun of a very familiar 'structure versus agency' debate, where neither side can reach a satisfactory reconciliation of the other's strength with their weakness.

Wilkinson's uncritical use of evolutionary psychology has also drawn criticism, especially in regard to his interpretation of animal studies and ideas on the effects of social rank (Crinson and Yuill 2008). Making an attempt to trace how society and biology might interact is a very welcome move, in many respects. It is increasingly perceived within medical sociology that the relationships between sociological and biological processes require urgent attention (for more detail on this development see Bendelow et al. 2003; Williams 2003). Only by attending to how the two 'mesh together' can a full account of human health begin to be established. There are dangers in doing so, however. One of the dangers has possibly influenced Wilkinson, in that one can lapse into a reductionist, static and determinist understanding of human society, human minds and human behaviour. Evolutionary psychologists tend to posit a view of human behaviour as having been formed in and, crucially, being unchanged since the Pleistocene. The neurobiologist Steven Rose (2006) objects to the evolutionary psychologists' position. He highlights instead the dynamic, fluid and malleable nature of the human mind and brain, and suggests that all evolutionary psychologists offer is a 'Flintstone psychology'. Human action here is trapped at an almost arbitrary point in human history – a point where more than enough time has elapsed since for other perhaps more modern modes of behaviour to evolve.

Elements of Wilkinson's thesis can, therefore, be criticised and found to be lacking. The main reason for that, as Scambler (2001) suggests, is that Wilkinson calls off his search for causes too soon. The journey to discover the causes of health inequality is signposted but not fully travelled. More needs to be done to tease out the full depth and causality of inequality. Such a move would require getting to grips with deeper structural forces and in particular the role of social class. One can, however, sense that Wilkinson is not disposed to engage in such an activity. The reason, as Yuill (2010) suspects, is that he is keen, if not impatient, to get on and do something about health inequalities in a more direct way. Wilkinson's frustration with those who chide him for not plumbing deeper into society is evident in this response to neo-materialists Muntaner and Lynch:

> In an attempt to lay down boundaries and avoid an infinite regress into causes of causes, I simply stopped at saying that wider income differences carry health costs. Others could wrestle with the extremely complicated, but crucial, issues of how income distribution can be influenced. (2002: 361)

Overall, the criticisms are very useful, but do not detract from the main observation that Wilkinson advances, namely that inequality needs to be addressed – a point even his most trenchant critics also note (for example, Lynch et al. 2000). It is how any reduction in levels of inequality is effected that is important.

More of *The Spirit Level* than any of Wilkinson's previous monographs on income and health inequalities is devoted to offering solutions to the problems of income inequality. As Wilkinson and Pickett make clear in their introduction, the purpose of *The Spirit Level* is not simply to communicate academic discourses to other academics but to bring about real and lasting change.

Conclusion

The research presented here clearly indicates that there are consistent and persistent differences in class and health in contemporary society. Such differences are part of the array of inequalities to do with wealth, income and other resources. Perhaps it is in health that the social division of class is most evidently visible: the bodies of people are affected and changed by their location in society. The bodies of working-class people are more likely to age quicker, be more susceptible to illness and be much more likely to encounter limiting long-term conditions than those located higher in society. The evidence also strongly points to these health differences being explainable not purely as the result of the actions and choices made by individual people but by deep impersonal structural forces (for example poverty, income differences and access to resources) that are beyond their control.

Exactly how best to explain those differences is still open to debate. Currently, the focus is on whether psycho-social or neo-material explanations offer the best theoretical articulation of class and health inequalities. Each places an emphasis on different causes, whether it is to do with the experiences of living in an unequal society or with the iniquitous distribution of the resources that are necessary for good health. It may be that the two explanations could be 'combined' (as indicated by some commentators, such as Yuill 2005 and Williams 2003) to account for different aspects of health inequalities – though this would require considerable refining and clarifying of important points. This could allow us to see what causes inequalities in the first place (best explained by the neo-material explanation) and how those inequalities are experienced in everyday life (best explained by the psycho-social explanation). This is possibly where the sociology of class and health inequalities could go next, but one point appears certain: as long as a class society exists, so too will health inequalities.

Summary points

- Class is a complex and dynamic power relationship between people.
- Class differences can be measured statistically using two different methods: the Registrar-General's Social Class scheme and the National Statistics Socio-economic Classification.
- A man from social class I lives on average 7.5 years longer than a man from social class V. For women the difference is 5.7 years.
- For self-reported health, those from the most advantaged groups indicate higher levels of good health and lower levels of poor health than the least advantaged groups.
- Across just about every cause of early mortality, both class V men and women will exhibit higher levels of early death than men and women from class I.
- Mental health problems also affect a higher number of people from classes IV and V than from classes I and II.
- There exists considerable class inequality in the UK today.
- Poverty continues to be a social problem: though the situation is better than it was, poverty in the UK is still worse than in other European countries.
- There have been several attempts over the years to explain class and health inequalities.

(Continued)

(Continued)

- The classic Black Report looked at material, behavioural, cultural and artefact explanations.
- Current explanations centre on the psycho-social approach versus the neo-material approach.
- The psycho-social approach draws our attention to the stress of living in an unequal society.
- The neo-material approach draws our attention to the uneven distribution of resources.

Case study

Shopping is the worst part of the week for Laura. It isn't because she cannot afford, well most of the time, to feed her two children (Amy and Pete, three and two years old respectively), but the food that she fills her basket with is all from the supermarket's Basics range, the packaging of which is a radiant bright orange that just proclaims low-budget. All those aisles neatly packed out with the tempting ranges of food in the carefully designed and interesting packets were not for her. She wants to try them, to experience new flavours, and to have her children able to run around the supermarket and pull something off the shelf that they might want to try, but no. Shopping is a strict disciplined exercise where preference is very much a secondary consideration to necessity.

The trip to the supermarket is a chore too. It required two bus trips as the local corner shop was way too expensive, plus it only stocked canned goods – and there are only so many baked beans a girl can eat! The bus journey itself is not that unpleasant, the estate where she lives is by-and-large OK, but just a bit run down in places. Built in the 1960s it is a bit past its best. It was once a showpiece of urban redevelopment and a model of how social housing could be, all clean and spacious in comparison with the old Victorian housing that used to exist in this part of the city. There's always some affection in Laura's mother's recollections of the estate in those days. Perhaps not street parties every weekend, but people would at least know who their neighbours were, and by neighbours that meant pretty much people in the whole street, not just people either side of you as Laura knows now.

In fact, there are less and less people on the estate of late. There's the occasional boarded up property now where the tenants have left, no one else has moved in and the windows and doors have been sealed up using flame-retardant metal grilles, just in case there's another spate of fire-raising, usually bored kids (and not so young adults, too) dropping lit rags through letter boxes or a box of matches into a litter bin. That doesn't cause too much damage, though it can get serious.

Last year one of the empty properties, an empty three storey low-rise, was almost burned down. The local authority has also stopped spending so much on keeping the various common areas neat and tidy. Grass on the roadside verges needs cutting, it's becoming overgrown and messy, just making the whole estate less of a nice place in which to live.

Her estate though is quite different from the one just three stops away on the second bus she has to take to the supermarket, though it is a stop where nobody gets on or off. This estate is all single houses, with two cars or more in the driveway, and finished off with perfect gardens boasting neat green lawns. She would like to live there. Just looks so much nicer.

Her health is fine, could be better, but can't complain and definitely better than other people on the bus. There's always someone coughing (too many cigarettes or perhaps something else?) but mainly people look worn down or as they say round here 'done in'. What always surprises her is just how much some of her friends have aged of late. They look a good ten years older than they should, even the ones who eat OK don't smoke and keep themselves active. Laura puts her mind back on the shopping she's about to do, and the same routine of tightly focusing on what she can pick off the shelves and what she simply must ignore.

1 The above case study obviously refers to class (and gender to some extent as well) and health. Before thinking through the health issues identified in the other questions, reflect on class today – are there still class divides? What are the different classes? What is it to be, let us say, working class as opposed to middle class?

2 Think about the two different theories discussed in the chapter concerning psycho-social and neo-material approaches. Which theory best explains the situation of Laura and perhaps other people on her estate?

3 Referring to Richard Wilkinson and Kate Pickett's material on inequality, in what ways does the above case study reflect the lived experiences of inequality?

4 What suggestions could you make to improve the long-term health of someone like Laura? Is it simply a case of eating well and not smoking or are there any deeper changes that can be made to society that would be perhaps more effective in making people healthier?

Taking your studies further

This chapter will have helped you understand many of the key terms, concepts, theories and debates relating to class and health. Listed below you will find journal articles and books that will provide deeper and more detailed discussions of the points raised in this chapter. You will also find what is available on the companion website. This feature will offer you downloads of relevant material, plus links to useful websites in addition to podcasts and other features.

Recommended Reading

A useful selection of articles on class and health inequalities can be found in *Social Science & Medicine*, (2000) Volume 51 (7).

Elstad, J.I. (1998) 'The psycho-social perspective on social inequalities in health', *Sociology of Health and Illness*, 20 (5): 598-618.

Marmot, M., Ryff, C.D., Bumpass, L.L., Shipley, M., and Marks, N.F. (1997) 'Social inequalities in health: next questions and converging evidence', *Social Science and Medicine*, 44 (6): 901-10.

Muntaner, C. and Lynch, J. (1999) 'Income inequality, social cohesion, and class relations: a critique of Wilkinson's neo-Durkheimian research program', *International Journal of Health Services*, 29 (1): 59-81.

Scambler, G. (2002) *Health and Social Change: a Critical Theory*. Buckingham: Open University Press.

Wilkinson, R. and Pickett, K. (2009) *The Spirit Level: Why Equality is Better for Everyone*. London: Penguin.

Websites

The Equality Trust (lectures and other education material on inequality)
http://www.equalitytrust.org.uk/resources/multimedia

On the companion website

Williams, S.J. (2003) *Medicine and the Body*. London: Sage. Chapter 2 on "Structuring' bodies: emotions, inequalities and health.'

7

Ethnicity, race and health

Main points

- Many countries in Europe and North America are becoming increasingly multicultural.
- Research indicates that ethnic minority groups display an ill health burden. This is despite many ethnic groups having a younger age profile than the majority white population.
- The reasons for this burden of ill health mainly relate to socio-economic factors, the effects of racism and negative experiences of medical and health services rather than a genetic or cultural explanation.
- People from ethnic minority groups are more likely to have lower-paid and more insecure jobs, worse housing and greater chances of being in poverty than the white majority population.
- Racism is a common and defining experience for many ethnic minority people. The stress of this has a negative impact on health.
- Medical and health services can discriminate against ethnic minority people by providing either insensitive or inappropriate treatment.

Key concepts

Race racism ethnicity prejudice discrimination stereotypes institutional racism.

Introduction

Events such as 9/11, the ensuing 'War on Terror', migration from the new member states of the European Union, and the success of far-right political parties also across Europe has led to a strong focus on issues of ethnicity and identity in the opening decade of this century. Much of this is the consequence of increasing globalisation, which has seen the movements not just of consumer goods but also of people. This, on the one hand, brings about a richer, more diverse culture, with different traditions and ways of life fusing into new exciting forms, notably in the fields of fashion, music and food. To that end Beck has commented that 'world society has taken possession of our kitchens and is boiling and sizzling in our pans' (2002: 28). These are very positive contemporary examples of ethnicity and culture. On the other hand, there have been less positive developments. In the wake of the 9/11 and 7/7 attacks there has been an increase in 'Islamophobia' and the rise of far-right parties across Europe.

This chapter will focus on how ethnicity, in our global and fast-changing world, influences health, and on the variety of complexities that go with looking at such a sensitive area. There has been a wealth of research on ethnicity and health over the years. What much of the research indicates is that there is a burden of ill health among ethnic minority groups in the UK. Many people from ethnic minority groups report poor health and long-term limiting illness (see Figure 7.1). This is even more notable as ethnic minority groups tend to have a younger age profile than the white majority population. Summarising trends from the Fourth National Survey of Ethnic Minorities in England and Wales, Nazroo (1997: 32) noted the following:

- One in three reported less than good health, or long-standing illness, or that they were registered disabled.
- Almost one in six reported that their health limited their performance of moderate activities, or climbing one flight of stairs, or walking half a mile or carrying groceries.
- One in 25 reported a diagnosis of heart disease; while among those aged 40 or older, one in 10 reported a diagnosis of heart disease and almost one in six reported a diagnosis or symptoms suggestive of heart disease.
- One in 10 reported a diagnosis of hypertension.
- One in 20 reported a diagnosis of diabetes.
- Almost one in five reported symptoms suggestive of respiratory disease.

Researchers in the past often favoured explanations that drew attention to either genetic or cultural reasons for ill health. The implication was that there was something wrong with the biology of ethnic groups which predisposed them to certain types of ill health, or that the culture of the ethnic group was to blame. An indicative example of this older approach can be noted in research on South Asians and coronary heart disease (CHD) (Nazroo 1998). Work by Gupta et al. (1995) inferred that the predisposition

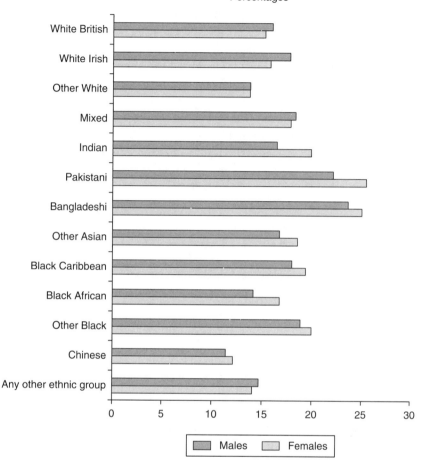

FIGURE 7.1 Age-standardised limiting long-term illness, by ethnic group and sex, April 2001, England and Wales

Source: National Statistics website: www.statistics.gov.uk. © Crown copyright

of South Asians to CHD was either something to do with their genetic make-up, or something in their cultural practices such as cooking with ghee, not exercising or not making the best use of medical services. Part of the reason why this 'victim blaming' came about was the research method used. Drawing on certain statistical and quantitative approaches, ethnicity here was treated in a stereotypical manner, casting all South Asians as genetically and culturally identical. Such approaches also ignored the socioeconomic context in which South Asian people found themselves, for example class and the effects of poorly paid jobs. Fenton and Charsley (2000) point out that the complexities, subtleties and sensitivities of understanding ethnicity are often ignored, or not fully appreciated, by the older positivist approaches. In the past few years, however, other researchers such as Ahmad (2000), Nazroo (2006) and Smaje (1996) have put forward a more challenging and sophisticated explanation of the complex way in which ethnicity, society and health interact. As Higginbottom usefully summarises, variations in ethnicity and health and ill health 'arise from the coalescence of complex factors such as migration, cultural adaptation, racism, reception by the host community, socio-economic influences and prevailing societal ideologies' (2006: 585). In this chapter we will look closely at how the health of ethnic minority groups is adversely affected by social context (socio-economic position, gender and racism) and not by faults in genes or culture.

Links

See Chapter 5 for more information on research methods.

Demographics

Western European countries are becoming increasingly multicultural and, in many ways, Britain is one of the most multicultural, with a substantial and diverse ethnic population. Though a great deal of ethnic minority migration into Britain happened in the 1950s, it is worth pointing out that there has been some form of ethnic population in Britain for centuries. We can find evidence of a black and Asian presence dating back to Roman times in Britain. Black North Africans who had been serving in Rome's legions in the third century AD lived and settled near Wallsend after finishing their time in the Roman army. Britain between AD 193 and 211 was ruled by the black Roman emperor Septimus Severius, who died in York and was cremated there at a time when York was the capital of Roman Britain. There are other examples throughout history. One has to remember that in the era of slavery there was a black population in Britain. For example, in St Mary's churchyard in Henbury near Bristol lies the grave of Scipio Africanus who died near there in 1720 aged 18 (see Figure 7.2).

Questions

Does it surprise you to learn that there has been a long history of black people in Britain? What does such information make you think about what it means to be British?

FIGURE 7.2   The grave of Scipio Africanus

Photograph courtesy of William Avery. Image sourced from http://commons.wikimedia.org/wiki/Image:Scripio_Africanus_grave.jpg

TABLE 7.1   Population, by ethnic group, April 2001

	Numbers	Total population (%)	Non-white population (%)
White	54,153,898	92.1	–
Mixed	677,117	1.2	14.6
Indian	1,053,411	1.8	22.7
Pakistani	747,285	1.3	16.1
Bangladeshi	283,063	0.5	6.1
Other Asian	247,664	0.4	5.3
All Asian or Asian British	2,331,423	4.0	50.3
Black Caribbean	565,876	1.0	12.2
Black African	485,277	0.8	10.5
Black other	97,585	0.2	2.1
All black or black British	1,148,738	2.0	24.8
Chinese	247,403	0.4	5.3
Other ethnic groups	230,615	0.4	5.0
All minority ethnic population	4,635,296	7.9	100.0
All population	58,789,194	100.0	

Source: (ONS 2005b: 1). National Statistics website: www.statistics.gov.uk. © Crown copyright

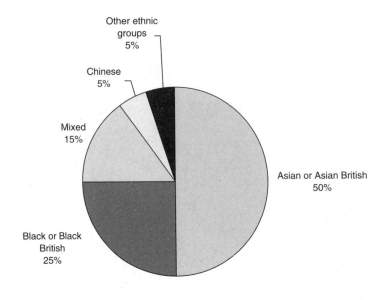

FIGURE 7.3   The non-white population by ethnic group, April 2001 (ONS 2005b: 1)

Source: National Statistics website: www.statistics.gov.uk. © Crown copyright

In Britain the 2001 national census revealed that 7.9 per cent of the population come from a non-white ethnic group (ONS 2005b). For the first time ever, a 'mixed' option was included in the census to reflect the increasing number of people in the UK who have parents from different ethnic backgrounds. The exact breakdown of population by ethnic group is laid out in Table 7.1, and the make-up of the non-white population shown in Figure 7.3.

Race, racism and ethnicity: definitions, debates and issues

Issues of **race** and ethnicity are complex and challenging to explore in any field of sociology. This is, as we shall see, due to the contentious and sometimes political nature of how we define and perceive supposed differences between people. In this section we shall explore how seeing the world as composed of different races is highly problematic and ultimately false. We will also look at how racism develops out of historical and social influences. Finally, we will question what can appear to be the relatively neutral concept of ethnicity, and point out that it too has several drawbacks.

Race

One aspect of modern life is that skin colour is often accepted or regarded as being a major way of seeing differences between people. This follows on from the idea that humanity consists of different races, in which there exist discernible and enduring genetic and cultural patterns that clearly separate one group of humans from another. This can be referred to as an *essentialist* perspective, where certain traits are seen as naturally given and outside social and historical influence. This implies that things are fixed and that people are born in a certain way that is with them for life. From a sociological perspective, however, this particular view can be challenged and shown to be false. We can also see how such a view is heavily influenced by racist prejudice and stereotyping.

First of all, can classifying humans into separate races be scientifically justified? The concept of **race** implies that there are different species of people, just as there are different species of animal. The scientific evidence indicates that there exist virtually no major differences between groups of humans. Biologist Steven Rose usefully summarises the genetic science as follows:

> The definition of race is essentially a social one, as in reference to Blacks or Jews. While there are differences in gene frequencies (that is, differences in the proportions in which particular genetic variants occur) between population groups, these do not map onto the social criteria used to define race. For instance, Polish Jews resemble genetically their fellow Polish nationals, non-Jews, more closely than they do Jews from Spain. Gene frequencies in Black Americans differ from those in Black South Africans. And for that matter, gene frequencies differ between people in North and South Wales, yet no one would think of classifying those two populations as two different races. This typological thinking has not disappeared: it characterizes, of course, the poisonous propaganda of racist political groups, and has not entirely vanished from popular scientific writing. (2005: 37)

What Rose is saying here is that people, regardless of exterior markers such as skin colour, are almost identical. Humans, as a life form, are fairly genetically homogeneous; one is likely to find more difference between people who are seen or see themselves as, let us say, Asian than between Asian people and people who are seen or see themselves as, let us say, white. This is not surprising as in evolutionary time *Homo sapiens* is comparatively recent, emerging out of Africa only *c.* 200,000 years ago. That is simply not enough time to evolve into different groups, species or races!

Rather than seeing differences between humans as being essential or natural, we must look to how differences are *socially* constructed over time and in different societies. The whole tradition of thinking in terms of race has a distinct history that is mired in prejudice and oppression. It also emerges out of specific historical and social circumstances. Using skin colour, or race, as a delimiter, or way of distinguishing one group of people from another, is historically recent. The first attempt to 'scientifically' classify people did not happen until the mid-1800s. This was the work of de Gobineau and was, at best, based on flimsy pseudo-science and carries no validity today. However, we must look a little further back in time to the rise and expansion of European colonialism and slavery from the mid-1600s to the early 1800s. As Blackburn (1998) has discussed, the need for cheap mass labour to work the new plantations in the Americas and the Caribbean

Race refers to biological differences between people based on skin colour and other physical features, though the actual differences between them genetically are extremely small. Ethnicity refers to the cultural heritage and identity of a group of people. Racism refers to the supposed racial superiority of one group over another.

led to the enslavement of millions of black Africans. The sheer brutal and bloody exploitation required some form of justification both on the plantations and in Britain, with many white working-class movements in Britain, such as Chartism, being opposed to slavery. So, starting as an oral tradition on the plantations, before becoming part of mainstream European thought, the racist idea that black people were of a lower order, perhaps even subhuman and therefore not allowed full human rights, spread and developed as part of this process of justifying the slave trade.

Prior to that period, the main ways of seeing differences between people have varied considerably over time. In the ancient world of Rome, Greece and Egypt, race and skin colour were not seen as important: instead the world was divided into civilised people and barbarians. Notably, what constituted being civilised was independent of skin colour, with barbarians including white Northern European people and civilised people including black North Africans. As mentioned before, key historical figures, such as the Roman emperor Septimus Severius, were black. Indeed much of the culture of the ancient world to varying degrees was, as Bernal (1991; 2001) has argued, a fusion of European, North African and Asian influences.

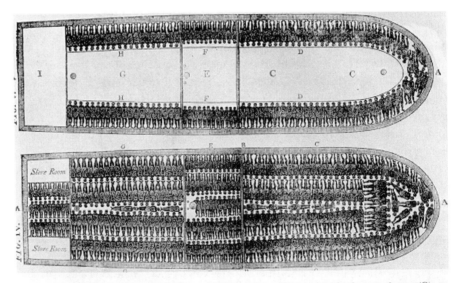

How slaves were stowed in the Brookes of Liverpool. The men's room (C) is to the right, the women's room (G) to the left, and the boys' room (E) in the center. The upper illustration shows the six-foot-wide platform on which slaves were ranged "like books on a shelf"; they had not space above them to sit up. The deck itself (lower illustration) was completely covered with rows of bodies. (From Clarkson's Abstract of the Evidence, 1791)

Figure 7.4   Anti-slavery leaflet from 1789

Figure 7.4 is taken from an abolitionist anti-slavery leaflet from 1789. It illustrates the brutal and inhumane way in which enslaved Africans were transported from Africa to the Americas. People were chained to platforms for weeks on end with no access to toilets or fresh air. Millions of Africans died on this transatlantic journey. British ports such as Bristol, Liverpool and Glasgow both directly and indirectly benefited from this trade.

Eamonn (Figure 7.5) belongs to one of the UK's fastest expanding ethnic minority groups. Born in Scotland, he is of mixed heritage with a white Irish mother and a black African father. In future years he will have an array of ethnic identities to adopt. He could choose, for example, to call himself Scottish or black Scottish or maybe black or black British. Or perhaps he might prefer Irish or African. In fact, he has a large number of ethnic identities he could choose and then discard throughout his life. Any ethnic identity he may select will be alongside other aspects of his identity too. For example, he'll be someone's son, someone's partner and so on.

FIGURE 7.5 Eamonn

Ethnicity

Given the problems associated with race, the concept of **ethnicity** is favoured today. With ethnicity there is no essential basis; reference is not to supposed biological or genetic traits, but rather to purely *social* phenomena. Ethnicity refers to a common cultural heritage that is socially learned and constructed. This means that as we grow up we take up and internalise what we see happening about us. So one sees certain ways of dressing and eating, for example, as being normal and adopts them as one's own.

In many respects the concept of ethnicity is a useful advance on, and correction to, the problems of race, with its emphasis on the social as opposed to the biological. However, ethnicity too can be problematic. We shall now look at how this is so, considering two main problems in the way that it can sometimes be (mis)used.

Questions

To which ethnic group, if any, do you regard yourself as belonging? What are the features (for example, dress, language, food, religion etc.) of your ethnic group? How much of a role, if any, does your ethnicity play in how you see yourself?

Static or fluid?

Ethnicity can be misused in a way that reduces culture to a static list of attributes, with the assumption that everyone who is identified as being in a particular ethnic group shares the same characteristics with regard to, for example, family, life, culture, food, and attitudes to illness and health services. This is seeing ethnicity as being like a shopping list or a 'cookie cutter', where everyone turns out the same. Ethnicity is far more complex than that. One of its complexities is that, like other forms of identity, it is dynamic, evolving and changing over time (Jenkins 2004).

It is useful here to mention that in the wider sociological literature on identity the idea of a fixed static identity is clearly rejected (Giddens 1991; Hall et al. 1993). What is emphasised is that identity is fluid. This means that we can switch between different identities (for example, being British or English, student or therapist, member of a youth subculture or churchgoer) depending on the context we find ourselves in and how we wish to present ourselves. In mainstream culture in the UK we see many examples of both the fluidity and the fusion of different ethnic cultures. Programmes like 'Goodness Gracious Me' played around with Asian and British stereotypes and introduced many new expressions into the English language, contributing to a way of speaking known as Hinglish.

Atkin et al. (2002) provide a useful example, in relation to disability, of these complexities and of how other forms of identity, in addition to an ethnic identity, can be important in deciding how people perceive themselves in society. Researching how South Asian deaf people negotiate their identity, Atkin et al. found that the people in their study did not see themselves in a singular way. Rather, they subscribed to a variety of identities depending on context. These multiple identities ranged from seeing their identity as part of a wider deaf community, to religious identities, and to a fusion of British and Asian identities.

Another useful example, this time concerning ethnic identity generally, is how Caribbean migrants thought of their identity in the late 1940s and how it has changed over time. Many early migrants, regardless of which Caribbean island they were originally from, saw themselves not as African-Caribbean (the currently preferred term) but as British. The following quote is from someone who arrived on the *Empire Windrush* in 1948 as part of the initial phase of migration from the Caribbean into Britain:

> I wouldn't say that we had our own identity. We were always British. In Jamaica I can remember, when it was the Queen's birthday or the King's birthday or the Coronation, everything was done the way Britain wanted us to. (Phillips and Phillips 1999: 12)

A unified and distinct African-Caribbean identity developed in Britain in response to the sometimes less than welcoming reception that early migrants encountered.

We can see the same fluidity and movement when it comes to ethnic majority identity – an area that is often forgotten when it comes to matters of ethnicity and health! Bond and

TABLE 7.2 Changes in Scottish identity in relation to British identity, 1992–2001

	1992	1997	1998	1999	2000	2001
Scottish not British	19	23	32	32	37	36
More Scottish than British	40	38	32	35	31	30
Equal	33	27	28	22	21	24
More British than Scottish	3	4	3	3	3	3
British	3	4	3	4	4	3
None	1	2	2	4	4	4

Source: Bond and Rosie (2002)

Rosie's (2002) work on Scottish identity also demonstrates the lack of a fixed idea of how Scottish people see themselves in relation to an overall British identity (see Table 7.2).

Questions

The above discussion talks a lot about fluidity, change and fusion. Identify ways in which both mainstream culture and your own personal life display elements of that fluidity and fusion. You may wish to think about TV programmes, dress, food and so on. Also, why is it important to be aware and knowledgeable about other cultures and ethnicities?

Ethnicity as too general

There is another distinct problem with ethnicity as a concept and how it can be used. The terms used in the UK are very loose and wide ranging in their coverage. 'South Asian', for instance, covers a huge geographic range with a population of millions, including India, Sri Lanka, Bangladesh and Pakistan. It also includes a variety of major languages (Punjabi, Gujarati, Pashto, Bengali, Urdu and English) and major religions (Hindu, Islam, Sikh and Christian). Such terms lack any real specificity and can miss out many important and telling differences within an ethnic group. This was suggested by Nazroo (1998) after breaking down the ethnic identity of 'Indian' into religious groups. He found that there were some differences in the reporting of fair or poor health. Indian Hindus, on average, reported similar levels, and Indian Christians slightly better, than the majority white population, while Indian Muslims reported, on average, worse health than all the previously mentioned groups.

In the US, Zsembik and Fennell (2005) have drawn attention to the difficulties associated with the concept of a Latino category. Here, again, a variety of people, also from a large and varied land mass, are brought together under one overarching heading. Zsembik and Fennell identify considerable and notable differences in culture, perceptions of health, social class and acculturation for different Latino people. So instead of this one overarching title of Latino, it would be more effective to break it down to identify Mexicans, Puerto Ricans, Dominicans and Cubans as separate groups.

Racism

Even though we have rejected the validity of race on the grounds that the concept is not soundly based in any real science, this does not mean that we can reject racism as a force in society (Bradby 1995). Racism is a defining experience for many ethnic groups in the UK, the US and elsewhere. As a concept it refers to one group holding itself to be inferior or superior to another group. Earlier we saw that ideas of race and racial superiority developed out of slavery and European colonial expansion. Even though the plantation system, which prompted the emergence of thinking in terms of white superiority over other groups of people, has disappeared, racism and all its problems still continue today. The current climate of the 'War on Terror' and wider conflicts in the Middle East have also increased tensions concerning Muslims in western countries.

Trying to capture the extent of racial prejudice in the United Kingdom is complex. On one hand various reports indicate that increasingly less people report themselves as being a little or very prejudiced when it comes to racial prejudice. The British Social Attitudes Survey in 2004 found that while nearly 40 per cent of respondents in 1983 self-reported some form of prejudice, this figure had decreased to around 30 per cent by 2002 (McLaren and Johnson 2004: 181). There is a complication here, however. When people are asked about their perceptions of racial prejudice, that is how much prejudice they perceive as occurring about them in society, they tend to report higher levels than indicated in the self-report findings mentioned above. So in the same survey 45 per cent of respondents reported that there was more prejudice in society than there had been compared to five years ago (McLaren and Johnson 2004: 182). In the 2009 survey this figure had increased to nearly 48 per cent (Park et al. 2010). Overall, the general picture may be optimistic in that racial prejudice may be decreasing but it still remains a very real issue within contemporary UK society.

The actual manifestation of racism and the form it takes in society have changed over time, though arguably the result is the same: the systematic disadvantaging of specific minority groups. In the early days of the slave trade racism centred on the supposed subhuman nature of enslaved African people, with claims that they were a lesser species of humans than white Europeans, and inferior to them in just about any conceivable way. At the high point of the British Empire in the late 1800s racism took on a paternalistic form with notions that colonised peoples required the guidance and help of supposedly more advanced and enlightened

Europeans. During the 1980s racism became more disguised and subtle, with the emphasis being on how the survival of indigenous British culture could be overwhelmed by the cultures of migrant ethnic groups. Prime Minister Margaret Thatcher, at the time, went as far as saying that British culture would be 'swamped' by the new groups arriving in the UK. In the wake of the attack on New York on 11 September 2001 and the ensuing 'War on Terror', 'Islamophobia' has been on the rise, with Muslims often portrayed as a potential threat, or having to justify aspects of Islamic culture in a way that other minority ethnic groups are not required to do.

Racism consists of three dimensions. First, there is **prejudice**, which relates to negative attitudes. In a day-to-day context this would mean name-calling on the street and putting forward opinions that denigrate an ethnic group. Next, there is **discrimination**, which relates to actions based on prejudice. This could mean, for example, preventing someone of an ethnic group from getting a job. Research by Noon (1993), for example, found that employers were less likely to employ someone with a typically Asian name than someone with a typically British name. Finally, in recent years in the UK one of the most highlighted and debated forms of racism has been **institutional racism**. The main focus on institutional racism has been in the wake of the MacPherson Report (1999) looking at the failures of the Metropolitan Police in investigating the murder of black student Stephen Lawrence. It is in this report that a very useful definition of institutional racism can be found:

> Racism can exist in the following forms:
> Prejudice – having a negative attitude about someone from another race or ethnic group.
> Discrimination – acting in a way that treats people from another race or ethnic group unequally.
> Institutional racism – the intentional or unintentional actions of a public or private body that result in people from ethnic minority backgrounds being discriminated against.

> The collective failure of an organisation to provide an appropriate and professional service to people because of their colour, culture or ethnic origin. It can be seen in processes, attitudes and behaviour which amount to discrimination through unwitting prejudice, ignorance, thoughtlessness and racist stereotyping which disadvantage minority ethnic people.
> (MacPherson 1999)

It is not just in the police force that institutional racism is evident. In the next section we will look at how prejudice and racist stereotyping within health and medical services adversely affect the health of ethnic minority people. Health professionals within the NHS also face institutional racism, with a variety of reports suggesting that health professionals from ethnic minority groups are worse off than white health professionals with equivalent training and expertise. This can range from unequal pay between white and minority doctors, to barriers in going to medical school, to South Asian doctors being over-represented in junior grades and unpopular specialities. Overall, as Coker (2001) points out, this represents a regrettable loss of skill and talent for the NHS.

> ## Questions
>
> What are your views on the levels of racism in society today? What do you think are the main issues and problems that we face in trying to bring about a more tolerant society?

Ethnicity, health and society

After looking at what we mean by ethnicity and some of its problems, plus levels and forms of racism, let us now see how all of this can affect the health of ethnic minority groups. Here, we shall look at class, the effects of racism, and the negative experiences that ethnic minority groups can have of medical and health services. What is important to bear in mind here is that all the following are not discrete 'either/or' influences, but can work together simultaneously. Indeed, there is considerable overlap between all three issues. Racism pervades both class and experiences of care. One of the reasons why so many ethnic minority people are located in lower social classes is, in part, the experience of racism during migration to the UK from the 1950s onwards. Often ethnic groups encountered discrimination that prevented them from occupying better-paid jobs. Racism is also apparent in experiences of health and medical care, where prejudice and discrimination – both intentional and unintentional – affect how staff perceive, and react to, ethnic minority patients.

Class

As discussed in the previous paragraph, there is considerable overlap between all three inequalities of gender, ethnicity and class. They quite often interact to produce multiple problems for many people, resulting in their health being adversely affected. This is very true for many ethnic groups where class, and the effects of social deprivation, are also of great importance. Much research in the past has ignored, or underplayed, the role that class has in the health of ethnic groups. Recently, though, some new research has sought to address that absence in our understanding of how ethnicity and class interact.

A great deal of evidence indicates that many ethnic minority groups in the UK experience social deprivation. Smaje (1995) and Karlsen et al. (2002b) identified that many ethnic groups live in socially deprived areas. Statistics (see Tables 7.3 and 7.4) on poverty routinely indicate that ethnic minority groups experience greater levels of poverty and unemployment than the majority white group in the UK.

From the evidence presented above, and by keeping in mind the material in Chapter 6 which deals with class and health, it appears that class should influence the health of ethnic minority groups. As we shall see this is very much the case but, as Nazroo (1998) warns,

TABLE 7.3 Economic activity, by ethnic group, UK

	Economic activity rate (ages 16–59/64)	Employment rate	ILO unemployment rate (ages 16+)
White	79.4	75.9	4.4
All ethnic minority groups	64.7	57.4	11.1
Mixed	70.0	62.2	11.1
Asian	61.9	55.4	10.6
Black	71.1	61.8	12.9
Chinese	58.3	54.1	–
Other ethnic groups	58.3	52.8	9.2

Source: SPIU (2002)

TABLE 7.4 Percentage resident in area of deprivation by quintile (Townsend score) and ethnic group

	White	Caribbean	Indian	Pakistani and Bangladeshi
Highest quintile	20.4	3.3	5.8	1.0
	20.2	5.1	9.5	1.6
	20.1	11.3	9.9	4.0
	19.4	8.0	26.3	12.7
Lowest quintile	19.8	72.3	48.5	80.6

Source: Nazroo (2006: 7). Reproduced by kind permission of Routledge

ethnicity should not be reduced to class. This means that we should not just drop ethnicity as a reason for people's poor health and claim that it is all down to class; we should see both as having very real and damaging effects. What the research reveals is that people from an ethnic minority group can be in the same class as people from the white majority group, but will be further disadvantaged and will be located towards the lower end of that particular class. So, we find, for example, that white people in the Registrar-General's classes IV and V have low mean weekly incomes, but people from Indian or African Asian, Caribbean, and – lowest of all – Pakistani or Bangladeshi ethnic groups have even lower mean weekly incomes (Nazroo 2006). Ethnic minority groups are also more likely to have more insecure jobs, more unsocial hours, and worse housing than white people of the same class. Class differences also exist within ethnic groups: ethnic minority people with non-manual occupations have better health over a range of indicators than those of the same ethnic group in manual occupations (see Table 7.5).

Links

See Chapter 6 for more information on class and health.

TABLE 7.5   Fair, poor, or very poor reported health compared with others of the same age, by socio-economic position and ethnic group, 2001

	White	Indian or African Asian	Pakistani or Bangladeshi	Caribbean
Occupational class				
Non-manual	21.5	19.9	30.2	25.0
Manual	22.6	27.4	35.1	29.4
No full-time worker in household	36.7	33.9	44.1	38.2
Unweighted base	2110	1782	1592	1060
Tenure				
Owner-occupier	22.6	24.4	34.7	26.6
Tenant	34.5	33.7	45.0	40.0
Unweighted base	2173	1848	1692	1077

For all four ethnic groups, *p* < 0.01 for both occupational class and tenure.

Source: Nazroo (2001: 117). Reproduced with permission of the copyright holders, Policy Studies Institute

The experience of racism

There is a growing body of research which shows that the experience of racism has a debilitating effect on health. Karlsen and Nazroo (2002a; 2004) in the UK, Krieger et al. (2005) in the US and Harris et al. (2006) in New Zealand, for example, have all come to the similar conclusions that we have to take the lived experience of racism seriously if we are to have a full and rounded understanding of what contributes to ethnic health inequalities. This racism can come in a variety of forms: the day-to-day racism of name-calling and prejudice; actual physical abuse and assault; and institutional racism. It is also important that it is not just the *direct* but also the *indirect* experience of racism that has an effect. This means that someone does not have to be name-called in the street or attacked: they simply need to have a perception that these things exist and that it could happen to them – in short, a fear of racism, and the worry and stress this creates (Karlsen and Nazroo 2004). In many ways indirect experiences of racism share an affinity with the stress-related psycho-social pathways of health that we explored in Chapter 6 on class and health.

This stress created by racism is clearly seen in research by Chahal and Julienne (1999). What they noted was that for black and ethnic minority people, racism was an everyday experience. This could have quite far-reaching and long-term consequences in their private lives and affected how they interacted with friends, family and the wider community. For example, worrying about and feeling stressed by racism could mean feeling anxious about leaving one's home at night, or allowing the children to play outside. Mundane tasks could become fraught with danger. One woman in the study said that she found it difficult to put the washing out during the day as this could lead to her being abused by a neighbour. Overall, the people in this study felt tired, worn out, stressed, depressed, vulnerable and isolated by their experiences of racist victimisation.

Questions

The above discussion points out that racism does not have to be directly experienced in the form of verbal abuse or assault, for instance, to have a negative impact on health; the idea that one could be subject to racism also has a similarly poor outcome for health. Why do you think this is so?

For ethnic minority people who have been either verbally abused or physically attacked, the chances of assessing their health as poor are greatly increased. Karlsen and Nazroo (2002b) reported that those who were verbally abused were around 50 per cent more likely to see their health as poor but those who had direct experience had just over 100 per cent greater chance of reporting their health as being poor.

Negative experiences of medical and health care

Reviewing a range of research and reports, Chahal (2004) concluded that medical and health care services can be problematic for black and ethnic minority people, with negative experiences of medical and health services being a common problem. This is particularly evident with mental health services. Black people are over-represented in mental illness statistics, and are more likely to be placed in secure wards and to receive different – if not poorer – treatment and care than whites. As ever, research findings beg the question of why is this so. Delving a little deeper we can see a picture of intentional and unintentional prejudice, racism of various kinds and a general lack of cultural sensitivity. To answer the question in more detail we shall look at why there is over-representation of black people in the statistics, how black people come into contact with services and what treatment is offered.

Pathways to care: ethnic minorities' initial contact with psychiatric services

One of the most common pathways for African-Caribbean people to come into contact with psychiatric services is via the police. From their research, Pilgrim and Rogers (1993) identified multiple interconnecting reasons. Black people, especially young black men, are more likely to be regarded as potentially threatening and/or dangerous than white people. These attitudes exist not only among the public, for the Stephen Lawrence Inquiry found examples of institutionalised racism within the Metropolitan Police Force. Here we see the police, an important part of the 'control culture' in British society, reflecting and acting on the wider racist attitudes that exist in society. Therefore, when the police come into contact with young black men they are more likely to react and interpret their behaviour in a negative manner. This negativity can extend to the judiciary. Pilgrim and Rogers also noted that black people have a different perception of services from white users, whether one of mistrust or of cynicism about the quality of treatment they might receive.

Treatment

When people from black or Asian communities are offered treatment, the form and quality of the services on offer can again be different from those offered to white service users. Reviewing the literature on treatment of ethnic minorities, Pilgrim and Rogers noted that 'Black people are treated in a more coercive and punitive way within the psychiatric system' (1993: 57). They cited various examples of research which indicated that black people, even when they were non-violent, tended to receive more medication over the period of their treatment, and that medication was more likely to include major tranquillisers. In addition, African-Caribbean patients were more often seen as potentially threatening or aggressive.

Problems exist for black and Asian people in aftercare and when living in the community. The ever-present problem of racism emerged clearly in Radia's (1996) study of Asians with mental health problems living in the four London boroughs of Brent, Harrow, Ealing and Tower Hamlets. Respondents here reported that they feared racial assault and abuse on the streets. Service provision was also noted to be poor and lacking in cultural sensitivity, with Asian people in this study often being subject to stereotyping by service providers. Common myths were that Asian people would be looked after 'by their own' and that services were not wanted because no one came forward. The lack of cultural sensitivity came through when conceptualising mental illness. Western notions of the mind and body being separate entities are not shared by Asian people, who see both existing as a whole. Fenton and Sadiq-Sangster (1996) have also noted this point. They found that South Asian women conceptualised mental distress using metaphors that shared images and expressions of mind and body. In their study, feelings of being stressed and of low mood were expressed as 'thinking-too-much-in-the-heart'.

Links

See Chapter 9 for more information on mental health.

Other research has also noted a lack of cultural sensitivity within service provision. Researching counselling providers in Glasgow, Leeds, Bristol and London, Netto et al. (2001) reported that a lack of awareness of cultural and religious factors could have a negative impact on the uptake and success of counselling services for Asian and black people. They suggested that services could be improved by increasing access to counselling for black people; by increasing the number of trained counsellors with appropriate experience and/or training in cultural sensitivity; by reviewing service provision in order to obtain feedback from black service users; and by encouraging the black community to question their own attitudes to mental health to make it easier for black people with mental health problems to come forward.

Irish people and mental health

So far we have concentrated on the experiences of black and Asian people, but there exists another ethnic minority in the UK that also experiences difficulties. This minority has a distinct problem, namely invisibility, because until quite recently they were classified as part of the indigenous white population. Here we are referring to Irish-born people living in Britain. Even though Irish-born people may outwardly appear to share the characteristics of native-born white people in terms of skin colour and language, there are many cultural subtleties that are overlooked by service providers and by society as a whole.

Irish-born people face the following problems:

- lack of services designed for Irish-born people
- high unemployment
- high levels of mental and physical health problems
- reduction in life expectancy on immigration to England. (MIND 2000b)

Conclusion

Current research and sociological thinking on race, ethnicity and health are beginning to develop a much more subtle and nuanced appreciation of the way in which various factors and social structures influence the health of ethnic minority groups in society. What is becoming clearer is that, to begin with, we must be very careful about making sweeping generalisations about terms such as 'race' and 'ethnicity'. Problems, stereotypes and, at worst, prejudices can often be bundled up in these concepts. For example, the concept of ethnicity can often depict a minority group as being culturally static, with other important divisions, such as class, being absent. As the evidence and research discussed in this chapter have indicated, this can be far from the lived experiences of people in minority groups.

We also saw that the major cause of ethnicity and health inequalities is not to be found in the particular cultures of the people in minority groups, but in racism. The negative effects can be experienced either directly (name-calling in the street) or indirectly (the anxiety created by anticipation of being subjected to some form of racism). This can also be present in care provision, with people from ethnic minority groups sometimes encountering prejudice and/or inappropriate services.

This illustrates once more that it is powerful social forces above and beyond the individual that shape and influence health, often more so than the choices and actions of individuals themselves.

Summary points

- There has been a black presence in Britain for thousands of years.
- The non-white population of the UK is now 7.9 per cent.
- Increasing numbers of people are from mixed backgrounds.
- Race lacks any scientific validity as a way of categorising and differentiating people. Genetically, people the world over are virtually the same.
- The concept of race is historically quite new and developed out of European colonialism and slavery.
- Racism can be a defining experience for many ethnic minority people.
- Ethnicity can be a more useful way of exploring different groups of people, with its emphasis on the social and cultural aspects of people's lives. It too can be problematic at times. Sometimes ethnicity can be used to imply that culture is static, and some ethnic classifications are too broad in their coverage.
- Class and socio-economic differences affect the health of ethnic minority groups.
- The health of ethnic minority people is often worse than the health of white people in the same class.
- Within the same ethnic minority group there are differences in health, with those from the non-manual occupation class having better health than those in manual occupation classes.
- The psycho-social effects of racism can have a strong impact on the health of ethnic minority groups.
- People in ethnic minorities can have negative experiences of health and medical services, encountering either inappropriate care or prejudice and discrimination.

Case study

Mike remembers what his dad told him about what he had to endure at work back in the 1970s. Being the first African-Caribbean person to work in the local council housing department, he had to deal with all sorts of abuse and disrespect. Sometimes this was out-and-out racism. A small group of people in the office often verbally abused him. On several occasions they left bananas or literature from far-right racist parties on his desk. What Mike's dad found worse though were the attitudes of other office workers, who, even though not openly hostile to him, always seemed a little suspicious. Mike's dad had to constantly make jokes about his skin colour in order to be accepted in any way. He hated having to act in that way as he found it demeaning. This added an extra layer of stress to an already stressful job. It was having to deal with all these issues that, Mike believes, led to his dad developing a heart condition in his late fifties. In fact, his dad had to take early retirement as a result of his poor health. To this day he still claims to feel quite poorly most of the time and not as healthy as he would like to be.

For Mike, many of these problems are firmly in the past. The office in which he works is like the rest of the city, with a mixed, cosmopolitan and diverse workforce.

He works alongside people who are white, Asian or African-Caribbean and who, like him, see themselves as British born and bred. He gets on well with just about everyone in his section and he faces none of the outward racism that his dad had to face. However, the more subtle forms of racism persist. Mainly, this is to do with the management. Despite the diversity of the workforce, the management are uniformly white. He has put in for promotion several times but each time he has been rejected. This is even though he has worked hard, has put in the hours and is respected by many of his colleagues as a good worker. Other people with a less strong profile than his have advanced up the ranks much quicker than him. He now suspects that it is something to do with his ethnicity. Regardless of how much he works, it just never seems enough. This is starting to get to him. Lately, he has found himself becoming more stressed and generally down.

1　What elements of the case study reflect some of the wider social changes that were discussed in this chapter?

2　Discuss the ways in which racism has had an effect on the health of both Mike today and his father in the past.

3　Besides issues to do with ethnicity, what other social factors could be exerting an influence on Mike's health?

Taking your studies further

This chapter will have helped you understand many of the key terms, concepts, theories and debates relating to race, ethnicity and health. Listed below are journal articles, books and a website that will provide deeper and more detailed discussions of the points raised in this chapter. You will also find what is available on the companion website. This offers downloads of relevant material, plus links to useful websites in addition to podcasts and other features.

Recommended reading

BBC Online. 'Race UK'. http://news.bbc.co.uk/hi/english/static/in_depth/uk/2002/race/.

Higginbottom, G.M.A. (2006) '"Pressure of life": ethnicity as a mediating factor in mid-life and older people's experience of high blood pressure', *Sociology of Health and Illness*, 28 (5): 583–610.

Karlsen, S. and Nazroo, J.Y. (2002) 'Agency and structure: the impact of ethnic identity and racism on the health of ethnic minority people', *Sociology of Health and Illness*, 24 (1): 1–20.

Karlsen, S. and Nazroo, J.Y. (2002) 'The relationship between racial discrimination, social class and health among ethnic minority groups', *American Journal of Public Health*, 92 (4): 624–31.

Karlsen, S. and Nazroo, J. (2004) 'Fear of racism and health', *Journal of Epidemiology and Community Health*, 58: 1017–18.

Krieger, N. (2003) 'Does racism harm health? Did child abuse exist before 1962? On explicit questions, critical science, and current controversies: an ecosocial perspective', *American Journal of Public Health*, 93 (2): 194–9.

Nazroo, J. (2001) *Ethnicity, Class and Health*. London: PSI.

Nazroo, J. (ed.) (2006) *Health and Social Research in Multiethnic Societies*. London: Routledge.

On the companion website

Fenton, S. and Charsley, K. (2000) 'Epidemiology and sociology as incommensurate games: accounts from the study of health and ethnicity', *Health*, 10 (4): 403–25.

Williams, S.J. (2003) *Medicine and the Body*. London: Sage. Chapter 2 on '"Structuring" bodies: emotions, inequalities and health'.

8

Gender and health

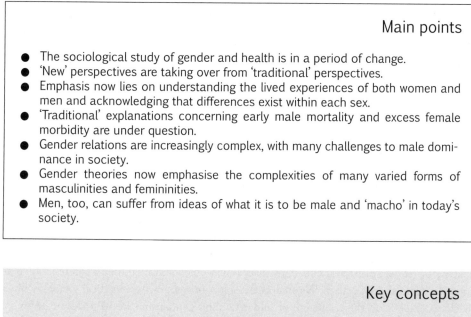

Main points

- The sociological study of gender and health is in a period of change.
- 'New' perspectives are taking over from 'traditional' perspectives.
- Emphasis now lies on understanding the lived experiences of both women and men and acknowledging that differences exist within each sex.
- 'Traditional' explanations concerning early male mortality and excess female morbidity are under question.
- Gender relations are increasingly complex, with many challenges to male dominance in society.
- Gender theories now emphasise the complexities of many varied forms of masculinities and femininities.
- Men, too, can suffer from ideas of what it is to be male and 'macho' in today's society.

Key concepts

Gender • patriarchy • inequality • masculinities • femininities.

Introduction

The study of gender and health has recently undergone a period of change and transition. New and interesting ways of thinking about how being a woman or a man affects your health are currently being developed and debated. This is in contrast with more 'traditional' perspectives of discussing gender and health, where the main perspectives could be easily summarised as 'men die and women suffer'. This was due to much of medical sociology in the past (mainly from the 1970s) putting forward the view that, when it comes to health differences between men and women, men experience higher levels of earlier mortality, while women live longer but experience higher levels of morbidity during their lives. The reasons for these differences were often explained by reference to paid and domestic work roles, as well as the wider, and often stereotypical, social roles which men and women held. Another important if somewhat unintentional feature of 'traditional' perspectives on gender and health was that, more often than not, gender meant women and not women *and* men. This was probably due to the influence of **feminism** in this particular area of sociological research.

Though traditional perspectives on gender and health produced a great deal of vital and interesting research, recently certain sociologists, such as Kandrack et al. (1991), Annandale and Hunt (2000) and Macintyre et al. (1999) have called for a rethink of how we both look at and understand gender and health. Much of this rethink has been prompted by two influences. First, we live in a society of increasingly complex gender relations. Many of the old assumptions about gender – for instance, the man as breadwinner going out to earn the family wage, and the woman staying at home tending to domestic chores – simply no longer fit today's society. There have been many other transformations, shifts and movements in how women and men relate to the home, to work and to each other. In the midst of all this change, women's and men's health is affected in new ways. Second, there is growing questioning of the theories used to conceptualise gender. The main point of contention is that we need to adequately understand how issues relating to gender affect both sexes and must take on board the varied experiences of men and women.

In this chapter, we shall take a journey through the research, literature and sociological perspectives on gender and health and, in doing so, we will make several distinct stops on the way. We shall begin with a review of what sociologists mean by gender, pointing to how ideas of what it means to be a man or a woman are not fixed but depend on the place or society in which you are situated. This discussion will then expand to consider some of the statistics that help us understand the situation of women and men today, before looking at some theoretical perspectives. We shall then look at how and where medical sociology finds itself, as it takes on the challenge of understanding gender and health in more complex times. Finally we shall look at how ideas of what it is to be masculine and feminine affect people's health.

Thinking about gender in contemporary society

Before we begin to look at wider issues of gender, it is useful to define the two key terms of 'sex' and 'gender'. **Sex** refers to the biological differences between men and women and how anatomical features lead to some being identified as male and some as female. On the other hand, **gender** refers to the social, cultural and psychological aspects of being a woman or a man. The two terms may be used interchangeably in some research and writing about women and men. In the rest of this chapter, we shall be quite strict in their usage and the definitions just given will be adhered to.

Let us now consider and think about what we mean by gender. For many people that will seem a rather obvious question to answer, with gender being decided by the biological body that we have. This line of thought also assumes that the types of behaviour that men and women engage in are decided by biology. Sociologists, however, have argued strongly that the answer is nowhere near as clear-cut as that. By comparing cultures in different places and across times we find that what constitutes being a man or a woman is *extremely variable*. All sorts of examples can be used to illustrate this. For instance, among the Wodaabe tribe, who live in the African country of Niger, it is the men who wear the make-up and act in what to western eyes would be a feminine manner.

Equally interesting examples can be found in the industrialised west. One gender stereotype, for instance, is that women are not suited to heavy industrial work and should not be employed in hazardous factories, but would be more appropriately employed as secretaries in safe office environments. During the Second World War the requirements of fighting the war turned that stereotype on its head. With many men away fighting at the front, there were few men left to do the heavy industrial work such as building aircraft or making munitions, which were vital for the war effort. As a consequence government-backed drives, in both the USA and the UK, attempted to get women into the factory to do that vital war work. In America, 'Rosie the Riveter' (Figure 8.1) spearheaded one campaign to attract women into the workplace. What's interesting about the image of Rosie is her depiction as being 'feminine', with headscarf and make-up, while at the same time displaying the very 'masculine' traits of the strong muscular arm and the factory overalls. The poster's tag-line 'We Can Do It!' is a very assertive statement about the capabilities of women. At the height of the war approximately 30 per cent of all working women in the US were in factories, with employers in 1942 increasing the number of jobs that they thought suitable for women from 29 per cent to 55 per cent of all occupations (Colman 1995). After the war this role reversal was not to continue, however, with women on both sides of the Atlantic being encouraged to leave the factory jobs that they had occupied during the war and to make the return to the domestic sphere.

> Gender refers to the social, cultural and psychological differences between men and women. Sex refers to the biological differences between men and women.

What the example of 'Rosie the Riveter' tells us is that what it means to be a man or a woman is not a fixed entity but is frequently defined by the needs and attitudes of a society at a given time. When American and British society needed female workers to meet shortages in the arms industry, attitudes changed to allow for that to happen; and when women

FIGURE 8.1   Rosie the Riveter

Image courtesy of US National Archives

were no longer required to fill those posts, attitudes changed again. It is not just society, or the needs of industry in the above example, which influence what it means to be a man or a woman. In the 1960s and 1970s, throughout Europe and North America, the rise of the Women's Movement saw the self-organisation of feminist women directly challenge prevailing social norms of what a woman's place in society should be. The old notions that the woman belonged passively in the home, looking after her husband and children, were brought into question, with women at this time fighting for and adopting more active roles, whether in the workplace or in their private lives. Indeed, many of the job opportunities and increased control over their lives experienced by women today are attributable to the success of the struggles of the 1960s and 1970s.

Questions

The above discussion looks at what it is to be a man or a woman. What do you think are masculine or feminine characteristics today? Do you see any changes in how men or women relate to each other in everyday life?

Theorising gender

Within the sociology of health and illness, how we theorise gender has shifted away from out-and-out feminist theories, which concentrated on how women are dominated by men, to theories that focus on gender relations and gender order. These theories look at how interactions between men and women are affected by the ideas of masculinity and femininity that pervade society (Annandale and Hunt 2000). This is not to claim that we should drop all the insights that feminist theories gave us – or to suggest, for one moment, that we have moved away from a society where gender ceases to act as an arbiter of power and privilege, particularly in favour of men. For instance, feminist theories, which provided a rich analysis of **patriarchy** (male domination), allowed us to understand how society privileges men on a variety of fronts. This, though, does not take into account the experiences of men and implies that all men are part of a 'unified' bloc, who all share similar dispositions and access to power and economic resources, for example. Current theoretical thinking on gender acknowledges that there exist many varieties of 'maleness' and masculinity in society (as well as 'femaleness' and femininity), which should also be acknowledged and theorised. Whitehead usefully summarises the many different expressions of masculinities that exist in the world today:

> from the 'gym queens' to suited politicians, from Boy George to Arnold Schwarzenegger, from the ageing leathered 'biker' to the ageing hippy 'drop-out'. From the gun-toting LA (or Manchester) gang member to the male nurse, from Rupert Murdoch to the black 'rapper', from 'Masters of the Universe' to the male charity worker, from the Muslim cleric to the atheist househusband, from Mike Tyson to Danny Glover, indeed from profeminist man to the Christian 'promise keepers'. (2002: 16)

Patriarchy refers to male domination in society and can be expressed both privately and publicly in culture, economics and politics, and through physical violence. Matriarchy refers to a society that is female dominated. See Chapter 1 for more on feminist theory.

Connell (2005) has provided a highly insightful theory of gender that brings an understanding of masculinity and patriarchy into an overall theory of gender relations and gender order. Central to his ideas is that we cannot understand masculinity and femininity unless we see them as related to and shaping each other. This relationship, however, is not equal and, by and large, it is men who continue to be dominant in society. This power is played out in the day-to-day interactions between men and women in their private and public lives and is informed by wider societal ideas of what it is to be masculine and feminine.

There exists, for Connell, a gender order in western capitalist societies (see Figure 8.2). At the top, and the most powerful element, of this gender order is **hegemonic masculinity**, to which all other forms of masculinity and femininity are subordinate. The concept refers to how one form of masculinity (in this case one which is healthy, heterosexual, wealthy, assertive, aggressive and white) is associated with power, being successful and being the form of masculinity that should be aspired to in western societies. By being the 'top dog', so to speak, this form of masculinity is hegemonic, which means it controls everything else. Some good examples of men who epitomise hegemonic masculinity are the British TV presenter Jeremy Clarkson, and in America the former actor and governor of California, Arnold Schwarzenegger. Next in the gender order is *complicit masculinity*. This is a form of masculinity that may not live up to the full expectations of hegemonic masculinity, but still affords a reasonable amount of power. We then see subordinated masculinities and femininities which are beneath both hegemonic and complicit masculinity in terms of power and status. *Subordinated masculinities* include gay men, and in terms of health, men whose masculinity is challenged or undermined by physical and mental illness. *Subordinated femininities* include *emphasised femininity*, which refers to women who comply with hegemonic masculinity; this involves matching up to hegemonic male expectations of attractiveness and femininity. In terms of health, this can mean, especially for older women, taking on care duties for children, disabled people or older relatives in the home. There also exists *resistant femininity* where women reject the demands and norms of emphasised femininity. This tends to be a less visible group of women (for example, lesbians and spinsters) in society, given the prevalence and profile of emphasised femininity.

Hegemonic masculinity refers to the dominant form of masculinity in society. Currently, this would refer to men who are healthy, wealthy, white and powerful and act in a 'macho' manner. Very few men live up to this expectation but it exerts a strong influence over both men and women.

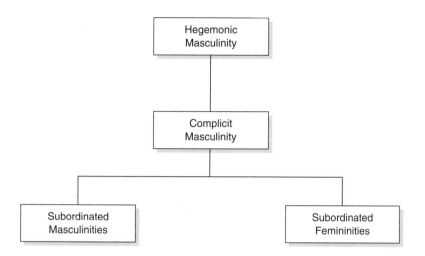

FIGURE 8.2 Connell's gender hierarchy

Gender relations today

A key theme throughout this chapter has been the increasing complexity of the many aspects of gender in contemporary society, whether this is to do with work, relationships or the home. In short, what we see today is that the deeper constraints on women (such as their sole focus in life being the home) are very much weaker, with women experiencing much more control and choice in their working and personal lives in comparison with previous generations of women. Parallel to the strengthening of women in society we see a weakening of male dominance in a variety of fields. For example, there have been changes in the economy, where the traditional male heavy manufacturing industries are giving way to female-dominated service industries. This is leading to a feminisation of the workforce.

This, though, should *not* be taken to mean that we now see complete equality of the sexes. Overall there are many signs of equality in some areas, but that has to be set against many other signs that things have not changed that much for women. If we look at some examples, this will become clearer. In terms of employment, we find that in the UK in 2005 each sex carried out 13.3 million jobs – roughly a fifty–fifty split of all jobs. On the surface this is a major shift, since in 1985 men performed 2 million more jobs than women (ONS 2006a). If we delve a little deeper we find inconsistencies. Even though there is strong female participation in the workforce (see Figure 8.3), the majority of those women will be employed part-time.

Another interesting complexity can be seen in the types of occupation in which women and men are located, and the disparities in their pay. What we see here is a picture of women making gains in some occupations but none in others. If we look at Figure 8.4, we

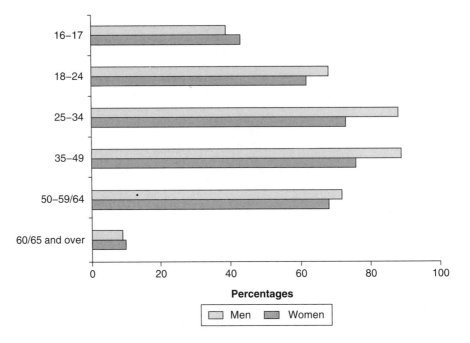

FIGURE 8.3   Participation in the workforce by age and sex (ONS 2004)

Source: National Statistics website: www.statistics.gov.uk. © Crown copyright

can see some of these trends. For example, there is increasing parity of women and men in middle-class professions and associated professions, with women also making gains in management. This, though, should be contrasted with more working-class occupations. Here we see a familiar pattern of men occupying the skilled trades and women in secretarial and administration.

If we turn now to the income gap between women and men we can see it beginning to close. Figure 8.5, on page 138, indicates that women are catching up with men. However, according to the Fawcett Society, it will still take another 85 years for women to completely catch up with men (Hall 2003)!

Understanding gender and health: at a crossroads?

Annandale and Hunt (2000) have recently pointed out that research in the study of gender and health is at a crossroads, with 'traditional' approaches giving way to 'new' approaches. Put simply, the *traditional approaches* often (though unintentionally)

Percentages

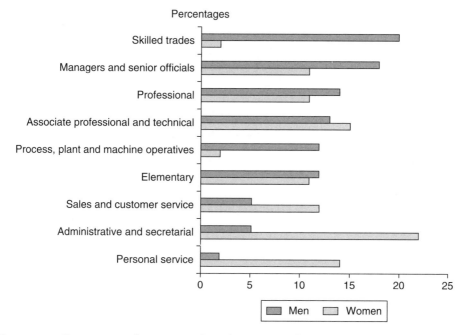

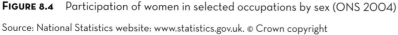

FIGURE 8.4 Participation of women in selected occupations by sex (ONS 2004)

Source: National Statistics website: www.statistics.gov.uk. © Crown copyright

put forward the view that men and women were located in very distinct and different social roles (notably, men in full-time paid work and women in the home). These social roles required them to act in certain ways, which were, generally speaking, good for men but bad for women. The *new approaches* hold that social roles may be 'masculine' or 'feminine' in orientation (such as running a business or looking after children) but a man may carry out a 'feminine' role (looking after the children), while a woman may occupy a 'masculine' role (running a business). The new approaches also focus on how men and women experience those roles and how those experiences affect their health. The more feminine a role, the lower status it tends to have, and this can lead to poor health. Performing feminine roles also carries much more pressure than performing male roles.

According to Annandale and Hunt (2000) we can identify 'traditional' and 'new' perspectives on gender and health. Traditional perspectives focus mainly on seeing differences between women and men, and focus on excess early male mortality and higher female morbidity. New perspectives focus on seeing the differences and similarities both between and within women and men, and acknowledge the increasing complexity of gender relations in contemporary society.

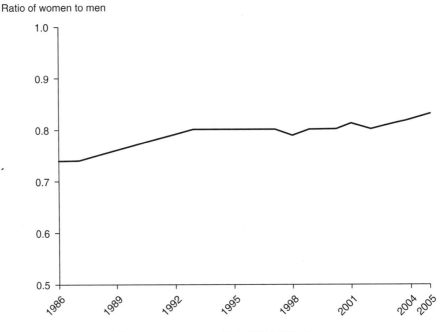

Ratio of women to men

FIGURE 8.5 Income ratio of women to men over time (ONS 2004)

Source: National Statistics website: www.statistics.gov.uk. © Crown copyright

Annandale and Hunt (2000: 27–9) usefully summarise the differences between what they see as traditional and new approaches to gender and health:

- 'Traditional' forms of research had the tacit assumption that what was good for men was bad for women when it came to health. 'New' research follows a more nuanced and subtle approach, and understands that similar circumstances may have *similar* or *different* consequences for the health of men and women.
- 'New' approaches are aware of the differences *within* men and *within* women. In 'traditional' research men, in particular, were treated as an undifferentiated group, where all men had similar health experiences.
- In 'traditional' research positivist, quantitative, statistical methods were predominant. In 'new' research the role of qualitative method is highlighted in trying to obtain an understanding of how the experiences of men and women shape their health. This does not mean abandoning quantitative approaches but understanding that alone they do not provide a full picture of gender and health.

We shall now look at some new thinking on morbidity and mortality rates for women. In the introduction we looked at how much traditional research and thinking made the observation that 'men die early and women spend more of their lives unwell'. The new thinking challenges some of these assumptions as to what causes these differences.

Gender and morbidity

One long-held view (for example, Hibbard and Pope 1986) is that women have higher morbidity rates than men. There have been different attempts to explain this over the years, for example:

- Women do experience more ill health than men because of the demands of their social roles.
- Women are more disposed to seek help than men.
- Women are more 'in tune' with their bodies.
- Surgeries are not male friendly and put men off seeking help.
- It is easier for women to adopt the sick role.

There may be something in the above explanations. Indeed, in Chapter 9 on mental health we see how attachment to, and experience of, certain roles can result in other levels of distress for women. However, if we turn to the statistical evidence on which the assumptions of higher female morbidity are often based, Macintyre et al. (1996; 1999) have raised a few concerns. They argue that on closer inspection of the evidence the actual picture of gender morbidity is very complex, and is very much dependent on where a woman or a man is in their **life cycle** and which particular type of illness you are considering. So, for example, younger males tend to report more long-standing and limiting illness than females. When it comes to type of illness we see a great variety and no clear pattern. Macintyre et al. (1996) also report no real sex difference for men and women of any age currently experiencing conditions such as diabetes, respiratory disorders or epilepsy.

Gender and mortality

Following on from the points raised above concerning morbidity, another long-standing perception, when looking at gender and health, is that women have some form of biological advantage in terms of life expectancy. In the UK, for instance, a female born in 2004 can expect to live until she is 81.1 years old, while a male born in the same year can expect to reach the age of 76.7 years (ONS 2006b). Such statistics strongly suggest that women do enjoy some form of biological advantage over men, but, again, we must exercise caution before making any firm statements. Mick Carpenter (2000: 49) makes several important points about always seeking to find differences between men and women when, in fact, there are many similarities in their life and health experiences. He notes that the life expectancy of both men and women has improved significantly since the 1800s (see Figure 8.6). Indeed, the gap between men and women appears to be closing, with men increasingly catching up with women as we enter the twenty-first century.

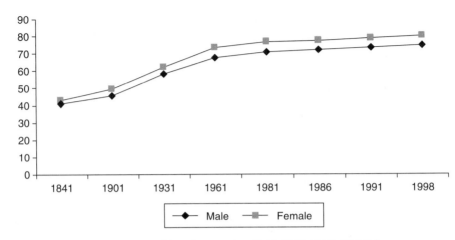

FIGURE 8.6 Changes in male and female mortality, 1840–1998 (ONS 2006b)

Source: National Statistics website: www.statistics.gov.uk. © Crown copyright

We should also consider that the sizeable life expectancy advantage that women experience in the UK is very much a western phenomenon. If we look at Figure 8.7, we can see that overall women do have longer lives than men in most countries, but this is extremely variable. On the one hand, in some countries, such as Malawi, the life expectancy for both women and men is very low, while in Algeria there is a negligible difference in life expectancy for women and men. The reasons for this are multiple and diverse. For example, it depends on the levels of health care a country can offer; on whether childbirth is safer; and on the levels of poverty and endemic illness, such as in Malawi, which faces widespread poverty and has many people infected with HIV/AIDS.

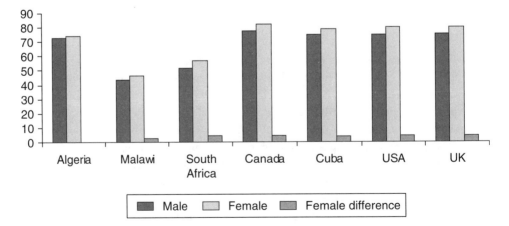

FIGURE 8.7 Life expectancy by sex and selected country, 2002 (United Nations 2005)

Bringing in men's health

One of the important shifts in the study of gender and health has been to acknowledge men and their experiences of health. It is, in some ways, ironic that the earlier research on gender and health focused almost exclusively on women, with little attention to men and their health. There have been calls by Banks (2001) and Doyal (2001), for example, for men's health to be more fully explored. In the past, male health was held to be unproblematic, perhaps even the norm, and men benefited from hegemonic masculinity. It is becoming clear that this is not the case. Men, too, experience distinct health problems and they themselves can suffer as a result from the expectations of, and challenges to, masculinity in contemporary society. In the UK, for example, there is strong pressure for young men to live up to a 'laddish' lifestyle, which involves demonstrating one's masculinity by engaging in potentially harmful and risky behaviours such as heavy drinking and driving fast cars. Indeed, many of the so-called 'lads' mags' are, arguably, replete with articles that extol such behaviour. The magazine *Nuts* (aimed at young men in their late teens), for instance, used to run a feature called 'Mate in a State', where readers were invited to send in photographs of their friends in highly inebriated states and caught in potentially compromising situations. The mortality and morbidity statistics show that one of the main causes of early death and injury for young men is alcohol related.

Williams (2003: 60–1) summarises the main reasons for an increasing interest in men's health:

- Men do care about health issues but find it difficult to express their fears.
- Socially constructed gender characteristics (in addition to biological risk factors) are important in shaping the capacity of men and women to realise their full health potential.
- Men face particular problems because of the relation between masculine identity and risk taking.
- Greater sensitivity to sex and gender is needed in medical research, service delivery and wider social policies, including medical school training and consultations between male doctors and patients.

Masculinities and health

One of the emerging themes in the research that looks at male health is how individual men relate to dominant forms of (hegemonic) masculinity and how that affects their health and frames their experiences of illness (Watson 2000). Here, we shall look at some examples of this relationship and how it better informs us about men and their health.

As we saw earlier, the traditional research on gender and health drew attention to greater levels of morbidity for women. Though much recent thinking casts doubt on many of these explanations, work by O'Brien et al. (2005) indicates the complexities that exist in how men seek help, and how ideas of masculinity influence their decisions. In their study they conducted 14 focus groups with men from a variety of backgrounds. The majority of the men, they found, preferred to be quite stoical in the face of illness and put off as long as possible seeking a consultation. Masculine ideas of being able to cope in the face of adversity, being able to endure pain and suffering, and not appearing to be weak or a 'sissy' were often voiced as reasons for keeping quiet about ill health.

There were, however, some interesting exceptions to the 'keeping-it-to-yourself' attitudes expressed above. Men such as the firemen in the study – whose occupations gave them access to a very powerful masculine identity – indicated no real problems in communicating their health needs.

Overall, mental illness came to the fore as the one condition where greater reticence was reported in seeking help for fear of being seen to be unmanly. In fact, admitting to mental illness appeared to be the one area that offered the most direct challenge to masculinity. However, Emslie et al. (2006) in their research found that there were examples of some men who would talk about mental illness, in this case depression. Those that did either employed very masculine imagery of seeing their illness as part of a heroic struggle, or were aware that experiencing depression had allowed them to acknowledge a 'feminine' vulnerability as part of their identity.

Links

See Chapter 9 for more on how gender issues affect mental health, for both men and women.

Conclusion

Complexity and change are motifs throughout this chapter, in terms of both gender relations in society and what sociology has to say about how those gender relations are reflected in the health of women and men. The traditional aphorism of 'men die, women suffer' that has been the dominant way of explaining gender inequalities has been demonstrated to be increasingly unhelpful. There are probably two factors at play here.

First, many of the general gender inequalities to do with pay and employment, for example, that played a part in the poorer morbidity of women are beginning to be addressed and certain positive shifts towards some form of equality are discernible. This, though, should be tempered and placed firmly in perspective: while this progress is welcome (if not long overdue) and significant, there is still *much* to be done to bring about full equality.

Second, there has been a reconsideration of gender as a theoretical concept. A more nuanced approach is now visible in much of the research. The work of Connell

(2002; 2005) has been highly noticeable. Men are being disaggregated from a homogeneous bloc, and different ways of being male, and their attendant status, have been identified. This allows insights into how the roles and the actions of both men *and* women affect their health.

Summary points

● Gender is not fixed but is heavily influenced by society.
● Gender relations are becoming increasingly complex, with women making gains in some areas but not in others.
● In theorising gender it can be more effective to think of the power differences between different expressions of masculinity and femininity.

Case study

The following extract is from research by O'Brien et al. (2005: 508). As mentioned earlier, this piece of research helps us understand further how masculinity influences men's decisions about seeking help for ill health. Read the extract and then consider the questions below.

Rory: I broke my thumb and it took me two days before I went to see a doctor …
          It was going septic, going green and purple and black and I was like, 'I'm
          not going to bother them.'
Jake: I think that's a male trait.
Nathan: Aye it's (puts on a very deep voice) 'I am man the hunter.' I think it's
          that.
Rory: I don't think it's that … It's just I couldnae go to the doctor's with
          that.
Nathan: If a woman cut themselves they'd be away to the doctor. A guy'd be
          like, 'I'll just go and get myself a bit of Sellotape and wrap it up.'
Rory: Aye. I put a bit of tape on it and carried on.
Nathan: That's just a man thing though isn't it?
Rory: Aye that's just a man thing. 'I'm hard, I'm daft, I'll cut my arm off and
          just grow another one back.'

1 First of all, outline what is meant by 'hegemonic masculinity' and note down the
  names of well-known men who exemplify such an expression of manhood.
2 In what ways are the men in the extract influenced by prevailing ideas of masculinity?
3 How could adhering to such ideas of masculinity be damaging for their health?
4 How do you think these same young men would talk about mental health issues?
5 What could be done to assist men in discussing their health?

Taking your studies further

This chapter will have helped you understand many of the key terms, concepts, theories and debates relating to gender and health. Listed below are journal articles and books that will provide deeper and more detailed discussions of the points raised in this chapter. You will also find what is available on the companion website. This offers downloads of relevant material, plus links to useful websites in addition to podcasts and other features.

Recommended reading

Annandale, H. and Hunt, K. (eds) (2000) *Gender Inequalities in Health*. Buckingham: Open University Press.

Courtenay, W.H. (2000) 'Constructions of masculinity and their influence on men's well-being: a theory of gender and health', *Social Science and Medicine*, 50 (10): 1385–401.

Green, S.E. (2006) '"We're tired, not sad": benefits and burdens of mothering a child with a disability', *Social Science and Medicine*, DOI 10.1016/j.scomed2006.08.025.

O'Brien, R., Hunt, K. and Hart, G. (2005) 'It's caveman stuff, but that is to a certain extent how guys still operate', *Social Science and Medicine*, 61 (3): 503–16.

Watson, J. (2000) *Male Bodies: Health, Culture and Identity*. Buckingham: Open University Press.

Williams, C. (2000) 'Doing health, doing gender: teenagers, diabetes and asthma', *Social Science and Medicine*, 50 (3): 387–96.

On the companion website

White, R. (2002) 'Social and political aspects of men's health', *Health*, 7 (6): 267–85.

Williams, S.J. (2003) *Medicine and the Body*. London: Sage. Chapter 2 on '"Structuring" bodies: emotions, inequalities and health'.

9

Mental health

Main points

- Many more people in contemporary society are reporting and experiencing distress and depression.
- Sociology helps us understand how mental health is framed in and by society.
- The attitudes of others and wider society greatly affect the well-being of those experiencing distress.
- Wider social inequalities are also visible in the distribution of diagnosed and reported mental health problems.

Key concepts

Mental health   stigma   attitudes   class   gender   ethnicity   suicide.

Introduction

In 2006 *The Depression Report* made some very important and telling points about the extent of mental health problems in the United Kingdom. Not only did the report state that of all causes of disability, whether physical or mental, 40 per cent were accounted for by mental illness, but it found that tens of thousands of therapists were required to provide the necessary level of service to treat and assist the thousands of people who experience distress (LSE 2006). This report represents part of a trend within official policy circles and among the general population to treat mental illness as a serious issue. Throughout time, mental health has been regarded with suspicion and sometimes fear within society, and has been seen as a lower-status field in which to practise by the medical profession. Much of this is to do with how social attitudes negatively frame mental illness. In previous centuries, for example, mental illness was seen as possession by demons, a curse by God. Even in more enlightened times it was the ultimate transgression against reason and rationality. As a result mental illness became stigmatised, the badge of the outsider and the deviant, associated with danger and violence.

Sociology has an important role to play in trying to understand the full intricacies of mental illness, especially when it comes to the ways in which society *influences* and *frames* both how we see mental health and illness and how society creates situations that can negatively impact on individuals' mental health. Busfield neatly summarises what sociology can offer the study of mental health and illness, and how sociology tells us about

> the importance of social processes in a range of areas: in the definition, boundaries and categories of mental disorder; in any adequate understanding of the factors that give rise to mental disorder; and in the understanding of the character of mental health practice and the professionals and others who shape that practice together with the ideas that underpin it. (2000: 554)

This chapter will explore many of the issues associated with mental health and illness. Much of the focus, as suggested above, will be on how mental health and illness are framed by society. A great deal of the research indicates that this framing (attitudes held by the general public, how people's behaviour is interpreted by others, and the influence of medical classifications and categories) can affect the lives of people with mental health problems much more than the symptoms of their particular condition. We will look at some of the debates that exist in relation to defining and identifying what is seen to be mental illness. Attention will also be given to the effect that social attitudes, whether expressed by official bodies or by the lay general public, have on people who are experiencing some form of distress. This will lead us to the theory of **stigma**, which helps us understand how people with certain traits and characteristics are made to feel unwelcome and excluded by society. We will also look at depression in some depth. This will allow us to consider some of the particular circumstances and issues that affect people who experience this condition. Finally, consideration will be given to sociological perspectives on suicide.

What causes mental illness?

Giving a clear and concise answer to the question 'What causes mental illness?' is highly problematic. Part of the reason for this is the complexities and uncertainties that surround the whole process of diagnosis and identifying mental illness in the first place. Unlike physical illnesses, there is often no clear-cut objective sign that someone is experiencing a mental illness. One cannot, for example, find a broken bone or a cell that has become cancerous.

Instead, doctors and psychiatrists have to rely on what people tell them – which is, in itself, highly problematic, as we shall see. McPherson and Armstrong summarise these concerns well, when they say:

> What is pneumonia or appendicitis or cancer can be agreed internationally with reference to the presence or absence of certain clearly defined physical characteristics. In psychiatry, however, there is no such external biological referent to act as an anchor for diagnosis. Essentially, psychiatry classifies on the basis of a patient's patterns of symptoms which might vary according to how they are elicited and interpreted. (2006: 50)

Because, then, we cannot always clearly identify what mental illness is, this makes the search for a cause all the harder. Lack of certainty means that no single authoritative answer can be put forward, and over the years we have seen many competing explanations come and go. Broadly speaking, explanations for mental illness fall into one of two camps: biological explanations and social explanations. These look in very different directions and see quite different reasons for the existence of mental illness, as outlined below.

Even though there are often no apparent organic signs, biological explanations (typically favoured by mainstream medicine) still privilege a focus on faulty genes or imbalances in the chemistry of the brain. There is, for instance, an association between low levels of serotonin and depression. This way of thinking, of looking for a biological cause, is increasingly reinforced by the proliferation of pharmaceutical interventions such as SSRIs (selective serotonin reuptake inhibitors) for treating depression, which suggest that if an illness can be treated by chemicals, then it must have a biological, organic basis.

Social explanations, on the other hand, fall into two general categories: social causation and social constructionist. The social causation perspective refers to how the various inequalities in society (mainly to do with ethnicity, gender and class) produce toxic levels of stress for some people. As a result of this stress, people may be 'tipped' into mental illness, whether it is a woman expected to bring up children on her own and keep down a job; or the experience of someone from an ethnic minority group of being racially abused by a neighbour; or the constant soul-destroying grind of poverty and not being able to lead the life that others enjoy. We shall look at some of these issues later in this chapter.

The other main social explanation is social constructionist. Mental illness, from this viewpoint, does not exist as a 'fact' or as 'real' and it has absolutely no organic basis. This sociological view is influenced by the work of Foucault, who has argued that there is no single incontestable truth that can be discovered and agreed on by everyone. Rather, society is constructed by the ideas and conceptualisations of both individual people and also, more importantly, certain powerful groups. Some groups, such as psychiatrists, are able to construct a discourse that privileges a certain viewpoint above others, which allows them to effectively rule out and rule in ways of conceptualising, for example, what constitutes mental illness. Constructing such discourses allows such groups to become dominant in society and allows them to regulate and control the activities of others. Such a perspective allows us to question the factual basis of what is deemed to constitute mental illness, which is useful given the lack of solid evidence by which psychiatry sometimes proceeds. It also points to the way in which, as with other aspects, medicine can discipline and gain control over our lives.

Links

See Chapter 1 for more information about Foucault and discourse.

Both biological and social explanations can definitely tell us something about mental illness. We have, however, to be careful here of not falling into the trap that either explanation on its own is sufficient to address the complexity of mental health and illness. What is certain is that mental illness does not fit into simple 'A-leads-to-B-leads-to-C' explanations. Rather, there is a complex interweaving of both society and biology, where both have to be understood as often working together in complex and dynamic ways.

Some of this complexity and dynamism is captured by Rose (2005) in his discussion of the causes of mental illness and how biology and society interact. He points out that just because a change in the chemistry of the brain takes place does not mean that the chemical change caused the illness. He urges that we must be careful in thinking about the processes which cause changes to happen. The example he uses to illustrate this point is that if someone has a headache, they take an aspirin. If we were then to check the chemicals in the person's brain in order to discover the chemical basis of a headache, we would find aspirin. Thus, according to the biological explanation, we would claim that aspirin causes headaches, because people who do not have headaches do not have the chemical aspirin present in their brains. Now, obviously, we know this not to be the case. What Rose is saying here is that, yes, chemical changes do occur, but they could equally be the *result* of other (in this case *social*) factors.

This takes us to an explanation put forward by Pilgrim and Rogers (1994), which acknowledges and develops that last point. They put forward a critical realist perspective on mental health and illness. This approach is useful in that it does not fall for the either/or impasse outlined above. Rather it brings in the consideration that to fully understand what causes misery and suffering in the world we have to be aware of one of the complexities of human life: that humans are simultaneously organic biological *and* social beings. This perspective allows us to see that both aspects of being human are important and that humans are not entirely reducible to either. What this means is that a critical realist perspective fully acknowledges the strong and influential role of culture, but does not say that it is all down to society; it also accepts the importance of medical information and research. However, crucially, it questions how diagnoses are framed by the social influences on the medical profession (this is explored further in the next section). Finally, a critical realist perspective accepts that biological processes are at work but, like Rose (2005) as outlined above, attempts to place those processes in a wider context where social factors may be the cause of biological changes.

Links

Chapter 1 provides an overview of sociological theories and perspectives.

Attitudes to and constructions of mental health and illness

We usually accept medical terminology and classifications as given, that is, as being fact, value-free and scientific. Various sociologists and other writers, however, have challenged these notions. This is because medicine (like every other aspect of human activity) takes place within a social context. This social context influences how people think, in all sorts of subtle and not so subtle ways. Those that work in medicine, such as doctors and psychiatrists, can also be quite easily influenced by, and in turn play an important role in, prevailing social attitudes. It is useful to remember this when thinking about mental illness and the way it is framed in and by society, especially when someone is judged to be acting in an 'unusual' and 'problematic' manner; for those judgements, made by doctors and psychiatrists, may be based not on purely neutral 'scientific' criteria but on social values and cultural norms (Foster 1995).

One useful example is the way in which both psychiatry and society have changed their perception of homosexuality. Until relatively recently, being gay was considered and framed as a form of mental illness. Gay men, for example, could find themselves on the receiving end of quite draconian interventions such as incarceration. During the 1960s, however, social attitudes towards homosexuality changed, partly due to the activities of campaign groups such as the Gay Liberation Front and events such as Stonewall when gay people fought back against police harassment. As the stigma and stereotyping diminished, so did the view that homosexuality was an illness rather than just one of the many forms of human sexuality.

Many myths and unhelpful images surround people deemed mentally ill. One common misconception is that people diagnosed with schizophrenia have a 'Jekyll and Hyde' personality, whereby they are sane and rational at one moment and violent and deranged the next (Angermeyer and Matschinger 1999). Unfortunately, these negative images appear to be widespread and persistent. Early research by Star (1955) identified negative stereotypes in the US, while similar work by Hall et al. (1993) in England found people possessing similar attitudes nearly 40 years later. Wider representations of mental illness also conflate and confuse mental illness and danger. More recently, Jorm (2000), researching in Australia, has found that many members of the public have a very limited knowledge of mental illness. Using vignettes of someone with depression or schizophrenia Jorm found that few people could identify the depicted mental illness according to medical classifications: only 39 per cent correctly identified depression, and even fewer, 27 per cent, correctly identified schizophrenia.

'Mental imbalance' often characterises many a movie or soap series villain. These are not just neutral images, however, that are contained within the safety of the cinema or the TV screen, but form beliefs and constructs held by people in everyday contexts. In turn these social stigmas increase the stress of those with mental illness and exacerbate feelings of social exclusion and social distance.

The *Counting the Cost* survey by Baker and MacPherson (2000) for MIND highlighted the extent of stigmatising images and the effects they had had on people with mental illness. For many respondents to the survey the social stigma was harder to deal with than the symptoms of their particular condition. Some key results from this survey are summarised below:

- 73 per cent of respondents felt that the media had been unfair, unbalanced or very negative over the previous three years
- 12 per cent felt that the media had been fair, balanced or very positive
- 50 per cent claimed that poor media coverage had a negative impact on their mental health
- 24 per cent experienced some hostility from neighbours and their local communities as a result of media reports. (2000: 5)

Questions

Why you think mental illness attracts such negative imagery?

Negative views of mental illness and mentally ill people are also evident among young people. The *Tomorrow's Minds* survey reached a similar conclusion on stereotyping and **prejudice** (Baker and MacPherson 2000). Sixty per cent of young people in the survey admitted to using abusive terms such as 'psycho', 'schizo', 'nutter' or 'loony' to describe mentally ill people.

Historically, these images of mental illness have their roots in ideas of demonic possession (Scheff 1966) or the loss of rationality (Foucault 1967). Currently, negative images of mental illness are presented in newspaper articles, films, documentaries and popular dramas. Again, we see a dominance of stereotypes and misleading images. Philo (1996) noted that the majority of images were associated with violence, particularly violence towards other people, though also to self. The dominance of so many negative images in the media is not necessarily to do with the prejudiced attitudes of programme makers; rather, it is to do with the restraints imposed by the format of television shows, especially soaps. Programmes are restricted to half-hour slots, have multiple plotlines and need to provide dramatic entertainment that unfolds over a relatively short period. Realistic portrayals of mental illness, with all the various subtleties and intricacies that distressed individuals experience, are therefore ignored or glossed over. In addition, the need for storylines to develop, peak and pass quite quickly may result in a very unrealistic portrayal of an illness, how it develops over time and how it can affect someone's life.

Stigma

Goffman is probably one of the best-known sociologists to have studied and theorised how certain groups of people attract stigma. His humanistic and sympathetic work focuses on why certain attributes of an individual or a group deny them full acceptance in given situations and lead them either to be excluded or to be left with a feeling of not 'fitting in'. Goffman (1968) classifies stigma into three broad groups:

- *physical stigma* – mainly to do with aspects visible 'on the surface' of people, for example facial scarring, a physical impairment or an amputation

> Stigma refers to an attribute that 'discredits', or prevents, someone's full acceptance in a particular situation.

- *personal/character stigma* – mainly to do with aspects 'below the surface', for example drug use, sexuality or mental health
- *social stigma* – belonging to a particular group or ethnic minority.

Questions

Can you identify conditions, mental or physical, that could be potentially stigmatising? Try to figure out why they could be stigmatising.

Like other symbolic interactionists, Goffman seeks to explore the subtleties and intricacies of how people present themselves to the outside world, especially if their identity is in some way 'spoiled' or stigmatised. How that identity can be spoiled or stigmatised varies greatly. Sometimes it is highly visible, in the case of facial scarring for example, or it can be highly invisible, such as a history of depressive episodes. Whatever it is, it may completely alter social identity. In some respects we all have something in our lives that we wish to keep hidden, or pieces of personal information that we manage in certain ways so as to maintain a particular 'face' to those about us.

Another aspect of Goffman's notion of stigma is that it is highly relational, depending on the situation in which we find ourselves. The previous section outlined how people experiencing mental health problems are portrayed in a negative light, and, if their status is known, in certain situations the effects could be quite damaging. If, let us say, a person was with others who shared similar mental health problems then the stigma would be reduced or non-existent. Notions of what is normal, or what stigma is, are thus highly contextual; each of these labels is socially constructed and has no inherent or natural basis.

Passing refers to attempts to conceal a potential stigma and prevent its disclosure.

People respond in a variety of ways to a potentially stigmatising condition or situation though, as Goffman argues, this can depend on how concealed or 'displayed' the stigma is. For those with a concealed or concealable stigma, an attribute that Goffman terms 'a discreditable stigma', there is the possibility of managing, manipulating or presenting information so as to avoid revealing the stigma. This is termed **passing** and entails devising a routine. This routine may involve being careful about what one talks about, where one goes, what one wears and so on – basically managing daily life so as to keep potentially stigmatising information secret.

Goffman points out that trying to maintain this round of secrecy can come at a terrible cost and be quite emotionally draining and demanding. There is always the chance of letting information slip or being discovered, and the consequences, real or imagined, would then have to be endured.

As persuasive and elaborate as Goffman's ideas are, he has been criticised for not acknowledging the material basis of stigmas and for overly reflecting on the individual. His ideas do, however, provide a challenge to health professionals as he stresses the importance of constructing identity. As the work by Baker and MacPherson (2000) illustrates, the social stigma of a condition can at times be more of an issue for someone with a mental illness than the condition itself. We need to be aware of how the social framing of mental health and illness affects the lives of people who are experiencing distress.

Mary provides an example of stigma and passing. She encountered severe mental health problems shortly after leaving university with a degree in plant science. Feeling very depressed, she found herself unable to leave her flat and even to attend to her personal hygiene. After several years of drug therapy and counselling she became more socially confident and able to deal with aspects of her mental health. She soon reached the point where she wanted to start working and perhaps catch up with old friends again. However, she did not want them to find out about her mental health problems and was worried that they might find her strange or dangerous. The potential problem was made worse by having a gap of several years in her life when she was ill and did not start a career like so many of her old university friends. Fortunately, she managed to find a job working in the greenhouses of the local botanical gardens. Her job involved routine repair and cleaning activities, even though she was qualified to take on more complex and demanding work. The job, though, gave Mary the cover of saying that she was working in the botanical gardens, making it sound as if she was currently in work of an appropriate level for a graduate with several years' work experience, even though it was not. This made it easier for her to catch up with old friends as she could pass herself as 'normal' and hide aspects of her biography that she did not want revealed.

Patterns of mental health and illness

As mentioned in the introduction to this chapter, mental illness affects a wide cross-section of people of different ages, sexes and ethnicity. Nevertheless, certain conditions tend to be found in some groups more than in others and certain people, for a variety of reasons, are more at risk. Overall, mental illnesses are fairly common. The most widespread form of mental illness is depression. A summary of the statistics indicates that:

- around 300 people out of 1000 will experience mental health problems every year in Britain
- 230 of these will visit a GP
- 102 will be diagnosed as having a mental health problem
- 24 will be referred to a specialist psychiatric service
- six will become inpatients in psychiatric services. (MIND 2000a)

It is quite apparent from Figures 9.1 and 9.2 that there is a tendency for mental illness to be distributed unevenly across the class scale, and in particular amongst women. In the research this association between social class and mental illness has long been noticeable. Early researchers such as Faris and Dunham (1939), in their study of the various residential zones of Chicago, observed that schizophrenia was more frequent among working-class people. Slightly later American work by Hollingshead and Redlich (1953) also identified class factors in relation to mental disorder. The now classic work by Brown and Harris (1978) similarly noted class differences: they came across higher rates of depression among working-class women with children than among their middle-class counterparts.

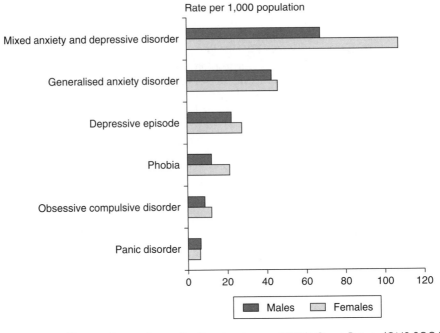

FIGURE 9.1   Weekly prevalence of neurotic disorders by sex, 2000, Great Britain (ONS 2006a)

Source: National Statistics website: www.statistics.gov.uk. © Crown copyright

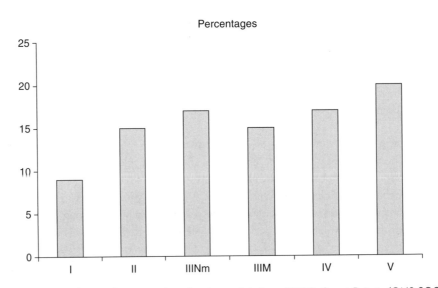

FIGURE 9.2   Prevalence of neurotic disorders by social class, 2000, Great Britain (ONS 2004)

Source: National Statistics website: www.statistics.gov.uk. © Crown copyright

Ethnicity and mental health

There are a number of explanations for why people from black and other ethnic backgrounds appear to have higher rates of mental illness and a different, often coercive, relationship with services. These explanations include:

- racist and prejudiced attitudes on the part of service providers and agencies of the state, such as the police
- lack of cultural sensitivity
- more frequent exposure to stressors in the form of, for example, unemployment
- adjusting to a new society if recently arrived
- racism generally.

Links

These issues are discussed in greater depth in Chapter 7 on ethnicity and health.

These explanations are useful when trying to understand the situation of people from ethnic minorities in relation to mental illness. However, Pilgrim and Rogers (1993) point to another, related concept that may help us in this context. They draw on Foucault's concept of seeing madness as part of the 'other', that is, groups of people who are regarded as being outside the norms of society and as constituting a threat to the order of society. In previous times people with mental illnesses were excluded from society, banished to the Ships of Fools that traversed European waterways in the Middle Ages, or to the asylums of the Victorian age. Here we see, they argue, a relationship between new racism and psychiatric discourse. In the new racism many of the explicit old racist practices of viewing black and Asian people as subhuman have given way to viewing people as a threat to 'British' social and cultural identity. This idea was noticeable during a speech made by Conservative MP John Townsend in the 2001 UK general election when he claimed that immigration was undermining Britain as an Anglo-Saxon country. The new racism also deals with this supposed threat to social and cultural identity by using exclusion, this time by excluding black and Asian people from full social acceptance into British society on grounds of non-Christian religions, diets, involvement in terrorism, or other 'non-western/British' aspects of identity behaviour. Thus psychiatric practice reflects, in its treatment of black and Asian people, wider aspects of racism within society by further excluding these groups from full social participation by identifying their behaviour and activities as pathological and insane.

Gender and mental health

Every review of the literature concerning sociology and mental health reaches the same conclusion when discussing gender: that women always display higher rates of certain mental illnesses than men (Bebbington 1996; Foster 1995). Much research has attempted to explain this particular phenomenon, with various results. Some explanations point to measurement artefact effects and to men seeking alternative outlets, such as drink, that mask depressive disorders; others point to role strain and conflict; while yet others indicate that social factors, such as poor housing or social class, are the cause.

Gender refers to the cultural differences between men and women, while sex refers to physical differences.

Other explanations point to the pressure on women to conform to prevailing norms of femininity and attractiveness. For example, the BMA (2000) warned that media images of very thin models and celebrities could have very damaging and negative effects on young women's perceptions of their body image and their self-esteem, which could lead to feelings of distress and anxiety.

Links

See Chapter 8 for more information on gender and health.

Measurement artefact means that women exhibit higher rates of mental illness than men because the design of questionnaires and the way data are collected produce a 'statistical mirage', which artificially generates a problem where there is not one. Earlier work by Gove (1984), among others, indicated that faults with the way in which data were collected meant that women appeared to exhibit higher rates of depression.

In a substantial review of the literature relating to women and depression, however, Bebbington (1996) and Nazroo et al. (1998) argued that there was little evidence of measurement artefact being responsible for the high levels of recorded depression in women. In their carefully constructed study, Nazroo et al. (1998) demonstrated that women did report more depressive episodes – whether distant, mild or exaggerated episodes. There was little evidence for men masking their depression by turning to alcohol or substance abuse, as had been suggested by other studies.

What Nazroo et al.'s research pointed to was the effect that gender roles and life events had on men and women. Looking at a range of crises that related to children, reproduction, housing, finance, work, marital issues, crime and health, the researchers concluded that women were more likely to develop depression if a crisis involved children, housing or reproduction. The chance of depression was increased if a woman's role identity meant that she attached greater importance to those areas. So if, for example, a woman feels a particularly close attachment to and sense of responsibility for children because of her role identity, then the chance of depression is much greater if there is a child-related problem, such as difficulties at school or drug misuse. For crises involving finance or work, marital issues, crime or health, there appeared to be no gender role difference.

One of the best-known pieces of sociological research on women and mental health was carried out by Brown and Harris (1978), who sought to analyse the relationship between social factors and mental health in the Camberwell area of London. From their research they developed a multifactorial model (Figure 9.3) which attempted to explain the intricacies and subtleties of why some women develop clinical depression while others, living in similar conditions, do not. The model contains the idea that the onset of depression (the dependent variable) will occur if other factors are present (the independent variables). Key components of the model are:

- *Current vulnerability factors.* These factors relate to events that have happened in a woman's past and indicate whether or not she may be more susceptible to depression. Brown and Harris identified four vulnerability factors:
  - losing a mother before the age of 11
  - presence at home of three or more children under the age of 15 years
  - absence of any confiding relationships, particularly with the husband
  - lack of full- or part-time job.

- *Provoking agents.* Here Brown and Harris identified various events that could occur in a woman's life, which could then trigger a depressive episode. The events mainly relate to loss and disappointment, e.g. death, losing a job or discovering a partner's unfaithfulness. Ongoing difficulties were also noted as being contributory; they included dealing with a variety of 'background' problems ranging from housing problems to headaches.

- *Symptom-formation factors.* Women over 50 years of age and women with low self-esteem were at greatest risk of developing depression.

One way of thinking about this approach is to imagine someone on a tightrope. The chances of falling are increased if there are any existing vulnerabilities, which means that the tightrope begins to sway, making it harder to maintain a sure footing. There is an even greater chance of falling if a provoking agent such as an adverse life event comes along and impacts on the person, making it likely that they will be knocked off. Finally, any possibility of staying on the rope may be diminished if balance is poor due to low self-esteem.

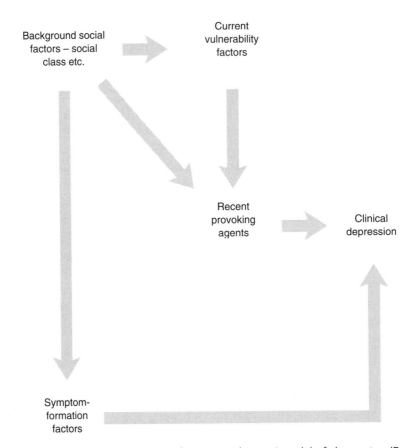

FIGURE 9.3   Schematic representation of Brown and Harris' model of depression (Brown and Harris 1978: 265)

Focus on depression

Depression is becoming an increasingly common condition in industrial capitalist societies such as the UK. Psychologist Oliver James (1998) points to the increases in the amount of depression in British society since the 1950s. He goes on to make the highly apposite point that even though we are now, in many ways, richer economically we are definitely poorer emotionally. This, he argues, is due to the tendency of contemporary society (mainly through hyped-up media images) to heighten our expectations of what life should be about – expectations which are ultimately impossible to fulfil. This leads to a depressing 'gap' between where we think we should be in life and where we actually are, or, as James puts it, we think we are losers even though we are winners.

One problem, when discussing 'depression', is the term itself. In lay usage we use the word to describe and refer to a vast variety of states and feelings in everyday life. So, for example, you could claim to be feeling depressed after your football team loses yet again on a Saturday afternoon, or when the essay you feverishly worked on receives a lower grade than you'd hoped. The emotional states indicated in these two examples will be highly unpleasant and perhaps lead to some, albeit temporary, change in behaviour, for example, having a cry or wanting to be on your own. This is quite different from what is meant by experiencing depression as a mental illness. Through confusion between the states of everyday blues and the illness of depression, many of the subtleties and issues which face people with clinical depression are lost. The severity of the condition and the experiences that people with depression go through may be unfairly diminished and not taken as seriously as they would be if the person was, for instance, experiencing a severe physical illness instead.

Depression is, therefore, considerably more than feeling just a little down or blue. People with clinical depression experience a highly distressing and debilitating combination of mental *and* physical symptoms that can last over a period of months or even years. In terms of mental states and emotions, people with depression experience a substantial reordering of how they think, see themselves and perceive others. Their thinking changes in that they interpret the world very negatively and see everything in the worst possible and most despairing way. Frequently, people with depression are acutely sensitive to the smallest of things. So, for example, if a friend does not sit next to them in a lecture this can be taken as a sign that nobody likes them and that life is terrible. What is important here is that this change in thinking cannot be 'snapped out of', as is sometimes popularly thought. Such changes in thinking often seem beyond the control of the person with depression. They wish they could stop thinking in such a negative and horrible way but find it almost impossible to do so. The following quote from someone with depression illustrates this point:

> It is so total … There is no reason to wake up in the morning. I just let the blinds stay down … Sometimes I wonder what life will be like, where I can find a fixed point, a hold to my life. (Kangas 2001: 86)

At worst, changes in thinking can take the direction of suicidal thoughts where taking one's life begins to appear as a 'suitable' way of dealing with life's problems. These thoughts are deeply despairing. We examine sociological perspectives on suicide later in this chapter.

As well as all the changes in thinking, there are considerable physical changes. Among the more common changes that affect the body are exhaustion, difficulties in sleeping, loss of appetite, loss of weight, and loss of interest in sex. These physical changes indicate how the differences between physical and mental illness are not so clear-cut. Just because something is mainly seen as a mental illness does not mean that it is only experienced as a set of feelings. The same also goes for physical illnesses, which often have an emotional side to them too.

Throughout this chapter, there has been reference to how society views or frames mental illness. Depression is no exception, and there are considerable cultural differences in how people from a particular society frame this mental illness. In an American study, Karasz (2005) found that there were differences between European Americans and South Asian immigrants in how they viewed depression. Two key differences emerged. The European Americans were more likely to see depression as a disease and a medical condition, not related to any social context, while the South Asians had the opposite viewpoint: they saw depression more as an emotional response to what was going on in someone's life and tied very closely to social context. Other social and cultural differences have been noted elsewhere. Fenton and Sadiq-Sangster (1996) found that South Asian women expressed depression in physical terminology, for example saying that they had a pain in their heart with little or no allusion to feelings or thoughts. What should be noted here is that just because different cultures frame depression in different ways does not mean that one is more accurate and correct than the other. All that this demonstrates is how social influences affect our ways of expressing our moments of suffering and anguish.

Suicide

On 8 April 1994 musician Kurt Cobain decided to take his own life and joined the list of various rock stars who have died early. His death was not an isolated tragedy, a one-off, but an instance of a trend that had been growing from the 1990s onwards: the increase in young male suicide. Even though UK suicide rates as a whole are down from the early 1980s, the suicide rate for young men has increased since 1982 by 67 per cent for young men aged 15–24, accounting for 20 per cent of all deaths for young people in that age group (MIND 1999). The highest rate for suicide, though, is still found among older men. Suicide often appears to be an unfathomable act, impervious to analysis or systematic understanding. After all, how can any research be carried out on an action that takes place in isolated and lonely circumstances, where the subject is someone whose life has reached the place where ending it appears a valid choice?

> ## Questions
>
> Do you think that there is glamour attached to the suicides of successful artistic people? If so why?

There has been much (perhaps too much, some would say) sociological work on suicide, mainly because of early work by functionalist Emile Durkheim. Durkheim used suicide as an example of how the most apparently individual of acts can be opened up to sociological investigation. First published in 1897, *Suicide: A Study in Sociology* was the first sociological attempt to systematically understand suicide (Durkheim 1970). Without denying that individual circumstances could affect a person's decision to take his or her own life, Durkheim noticed patterns in suicide rates between countries and between different groups in the same society. Protestant countries had higher rates than Catholic countries, while Jewish societies had the lowest suicide rates of all. What was also notable was the constancy of relative suicide rates between countries. After further analysis Durkheim identified four different types of suicide:

- *Egoistic suicide.* If an individual was not sufficiently integrated into society then they were at a higher risk of suicide. This explains why Protestants were at greater risk than Catholics. The Protestant faith emphasises individualism, while Catholicism emphasises community, with greater integration for a community's members. In addition, people who were unmarried or childless were more likely to commit suicide than the married and those with children, because of the former's lack of integration with a family unit.
- *Anomic suicide.* The opposite of egoistic suicide, this occurs where a society fails to regulate the individual, for example when a society collapses and all the usual norms and patterns of life fall apart, leaving people bewildered and unsure of what is happening. The classic example of this is the 1928 stock market crash that just about devastated American life, with people losing security, savings and their homes. Here the loss of all that was considered normal led to an increase in suicide rates.
- *Altruistic suicide.* Here a sense of duty, linked to a high level of integration into a particular society, leads someone to take their own life. There are numerous examples around the world: the Japanese kamikaze pilots who flew their planes directly into American battleships in an attempt to sink them during the Second World War; the Hindu practice of suttee, where a wife kills herself at her husband's funeral; and the Irish Republican hunger strikers, such as Bobby Sands, who starved themselves to death in pursuit of their political beliefs.
- *Fatalistic suicide.* This form of suicide refers to the despair of living in a highly regulated society with no opportunity for personal freedom and control. It is very rare in contemporary society and Durkheim only included it for historical interest. Mainly applying to highly restrictive societies, this type of suicide could be seen among slaves in ancient slave societies.

Links

Chapter 1 discusses functionalism in more depth.

As with any other groundbreaking and important piece of sociology, Durkheim's theory of suicide has attracted much debate, with many proponents and opponents. Some critics point out that suicide statistics are notoriously unreliable. Coroners or doctors may record a death as due to some cause other than suicide, in an attempt to avoid problems for surviving family members. Other critics point out that his observations could not always be proved or researched properly.

The strongest critique, however, came from interpretive sociologists such as J.D. Douglas (1967). He put forward two points:

1 All suicide statistics should be treated with caution, as there may have been collusion between officials who record and categorise deaths, and family and friends. The degree of integration here may affect the decision. The more integrated the suicide in a social group, the greater the possibility of a cover-up taking place.
2 Durkheim failed to take into account the motive for and meaning of the suicide. Suicide can be a way of communicating revenge, eliciting sympathy or dealing with guilt, or a way of meeting cultural obligations. This information could be elicited by studying diaries and suicide notes.

Links

Chapter 1 discusses interpretive perspectives in greater depth.

More recent sociologists have criticised theories of the interpretive approach of sociologists such as Douglas, and sought to construct more elegant and sophisticated theories of suicide. Taylor (1989; 1990) also agreed that statistics are unreliable and noted, in a study of deaths in the London Underground, a number of contributory factors that could lead to a death being recorded as a suicide or not. These included whether or not the person had a history of mental illness, or the views and opinions of people who knew the deceased. If the coroner asked a close friend or family member then suicide would often be denied, while if the coroner asked a casual acquaintance then a verdict of suicide was more likely.

Taylor then went on to identify four different types of suicide. The categorisation is similar to Durkheim's, but Taylor's emphasis is less on social factors and more on what people think of themselves and their relationships with others – and the certainty or uncertainty of these feelings is important. These suicides divide into two main categories: ectopic, which relates to a person's view of him/herself; and symphisic, that is concerning the person's relationship with others.

Ectopic suicides (self)

- *Submissive suicide.* This occurs when someone has decided that there is no point in going on and that their life is at an end. This may be because of the death of a loved one, or because of terminal illness. Any attempt at suicide is carried out with the full intention of taking one's life and may take place in an isolated place so as to avoid the chance of discovery.
- *Thanatation suicide.* This relates to feelings of uncertainty, and the attempt at suicide is not as earnest as a submissive suicide, the person leaving it to chance as to whether they actually die or not.

Symphisic suicide (relationships)

- *Sacrifice suicides.* Here the person takes their own life in order to make others, such as partners or former lovers, feel guilty or incur censure from friends and family. Any suicide note will indicate on whom the blame for the suicide rests.
- *Appeal suicide.* This occurs when someone is uncertain how others feel about them. The person who attempts suicide is not necessarily trying to end their life, but is testing the reactions of others. The suicide attempt may be staged in such a way, in front of others for example, as to enable the person who is making the attempt to see how much someone else cares about them.

Questions

Which of the above theories do you find the most satisfactory in attempting to explain suicide? Provide justification for your answer.

The above three sociological theories of suicide present interesting and different perspectives on why people decide to take their own lives. Each has a particular strength or weakness, and in many ways a combination of all three provides some useful insights into why people attempt suicide. Durkheim offers useful ideas on how social pressures and wider aspects of a society affect suicidal behaviour, while Douglas cautions against accepting suicide statistics at face value and urges us to look at meaning. In Taylor's work we find explanations of why some people leave notes, or attempt suicide in a variety of locations with different levels of secrecy or openness.

Conclusion

A theme running through this chapter has been how distress, suffering and mental health issues are framed and very much influenced by society. This extends from trying to define what is meant by mental illness and the ways in which wider attitudes (and prejudices) impinge on official discourses and perspectives, to the difficult experiences of people with mental health problems and the ways in which they can be stigmatised by wider society. Indeed, for many people who feel depressed or experience other issues with their mental and emotional well-being, it is the reactions of others that can cause them more problems in their day-to-day lives.

We have seen once more that, as with other aspects of health, there exist great social inequalities. Women, working-class people and people from minority ethnic groups all appear to report higher levels of distress. Again, social influences are at play here. We can see the pressures created by expectations of what it is to be feminine, the experiences of stress and poverty, or the results of racism all having potential negative consequences. This chapter has highlighted that mental health has to be understood in its widest context, with sociology providing insights into the social processes that influence and define the misery and suffering of many people in society today.

Given the higher profile of mental health issues and well-being in contemporary society, it appears that interventions in improving and maintaining good mental health have to take place at a social level just as much as, if not more than, at a personal level.

Summary points

- Mental illness, particularly depression, is common in contemporary society.
- Many people hold negative images of mental illness. These negative images often associate mental illness with danger, whether to others or to the mentally ill person. Media portrayals of mental illness are often similarly negative. The stigma created by negative images can have an adverse impact on people with mental illness.
- Ethnic minorities have a different experience of mental health care than do white people. African-Caribbean young men are more likely to be perceived as difficult or violent and more likely to enter mental health care via the police. Cultural stereotyping and racist attitudes affect the care of people from ethnic backgrounds. This also includes white ethnic groups, such as Irish people.
- Women have a different experience of mental health care and mental illness from men. Women tend to have higher rates of depression than men. Stress created by attachment to gender roles is likely to be the cause of those higher rates.
- Overall suicide rates are decreasing, but suicide rates for young men aged 15–24 are increasing. Various sociological theories point to a variety of reasons as to why people take their own lives. Durkheim stresses social and cultural factors; Douglas warns against accepting statistics at face value and emphasises the need to understand individual meaning; while Taylor looks at feelings of uncertainty and certainty with self and others.

Case study

John has recently been relocated into a community hostel that helps those with a variety of mild and non-violent mental illnesses to reintegrate into society. The hostel is situated in a reasonably affluent suburb near a sizeable public park.

It was during his fourth year at university that John first came into contact with the psychiatric services. Until then John was a fairly standard student, competent but not especially noteworthy. This was probably due to his participation in a rather hectic social life in which he appeared to be one of the prime movers. This particular group of friends clubbed quite extensively at the weekends and some of the group took drugs. As he himself remarked to a case worker: 'Yeah, drugs were part of what we did at the weekends but it was nothing serious – dope mainly and speed. Well, speed most Fridays and Saturdays just to help us get that extra energy boost.'

In his third year one of this group was killed in a random accident. They had been out on a Friday night and John had encouraged everyone to try and drink and smoke as much dope as possible. After the club closed they headed down to the nearby beach to watch the sun come up. It was there that John's friend slipped on a rock and fell to his death. Strong feelings of guilt overcame John as he felt to blame for the accident. He gradually became more withdrawn from his friends, and his use of alcohol and soft drugs increased. At the start of his fourth year a relationship with another student fell apart. She found his increasingly pessimistic moods difficult to handle. In addition, his overall behaviour was becoming more compulsive: he constantly analysed what lay behind her words and actions. Invariably, all his con- clusions were negative and he firmly believed that she was bored with him. After she left he ceased attending classes and his coursework suffered. He spent most of his time in his flat, unable to sleep and constantly fixating on what he had done wrong in his life. One night in an attempt to sleep he drank half a bottle of whisky and took some sleeping tablets. A flatmate found him unconscious on the living-room floor and rushed him to hospital.

In the following weeks he was advised to see a counsellor and was referred to cognitive therapy. He made some progress, but as the year went on his university friends finished their courses and moved out of the area. This left John feeling alone and isolated. Consequently his problems returned, and this time he was placed in the local psychiatric hospital. The seven months that he spent there seem to have made some difference to him. In his stay there he responded well to medication and to the various therapies, and hints of his former self appeared. At various social events the charismatic aspects of his personality, which had been quite strong during his university days, surfaced. However, the outside world still seemed problematic to him and he found it difficult to be among large groups of people on his own. In addition to this he had nowhere to stay, as he was no longer entitled to student accommodation.

It was then decided that the hostel was the best place for him as his family might find it difficult to care for him. His father had left home to set up a new

(Continued)

(Continued)

life for himself and his new partner, a former office colleague, and his parents divorced. As a result of the separation John's mother developed severe long-term depression and found life generally difficult to cope with. Recently she had been experiencing some ill effects from a course of Fluoxetine prescribed by her doctor. This led to her taking several days off work from the department store she worked in. Management were reasonably supportive but a proposed restructuring of the department was causing her some anxiety because of the possible loss of a part-time assistant, which would increase her workload. It was proposed that John's father might help to care for him, but John did not feel that he was ready to re-establish such a relationship with his father as he still felt some ambivalence towards him for leaving the family home.

Life at the hostel had until recently been going reasonably well. John was managing to socialise again and felt confident about interacting with the world at large. In fact, he had managed to get to know some local people his own age. They knew he was at the hostel but he claimed that he was a worker there, and with his quick wit and outward appearance of calm there was no reason to doubt this. However, one day in the nearby supermarket John suddenly felt quite anxious and rushed out of the store, discarding his shopping as he left. This was witnessed by one of his new friends who started to have doubts about John's true identity.

1 Discuss how John's sense of identity has been affected by his mental illness. How important is maintaining a sense of identity for John?
2 What has happened in his mother's life that has led her to feel depressed? Which theory could help us understand her situation?
3 What passing technique does John employ?
4 If you are a health professional student, what type of involvement would you have with someone like John?
5 The assumption is that John is white, but how might his treatment and subsequent care and recovery have been different if he was a young African-Caribbean male?

Taking your studies further

This chapter will have helped you understand many of the key terms, concepts, theories and debates relating to mental health. Listed below are journal articles, books and a website that will provide deeper and more detailed discussions of the points raised in this chapter. You will also find what is available on the companion website. This offers you downloads of relevant material, plus links to useful websites in addition to podcasts and other features.

Recommended reading

Busfield, J. (ed.) (2001) *Rethinking the Sociology of Mental Health*. London: Blackwell.

Goffman, E. (1968) *Stigma: Notes on the Management of a Spoiled Identity*. Harmondsworth: Penguin.

MIND. http://www.mind.org.uk/. This website has a wealth of useful and interesting information.

Philo, G. (ed.) (1996) *Media and Mental Distress*. London: Longman.

Pilgrim, D. (2005) *Key Concepts in Mental Health*. London: Sage.

Pilgrim, D. and Bentall, R. (1999) 'The medicalisation of misery: a critical realist analysis of the concept of depression', *Journal of Mental Health*, 8 (3): 261–74.

Pilgrim, D. and Rogers, A. (2005) *A Sociology of Mental Health and Illness*. Buckingham: Open University Press.

Prior, L. (1993) *The Social Organization of Mental Illness*. London: Sage.

On the companion website

Muntaner, C., Eaton, W.W. and Diala, C.C. (2000) 'Social inequalities in mental health: a review of concepts and underlying assumptions', *Health*, 4 (1): 89–113.

10

Sexualities and health
With Megan Todd

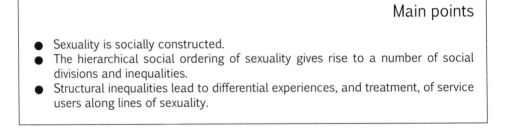

Main points

- Sexuality is socially constructed.
- The hierarchical social ordering of sexuality gives rise to a number of social divisions and inequalities.
- Structural inequalities lead to differential experiences, and treatment, of service users along lines of sexuality.

Key concepts

Sexuality • health • heteronormativity • inequalities.

Introduction

The topic of sexuality in relation to health and inequality remains relatively neglected, and perhaps even taboo. Arguably, sexuality has often been secondary to other important issues such as class, gender and ethnicity. As we shall see, this can have potentially serious consequences for the well-being of many service users. This chapter aims to introduce readers to the topic of sexuality by considering the diversity of sexuality in order to provide a deeper understanding of the implications for workers in the field of health and social care, thus enabling them to work better with a range of service users. Although this chapter will focus mainly on lesbian, gay and bisexual lives, there is not an assumption that heterosexuality is the norm; all sexualities, including heterosexuality, need explanation.

> Sexuality is often presented as the most natural and private aspect of identity. Social constructionists would argue that sexuality is shaped by social structures. What is considered normal changes over time and between cultures (Weeks 2003).

One reason why it is problematic to write about sexuality is that the available terminology can be difficult to negotiate, is often inadequate and can so easily offend. Before we begin the chapter proper, therefore, it may be useful to have a brief discussion about terminology. *Sexuality* in this chapter refers to sexual identity or orientation, rather than simply sexual activity. Where possible, the term 'homosexual' has not been used; this is because it is derived from nineteenth-century sexology and exhibits many negative connotations associated with medicalisation. Instead, where possible the terms 'LGBT' (lesbian, gay, bisexual and transgender) or 'lesbian' and 'gay man' are used because these are the terms more usually used by the lesbian and gay communities. Also used often is the phrase 'coming out' to refer to those (LGBT) people who acknowledge their sexuality openly, and the related 'closeted' (someone who has not come out of the closet). It is also important to recognise that coming out is not a one-off event: decisions about when and where to disclose one's sexuality can be a daily experience. Partly because a chapter of this length cannot do the topic justice, and partly because it is not necessarily about sexual identity, no specific discussion about transgender and transsexual health issues is included. Readers seeking to find out more about this area are advised to look at the burgeoning literature elsewhere (Hines and Sanger 2010; Stryker and Whittle 2006).

We also need to proceed with caution when using statistics. First, we do not know how many lesbians and gay men live in the UK; current statistics – which suggest roughly 5–7 per cent of the population are gay – are likely to be underestimates. Despite a recent raft of policies aimed at moving towards equality, we still live in a *heteronormative* society where gay men and lesbians are relatively marginalised and often hard to reach. Thus many people are not 'out' and may not label, or indeed recognise, themselves as gay or lesbian.

Heteronormative refers to the assumption that heterosexuality is the norm, is natural and superior. Consequently anything else is rendered marginal or abnormal. In order to think usefully about sexuality, we first need to consider the ways in which gender, sex and sexuality are inextricably linked. **Gender** is often understood as a system which divides society into two categories – masculine and feminine – and is relational, in that one cannot understand what is meant by 'masculinity' without having some notion of what it is to be 'feminine' and vice versa. Gender is something which organises virtually every aspect of our lives without us thinking about it. Sometimes it is difficult for us to see it in operation precisely because it is everywhere: we declare our gender when we walk into public toilets or changing rooms, and it's stated on our birth certificate, driving licence and passport. Because of this, gender can seem natural. However, much research (for example Margaret Mead's (1930) observations in Papua New Guinea) highlights the fact that gender is not expressed in the same way across the globe or over time. We can therefore argue that gender is **socially constructed**; it is often conceptualised as the social and cultural expression of sex. The binary system, crucially for feminist thinkers, operates as a set of hierarchies, in that we tend to privilege the masculine over the feminine. It is therefore a system of power and not just about observable differences and similarities. Understanding that gender is socially constructed, however, means that there is potential for change: the system has not always operated in this way and need not continue to do so.

Links

More information on gender can be found in Chapter 8.

When gender is used in feminist analysis, it is defined in relation to **sex**. Feminist thinkers were the first to separate gender from sex. In our society, we recognise only two sexes – male and female – but it is important to state that this is not a universal approach to sex. Sex is often conceptualised as the natural, or biological, differences between men and women. This binary system may not be as stable as we might think: if you were to take a cross-sample of society and test people's chromosomes, hormones, genes, physiology and so on, very few would fit into the 'ideal' male or female categories. Many sociologists would argue that how we categorise sex is also influenced by culture.

Ideas about **sexuality** are intimately tied up with gender and sex. Heterosexuality is viewed, in contemporary western society, as the appropriate or proper expression of gender. A truly 'masculine' man is heterosexual. Within western society, it is argued, we privilege men; male sexuality is acceptable in itself. By contrast, appropriate female sexuality is passive and is synonymous with the reproductive role; motherhood is the only acceptable expression of female sexuality. Heterosexual sex (penetration of a vagina by a penis) in our society is deemed to be real sex or natural sex. This is reflected in our legal codes; it is only recently, for example, that UK law has broadened the definition of rape to include the penetration of an anus (so men can now be legitimate victims of rape). To date, women cannot be guilty of perpetrating rape, as only forced use of a penis constitutes rape; use of fists, bottles or other instruments only qualifies as sexual assault. Heterosexuality is a powerful conceptual tool in society. Adrienne Rich (1980) refers to 'compulsory heterosexuality'; this is the idea that heterosexuality is the default or obligatory sexuality and is something which further subjugates women. Like sex and gender, sexuality is often thought to be an innate or natural essence of our identity. Social constructionists would argue that in fact sexuality is also shaped through social process. Heterosexuality and homosexuality are relatively recent concepts (1902 and 1897 respectively), being inventions of the Victorian sexologists. Early 'scientists' understood 'the homosexual' as a woman trapped in a male body, and they labelled this person as an 'invert' – in other words, someone who was not correctly gendered. This stereotyped view of gay men as effeminate and lesbians as masculine persists in dominant discourses, reflecting the fact that we can only conceptualise society along heterosexual lines. The new labels created categories which regulated our behaviours and created, for the first time, sexual identities. Before the invention of the homosexual and the heterosexual, we had a variety of acts which didn't necessarily define the individual. Foucault (1979b) has argued, therefore, that sexuality is historically and culturally constructed, rather than biologically derived. Our current system also, crucially, positions some sexualities as 'good' and others as 'bad'; heterosexuality is desirable and 'normal', whereas same-sex attraction has historically been read as symptomatic of sickness or sinfulness. One could say that society has rigid, and arbitrary, rules about what we can do and with whom. Having given some thought to terminology, we will now move on to consider some of the ways in which sexuality bears an important relation to health and social care.

Domestic and other abuses

An important consequence of living in a heteronormative world is that LGBT people are framed by their sexuality, unlike heterosexuals. Despite the fact that someone who has a lesbian identity may never actually have sex with another woman, she is seen, by the rest of society, as being overtly sexual. More attention is paid to lesbian and gay lifestyles than to heterosexual lifestyles. This means that more focus is given to the potentially harmful effects of a 'homosexual' lifestyle. Issues related to heterosexual lifestyles tend be discussed purely in terms of gender (Wilton 2000). In relation to this, we know that married men fare better than single men in terms of general health, for example, whereas single women live longer than married heterosexual women.

Sylvia Walby describes patriarchy as 'a system of social structures and practices in which men dominate, oppress, and exploit women' (1989: 214).

Years of feminist research have revealed that heterosexuality can place women in great danger. Studies consistently show domestic violence to be a significant social problem, with UK figures suggesting that one in four women will experience this form of abuse at the hands of a man (Walby and Allen 2004). From feminist perspectives, male violence against women is persistent and severe, and both reflects and maintains their unequal positions within society. **Patriarchy**, it was argued, could be explained as a consistent pattern of ideological and structural practices that serve to justify and perpetuate men's oppression of women. Patriarchy (and heteronormativity) also, it is argued, establishes hierarchies not only between women and men, but also between men and men and between women and women (Connell 2002). It has been argued that, consciously or not, all women are aware of their vulnerability to becoming victims. Even in the absence of a specific threat, awareness of vulnerability governs many women's lives and choices. Kelly, for instance, suggested that 'whilst not all women live in constant fear, many of women's routine decisions and behaviour are almost automatic measures taken to protect themselves from potential violence' (1988: 32). Legislation in relation to violence against women has arguably reflected patriarchal heterosexuality. Rape in marriage, for example, was not recognised as a crime in Scotland until 1989 and the rest of the UK in 1991; the assumption was that a woman was the property of her husband, and so marriage gave conjugal rights which could be forcibly taken if not freely given. Across the globe, women's subordinate status means that their physical and mental well-being is constrained. Women and girls are forced or coerced into having their genitals mutilated, or herbs inserted into their vaginas to tighten them in order to increase their male partner's pleasure. Most forms of contraception also carry health risks for those women engaging in heterosex. Indeed, so prolific are the abuses inflicted upon women that many have suggested that gender-based violence should be classified as a hate crime.

It took many decades of campaigning on the part of feminists to get the abuse of heterosexual women recognised as a crime. However, there are suggestions that this produced a dominant discourse about domestic abuse which rendered other groups invisible. We are only just beginning to acknowledge, for example, that men can be victims of abuse by their female partners. We are also just beginning to address the fact that domestic abuse is a significant problem within LGBT communities (Ristock 2002), although given that this is a stigmatised and hidden population, we must be cautious about statistics. For some, much feminist analysis of violence based on male privilege and power may seem irrelevant or inapplicable to same-sex relationships; this is one reason why there has been relatively little research in this area to date. Yet, while neither partner in a lesbian relationship, for example, enjoys male privilege and power, lesbians have other identity/power positions whilst living in a society that promotes hierarchy, power differentials, inequality and violence. These are endemic to patriarchy and can occur in all relationships lived in this cultural milieu. Additionally, same-sex relationships are directly influenced by other societal power inequalities that impact on all citizens – including sexism and those based in class, racial, ethnic and economic inequalities – as well as on interpersonal differences in power. Evidence points to the fact, however, that those services which provide help and support for victims of domestic violence do not have the awareness, training and provisions to cope with male victims or instances of same-sex abuse.

Another harm that occurs as a direct result of sexual orientation (either real or perceived) is anti-gay hate crime. Recent reports in Scotland have indicated a rise in homophobic hate crime, although it is difficult to assess whether this reflects an actual rise in offences or changes in reporting (Archibald 2011). What is clear is that it is a significant problem and one which can have additional impacts depending on ethnicity, disability and gender.

Drug and alcohol abuse

Use and misuse of tobacco, alcohol and other drugs appears to be higher among LGBT people (Drabble et al. 2005; Hughes and Jacobson 2003). One explanation may be related to the stress linked to living with prejudice and homophobia. Another reason may be that it is difficult for gay men and lesbians to enjoy taking part in the leisure activities that many heterosexuals take for granted. Recent studies, for example, have pointed to the difficulties and anxieties related to a gay man or lesbian becoming part of a (unquestionably heterosexual) sports team, with individuals being reliant on the goodwill and tolerance of heterosexual team members. As a result, in many towns and cities, gay areas have developed which offer a degree of safety and security. Such gay spaces tend to be heavily commercialised and revolve around pubs, bars and clubs, where it becomes difficult to avoid alcohol. This might also be an issue related to recruitment. The LGBT population, despite recent social and legal shifts, is stigmatised and thus is a relatively marginalised and hidden group. Many studies into LGBT lifestyles, therefore, recruit from 'gay villages'; thus a study into alcohol consumption is likely to encounter some heavy drinkers if the sample is taken largely from bars and clubs.

Health

Mental health

For decades homosexuality itself was considered a mental illness. Despite the fact that research findings have effectively collapsed any evidence for this belief, a significant number of psychiatrists and clinicians still maintain that homosexuality is an illness *per se*, or symptomatic of mental ill health. Research findings do suggest that LGBT men and women have a higher instance of mental health problems than the wider population (King and McKeowan 2003) – anxiety, depression, self-harm and suicidal behaviour being the main expressions of this ill health. Arguably it is homophobia, rather than being gay, which is the cause of such anxiety – with rejection, discrimination, exclusion and victimisation being identified as primary reasons for the ill health (Musingarimi 2008). A lack of appropriate social spaces, as discussed above, has also been cited as an additional source of stress for young LGBT people, particularly in rural areas. Studies into sexuality and mental health have shown consistently that the majority of those interviewed do not have faith in current health care providers and state they would prefer to see an LGBT-specific counsellor (Chakraborty et al. 2011).

Questions

Should LGBT people have separate provisions for health and social care? What might be the benefits of this and what might be negative consequences? What might an alternative be?

Breast and other cancers

One health issue which appears to be a particular problem in the lesbian community is breast cancer (Breast Cancer Care 2011). 'Over 1 in 12 lesbian and bisexual women aged between 50 [and] 79 have been diagnosed with breast cancer, compared with 1 in 20 of women in general' (Hunt and Fish 2008). It is important, however, to unpick the problem here. Lesbians are not at higher risk of breast cancer because they are lesbians. Rather, it is because there are certain characteristics associated with lesbian communities and lifestyles which place lesbian women at greater risk. These include childlessness (thus, crucially, not breast feeding), obesity and excess consumption of alcohol. Figures are extrapolated from small-scale studies, and, as discussed above, populations may well be drawn mainly from bars and clubs, given the relatively 'hard-to-reach' nature of the population. We do not know how many lesbians have breast cancer as the NHS does not routinely make a note of sexual identity. Neither do we know how many lesbians have children. Much research (e.g. Hunt et al. 2007) has found that lesbians continue to have negative experiences in health services despite anti-discriminatory legislation; thus there is a very real chance that lesbians suffering ill health do not seek medical advice or, if they do, do not wish to add to the stress by coming out (Fish 2010).

There is also a suggestion that lesbians are falling off the radar when it comes to cervical cancer. Many lesbians either believe, or have been told by medical practitioners, that they do not need to have smear tests. Certainly, it would appear that women who have never had sex with a man are at less risk of developing cervical cancer. First, however, many lesbians have had sex with men, either before they came out or after (despite neat labels, many people do not conform to rigid boundaries of 'gay' or 'straight'). New evidence also suggests that human papillomavirus (HPV), a cause of cervical cancer passed by sexual contact, can be transmitted by female-to-female sexual contact. In addition, smoking is a risk, and it is thought that lesbians are more likely to smoke or have smoked than heterosexual women.

STDs, HIV and AIDS

Certain groups in society are particularly at risk of contracting sexually transmitted diseases (STDs). Often, these groups are at risk because of misleading dominant discourses. For example, figures suggest that STDs and HIV are rising among older people. ACE (2002) has shown that more than 10 per cent of those men who are HIV positive are over 50. Partly, this is because they are less likely to use condoms as they do not perceive themselves to be at risk. In addition, post-menopausal women have thinner vaginal tissue and less natural lubrication which means their skin is more likely to tear. This is particularly worrying given that we know older people take longer to access services than younger people.

Much writing and research into gay sexuality and health has been concerned with *HIV/AIDS*. Similarly, much writing on HIV and AIDS has focused on gay men – thus, in part, perpetuating the myth that this is an issue that pertains only to the gay community. Certainly, many of the earliest cases involved young gay men and, as a result, many assumed that it was a disease which affected the gay community only. Some doctors called it gay-related immune deficiency (GRID) and the tabloid press in Britain, for example, referred to it as the 'gay plague'. Given that this was a time of more general homophobia, this assump-

HIV stands for human immunodeficiency virus, a retrovirus which infects and destroys the immune system; thus someone with HIV has reduced protection against infections and cancer. The disease can be transmitted in a variety of ways but the greatest risk is when semen is deposited in an anus or a vagina.

AIDS, or acquired immune deficiency syndrome, refers to the infection(s) which attack someone with an immune system weakened by HIV. Recent drug treatments used in the west have meant that HIV is now seen as a chronic rather than an acute condition.

tion was generally accepted, and led to the stigmatisation of the disease; this is another example of how 'homosexuality', the subject of many powerful sanctions, is contaminating by association (Plummer 1981). As Watney (2000) argued, the ongoing misinformation that HIV transmission is related to sexual orientation, rather than sexual behaviour, places the heterosexual community at risk. World Health Organisation (WHO) studies consistently show that, globally, HIV is spreading as a result of unprotected heterosex. Other groups who have recently been identified as at risk include asylum seekers and prisoners. Society's conceptualisation of 'real' sex as penile penetration and anything else as 'not real sex' has placed other groups at risk. For example, sex between women carries a low risk of transmitting HIV but it is not always safe.

Questions

Collect from the internet the annual reports of as many health and social care service providers as you can. Do they make reference to heterosexual, lesbian, gay or bisexual service users? What are the possible consequences for your own profession?

Ageing

Ageing in general is increasingly becoming an issue of importance, partly because we are an ageing population. In addition, with the recent coalition government in the UK, pressures on **older** people have increased and are likely to continue to do so. We know that older people are disadvantaged in the labour market, partly because they are perceived as being unable to learn new skills. Older people are more likely to live in poverty. It is also important to remember that older people are not a heterogeneous group with similar needs; they are a diverse group reflecting different social divisions. In other words, structural inequalities persist into old age. So, for example, issues of gender and class impact in older age: older women are more likely than older men to live in poverty, and older working-class people are more likely to live in poverty than older middle-class people. In a youth-oriented society, older people become marginalised and invisible. Recent stories about the representation of older women on television show how this is something which arguably impacts on women especially, where older women are deemed to be less attractive and less acceptable than older men (Cochrane 2011). Stereotypes about older people abound in our society. We tend to perceive older people as vulnerable, incapable and asexual (Gott 2005). These dominant discourses about sexuality in later life can have serious consequences for older people's quality of life. Positioning sexuality in later life as unnatural, shameful or disgusting can have the effect of rendering it invisible; this, of course, not only affects older people's sense of self, but also excludes them from the services and resources available to them.

There is not always agreement about what constitutes *older* in research. For some this includes those individuals who are 65 and above. For others, including many who research into older LGBT people, the term refers to 50 plus. Until recently, little effort had been made to explore the lives of older lesbians and gay men, and the area has remained relatively unexplored in health and social care work. There is, however, a small but growing body of research which allows us to look at the LGBT experience of growing older in relation to the heterosexual experience. Older LGBT individuals are, for instance, more likely to live alone, to age as a single person and not to have children. This means that compared to their heterosexual counterparts, many lack key social support networks. Research has shown that many younger LGBT people rely on friendships forged in the LGBT community, these friendships forming 'families of choice'. Such communities, however, are increasingly commercialised and youth oriented, meaning that older LGBT people may not be welcome. They are also, arguably, more in need therefore of formal services. Although the twenty-first century marks, in many ways, an unprecedented age of positive legislative and social change for gay men and lesbians (e.g. the Civil Partnership Act 2004; the Equality Act (Sexual Orientation) Regulations 2007), it is important to acknowledge that many older lesbians and gay men have lived through less liberal times. They will have experienced not only informal discrimination but also formal discrimination – and this will impact on their use and experience of health services. The defection of Burgess and Maclean in 1951, for example, directly and indirectly impacted on the lives of many gay men and lesbians. The central scandal was the fact that these were two upper-class English men defecting to the Soviet Union – but the revelation that they were gay was used to cement the outrage, and perhaps even to explain it (Vargo 2002: 83). The combined fear of communism and homosexuality was a pervasive one in the 1950s. In England and Wales, the arrest of gay men rose by 50 per cent between 1950 and 1955 – in part as a result of deliberate 'sting' operations, with homosexuality frequently being linked to general subversiveness and threats to the nation (2002: 103). Awareness of the fact that a homosexual identity was a stigmatised one, as far as much of society was concerned, may well have impacted on the ability of lesbians and gay men to access services. Older lesbians, gay men and bisexuals are five times less likely to access services for older people than is the older population in general, because they fear discrimination, homophobia and ignorance and believe that they will have to hide their sexuality. Older lesbians and gay men experience an unfortunate paradox. They live in a time of increasing sexuality, and at a time when arguably it is easier to be gay; yet they also live in a society where they are told older sexuality is distasteful. In addition, as older members of the LGBT community – a commercialised, youth-oriented population – many older LGBT people feel marginalised. This sense of isolation, marginalisation and invisibility impacts on many aspects of older LGBT lives.

Domestic abuse

As we have already seen, domestic abuse among LGBT people is a significant problem. Older same-sex couples suffer both direct and indirect discrimination in relation to this (ACE 2002a). If the image of the older lesbian and gay man as depressed, isolated, desperate, and sexless is prevalent (Ginn and Arber 1995), if risks are associated with an 'out' identity in certain circumstances, and if there is little sense of support from LGBT communities – for example, if you feel your values are derided or you are just 'too old' to enjoy yourself – this may mean that there are few safe spaces in which to discuss same-sex domestic violence. The views of older lesbians and gay men as isolated, desperate and perhaps vulnerable may also render particularly invisible the potential perpetrators of domestic violence.

Elder abuse

Societal reluctance to acknowledge that older people engage in sexual activities results in the invisibility of their relationships. This means that when domestic violence happens in relationships involving older people, it tends to fall under the umbrella term 'elder abuse' (O'Keefe et al. 2007). This is especially so for LGBT elders who are more likely to keep their sexuality hidden.

Bereavement

The death of a loved one is a difficult time for anyone. Being an older LGBT person at such a time can present additional anxieties (Age UK 2010). Many of the issues discussed previously about 'coming out' apply here, as experiencing a bereavement may require constant 'coming out'. This may be especially problematic for many, especially older, LGBT individuals who are less comfortable in disclosing their sexuality to service providers. Despite recent formal recognition of same-sex partnerships, many LGBT people suffer lack of recognition of their relationships by families and, in some cases, agencies. Again, many have felt that gay-specific counselling would be desirable.

Care and the older LGBT person

For many of us, 'home' represents a sanctuary, a safe place to retreat, somewhere we can 'be ourselves'. Home can also be seen as an important site for constructing our identity, so that it becomes not just a space but also somewhere with social meaning. As we have already seen, many LGBT people experience a constrained sense of self in the public sphere, so the home may well have additional resonance. Asking for and accepting help in the home may therefore be especially hard for older LGBT people. Research has highlighted that older LGBT people receiving care in the home experience many difficulties (Pugh 2005). Many older gay men and lesbians have expressed concern that they would be subject to a disapproving or policing 'gaze', and consequently have had to de-gay or de-dyke their flat before a visit, for example by hiding 'incriminating' CDs. Other studies have begun to look into the issue of residential care homes. Heaphy et al. (2004) found that many lesbians and gay men feared getting older and having to enter care homes because they believed their sexuality would not be understood. There is evidence, for example, that many LGBT couples in care homes find their relationships are not recognised. As a result, LGBT-specific care is something desired by many older LGBT individuals. Such examples point to the fact that perhaps generic providers for older people need to make specific efforts to ensure that older lesbians, gay men and bisexuals feel included; that they feel able to access services on their own terms, without fear of discrimination; and that the information and services they receive are relevant and responsive to their circumstances and needs.

Questions

Identify and discuss in what ways might older LGBT people suffer from discrimination?

Conclusion

Clearly, the relationship between sexual orientation and health is a complicated one – and an important one. The historical stigmatising of LGBT sexualities, and the promotion of heterosexuality, have served to regulate and police intimate lives. This has led to problematic health and social care provision for many lesbian and gay service users. LGBT service users do not demand special treatment; rather, they have particular needs which require to be dealt with in appropriate ways. By thinking critically, challenging notions of 'normality' and 'acceptability' and engaging in reflective practice, you should have the skills to apply good practice to a variety of situations.

Summary points

- All sexual identities are socially constructed and ideas and ways of being sexual are very much tied into the culture and norms of a society. There is, therefore, no 'natural' sexuality.
- When discussing sexuality it is important to remember that all people possess a sexuality.
- Western society tends to be heteronormative, where there is both a direct and indirect assumption that everyone is heterosexual and that a particular social construct of sexuality is correct and superior to other forms of sexuality.
- LGBT people can encounter problems with health and social services that are geared for the needs of heterosexual people.
- Older LGBT people may find that that they may lack informal sources of social support.
- There are higher rates of mental distress, and alcohol and substance use, in the LGBT community and these higher rates can be attributed to the psychosocial stresses of discrimination and prejudice.

Case study

Breaking up is never easy and for Francesca the end of her two-year relationship with Claire was hitting her hard. She had thought all was going well. Last summer had been wonderful, touring round various English music festivals before a week's holiday clubbing in Spain. They had even talked about making that next big step and perhaps moving in together. In fact, they had gone as far as looking at flats to rent. That had been mostly fun, but also annoying, especially when landlords thought

(Continued)

(Continued)

she and Claire had misread the advert for the flat and not picked up it was only a single-bedroom property, and therefore not suitable for two girls to share. In fact, one landlord had been distinctly uneasy all the way through their visit and texted them shortly afterwards to say that someone else had just signed the lease for the flat and was very emphatic that they should now look elsewhere.

Then last August it all went wrong. Claire had been acting a little more distant than normal for a few weeks and then suddenly in a fit of tears announced there was someone else that she had met and she had to break the relationship off. Francesca found herself becoming increasingly depressed. All the day-to-day tasks became too difficult and she began to stay in bed for as much of the day as she could. Then, last month there had been a terrible run-in with Claire. Francesca saw her in the local shopping mall. It was strange to see her and she felt this powerful urge to talk to Claire as she hadn't seen her for a while. She only intended to say hello, but instead found herself breaking down in tears and trying to give Claire a hug. What had hurt most was Claire pushing her away. 'Not in public!' Claire had said under her breath as she walked away.

A few weeks ago she had decided to visit the local surgery to seek help for what she had decided was the depression she was experiencing. It was not always possible to see the same doctor each time and this introduced a problem for her, in that she had to come out when she summarised what had been happening to her. Francesca remembered what it was like to come out the first time. It was not the actual moment of coming out that had been painful or stressful. It was actually a complete relief, and she experienced a sense of elation on telling her parents when she was in her mid-teens. What was really problematic was the build-up, the tension of rehearsing what she was going to say and her mind running through all the possible scenarios of what could happen: acceptance, rejection or denial. So, every time she visits the local surgery for an appointment she remembers those emotions and tensions, wondering how she is going to be received by the doctor when she politely corrected their assumption that it was a woman not a man who had left her.

Questions

Before discussing the more health-specific questions below, discuss the extent of prejudice and discrimination encountered by LGBT people in contemporary society. In what ways do you think this particular case study of Francesca exemplifies any common experiences of LGBT people?

Why may the situation of having to come out every time Francesca visits the local doctors be difficult for her?

In what ways might a specific LGBT health-service be of benefit for Francesca and other LGBT people?

Taking your studies further

This chapter will have helped you understand many of the key terms, concepts, theories and debates relating to sexuality and health. Listed below are journal articles, books and a website that will provide deeper and more detailed discussions of the points raised in this chapter. You will also find what is available on the companion website. This feature offers you downloads of relevant material, plus links to useful websites in addition to podcasts and other features.

Recommended reading

Fish, J. (2006) *Heterosexism in Health and Social Care*. Basingstoke: Palgrave.
Hawkes, G. (2002) *A Sociology of Sex and Sexuality*. Buckingham: Open University Press.
Richardson, D. (2000) *Rethinking Sexuality*. London: Sage.

On the companion website

Gilbert, E., Ussher, J.M. and Hawkins, Y. (2009) 'Accounts of disruptions to sexuality following cancer: the perspective of informal carers who are partners of a person with cancer', *Health*, 13(5): 523–41.

11

Sociology of the body: chronic illness and disability

Main points

- The body is not simply a biological entity only understood by the natural sciences.
- Perceptions of the body, what we do with our bodies and how the body is regulated are all influenced by society.
- Morality is attached to the presentation of the body in contemporary society, with thin bodies perceived as 'good' and overweight bodies perceived as 'bad'.
- Chronic illness leads to 'biographical disruption', where the 'taken-for-granted' aspects of life and identity are thrown into question.
- The medical model of disability locates the causes of disability in the individual body.
- The social model of disability sees the causes of disability as a form of social oppression and discrimination.

Key concepts

The sociology of the body   embodiment   the civilised body   identity   chronic illness   normality   stigma   biographical disruption.

Introduction

The sociology of the body addresses how we use our bodies, considers how we engage with them and, fundamentally, seeks to understand the nature of the physical body. The key point to bear in mind is that the body is both 'natural' and the product of its social environment.

This chapter concentrates on the *sociology of the body* and what it can contribute to our understanding of health and illness. While there will be a strong emphasis on a theoretical approach to the human body, there will be equal coverage of the significance of embodiment through an examination of the impact of living with chronic illness and disability.

Key issues in the study of the body

Until relatively recently sociologists shied away from theorising and researching the human body. The reasons for the reluctance is twofold. First, there is an unwillingness to be caught up in biological and determinist explanations of human behaviour. Sociologists have, for example, chosen to study gender rather than sex differences. Sex is often used to defend inequalities between women and men; the concept of gender, on the other hand, removes the problem of the bodily differences and draws our attention to the social construction of 'male' and 'female' in terms of the values, beliefs and expectations placed on biological women and men.

The second explanation for the general reluctance to embrace the body stems from the historical and cultural origins of the discipline itself. As the opening chapter illustrated, the founding fathers of sociology were primarily concerned to explain the social changes brought about by urbanisation and industrialisation. Early sociological texts indicate a preoccupation with topics such as urbanisation, religion, paid work and the role of the state. Physical differences between people mattered less than inequalities of class and status. Differences such as those between women and men and between adults and children were seen as belonging to the 'natural' world, and were unchangeable and fixed. In recent times, however, sociology has developed to include topics such as sex and gender, disability, and the physical and biological aspects of our lives. In addition to changes within the discipline of sociology, a number of social and cultural shifts have taken place which have resulted in a renewed interest in the human body. The body has ceased to be the preserve of the medical and scientific world and has become a major concern for sociologists. Table 11.1 illustrates the main trends and developments.

Bodies are central to everything that we do and yet this centrality seems to have resulted in attitudes that very much take the body for granted; the body is so obvious it is hardly worth comment.

> If one thing is certain, it is that we all have a body. Everything that we do we do with our bodies – when we think, speak, listen, eat, sleep, walk, relax, work and play we 'use' our bodies. Every aspect of our lives is therefore embodied. Sometimes we may be more aware of our bodies than others but from the moment we wake, we are to a greater or lesser extent, consciously or sub-consciously relying on our bodies. (Nettleton and Watson 1998: 1)

We have highlighted the significance of the body as a subject for students of sociology by emphasising the central role played by our physical selves in all that we do. Sociologists also seek to 'see' the body in more than purely physical and biological terms, drawing

TABLE 11.1   Bringing the body to the fore

Body politics: Recognition that the physical body has a social and political status such that a different body (whether that is female as opposed to male, or a body with a disability) helps determine an individual's life chances. The feminist movement and the disability movement have played a central role in attempting to ensure that people have power over their own bodies

Demographic changes: An increasingly ageing population draws attention to the physical changes arising from the ageing process and the consequences of living with an ageing body

The prevalence of chronic illnesses: There has been a significant change in what Nettleton and Watson refer to as 'the disease burden'. Infectious diseases have now been replaced by chronic and degenerative conditions, many of which raise important questions about how a physically changed body impacts on our sense of identity and how people live with pain and discomfort

Consumerism: An increased emphasis on the appearance and health of the body. People are concerned about maintaining their bodies in good condition and purchasing goods to help them do so. In this context, 'good' suggests youthful, slim and active

Technological changes: Physical limitations of the body can be overcome, appearance changed, organs and limbs repaired and replaced. It becomes increasingly difficult to distinguish between the 'natural' body and the 'technological' body

The body as an expression of our identity: The body becomes a means to express an identity. Diet, exercise and lifestyles can be portrayed as 'moral' or 'immoral' and 'irresponsible'

Source: adapted from Nettleton and Watson (1998: 4)

our attention to the two key 'social' aspects of the body. The first of these is the impact of environmental, cultural, social and political influences on the body, while the second is the knowledge that the body is shaped by certain dominant discourses such as medicine. Chapter 6 examines inequalities in health and presents evidence that indicates a relationship between social class and patterns of morbidity and mortality. Social class can be used as an indicator of the types of illnesses people experience, as well as their life expectancy. Historical evidence reveals that body shape and stature are influenced by environmental factors. Birke (1992: 74–5) suggests an almost circular process where (a) biology, (b) environment and (c) the outcome all interact to transform one another. In her example, genetic inheritance interacts with nutrition to produce the final height of a child. Importantly, however, the final height of the child then influences the genes he or she passes on, which then interact with the environment – and so the process goes on. The second sense in which sociologists understand the body is in terms of our knowledge of the social construction of the physical. There is an inherent danger in understanding the body as only a social construction as this may impede the study of the body as a real and physical entity. Nettleton and Watson (1998: 2) point to a tendency for the sociology of the body to suffer from

> Embodiment refers to the experience of living through and with the physical body. Our experiences are essentially embodied. For example, we experience pleasure and pain through the body. Feelings of happiness and sadness are as physical as they are emotional.

theoreticism, where there is little or no reference to the empirical evidence about the lived experience of **embodiment**. This chapter will overcome this with a detailed consideration of the embodied experience of living with chronic illness.

Questions

Can you identify how and when you are most aware of your body?

The civilised body: a controlled body and a 'clean' body

This section seeks to explore concepts of privacy and of the civilised, clean body. Views on what is appropriate bodily behaviour and who has access to our bodies have a key bearing on the delivery of health care as well as on our experience of illness. The physical examination of the body is central to the practice of medicine: it is this that allows practitioners to investigate whether or not the body is functioning normally. Doctors, nurses, physiotherapists, opticians and dentists are all required to touch the body, sometimes in intimate ways. Illness often entails losing some control over bodily functions. Migraine, for example, can cause uncontrollable vomiting, and food poisoning can lead to uncontrollable diarrhoea. Physical incapacity can necessitate the use of a commode, thus requiring someone to share what is not only an intimate act but also one that has overtones of being unclean. How we negotiate access to other bodies and how we think of our own are, therefore, key issues for the sociology of health.

As Nettleton and Watson (1998) have stated, we all have bodies and everything that we do, we do through them. All bodies have the same basic needs in terms of food, water and sleep. We must all remove waste from our bodies in the form of urine and faeces. Whether through illness or over-indulgence, our bodies vomit and we have little control over this. All bodies have the same basic components but differ in size, shape and colour. These are all fundamental human experiences and activities and yet, particularly in contemporary western societies, the body and its functions are regarded with a degree of shame and embarrassment.

To explore these concepts in more depth we will examine the work of Norbert Elias, first published in 1939, in relation to manners and the development of 'civilised' society. Elias' (1982) historical account of the **civilised body** examines the development of preferred ways of behaving and of control over the physical functions of the body. Regulation of the body came to be associated with higher social status and

> The concept of the civilised body was developed by Norbert Elias. The term is used to denote a historical and cultural shift whereby the body is subject to increasing restraints that appear to limit the 'natural' body. The development of rules around eating manners is an example of how the body has become 'civilised'.

refinement. Nettleton (1995: 116–17) argues that the civilising of the body involves three progressive elements:

- *Socialisation.* People learn to conceal the natural functions of the body. We come to 'know' that certain functions such as defecating or vomiting are essentially private and potentially distasteful to others.
- *Rationalisation.* We prize our ability to control our emotions. Anger may be felt but only expressed in an acceptable way.
- *Individualisation.* Individual bodies are seen as separate from others. We demand a degree of personal 'social space' and privacy.

The development of ideas about the civilised body also demonstrates a concern to distinguish between human and bestial behaviour (Hawkes 1996: 20), and accords with Enlightenment notions about the higher self being associated with the mind and the base self with the body.

The work of Elias helps us to understand why people find intimate medical examination potentially embarrassing and why an inability to control the basic functions of the body can lead to stigmatisation. Control over our most basic bodily functions is something we require even in young children. As Nettleton suggests above, **socialisation** into the norms of any society entails learning that certain types of behaviour are private and potentially shameful when performed inappropriately. Mayall (1996) notes that much of the socialisation process is about teaching children to control their bodies and to be civilised. Young children are taught appropriate table manners, toilet trained, and taught the necessity of sitting still in preparation for schooling. Even at an early age, then, the importance of bodily control is underlined. Equally, the essentially private nature of the naked body and of sex is an implicit part of the concept of the civilised body. In her study of sex and sexuality, Hawkes (1996) argues that in medieval times nudity was not a source of shame and that sexual matters were discussed without any sense of embarrassment. She notes, too, that accompanying 'couples to the marital bed and celebration of the consummation were customs that persisted well into the seventeenth century' (1996: 22). After that period both nudity and sexual matters were moved 'behind the scenes', appropriate only in private (1996: 23).

Questions

Identify examples of when the body is subject to regulation and control, in both medical and non-medical settings.

How then do health practitioners deal with the potential discomfort that arises from physically intimate examinations? According to Lawler (1991), nursing staff have adopted a number of strategies to cope with potential embarrassment and shame, both on their part and on the part of the patient. A number of rules appear to govern such encounters. The first is that patients should comply with requests for examinations because they are dependent on nursing staff. Here it is helpful to refer back to Parsons' model of the sick role because it too justifies access to the patient's body on the grounds of expertise on the part of the practitioner. In addition, the practitioner's own professional code of conduct is, arguably, meant to protect the patient from potential abuse and exploitation. By maintaining a degree of professional distance, the situation may be depersonalised. Lawler (1991) also argues that patients themselves are expected to maintain a degree of modesty, while the nurse attempts to protect the patient's privacy.

Maintaining personal hygiene when ill often requires assistance with bathing, but it is common for nursing staff to allow patients the option of cleaning their own private parts. It is ironic that while much of modern health care is premised on practices such as holistic care, being attended to by a named carer, and attempts generally to break down the barriers between patients and staff, it seems that there are some circumstances when a professional and distanced stance is appreciated by both parties.

Questions

What are your experiences either as a patient being examined or as a practitioner undertaking an examination of a patient?

Chapter 3 dealt with the subject of the new public health movement, emphasising the extent to which governments are concerned with controlling individual bodies as well as the social body. Behind these developments lies the fear that without regulation bodies would be out of control. Disease and contamination of the body have been central concerns of the public health movement. Lupton (1994), for example, writes of the economic and political implications of disease in terms of absence from work.

Our discussion of **medicalisation** illustrated the way in which it is not just unhealthy bodies that come under the scrutiny of the medical profession; there is an important sense in which we are all judged to be 'at risk'. The issues of cleanliness and hygiene are important illustrations of this trend, because there is considerable emphasis on preserving health through cleanliness. Lupton provides an interesting historical account of just how our concept of cleanliness has changed over time:

Consider the following examples of how, at varying periods in time, the body was kept clean and safe from infection and make a note of your personal reactions to them:

- Being 'clean' meant that those areas of the body seen by others were free of dirt.
- Washing was 'dry' in the sense that a cloth was used to rub the face and hands.
- Bathing was not an option; immersing the body in water was thought to weaken it as the liquid might invade the body.
- Once bathing became an accepted practice, cold bathing was preferred as it was thought to toughen and invigorate the body.
- The use of 'cosmetics' such as perfume to scent the body was seen as frivolous. (1994: 33–4)

These examples of hygienic practices are in marked contrast to the values prevalent in most western societies. Personal hygiene is both desirable and, it might be argued, possible with the provision of indoor plumbing. We all sweat as a means of cooling the body down, yet the smell of sweat is shunned. Instead, we attempt either to prevent our bodies sweating (through the use of an anti-perspirant) or to mask the smell if the body does sweat (through the use of deodorant). Media images reinforce the message that bodies that are clean and perfumed are desirable bodies.

The desire for cleanliness extends beyond our bodies to our homes. The nineteenth-century push to improve the health of the nation focused primarily on instructing mothers in childcare practices and, significantly, in domestic hygiene. According to Hawkes, 'a good mother kept a clean home. Whiter whites were a sign of superiority' (1996: 97). The multitude of products that claim to be anti-bacterial or effective in combating the invisible threat of germs bears testimony to our fear of dirt and the negative moral connotations that attach to a lack of hygiene. Lupton (1994) argues that modern standards and beliefs about cleanliness are characterised by a fear of invisible germs and viruses. She comments in particular on a near obsession with the cleanliness of toilets and the desire to have a visible indication of cleanliness 'displayed by a bright blue chemical being released every time the lavatory is flushed' (1994: 35).

Among commentators on the sociology of the body, it appears to be accepted that we as a population are obsessed with hygiene and cleanliness. There is some evidence to suggest that this view is simplistic. Recent outbreaks of salmonella and the spread of hospital-acquired infections have revealed hygiene practices that are far from perfect. Professor Hugh Pennington of the Bacteriology Department of Aberdeen University has been particularly critical of poor hygiene practices around the home. Among his main concerns is the use of washing-up bowls and reusable dishcloths.

> Professor Pennington said that placing chopping boards and knives teeming with germs together with plates and glasses in a plastic bowl created the ideal environment for the spread of bugs.
>
> The experts said disposable paper cloths should be used instead of tea towels that could easily spread infection.
>
> They also recommended using 'good old fashioned bleach' in the kitchen rather than newer anti-bacterial products that were only vaguely effective. (BBC News 2000)

The beginning of 2002 heralded a major health crisis for hospitals in Scotland, as hospital-acquired infections in general and the MRSA bug in particular led to the closure of the Victoria Infirmary, Glasgow, to all new admissions. Once again, the problem appeared to be poor hygiene practices. Hugh Pennington commented that infection control was being severely compromised by lack of basic hygiene practices, such as doctors and nurses failing to wash their hands between treating patients.

The discussion above has highlighted the ways in which bodily functions and intimate access to the body can present barriers in the caring relationship. It has been suggested that shame and embarrassment about the body are not natural but are socially cultivated, and the work of Elias has provided an insight into the development of concepts of the 'civilised body'. Our discussion now takes us on to images and perceptions of the 'perfect' body.

The sculptured body: creating perfection

Images of bodily perfection, most often images of women, are powerful but never static. Whether it is the voluptuous bust, tiny waist and rounded bottom of the nineteenth century, the androgynous figure of the 1920s, the curves of Marilyn Monroe, or the taut, lean and muscular body of Madonna, images of how female bodies should look are powerful reminders of the extent to which people have aspired to the perfect body. The purpose of this discussion is to examine how and why people have tried to attain that 'good' body. A later discussion of disability and chronic illness will pose equally powerful questions about what happens when bodies are not and cannot be made perfect.

Diet is perhaps the most obvious way in which we control the size and shape of the body. As Lupton comments: 'skin tone, weight, strength of bones, condition of hair and nails are all commonly said to be directly affected by diet' (1994: 40). An increasingly important aspect of diet is the desire to limit the intake of food. Bordo (1990: 83) argues that types of fasting have been common throughout history, and are usually characterised by control over the body's appetites or by a religious desire to purify the flesh. However, she notes a significant shift during the late Victorian era, when 'for the first time in the West, those who could afford to eat well began systematically to deny themselves food in the pursuit of an aesthetic ideal' (1990: 83). So began what Bordo has described as the tyranny of slenderness.

In common with others, Bordo argues that body size is underpinned by a code of morality. The possession of a slender body suggests that the individual is in control of their body and their life. To achieve the 'perfect' body requires considerable time, effort and determination. Geri Halliwell recently achieved what she described as her ideal body – a body very much thinner than her previous form, and made possible only with a strict diet and considerable time in the gym. In contrast, Helen Fielding's heroine, Bridget Jones, overeats, smokes and drinks in response to what she sees as an unfulfilled life. Renée Zellweger, the actress who played Bridget Jones in the two films so far, soon shed the extra two stone put on for her role, reverting to her original size 6 in contrast to the 12 of the heroine. It is interesting to note that almost half of all women in Britain take a dress size 16 or over. Benson suggests that the body is increasingly seen as an indicator of a person's moral character.

> The bad body is fat, slack, uncared for; it demonstrates a lazy and undisciplined 'self'. The good body is sleek, thin and toned. To have such a body is to project to those around you – as well as to yourself – that you are morally as well as physically 'in shape'. (1997: 123)

In the same vein, a muscular body has become what Bordo describes as a 'cultural icon':

> The firm, developed body has become a symbol of correct *attitude;* it means that one 'cares' about oneself and how one appears to others, suggesting willpower, energy, control over infantile impulses, the ability to 'make something' of oneself. (1990: 94–5)

Links

The desire (and ability) to control and discipline the body is seen as a characteristic of postmodern society, discussed in Chapters 1 and 4.

Themes of controlling the body through willpower and discipline are frequent in accounts of people with eating disorders – a term which covers a range of behaviours from systematically starving the body, to overeating, and finally to eating and purging the body through vomiting or the use of laxatives. Although there is not the space here for a detailed discussion of eating disorders, a number of points can be made about the denial of food and the desire to assert power and autonomy. Benson (1997) describes the refusal to eat as 'an inescapably political act' because it is most often associated with asserting control and/or registering a protest. The use of hunger strikes as a political protest is common (Yuill 2007) and, at the other end of the spectrum, a child's refusal to eat is a clear sign of defying parental authority. It has been suggested, therefore, that eating disorders such as anorexia may be a way of exercising power over the body, food intake being perhaps the only area of choice open to a person. Bordo (1990) examines limiting food intake in the context of a general cultural fear of 'fat' as an indicator of losing control over the body. In this sense, bodies have to be not only slender but contained, in the sense of minimising bulges and flab (1990: 88–9):

> Areas that are soft, loose, or 'wiggly' are unacceptable, even on extremely thin bodies. Cellulite management, like liposuction, has nothing to do with weight loss, and everything to do with the quest for firm bodily margins. (1990: 90)

We have, thus far, concentrated principally on diet as a way of regulating the size and shape of the body, as well as being an indicator of a personal morality: thin bodies represent controlled and cared-for bodies; fat bodies suggest some sort of moral failing. There are, however, other ways in which the body can be managed and sculptured. Surgical intervention, most commonly in the form of cosmetic surgery to alter appearance, is an obvious example. Parts of the body can be enlarged or changed in appearance, as in the practice of breast enhancement. Far more radical, however, is the case of gender realignment, or sex change. Complex surgical procedures, combined with the use of hormones and counselling, can help a person complete the transition from male to female or vice versa. The body, and in particular the genitalia, are the most obvious indicators of our sex.

Paul Hewitt writes movingly of his own experiences as a female-to-male transsexual: 'It is not that I *want* to be male. I *am* male, and, like all transsexuals, I experience an overwhelming urge to bring the gender of my body into line with the gender of my mind' (Hewitt and Warren 1997: 75). Changing his outward appearance allows Hewitt to pass as a man. Male dress, haircuts and clothes all play an important part in signalling to others that he is male, but more fundamental changes are needed: the possession of an artificial penis and the removal of both breasts. This alone should be evidence that the body is the ultimate means of displaying who we are to others.

Questions

Which new technologies have made us rethink our understanding of our bodies?

The 'failed' body: ill health and disease

We now continue these themes, but move on to an examination of the ways in which disability and chronic illness transform the body and personal identity.

Increasingly, most heavyweight newspapers carry a regular column written by someone with some form of chronic illness, providing insights into their life and the challenges that chronic illness brings. Also, with the widening use of the internet, people with chronic illnesses set up and write their own blogs. These discuss various aspects of living with a variety of illnesses (Hardey 2002; Seale 2005). Many blogs or columns are written from an 'open secret' position, in that both writer and reader know that at some point the author may well die. Over the years we have seen columns and books dealing with, for example, HIV/ AIDS (Oscar Moore with *PWA* – people with AIDS) and breast cancer (Ruth Picardie with *Before I Say Goodbye*). These glimpses into the life of someone with a long-term, probably fatal condition are deeply moving, and readers feel a strong sense of attachment to the writer. Such articles and serials are also indicative of how chronic illness is moving centre stage in terms of the general awareness of health and illness. Most people in the UK now will die of a chronic illness rather than from an infectious disease – many more than in previous centuries. The increase in the number of people with chronic illnesses raises several important issues:

- The dominance of medical science and its ability to cure all is challenged; its weaknesses and limits are exposed.
- The person with a chronic illness has to reconstruct aspects of their life and identity when facing a condition that will become a fundamental part of their existence.

We can see these concerns in this extract from Picardie, when she is corresponding with a friend about forthcoming treatment and her wider anxieties about her family:

> The latest news is that I didn't have the second lot of chemo yesterday, because my white blood cell count is still crap – they went in 'all guns blazing' (direct quote from oncologist) first time round and it was obviously OTT ... Meanwhile, my hair is falling out with amazing rapidity – I estimate total baldness will be achieved by the weekend, so the whole thing will have happened in a week. It's getting awfully expensive – had my hair cut ultra short on Monday, and reckon I will have to have it shaved on Friday. I was a bit freaked out at first – it's really alarming running your hand through your hair and handfuls coming out. Makes you look sick, feel that you are dying, etc., which I am not ... Meanwhile, I am asking everyone I know to buy me a hat. I hope I don't frighten the children – I imagine I'll look pretty weird. (1993: 1)

In this extract, Picardie records her ambivalence toward the chemotherapy treatment, which was, at that time, resulting only in hair loss. She is also battling to maintain 'normality' by seeking to minimise the impact and disruption that being bald may have on her children. These themes of identity and maintaining a 'normal life' will be explored in this section. Sociologists such as Anselm Strauss, Ilene Lubkin and Michael Bury have developed useful perspectives and ideas for understanding the many complexities and subtleties that surround people with chronic illnesses in contemporary western societies. Much research has focused on how people readapt their lives, organise resources and present themselves to the outside world.

Questions

Find some examples of people discussing their lives with a chronic illness, whether in a book, newspaper or online. Identify trends and issues in what they discuss. What insights do they give you into such a life?

In particular we will look at the work of Bury (1991) and the following concepts he has devised that help us sociologically explore chronic illness:

- biographical disruption
- adjusting to the impact of treatment regimens
- adaptation and management of illness.

Before going any further, it should be emphasised that we are not looking at a formal model or stages that people go through as their lives with a chronic illness unfold. Rather, we are looking at issues that face them at various points during their lives. The various concepts listed above should be seen as *emergent* and not *sequential*. This means that there is no ordered 'timetable' as to how a condition develops over time – what symptoms a person with a chronic illness will experience and when they will experience them. For example, with multiple sclerosis people with the condition often have no idea how the illness will develop in their life. There is almost a 'randomness' in when symptoms appear or emerge and how people will have to respond to the changes that those symptoms bring to their life when they appear.

Biographical disruption

Biographical disruption is a core concept in the sociological study of chronic illness, and has helped to illuminate and explore the lived experience of people with chronic illnesses (Williams 2000). In this section, we will look at what biographical disruption means and entails, as well as the subtleties and nuances that go along with it, before moving on to some of the criticisms that have been made.

First of all, let us turn to looking at what biographical disruption means as a concept. Think of your life as narrative, as a story that has been partially written, with past events apparently well defined and recorded, the present unfolding,

> Biographical disruption refers to a destabilisation, questioning and reorganisation of identity after the onset of chronic illness.

and the future a set of plans, ambitions and hopes. Now imagine that personal biography being radically altered as you learn that your body is failing: cells are under attack, or your brain is sending out a series of bizarre signals that prevent your limbs functioning as they once did. Suddenly, all that narrative, that 'biography', you have constructed for yourself and hope to build for the future is thrown into doubt. The present now has to be renegotiated (worked out), the future seems doubtful and the past is a strange place. In short, you have to face a disruption in your concept of self and in your 'own biography'. This is something that Charmaz (1983) has described as the 'loss of self', where you see your former self crumble and disappear. Frank (1995), too, has used similar dramatic language to capture an image of the wreckage of one's life following the onset of chronic illness.

Questions

Think of your life as a narrative. What has been written so far and what have you plotted out for the future?

For someone with a chronic illness, biographical disruption often entails a reorganisation of their life on many levels; various ideas of self and of relationships with family, friends and colleagues will be challenged and re-evaluated. Within the biographical disruption of life the individual will have to deal with the *consequences* and *significance* of the illness (Bury 1997). We can see some of this, for example, in a study on multiple sclerosis (MS) by Boeije et al. (2002). They found that for the people in their research many parts of their lives, which they held to be important as part of their self-identity, had to be reconsidered. One useful example is that of Marc, a young man in his early thirties, who was dedicated to his job and was a keen windsurfer – an activity that was a key part of his social life (2002: 886). The changes in his body brought on by the MS meant that he was unable to go to work and to socialise as he had before the onset of the condition. To deal with these issues he began to relish having free time, something he thought he would be unable to do, and he developed new hobbies with friends such as playing cards. As Marc says:

> When I was working I was almost a workaholic. So I thought that I would go crazy sitting at home all day. But I still know how to enjoy things, it's wonderful having all these days off. Beforehand, you don't expect that to happen, but I've got such nice people around me and I often have visitors. That never seems to stop. I can open the doors with my remote control from my bedroom, which is ideal. I have contact with all kinds of people, including fellow sufferers. (2002: 886)

The actual symptoms of a condition will affect everyday life. Someone, for example, with temporal lobe epilepsy (or petit mal epilepsy as it was formerly called) may have to live with the uncertainty of not knowing when or in what context they may have an absence (Iphofen 1996). This can make certain social situations fraught with risk in terms of safety or, more importantly, of breaking social norms. For other conditions, there are issues of self-care and managing symptoms on a daily basis. As mentioned in Chapter 1, illness also has cultural and metaphorical significance. People with chronic illness may have to respond to the way in which their culture and society perceive their condition. Certain conditions carry a social stigma when the illness is connected with undesirable states or social deviance. Younger people with arthritis feel that they are ageing prematurely (Singer 1974), while people with HIV/AIDS could be stigmatised as 'junkies', given the association of HIV/AIDS with substance use, for example. It is important to note here that it is not the person with chronic illness that is 'the problem', but rather societal attitudes and the way in which the physical environment is shaped. We will explore this highly important and fundamental issue later in this chapter, when we look at disability.

There has been some debate surrounding the assumption that biography is always disrupted after the onset of a chronic illness. Pound et al. (1998) have argued that for older people the development of a chronic illness (stroke, in their research) was in some ways expected and regarded as a 'normal crisis'. The impact of the stroke, and the consequent disruption of biography, was lessened by the fact that it was just one of many 'disruptive' issues (such as poverty and poor housing) that faced this group of people. Faircloth et al. (2004) also explored this idea of age and other factors in studying how people could minimise biographical disruption. In their study, also on stroke, they too found that age reduced the disruptive effects of stroke on older people's understandings and perceptions of who they were and their wider identity. They also found that the presence, and a history, of other illnesses (such as diabetes) and knowledge of stroke (typically seeing it happen to other people) also helped people who had experienced a stroke view it as a normal part of life. Thus, they were better set to handle the changes in their lives that having a stroke entailed. To some extent having a stroke was part of the 'biographical flow', where chronic illness was just part of the rhythms and expectations of everyday life, especially, in this case, for older people.

Schnittker (2005) noted that age could act as a factor in lessening disruption for someone with a chronic illness generally. He found that depression as a consequence of chronic illness seemed more likely to affect people who had become chronically ill when younger rather than those who had become chronically ill when they were older. This was possibly due to older people having developed more complex emotional skills over their life course, which could help them cope with illness.

Reviewing the literature on biographical disruption, Williams (2000) has offered further refinements to this core concept. Following Pound et al. (1998), he suggested that chronic illness cannot be seen exclusively as *disruption* but could be viewed as *continuity*, where chronic illness is expected and regarded as normal due to age and class. In the case of gay men with HIV/AIDS, for instance, the onset of infection or the development of non-symptomatic HIV can also lead to an affirmation of political identity, something that Carricaburu and Pierret (1995) describe as 'biographical reinforcement'. Williams cites other examples, too numerous to mention here, but all with the same theme: that the context of someone's life has a strong bearing on how disruptive a chronic illness will be.

Questions

Discuss the concept of biographical disruption. How accurate do you think it is in exploring the experiences of people with chronic conditions?

Impact of treatment regimens

One major adjustment that inevitably comes with a chronic illness is incorporating medical and clinical treatments into daily life. We will look here at how treatment regimens can impact on a person with a chronic illness and also why people with a chronic illness do not always go along with what they are told to do by medical experts and therapists. A key point here is that what a health professional thinks is the best form of treatment or therapy may not be accepted by someone with a chronic illness for a whole host of complex, but legitimate, reasons as the best way forward. For example, someone with MS may be encouraged by a therapist to use a wheelchair. This may be a sensible course of action from the therapist's perspective, as it allows the person with MS a degree of mobility that they may not currently have. For the person with MS, however, a wheelchair may signify a massive change in their life, on both a symbolic and a personal level, with using a wheelchair being a very strong indicator that they are becoming a disabled person and are no longer the person they once perceived themselves as being.

There are two main ways in which treatment regimens impact on people with a chronic illness. Treatment regimens that are part and parcel of living with chronic illness vary widely both in the form they take (for example, having to use a stoma, having regular dialysis or taking a variety of medication) and in the impact they may have (more of which later). Such impacts can be either affective (to do with people's emotions and how they see themselves) or instrumental (reorganising time and learning to manage technology and medication), though these attributes overlap to a great extent.

If we look at *affective* changes first of all, what we see is that treatment can alter how you think about yourself both in relation to your past biography and in relation to other people – particularly if the treatment has potentially stigmatising consequences. MacDonald (1988), for example, observed that for people with a colostomy, following treatment for rectal cancer, there was a strong tendency to conceal information about their stoma. The patients felt that the odours, noise and dealing with the bag in public places were potentially disruptive to normal social intercourse. These patients with rectal cancer were further stigmatised in a variety of ways. In addition to having to negotiate the stigma of cancer, they also broke cultural taboos concerning faeces and their disposal. As a result, social situations became fraught with risk, with patients seeking to minimise the impact of the stigma, fearing embarrassment or disgust. Overall, for these patients, there was some impairment of quality of life, even if they had managed to deal with the socially perceived 'problems' of their stomas in some way.

When someone is involved in long-term treatment or therapy there exists the problem of what Robinson (1988) terms the 'medical merry-go-round'. Here the person with a chronic illness experiences emotional highs and lows as their expectations of what treatment will deliver go up and down while they circle through various forms and stages of treatment or medication, in a way that is similar to an old-fashioned carousel ride where the horses go up and down and continually move in a circle. This can be very emotionally and physically draining and exhausting. Research by Wiles et al. (2004) provides a useful example of this. Looking at people who were undergoing physiotherapy after a stroke, Wiles et al. found that clients had to manage feelings of potential disappointment when their time with the physiotherapist was at an end. Though the patients usually felt disappointment at no longer receiving 'physio', they often left with high expectations that their future recovery was going to continue and their overall function improve – something that, given the uncertainties of stroke recovery, may be unlikely to happen. Wiles et al. draw attention to the need for therapists to be wary of the emotional aspects of a client's therapy as part of the therapy process, as well as how to manage feelings of optimism and disappointment.

If we turn now to the *instrumental* effects of treatment regimens we can see that compliance/adherence to medication, meeting the demands of clinical appointments and using medical technology can also be very complex. Compliance/adherence to medication used to be regarded as almost a straightforward example of medicalisation within medical sociology, where the medical world took over another part of someone's private life-world. There has been a shift lately, however, in thinking about how people with chronic conditions relate to medication. Instead of being seen in 'black-and-white' terms, as meekly following what they are told, people are now seen as thoughtfully engaging with the medication as part of their wider adjustments to changes in the self brought about by chronic illness.

This means that it is not a simple case of the medical expert giving out advice or instructing someone in what to do and that person going meekly along with what they have been told. Such an idea is evident in Parsons' concept of the sick role, which is discussed in Chapter 3. Increasingly, as Pound et al. (2005) note, people adopt a strategic position on medication and treatment, whereby they will often see how well treatment regimens work in the context of their lives before deciding whether or not to comply. As a result health professionals have to develop more flexible and fluid ways of interacting, adopting a variety of roles and approaches to encourage people with chronic illnesses to engage with and adopt certain treatment regimens. This may entail health professionals acting as 'educators, detectives, negotiators, salesmen, cheerleaders and policemen' (Lutfey 2005: 421) when working with clients.

Adaptation and management of illness

From the discussion so far, we see that chronic illness can have a considerable impact on your life. Aspects of your life may be thrown into question and have to be re-evaluated, while the treatment for the condition can produce a whole host of potentially stigmatising situations. Within this context people with chronic illnesses nevertheless seek to maintain some sense of self and identity. In the earlier quote from Picardie there was evidence of how she dealt with hair loss by having her hair cut short in an attempt to appear 'normal'. Bury (1991) describes these responses as coping, strategy and style:

- *Coping* is a term used in a variety of contexts, commonly when someone is coping with the illness, whether successfully or not. It can also take on emotional dimensions and relate to how someone is holding on to certain aspects of identity.
- *Strategy* is the particular actions or resources someone utilises to deal with problems created by the illness and by social responses. Strategies can range from breaking the day down into manageable chunks to avoiding the general public in order to minimise the risk of stigma.
- *Style* is how one presents oneself to the social world in an attempt to maintain aspects of self.

Disabled people and disability

As always in sociology it is useful to explore how a particular phenomenon is defined and to critically appraise the words that are used to describe that phenomenon. The reason for this is that language is never neutral; words do not simply hang in the air and have no effect on the real world. Language, rather, is very powerful; the words used and how something is conceptualised can have very serious consequences for people, and language is much more than an exercise in 'political correctness'. The main reason is that how a social phenomenon is defined and conceptualised influences and conditions what follows in regard to how certain people are perceived by others, their standing in society, or what form of care or therapy is made available. This relationship between language or concepts and the lives of people is highly relevant for people with disabilities. Consider the following terms and expressions that are commonly used in connection with disabled people:

- cripple, crippled
- handicapped
- deformed
- invalid
- 'something wrong'
- the disabled.

Some of the above immediately appear to be offensive at the very least. 'Cripple' and 'deformed' are probably the worst in that respect, filled with connotations of someone being less than a 'whole' person, and possibly therefore worthy of pity or charity, and definitely not worthy of full social acceptance. Even though initially 'the disabled' as a term may seem to be more acceptable, it too is problematic. The definite article 'the' is at fault, as it implies that there is no person there, simply a medical condition with no personal narrative, identity or desires. Moreover, such expressions imply that everyone who is disabled has a uniform experience regardless of gender, class, ethnicity, age, sexuality or impairment; people with disabilities are seen as an undifferentiated homogeneous block. That is why terms such as 'disabled people' or 'person with disabilities' are used. These terms reintroduce the humanity and therefore rights of citizenship and broader human rights.

The above discussion is steering towards different approaches in thinking about disability. What is being opened up here is a very fundamental question: what is disability? As we shall encounter shortly, there are two broad answers to this question. One suggests that disability is the limitations of a person because of some form of physical difference or impairment *located in their body*. Another, instead, refers to disability arising out of the barriers and attitudes *located in society* with which people with impairments are presented on a daily basis. What we have here are two very different accounts of what constitutes disability, one focusing on the person and the other on society. The acceptance or privileging of one answer over the other entails different understandings of disability and different relationships with disabled people.

The first answer identifies that disability occurs in the body and therefore can be regarded as a medical condition. Interpreting disability as a medical condition implies that the individual with an impairment is almost at fault – that there is something wrong with *them*, and they are in some way deficient. The way to improve the lives of people with disabilities is to therefore focus on changes that can be made to their bodies. Since medical technology cannot offer complete 'cures' for many disabilities, people with disabilities have to accept the limitations on their lives, tragic as that may be. This position also infers that people with disabilities are reliant upon other people to help them, as they are limited in what they can achieve in everyday life because of their disability.

The second answer, which looks towards a social explanation, implies quite a different orientation towards disability. The fundamental premise of this approach is that the lives of people with disabilities are made difficult by the way that society, in terms of both built spaces and social attitudes, is constructed. Remove those attitudes and reorganise physical space, and the problems disabled people encounter are greatly reduced if not no longer present. In certain respects this position shares many similarities with other groups in society who encounter or have encountered discrimination because of some socially defined difference. In the 1960s in the United States of America, black people in some southern states, for example, encountered segregation on a daily basis, where they were not permitted by law to eat in the same restaurants as white people or sit in the same seats on a bus as white people. The only reason black people could not do these things was because of racist attitudes. So what is the difference, it could be argued, between this experience and that of disabled people not being able to access restaurants or public transport? All that is required is a different approach to design and a different mindset, and there would be no problems. This does not happen because of a form of prejudice which parallels racism, in this case disablism, which perceives disabled people as being inferior and therefore excluded from the rights that everyone else enjoys. Disability here becomes an issue of civil rights that requires changes to society – changes that can be led by disabled people.

The two different outlooks on disability sketched out above form the basis of different models of disability as advanced by disability activists and academics such as Oliver (1990; 1993) and Barnes (Barnes et al. 1999). The first viewpoint is referred to as the medical model and the second as the social model. The two models importantly are not intended by their authors to be value-free, neutral observations of the world; they are instead deliberately judgemental. The **medical model** is a negative and discrimina-

> The medical model refers to a negative perception of disabled people that identifies disability as being located in the body of the person, related to a physical deficit, therefore requiring the disabled person to rely on the help of others. The social model focuses on disability being located in barriers created by oppressive and prejudicial social attitudes and in the design of the built environment.

tory perspective that holds a static and fatalistic understanding of disability: *that's how life is, how unfair!* By contrast the **social model** is a positive and emancipatory perspective that seeks to offer a way for disabled people to bring about meaningful changes in their lives: *life's unfair, let's go and change it and make it fair!*

Over time the medical model of disability has lost out to the social model in many respects. Allied health professionals, such as occupational therapists, physiotherapists and nurses, advocate the social model when working with disabled people. We can see the influence of the social model in legislation such as the Disability Discrimination Act 1995 and the Equality Act 2010 which place the onus on organisations not to discriminate against disabled people and to make buildings accessible (though in practice not always as accessible as they could be).

There are many reasons for the success of the social model. One of the main reasons is that by refocusing the cause of disability away from the individual towards society, the model allows for a wider understanding of the relationships between society and disabled people, exploring dynamics of power, identity, culture and oppression (Shakespeare 2006). The social model also played a fundamental role in providing a political analysis of disability which helped in building and framing the disabled civil rights movement where disabled people organised on their own terms to challenge the prejudice and discrimination prevalent in society.

There has been growing criticism of the social model in recent years, however. The main point of departure is that the social model overemphasises the social, and holds that all of the issues that negatively impact upon the lives of disabled people are to be found in society; the upshot is that changing society would eliminate disability. What sociologists such as Tom Shakespeare (2006) and Williams (1999) have countered is that such a strong perspective on the social aspects of disability ignores the very real problems of suffering and pain caused by physical impairments and the whole subjective, personal experiences of disability. The body of disabled people in effect 'vanishes' in the social model. Making this observation – that the body and therefore the biological have to be taken into account – is not to reject the contribution that the social model has made in understanding the situation of disabled people in society, or to suggest that improvements in civil rights and changes in social attitudes concerning disabled people are unnecessary. Far from it: there is still much in society that remains oppressive. It is rather to acknowledge that a more effective and holistic model of disability would include an understanding of the physical and biological aspects of disability, but importantly also an appreciation of how those biological aspects of disability interact with the social aspects. This is actually quite an important statement. Disability is not a bit of both, 50 per cent biological and 50 per cent social; rather disability, and what it is to be disabled, are a state of being that emerges out of various interweaving and interacting social and biological processes. Shakespeare captures the aforesaid very elegantly:

> The approach to disability which I propose to adopt suggests that disability is always an inter-action between individual and structural factors. Rather than getting fixated on defining dis-ability either as a deficit or a structural disadvantage, a holistic understanding is required. The experience of a disabled person results from the relationship between factors intrinsic to the individual, and extrinsic factors arising from the wider context in which he or she finds herself. Among the intrinsic factors are issues such as: the nature and severity of her impairment, her own attitudes, her personal qualities and abilities and her personality. Among the contextual factors are: the attitudes and reactions of others, the extent to which the environment is ena-bling or disabling, and wider cultural, social and economic issues relevant to disability in that society. (2006: 55–6)

Learning or intellectual disabilities

Learning or intellectual disability provides a useful example of many of the themes dis-cussed above, illustrating the relationships between prevailing social attitudes, disability and impairment. Estimates indicate that there are somewhere in the region of 145,000 adults and 65,000 children with severe or profound learning disabilities in England, and a further 1.2 million people with mild or moderate learning difficulties (Department of Health 2001). It is in the history of people with learning disabilities that the inter-actions of impairment and society are most noticeable; this illustrates the importance of Shakespeare's (2006) point, outlined in the previous section, that the wider cultural issues relevant to disability shape the lived experiences of disabled people. For people with learning disabilities, as Race (2002) outlines, there is a history of moving from reasonable tolerance in the pre-industrial age, to being regarded as problematic during the early stages of the Industrial Revolution, to being seen as a threat to the integ-rity of the white English race in the Victorian period and needing to be isolated from the rest of society, and finally to increasing but still incomplete acceptance again today. These changes in how people with learning disabilities were understood and received by society were driven by developments and trends in society's attitudes to disability in one measure, but also by the wider cultural dynamics that informed the times. In the pre-industrial age, before science became the main way of understanding the world and supernatural explanations dominated, those who were considered to be fools because of impairment were regarded as possessing special and mystical insights into the nature of things and into the complexities of the human spirit. We can glimpse the position of people with learning disabilities in a different age in the plays of William Shakespeare, where often the court fool imparts wise advice gained from his 'different' perspective on the world to the King or lead characters. In the industrial and scientific times of the Industrial Revolution and the Enlightenment, people with intellectual disabilities were not so accepted. They were seen to be out of sync with the new mechanised rhythms of the workplace; they were alienated from the new techniques of mass production, and their apparent lack of reason offended rationalism. Later in the Victorian period the Eugenics movement, a pseudo-scientific and racist approach to matters of ethnicity and what would become genetics, centred on the need for racial purity and held that the fine English stock could be contaminated by the external threat of inferior races (typically people from outside western Europe) or the internal threat of the 'feeble minded'. At this point in history it became common to see that the 'solution' for people with learning disabilities was isolation and segregation from society in order to prevent their genes infecting the wider population.

We can witness something of this time in the genesis of the term 'Down's syndrome', which is now used to denote the condition emerging out of genetic 'damage' to chromosome 21. When physician John Langdon Down first described the condition in the 1860s he did not apply his own name to it. He instead drew on the prevailing view of the times that there were lesser races and decided that people with Down's syndrome bore some resemblance to people from Mongolia; hence the older term 'Mongolism'. In the mind of the nineteenth century there was a connection between people with 'lower' minds and the 'lower', in this case Far Eastern, races (Gould 1980).

Links

For more on history and health see Chapters 2 and 15, where some of the general historical issues mentioned above are discussed in greater depth.

Throughout all the twists and turns mentioned in the above historical sketch, the objective reality concerning the nature of learning disability as an impairment remains in many respects 'stable'. Thus the movement of people with intellectual disabilities – from being part of the community, to being rejected, and back to being seen once more as part of the community – is dependent on changing social attitudes and not on impairment (Goodley 2001).

The above discussion has made claims that there is a move in contemporary society for people with learning disabilities to be included in the wider community. Achieving this ambition is not necessarily straightforwardly unproblematic, and many of the negative images attached to people with learning disabilities still remain. Rooney (2002), for instance, points to issues of being *meaningfully* part of a community. Just because someone is deemed to be in a community setting, often by virtue of not being in an institution, does not mean they are necessarily part of a community in terms of relationships with other people and local social systems. As with wider disability issues, stigma remains a defining experience for many people with learning disabilities. Full inclusion cannot be considered to have been achieved till that negative relationship has been overcome.

Conclusion

This chapter has shown that the human body is not just a biological entity but is inextricably bound up with society, culture and history. Much of how we project our identity and develop a sense of self that is important and vital in our everyday interactions is performed through and with our bodies. This use of the body is becoming more central in the consumerist society in which we live, where a thin, toned body adorned in the most current of fashion styles is presented as being highly desirable. Television shows, magazines and commercials extol the supposed virtues of such an appearance. Obviously, only a very few people (usually celebrities with financial and other resources) can obtain that look, and the pressure to conform to such appearances can result in misery and suffering for many people.

The importance of the body in identity is brought into sharp relief in relation to chronic illness. Here, the emergence of symptoms and changes in the body disrupts the sense of self and can challenge how we see our lives. This can lead to all sorts of re-evaluations of identity and how to lead a life with the destabilisation that chronic illness can bring. This 'pessimistic' take on chronic illness should, however, be tempered by research that indicates that sometimes chronic illness is 'not that bad'. Age and class, for example, can provide an emotional resilience and acceptance of chronic illness.

The body and identity are also visible in disability issues. Sociological perspectives focus on disability as the outcome of prejudicial and discriminatory social attitudes and perceptions. Bodies that do not match or that are 'different' from an able-bodied norm are devalued, and disabled people's identities are given a lesser social status. Disabled people have advanced a civil rights agenda to counteract many of the negative and oppressive structures that act against them being fairly treated in society.

Summary points

- The taken-for-granted status of the body has detracted from the significance of the body for students of the sociology of health.
- Human experiences are essentially embodied and this is most true of health and illness.
- The body is a bearer of values and a means of representing our identity to others.
- The civilised body is one that is controlled in terms of both bodily functions and displays of emotion.
- The limits of the physical body are constantly being extended as scientific advances allow us to alter the appearance of our bodies and to replace diseased organs.
- Ideas about the body are underpinned by normative concepts of the 'good' and 'bad' body, the former being associated with bodily perfection.
- Any form of disease, but particularly chronic and terminal conditions, brings into stark reality the limits and fallibility of the human body.
- A 'failed' body forces individuals to reassess their lives and sense of identity – though this is not necessarily a negative experience.
- Disability is a combination of environmental, social, cultural, material and physical factors. Acknowledging disability in this way asks fundamental questions of health professionals when interacting with disabled people.

Case study

Consider the following case study and then answer the questions below.

James was diagnosed with rheumatoid arthritis around the time of his eighth birthday. The condition has meant that at times his mobility has been severely affected. Games and sports at school were something that he had to miss out on. Writing for long periods in exams became impossible in his final year and so he produced his work on a laptop in a room separate from the rest of his classmates. After finishing school, James wanted to enter a career in hotel management, but this proved impossible as the work involved a considerable amount of time spent on one's feet, something James could not do without being in severe pain. Instead, he chose a clerical post in the Civil Service which would allow him to be seated for much of the day and to use a PC instead of physically writing.

1 Mobility was a problem for James from an early age. What kinds of activities and experiences do you think he might have missed out on compared to other children his age?

2 How might you apply the concept of 'biographical disruption' to James' experiences as a young adult?

3 What kind of knowledge would you have expected James to accumulate about this condition? How would this differ from the knowledge of the clinician, and what, if any, would be its relevance to anyone treating James?

Taking your studies further

This chapter will have helped you understand many of the key terms, concepts, theories and debates relating to the body. Listed below are journal articles and books that will provide deeper and more detailed discussions of the points raised in this chapter. You will also find what is available on the companion website. This offers downloads of relevant material, plus links to useful websites in addition to podcasts and other features.

Recommended reading

Barnes, C. and Mercer, G. (2003) *Disability*. Cambridge: Polity.

Bordo, S. (1990) 'Reading the slender body', in M. Jacobs, E.F. Keller and S. Shuttleworth (eds), *Body/Politics: Women and the Discourse of Science*. New York: Routledge.

Bury, M. (2001) 'Illness narratives: fact or fiction?', *Sociology of Health and Illness*, 23 (3): 263–85.

Hawkes, G. (1996) *A Sociology of Sex and Sexuality*. Buckingham: Open University Press.

Hockey, J. and James, A. (2007) *Embodying Health Identities*. Basingstoke: Palgrave Macmillan.

Pound, P., Gompertz, P. and Ebrahim, S. (1998) 'Illness in the context of older age: the case of stroke', *Sociology of Health and Illness*, 20 (4): 489–506.

Shakespeare, T. (2006) *Disability Rights and Wrongs*. London: Routledge.

Shilling, C. (2003) *The Body and Social Theory*, 2nd edn. London: Sage.

Shilling, C. (2007) *Embodying Sociology: Retrospect, Progress and Prospects*. Oxford: Blackwell.

Williams, S.J., Bendelow, G. and Birke, L. (2003) *Debating Biology: Sociological Reflections on Health, Medicine and Society*. London: Routledge.

On the companion website

Frank, A.W. (1997) 'Illness as moral occasion: restoring agency to ill people', *Health*, 4 (1): 131–48.

Williams, S.J. (2003) *Medicine and the Body*. London: Sage. Chapter 5.

12

Health, ageing and the life course

Main points

- Old age and ill health are not necessarily synchronous, with the majority of older people living fit, healthy and active lives.
- Older people can be subject to ageist stereotyping and this can impact on identity and sense of self.
- It is important to understand ageing as taking place in biographical and historical time. Experiences across the life course strongly influence the health of older people.

Key concepts

Ageism • attitudes • Third Age • life course • biographical and historical time • the body.

Introduction

Throughout Europe and North America more and more people are living into old age as the post-war baby boom generation reaches that phase of their lives. In the UK, for example, in 1951 there were 13.8 million people over the age of 50; this compares to 20 million over 50 in 2003 (ONS 2005a: 1). Figure 12.1 displays other important and significant ways in which the age composition of the older population has changed in the UK, comparing 1951 to 2003 and projecting ahead to 2031. This increase in the number of older people in society is visible in developing nations too, with the United Nations predicting that by 2050 older people will comprise 20 per cent of the population in developing regions. This demographic shift raises many interesting issues and challenges both for society and for the sociological study of what it means to be an older person. As will be explored in this chapter, being older is not a simple case of having grey hair, experiencing worsening health and living alone, as popular stereotypes sometimes hold; it is a complex mix of lifestyles, social perceptions and levels of health.

Ageing in society: a general overview

The body begins to age, change and develop from the moment of birth until its eventual death. This, though, should not be read as meaning that ageing is purely a biological phenomenon driven entirely by alterations to the surface layers of skin and hair paralleled by decreasing mental acuity and all-round physiological decline. Rather, ageing, as a phase of one's life, is the product of three factors that all weave together: biology, psychology and the social. Each of these factors can exert an influence on the others. So,

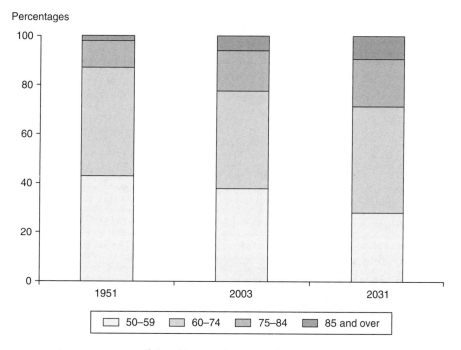

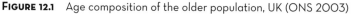

FIGURE 12.1 Age composition of the older population, UK (ONS 2003)

Source: National Statistics Website: www.statistics.gov.uk. © Crown copyright

for example, going grey may be a physical sign of ageing in some sense, but it depends on the society of which one is a member as to whether having grey hair means someone is deemed to be 'old' and should be treated in a different way from someone who does not have grey hair. It is through the social that experiences of, perceptions about and attitudes towards what it is to be old and what is regarded as being old are mediated and created. Similarly, a society can exert such pressure and stress on someone that this hastens their biological ageing. Among the more overt social aspects of ageing in society are certain negative attitudes expressed by individuals. It is to a discussion of **ageism** that attention turns next.

Ageism

In other chapters we have looked at discrimination and prejudice in the form of sexism and racism. We saw how socially created perceptions of people's characteristics (their sex or ethnicity) act as barriers that prevent women and people from ethnic minority groups having a full and equal place in society. Such barriers can have a negative and harmful effect on their health.

Ageism is yet another example of the many prejudices that exist within society. In popular culture there are many examples of this stereotype. A useful example is, arguably, Abe Simpson, the grandpa character in 'The Simpsons'. In the episodes in which Abe appears the comedy content is generated by Abe falling asleep at inopportune moments or embarking on long rambling stories about his youth. Instances such as these match popular stereotypes that all old people are 'demented' and in poor health.

Ageism

comprises: (1) a set of beliefs originating in biological variation related to the ageing process; (2) the actions of corporate bodies and their agents, and the resulting views of ordinary people.

It follows that:

(a) ageism generates and reinforces a fear and denigration of the ageing process, and stereotyping presumptions regarding competence and the need for protection;

(b) in particular, ageism legitimates the use of chronological age to mark out classes of people who are systematically denied resources and opportunities that others enjoy, and who suffer the consequences of such denigration, ranging from well-meaning patronage to unambiguous vilification. (Bytheway and Johnson 1990, cited in Bytheway 1995: 14)

Ageism is, however, more than just finding old people amusing. It can take many other forms as well. At its worst it can be structurally located and act as a barrier to older people receiving appropriate health care. Age Concern England (ACE 2002b) has noted the presence of two forms of ageism within the NHS. The first is *direct ageism*, namely instances when actual policy or guidelines prevent someone from receiving appropriate health care based directly on their age. This is a very overt and easy-to-identify form of discrimination. The other form of ageism, *indirect ageism*, is more subtle and is concerned with attitudes and assumptions that the health of older people is less important than that of younger people.

Questions

Identify positive and negative portrayals of older people in society. Which type of image is more frequently visible? Why do you think there is prejudice and discrimination against old people in current society?

Bodies and ageing

Despite the fact that this is the fate of us all, old age is often associated with negative images and attitudes. The earlier discussion of the sociology of the body illustrated the importance of our physical self for our sense of identity, and from this it is possible to see that the visible signs of ageing (greying hair and developing wrinkles, for example) act as a set of symbols, which can be read in often prejudicial and negative ways in society. This is especially so in a consumer society where an old body is often perceived as a less socially valued and acceptable body than a young, fit, fat-free and athletic body. Indeed, the ever-increasing range of cosmetics offering to hold back the onset of the signs of ageing is another way in which both the body is commodified (essentially one is compelled to purchase a youthful face and body) and youth is prioritised. Youth is clearly associated with notions of optimum physical performance (hence sports people are 'old' in their mid thirties), cognitive ability and attractiveness. In contrast, old age is seen as a period of decline marked, for example, by loss of height and by wrinkled skin. This social impulse to maintain youth is especially problematic for women who, unlike men, are likely to be judged on their physical appearance – their looks – rather on any other criteria.

The continuing importance of the body and images of ageing can also be seen in the next example. One of the most important activities that we do with our bodies is to dress and present it with clothes that accord with what we wish to say about ourselves and what we believe to be socially appropriate. This can be a difficult balancing act at any stage of one's life, given the strong pressure to meet certain consumerist and cultural expectations. There are, though, certain issues that older people have to negotiate when they choose what to wear. Twigg (2007) draws our attention to how clothing is 'age ordered', with certain styles of clothes deemed both age appropriate and a signifier of age. In some respects, this can be seen as an informal policing of how older people (women in particular) present themselves as they grow older. Often this means a toning down of style and opting for less 'flamboyant' styles. Twigg (2007: 296) uses an example from research by Holland (2004) to illustrate this point. Here, women who have an alternative style of dress (for example, grunge and Goth styles involving dreadlocks, piercings and tattoos) indicated a sense of apprehension about having to alter their appearance as they grew older. The women in this study were worried that their alternative stylistic difference, which was an important part of their youthful identity, would be seen as being 'grotesque' if they maintained it into their middle years and beyond. The two phrases that sum up the association between youth, attractiveness and age are 'growing old gracefully' and 'mutton dressed as lamb' (Fairhurst 1998: 261). Both phrases make assumptions about age-appropriate actions and appearance. Mutton is older, tougher meat than youthful and tender lamb. Fairhurst's respondents all interpreted 'mutton dressed as lamb' as the wearing of 'inappropriate clothes, hair, make-up or jewellery' (1998: 262).

Featherstone and Hepworth (1993) also draw our attention to the largely negative terms used to describe older people. Such words include 'wrinkly', 'gaga', 'biddy', 'fogey' and 'geriatric' (1993: 308). The biological process of ageing is 'shaped or constructed in terms of symbolic imagery, both verbal and non verbal' (1993: 308). Words and images are used as stereotypes to make sense of and describe the experiences of older people. The danger of such stereotypes is that they fail to reflect the complexity and diversity of people's experiences of ageing.

These negative images of old age can permeate all aspects of ageing in society. One of the most common stereotypes is that old age is synonymous with decline and dependency, and that ageing is *itself* a disease or illness. These assumptions provide a useful starting point for a discussion of the assumed association between old age and ill health. As we will go on to discuss, many older people, on the contrary, enjoy a life relatively free from sickness and dependency. The same negative stereotyping of individuals on the basis of sickness and dependency can, arguably, be seen in relation to people with disabilities. Such an association may, therefore, lead us to conclude that it is the assumption of dependency and of an inability to perform socially that is the source of the discrimination rather than the actual age of the person.

Thus far we have given consideration to images of old age. The following section is concerned with placing those images within a theoretical context. The aim of this discussion is to illustrate through a sociological analysis that, much more than simply a physiological experience, age is fundamentally a social experience.

Sociological theories of ageing

Sociology offers a number of perspectives, all of which seek to explain the social situation, status and role of older people. **Disengagement theory** offers what might appear in the twenty-first century a rather dated perspective on ageing and the role of older people. Cumming and Henry (1961) suggested that as people reach old age they gradually disengage from society, in terms of their social contacts, roles and responsibilities. The process of disengagement prepares the older person and society in general for the ultimate disengagement in the form of death or incapacity (Bond et al. 1993: 32). Disengagement theory is based on a broader functionalist perspective of society with its emphasis on the roles, responsibilities and values that ensure the smooth running of the social structure. By disengaging, for example through retirement from the paid workforce, individuals cease to be essential to the functioning of the social structure. On this basis their death does not result in any significant disruption since older people have ceased to be part of the workforce.

Bond et al. (1993) highlight a number of problems with this perspective on ageing. They argue, first, that disengagement theory condones the social isolation and marginalisation of older people, which for many results in poverty and loneliness. Second, they suggest that this theory is based on an assumption that disengagement is a natural and inevitable occurrence. It is possible to argue that the theory is essentially ageist in the sense that it assumes identical experiences for all older people. However, as Bond et al. (1993: 32) point out, many older people may still be actively engaged in society, while for others old age is part of a lifelong experience of non-engagement and social isolation. The final criticism that can be made of disengagement theory is its failure to appreciate that certain social practices (such as enforced retirement from the paid workforce) and cultural values (ageism) combine to ensure that disengagement does become the experience of many older people. In this sense, we can perhaps appreciate that disengagement is the consequence of a specific set of social arrangements rather than a natural and inevitable part of the experience of ageing.

> Disengagement theory states that older people relinquish their roles in society so as to minimise social disruption as they approach their final years.

Links

Disengagement theory is closely related to the functionalist perspective outlined in Chapter 1.

In contrast to disengagement theory, an alternative explanation of the experience of older people centres on the social creation of dependency. The essence of this approach is that older people are constructed as dependent on the state, primarily through exclusion from the paid workforce. Such exclusion also means that older people are further isolated from a wide variety of social settings, relationships and networks. Data indicate that older people are one of the groups most at risk of poverty because of their dependence largely on welfare benefits.

> Dependency theory claims that older people's lives are restricted by poverty and not being able to access social and cultural resources.

The potential effects of retirement are, according to Bond et al., poverty and restricted 'access to social resources in the form of a reduction in social relationships' (1993: 34).

So far, the discussion has focused on what may be seen as pessimistic perspectives on ageing. We shall now turn to what might be regarded as more optimistic perspectives – where growing older opens up the possibilities of a phase in one's life that is filled with rich and rewarding experiences, free of the binds of work and other commitments. Such perspectives also draw our attention to some of the complexities of growing older in contemporary society, brought about by changes in welfare provision and the all-pervasive influence of consumer culture offering a range of possibilities on *how* to be an older person. Here, older people are seen to have more freedom to choose and decide their own identities and lifestyles.

Key to this more optimistic perspective is the work of Laslett (1987; 1989) and his concept of the **Third Age**. He is calling for a reworking of how society views the different stages of moving through life. Essentially, the Third Age involves a transition from various states of dependence to independence and from responsibility to increasing freedom and flexibility. So, the First Age is childhood, when we are dependent on our parents. The Second Age is the independence of being a mature person and being able to provide for yourself, but perhaps being hemmed in by the responsibilities of raising a family and holding down a job. The Third Age is a period of life between later middle age and early older age. It is marked by increasing freedom from the constraints of work and family concerns, and can also be a 'golden age' occupied with activities that lead to a sense of fulfilment, self-realisation and

> Third Age theory points to old age as being a 'golden age' where enriching and rewarding experiences are available due to freedom from family and work commitments mediated by a consumerist society.

personal growth. More recently, Laslett (1996) has added a Fourth Age, where physical decline and health problems begin to dominate the experiences of people in deeper old age, that is those above the age of 75.

The Third Age has been made possible by the increasing numbers, affluence and health of older people. This, combined with a consumer culture which blurs many of the distinctions between the age groups, has allowed older people to escape the social expectations of how they should lead their lives and to strike out and create identities of their own.

There are, however, criticisms of this approach. For example, Bury (2000) has raised objections that the research is 'data light', meaning that more research has to be carried out to see if this Third Age is actually happening, or whether it is more of an idea of what could happen given the changes indicated above. Another criticism is that this phase of self-realisation after one has retired is only open to those with the financial means to accomplish it. One could argue that poverty still affects the lives of many older people, thus effectively preventing them from engaging in the consumerist activities that are so much part of the Third Age. Just over 20 per cent of pensioners are living in poverty (ONS 2005a), though this is worse for older people from ethnic minority backgrounds and people in deeper old age.

Questions

Which sociological theory of ageing do you find the most persuasive, and why?

Health and the life course

As was outlined above, there is often an almost taken-for-granted association between ageing, disability and ill health. The reality is far different, with many older people living healthy active lives, especially the 'younger' old. Table 12.1 indicates that many older people remain free of any long-standing illness or disability. For example, while just over 47 per cent of women aged between 65 and 84 did report a long-standing illness or disability, just under 53 per cent did not and, one can assume, enjoyed reasonable health (ONS 2005a). A closer examination of these figures does, however, reveal some subtle but important differences. In terms of gender, older women experience more health problems than men of the same age. It is also clear that some distinction should be made between age groups within the catch-all category of old age. Field (1992) draws a distinction between the 'young old' and the 'old old', the former below 75 and the latter over 85. Although the cut-off points might seem a little arbitrary, they are nevertheless helpful in identifying a trend towards increased levels of disability and ill health among older people over the age of 75 (1992: 276).

TABLE 12.1 Older people reporting a limiting long-term illness, by age and sex, England and Wales, 2001 (%)

	50–54	55–59	60–64	65–74	75–84	85 and over
Men	19.9	26.7	37.4	42.9	56.0	70.2
Women	21.1	27.5	32.1	40.6	58.9	78.3

Source: ONS (2005b). © Crown copyright

Being old is simply – and obviously – not just always having been a certain age for all one's life. Older age is just another of the many elements and phases that go to make up one's life. How that life is lived, however, greatly influences health in the older years, in terms of both developing long-term illness or disability, for example, and shaping how illness and health are experienced and perceived. A useful concept in trying to understand this relationship between health and old age is that of the **life course** (Hockey and James 2003). In the past, moving through life was conceptualised as being similar to a cycle and commonly expressed using the term **life cycle**. Aspects of moving through life in this context were seen as inescapable certainties in life encountered by every generation. This included such events as school, work, marriage and starting a family. Overall, life-cycle approaches conceive life as being a set of rigid stages that one goes through without any variance or personal choice. In contrast, life in this current phase of modernity has become increasingly complex, fluid and fragmented. The certainties that are implied in a life-cycle approach are no longer with us and there can exist great varieties in how people experience and choose to live their lives. So, for example, people increasingly do not always enter into marriage or may delay having children, if they make that decision at all. By seeing life as a *course* that one takes through life where one has a certain latitude in making choices, rather than a *cycle* over which one has little control, such variety can be easier to understand.

Regarding ageing in the context of both 'biographical' and 'historical' time is important to the life-course approach (Bury 2000). Biographical time refers to the personal events in your life; for example, developing relationships, or choosing to go travelling, or what you did at university. Historical time refers to the events and social attitudes that mark particular phases in history; for example, the Second World War, or the changes in attitudes towards sexuality that took place in the 1960s. Though biographical time and historical time may seem quite different, they do relate to each other. Historical time can set the scene for what happens and unfolds in biographical time, giving a particular generation a shared set of beliefs and common experiences.

Life cycle is a concept borrowed from natural science and implies a series of set rigid stages that humans move through in their lives. Life course as a concept points to the increasing fluidity and fragmentation of contemporary society and reflects the fact that old certainties of what one does at certain points in one's life are increasingly unstable.

Questions

Sketch out your life course so far. Identify both your biographical time and the historical time in which you live. What aspects of historical time help shape the identity of your generation?

Thinking of ageing in this way helps us to understand older people's health in two main respects. First, acknowledging a biographical element allows us to see that not all older people are a homogeneous social group and alike in all manner of ways. Rather, it draws attention to the importance of difference and how people can age in the same historical time but do so in their own individual way and how events in their past affect their health in the present. Second, the historical element can help us understand that people are part of a particular generation and that the experience of being part of that generation (this is called a *cohort effect*) shapes their health beliefs and attitudes towards illness. Ultimately, though, it is the human body on which the experiences of both biographical and historical time will be 'recorded' in terms of good or bad health in older age. Blane et al. usefully summarise this point:

> The body can be seen as a mechanism which stores the past benefits and dis-benefits to which it has been exposed, either because damage at a critical period of development causes irreparable loss or because the effects of various types of damage accumulate over time. (2004: 2171)

So, for example, coming from a deprived background in childhood and working in an occupation that was tightly supervised and low in control could lead to poor health for an older person. Conversely, the opposite – material stability and an enjoyable career – is much more likely to mean good health for an older person. These are themes that we have explored in other chapters and that indicate, once more, how social influences, such as class, strongly influence health. Berney et al. (2000), for instance, found that both negative material and psycho-social factors from childhood onwards can greatly impact on our health as we become older. From the residential and occupational histories of 294 people aged between 63 and 78 they found differences in social class and gender for health that were related to the lived and working experiences of the people in the study.

Links

See Chapter 11 on the body for more discussion of sociological perspectives on the body and chronic illness.

A useful illustration of how life-course experiences and events impact on health can be found in the following extract from research by Sanders et al. (2002) into the experiences of older people with painful joints brought about by osteoarthritis. What is evident here is how this interviewee clearly saw her current poor health as the outcome of the hardship that had been a defining feature of her life:

I've always done a job that involves a lot of steps and kneeling, and I've always worked because we had this old house that was condemned and you couldn't get new houses during the war, and when my husband came out of the army, we didn't have much money, he was on the buildings so … I used to do part-time work. And I done over there 15 years picking mushrooms across the road part time whilst the children were at school. And after that finished I went in different shops just working odd hours so that I was here when the children were here. Whether it was the wear and tear on the knees. But anyway, after about 20 years, I was walking on two sticks, you know during the time I was was working. (int. 8, 82 years, occupational class IV) (2002: 235)

The life course also shapes how older people come to view and experience illness. In Chapter 11 when we looked at chronic illness we noted the research of Pound et al. (1998). They found that for the older people in their study, who had survived a stroke, possible disruption to their lives was lessened by their attitudes. As a generation their experiences of historical time had been of self-denial and coping with the problems life presented to them due to living through the privations of the Second World War. It was these events that forged a common stoical approach to life. For this generation, a health problem was no different from the many other problems they expected to encounter.

Dementia

As has been stressed throughout this chapter, being an older person does not automatically entail being ill. This is a popular misconception, for the majority of older people enjoy fulfilling and healthy lives. There are, however, certain conditions that do affect older people more than other sections of the population. One of these is dementia, which currently affects one in 88 of the general population, one in 20 people over 65, and one in five people over the age of 80, and is a major cause of disability in older age. Dementia refers to a variety of degenerative conditions affecting the higher functions of the brain, with memory loss being one of the most unsettling symptoms both for people with dementia and for their families. Out of the 100 different forms of dementia the most common are Alzheimer's disease, vascular dementia, and dementia with Lewy bodies. In this section we shall mainly focus on Alzheimer's disease.

Dementia demonstrates a point that was made earlier. that ageing is the result of social, biological and psychological influences. Undoubtedly dementia has a biological basis, with a variety of causes including, for example, changes in the brain chemistry, restriction of oxygen to the brain, and degeneration of nerve cells and brain tissue. It also has psychological aspects, the most notable being memory impairment. Some aspects of dementia are, however, very social in their effects and create issues for maintaining a sense of who we are and how we relate to other people. It is to these issues that we now turn.

As a degenerative condition the effects of dementia unfold over time, beginning with disturbances in memory and progressing to substantial or complete memory loss in addition to physical frailty, speech impairment and emotional disturbance. This corrosion of memory and intellectual function can cause a potential destabilising of self and identity. In effect, someone can lose the memories of their life and the facets of their personality that make them what they are, and this has implications for their ability to function as a social being. Much of how we communicate with others is based on how we present ourselves in conversations, for example. During such interactions what we say, and how we respond to the prompts and questions of others, communicate how we wish to be seen. Dementia can make this whole situation problematic. Either the person with dementia finds it difficult to engage in the expected way or the person they are interacting with is unable to adapt to the person with dementia.

People in the early stages of dementia have an awareness of the changes and transformations that are taking place in their lives as the condition begins to alter their memory and other cognitive functions. This is a difficult and worrying phase, not just because of the changes they detect in themselves, but also because of the changes in how other people react to them. Langdon et al. (2007) found that a variety of issues could cause concern for people in the early stages of dementia. For example, the actual name of the condition could cause upset. 'Dementia' sounds very similar to the word 'demented', with its implications of being 'without mind'. This could, the people in the study reported, lead to them being viewed by others as being 'short on top', 'a bit funny' or 'crackers'. Being seen negatively, or stigmatised, by others could cause unease in other ways, too. Revealing their diagnosis was fraught with risk as it was feared that other people would not really understand the condition, as this extract from a woman with dementia illustrates:

> I haven't told anyone. I think they will treat me differently. I wouldn't be upset though, it depends what they know. If they have heard about it and don't understand they would treat me differently. They think it's something bad – they would scorn you and not want to come near you and fully believe you are like that. (2007: 995)

Links

See Chapter 9 on stigma and how social attitudes can have an adverse effect on people's sense of identity.

Ultimately, the almost complete loss of memory leads to a 'social death', where the physical body is still alive but the self is, in many ways, no longer there. One has to take care not to see 'social death' as an absolute state. Often it can depend on the views of other people, particularly relatives and carers who, for a variety of legitimate and personal reasons, may not share an 'objective' assessment that a loved one has undergone a 'social death'. Also, as Sabat (2001) points out, for people with Alzheimer's disease, personhood and the self are not completely 'wiped out'. He stresses that many aspects of some form of self continue to be present; that ignoring them is to deny the person's humanity; and that as much as possible should be done to support and nurture the sense of self of someone with dementia.

Sweeting and Gilhooly (1997) found many complexities and subtleties in how carers managed their encounters and relationships with a spouse or family member with dementia. Their research uncovered various strategies that carers had developed, focusing on a combination of believing and behaving as if a loved one was socially dead. This could mean stating openly that the person with dementia might be better off if they passed away, for instance, while perhaps caring for that person on a physical rather than a social or emotional level. Other carers in the survey adopted a different strategy: while accepting that the person they were caring for was socially dead, their behaviour towards that person was otherwise. This entailed carrying on as much as possible with life as it had been prior to the onset of dementia. For example, they would make sure that the person with dementia was always included in social interaction and that familiar activities, such as the playing of bingo, still went ahead. A third group believed and behaved as if the person with dementia was not socially dead.

The above discussion has sought to highlight the range, extent and consequences of disease and disability among older people. It is clear that while there are specific conditions associated with the onset of old age, many people experience an old age relatively free of such complaints. Significantly, the consequences of disease and acute conditions may be considerably different for older people than for the younger population. Older people have a greater tendency to experience multiple pathologies, with each condition compounding the one before. Their health experiences have also to be considered within a social context where ageing is seen in negative terms and assumptions are made about the inevitability of disease and decline as part of the ageing process.

Conclusion

The main message both from this discussion and from the current research is that old age does not automatically equal infirmity, disability or poor health. Indeed, the majority of older people lead active and healthy lives. What do create issues and challenges for older people are the negative stereotypes and images attached to being old in contemporary society. Ageist attitudes still persist, whether these are expressed in the actions of private individuals or institutions.

What it means to be older in the early part of the twenty-first century is quite different from other times. Being older now can be (for those with the requisite resources) a phase in life where ambitions and life goals can be realised. Old age does not automatically mean poverty or deprivation. The increasing numbers of older people allied with the rise of a consumerist society, through which they can express their identity and sense of self, will hopefully lead to a re-evaluation of how older people are perceived and understood.

Summary points

- Old age is an inevitable phase of human lives, yet can be subject to negative ageist attitudes.
- The vast majority of older people enjoy healthy active lives and it is incorrect to assume that old age automatically means poor health.
- What it is to be old in contemporary society is changing, with many older people enjoying a 'golden age' in their lives made possible by access to consumer culture.
- The life course is a combination of historical and biographical time.
- Older people's lives are influenced by their experiences over their life course. Those with employment histories that are low in control and status tend to have poorer health as they age.

Case study

Joan's first memories as a very young child of five are of an air raid during the Second World War when she was growing up in Glasgow. She remembers the sound of the sirens and the deafening explosion of a bomb falling on her street. She also remembers her mother constantly telling her off for wasting things, whether it was food, clothing or just about anything. But that was all part of the scarcity of the war years and in the rest of the 1940s when she was growing up. This culture of thrift and saving up for a rainy day made a big impression on her. These were to be values she would hold throughout her life.

In early 1961 she met Dave, who asked her to marry him a year later. Life in the 1960s was a great deal more pleasurable than it had been previously. Dave and Joan managed to find themselves well paid jobs and, even though, Joan still saved and was always reluctant to buy anything she considered unnecessary, they both enjoyed themselves. Music was a particular pasttime. First it was the Beatles, and then some of the more obscure and alternative American bands as the 1960s progressed. Despite her thrift, Joan had one passion: clothes. She remembered her own mum as only having one or two outfits, but now there was so much choice and each season had new styles, and there was so much more to buy than ever before.

(Continued)

(Continued)

Life carried on in this vein into the 1970s. Now in their early 30s Dave and Joan began a family of their own. All went well, Dave had promotion at work and they gained a modest level of affluence. Not enough, perhaps, to regard themselves as well-off, but definitely as comfortable. Life progressed reasonably well during the 1980s, but Joan and Dave noticed that the Conservative government of the day was making changes to the welfare state, and many of the sureties of state provision that they assumed would be there as they grew older were beginning to be rolled back. The ability to save and be good with money learned in her early life served Joan well, however. She made sure that enough money was put away each month in a private pension plan and other investments.

In the early 2000s both Joan and Dave retired. With their children now mature adults leading their own lives and away from home, Joan and Dave found that they had both free time and enough financial resources to do something with that time. Joan found that she could rekindle her youthful penchant for clothes and dressed very stylishly, though she always felt tentative about trying on anything that was too 'young' for her. She and Dave also began to do some travelling. They had a holiday in San Francisco. This allowed them to realise a lifetime ambition: visiting the city where so many of their favourite bands came from during the 1960s.

Lately, as Joan is now in her early 70s, she's noticed that she's beginning to feel a little tired more often, and finding it much harder both to move around her house and go about in town. This is unsettling for her as she always liked to be active. She also dislikes the idea of how other people act towards her. The other day someone called her an OAP; that made her feel old. But, as she herself always points out, life is what you make it.

1 Which of the three sociological theories concerning ageing best fits this case study?
2 Identify how Joan's experiences in both biographical and historical time have influenced her life.
3 In what ways has consumerism been a part of Joan's life?
4 Why is the presentation of the body so important in contemporary society?

Taking your studies further

This chapter will have helped you understand many of the key terms, concepts, theories and debates relating to health, ageing and the life course. Listed below are journal articles and books that will provide deeper and more detailed discussions of the points raised in this chapter. You will also find what is available on the companion website. This offers downloads of relevant material, plus links to useful websites in addition to podcasts and other features.

Recommended reading

Gilleard, C. and Higgs, P. (2005) *Contexts of Ageing: Class, Cohort and Community*. Cambridge: Polity.

Hepworth, M. (2000) *Stories of Ageing (Rethinking Ageing)*. Buckingham: Open University Press.

Hockey, J. and James, A. (2003) *Social Identities across the Lifecourse*. Basingstoke: Palgrave Macmillan.

Tulle, E. and Mooney, E. (2002) 'Moving to "age-appropriate" housing: government and self in later life', *Sociology*, 8 (36): 685–702.

On the companion website

Bond, J., Peace, S.M., Dittmann-Kohli, F. and Westerhoff, G. (2007) *Ageing in Society: European Perspectives on Gerontology*. London: Sage. Chapter 6.

SECTION 3

Contexts

13

Places of care

Main points

- Health and social care occurs in distinct places, and these places can exert influences over that care and the quality of life for the people receiving that care.
- Many sociological theories draw attention to the problems of institutional care, which at worst can result in a loss of identity and residents becoming institutionalised.
- Recent shifts towards community care bring fresh challenges. There exist problems in defining community, and evidence suggests that community involvement is giving way to increasing individualism.
- Informal care given by friends and family is an important feature of supporting and looking after people in the community.
- The act of caring can bring about changes in the home and in relationships between those who receive and those who give care.

Key concepts

Organisations   bureaucracy   informal routines   surveillance   resistance
institutions   institutionalisation   community   community care   care and carers.

Introduction

All health care takes place in some spatial context or location, whether it is a hospital, an institution or the community. Each of these contexts brings with it a range of issues and challenges, all of which are open to sociological interpretation. This chapter will begin by looking at organisations generally and evaluate some of the major theories that attempt to understand institutions. Max Weber's classic theory of rationality and bureaucracy will be outlined, followed by Michel Foucault's views on the organisation of physical space and surveillance. How people subvert and manage to bend the rules will be examined next.

Where health care takes place is often decided by social policy, and since the introduction of the NHS and Community Care Act 1990 there has been a shift towards caring for people in the community as opposed to institutional settings. Critiques of institutional or asylum care will be discussed, focusing on the work of Foucault and Andrew Scull. More attention will be given to Erving Goffman's seminal work on institutionalisation and the negative effects of institutional care. Care in the community was proposed as an alternative and better form of care. However, it too is problematic. One difficulty is in trying to define what a community really is, with multiple and different uses of the concept in existence. Even if a definition can be agreed upon, there still exists a debate about whether community care actually changes anything, and some comments will be made on how the community may just be an extension of the institution. Finally, there will be some discussion of the many issues facing carers in the community, highlighting what care involves and some of the problems facing carers.

Organisations

For many people the hospital is still the expected place or context for the provision of health care. Like many other examples of large organisations, hospitals have complex bureaucracies, operate surveillance, and often involve the management of thousands of bodies. Unlike other examples of large organisations, however, they are expected to effect a positive physical or mental change in some of the people who enter through the front doors. This means that although we can use an array of sociological perspectives to understand large institutions, we must also pay attention to the differences that arise from them making life-or-death decisions about people. Attention will be given to the classic work of Weber on bureaucracy and organisations. How the physical layout of a hospital and use of surveillance affect patients and staff will be examined with reference to the work of Foucault. How people 'subvert' organisations will also be discussed.

Weber, organisations and bureaucracy

The ideas of Weber (1997; 2001) about rationality are a useful starting point. Weber, writing at the turn of the twentieth century, saw all human activity as purposeful, and in investigating society it is important to try and identify what meanings people attach to what they do; he termed this *Verstehen* or understanding. To this end he identified the following three forms of action:

- *Affective or emotional action.* This is action that results from an individual emotional state at a given time. If we feel happy and caring we may wish to spend longer with a patient or be more caring than we might if our mood was bad.
- *Traditional action.* We engage in certain forms of activity because we always have, to the extent that we may be unaware that we are doing it. An example of this could be the British habit of saying 'sorry' or 'cheers' in a variety of situations even though we might not actually want to apologise or wish someone good health.
- *Rational action.* This is purposeful activity where there is an intended outcome to our actions. To achieve particular ends we must also take into account what we need and what the best way possible is of reaching our intended outcome. An occupational therapist devising a treatment plan, working out what goals a client can reach and what is required to reach those goals, is an example of this.

For Weber the key to understanding the modern capitalist period was the increase of rationalisation in every aspect of life. He saw a move away from spontaneity and the outward expression of emotion towards a society in which every aspect is governed by rules, procedures or non-spontaneous practices, all grounded in logical, rational science. To this end he characterised mankind's condition in modernity as living in an 'iron cage'.

Weber's analysis of bureaucracy and organisations is distilled into what he termed an *ideal type*. By ideal type he does not mean what an organisation should be but rather a pure form by which to measure a particular organisation. The closer to this ideal, the more effective the organisation will be:

- *Everybody knows what they are meant to do.* Everyone in an organisation should have a clear knowledge of what they are meant to do and what their responsibilities are.
- *It's clear who is in charge and who you are accountable to.* Effective organisation requires effective leadership, which operates in a clear-cut, hierarchical manner.
- *Everybody follows the rules.* There are clear procedures and guidelines for whatever is undertaken within the institution.
- *Those in an organisation act with as little emotion as possible.* Decisions are based on the rules and not on personal whims or desires.
- *Your position is a result of how well you can do the job.* This reflects your knowledge and expertise.
- *Work and home are entirely separate spheres.* No aspect of the organisation is owned by an individual and what happens in work cannot be used for private gain.

Questions

Do you recognise any of Weber's ideas in places where you have worked or had placements? If you do, did these make for efficient organisation?

Links

Chapter 2 discusses the ideas of Foucault further.

Physical layout, surveillance and Foucault

Every hospital is a specifically designed building, with certain features that aid its particular function. In hospitals we find rooms that are designed or designated as treatment rooms, operating theatres or consultation rooms. This may seem a useful and logical way of organising space so as to manage the complexities and functions of hospital work. Foucault (1970; 1979a), however, argues that the design of architectural space is not always for some neutral utilitarian function, but often reflects power balances, authority and ways of controlling people. Prior (1993) discusses a mental health hospital built in the 1950s where there existed separate wards for black and white people, with fewer separate facilities for black people. This is a clear example of how prevailing racist attitudes at the time were made 'concrete' in the construction of a building, with the intention to enforce a particular racist discourse on the people who were sent there for 'care'. Modern-day hospitals may not possess such obvious examples of control, but space is managed for specific reasons. In NHS hospitals, in particular, most space is highly impersonal, with people on large open wards. Senior figures often have their own spaces that are at a distance from the rest of the staff to indicate their higher power and status.

Questions

Next time you are in a hospital or a surgery, look at the layout of physical space. Are there any power relationships that you can detect? Is the space organised so as to facilitate control over those who use it?

The most useful aspect of Foucault's work is on **surveillance**. Part of every modern organisation depends on, and subjects bodies to, surveillance. Surveillance can be seen to exist in two different forms:

Direct observation

This is where people are directly monitored or observed either by a superior or by someone in a position of authority or responsibility. Again, think of a hospital ward and how the actual space (see previous comments) is set out so that someone can monitor what is going on. In addition to making sure that the patients are receiving care and their health is not at risk, surveillance also checks that they are behaving themselves and acting in a manner that complies with the rules of the institution. There is also surveillance of staff, to make sure that they are working and performing their tasks. This may sound innocuous but Foucault maintains that it creates a form of control whereby people become compliant to forms of authority or power.

Written records

An increasing and ever-growing aspect of contemporary life is the vast amount of data, whether electronic or written, that is kept about us. Each of us accrues numerous records concerning tax, educational attainment, criminal records, career progress, health and so on. These records are a more insidious method of control, as what is written down can have a dramatic effect on areas such as career and employment. In a health care context vast amounts of information can be kept about an individual. This information could have a bearing on how well someone is cared for and treated when they have, for example, potentially stigmatising conditions such as HIV or some form of mental illness.

Blau and informal routines

This outline of the various theories about organisations so far may give the impression that either we are like *Star Trek*'s 'The Borg', living as completely perfect rational, emotionless drones working for the greater good of the collective or organisation, or we are being constantly monitored. However, other studies, and Foucault himself, noted that people develop ways of subverting the routines and overall controls of organisations. The more sociologists studied organisations, the more they found layers of subtlety and nuance that were missing from Weber's account.

Peter Blau (1963), for example, found that instead of workers rigidly sticking to the rules and complying with the bureaucracy, a whole host of informal working practices could develop. These informal practices, *contra* Weber, could actually improve the overall working of an institution. Often the complexities of what an organisation has to deal with cannot be covered by contingencies in the bureaucracy and a certain flexibility is required, though never officially sanctioned. Workers may prefer these informal working practices as they can act as a relief or as a way of overcoming the effects of working for a potentially suffocating, alienating bureaucracy.

Technological changes can also have an effect on organisations and bureaucracies. The recent and massive expansion of the internet and computer-based technologies promises to change our working and private lives.

Questions

Have you encountered examples of working where informal routines were used that went against the formal rules? Do you think the informal routines produced a better, more efficient outcome than the formal rules?

Shifts in policy: the move from institutions to the community

In 1990 the NHS and Community Care Act came into being, which saw a change in the organisation of health and social care in the UK. As well as reorganising hospitals into trusts and introducing GP fundholders, the Act also brought about a shift away from caring for people in institutions to caring for people in the community. It was argued that people cared for in the community would receive a higher, more personally tailored standard of care than they would as anonymous faces within an institution. This shift in policy came about as a result of various influences that were ideological, political or financial. Research had shown that institutional care had inherent problems that could be damaging to the health and identity of those being looked after. Writers such as Goffman, and more recently Prior, have noted that individuals can become institutionalised by their extended stay inside long-term places of care.

Institutions, or asylums as they were formerly known, have long been a feature of care within western countries and their contribution to providing effective care has been much debated. Some authors assert that by a rational progress various innovators develop new and more humane and effective techniques, while other authors note that institutions fit into the existing patterns of social control and act as agents for dominant social groups or the needs of capitalism. The writers Foucault and Scull were proponents of this view.

Foucault's critique of institutions

For Foucault the history and development of the asylum or institutional care are linked with the growth of surveillance, discipline and notions of scientific rationality from the period of **the Enlightenment** onwards. He concentrates on how the focus of the 'other' shifted away from the lepers of the Middle Ages, who had been excluded from society, to the mad in the modern period. In the medieval period, leprosy and lepers were a pariah group, the 'other' of society, routinely excluded from social acceptance and admittance to everyday life. People who were mentally ill were regarded as possessed by demons or witchcraft. Later, the emphasis on scientific rationality and scientific investigation during the Enlightenment led to increasing classification, and consequently increasing control of the population. The mad, those designated as irrational and lacking in reason, now came under particular scrutiny.

Such a group posed a challenge to the new orthodoxy of rationality, and so it was they who were separated from society, this time not to leper colonies but to asylums and other places of containment (Pilgrim and Rogers 1993; Turner and Samson 1995).

Foucault highlights the use in the nineteenth century of English philosopher Jeremy Bentham's (1748–1832) Panopticon design for asylums. The Panopticon (the all-seeing eye) allows for the continual regulation and surveillance of inmates. A central tower allows observation of every cell whenever a guard or warden wishes. This gives the authorities great power to classify and control those in their charge.

Foucault is critical of what on the surface are seen as liberal and progressive forms of treatment. Figures such as William Tuke and Philippe Pinel are often credited with bringing the treatment of mentally ill people out of the Dark Ages and into the Enlightenment. Tuke founded his famous Retreat near York in 1796, where kindness and benevolence were to be the moral basis of treatment in place of the degrading, inhuman treatment that had existed before. Tuke wanted a 'desire for esteem' to replace 'the principle of fear' (Morgan et al. 1985: 152). A few years earlier, in 1792, Pinel had unchained the inmates of the Bicêtre asylum south of Paris and founded his *traitement moral*. For Foucault, though, these were not the humanitarian breakthroughs that they are sometimes represented as being. For him, it was the replacement of one form of control (physical) by another (moral). The mad were no longer bound with chains but with strict regimes and routines backed up by moral and religious teachings, a more subtle and insidious, but just as effective, form of control (Samson 1995). The purpose of these moral controls was to turn those in the asylum into 'docile bodies': manageable, controlled entities who posed no threat to the authorities.

Scull's critique of institutions

The Marxist writer Andrew Scull (1979) takes a different position from that of Foucault in that he concentrates on the needs of capitalism, on the medical profession and on the effects of urbanisation on the development of the asylum. For him the asylum was a 'dumping ground' for those superfluous to the needs of capitalism who did not fit into the new market-led economies that developed during the nineteenth century. The poor and unemployed who were capable of working were sent to the workhouses, while those who were incapable were sent to the new asylums. Thus the removal of potentially awkward members of society allowed for the smooth accumulation of capital.

Links

Chapter 1 discusses Marxist ideas further.

Scull also draws attention to the opportunistic nature of the emerging medical profession. By absorbing Tuke's ideas on moral treatment into its body of scientific knowledge, the profession was able to persuade Parliament to pass the County Asylums Act and the Lunacy Act of 1845. This gave the medical profession a monopoly in the field of madness, and since they now had the power to define madness, as well as control it, they could ensure a steady clientele for their services (Pilgrim and Rogers 1993; Turner and Samson 1995). Throughout the nineteenth century there were substantial increases in the number of people inside asylums or classed as insane:

- In 1849 there were 27,000 inmates in 23 asylums.
- In 1909 there were 105,000 inmates in 97 asylums.

Both Foucault and Scull offer a view of the rise of the asylum that counters notions of a steady, value-free evolution of care for mentally ill people. For these writers, wider social and cultural forces influence and shape the development of institutions and asylums.

Goffman's critique of institutions

Whatever the origins of asylum care historically, there was a reappraisal of the effectiveness of institutions in the twentieth century, especially in the post-war period. During the 1960s the 'anti-psychiatry movement', which included writers such as R.D. Laing and Thomas Szasz, started to challenge assumptions about the nature of mental illness and its treatment, favouring a more open, patient-centred approach. Alongside this challenge to psychiatry, Goffman questioned the role of the asylum. In his seminal text *Asylums* (1961) he sought to delve beneath the surface of psychiatric institutions and expose the problems that asylum and institutional care could create. His basic premise was that the needs of the institution came before the needs of the patient and this resulted in a change of identity for the patient. In becoming institutionalised, the patient's whole personality is transformed into a shadow of its former self, and motivation, independence and individuality are lost.

Goffman begins his analysis by observing that we live in a world of institutions, whether workplaces or religious, educational or military establishments. However, there are some institutions in society that are different. These he terms 'total institutions'. In these all the normally separate parts of daily life (such as eating, sleeping or leisure activities) take place in one setting: 'He suggested that the key process – the totality – was established by collapsing the normally separate social spheres of work, home and leisure, into one monolithic social experience' (Morgan et al. 1985: 157). As a result patients inside a mental hospital can lead lives as a 'batch' – a term Goffman borrows from animal husbandry. Individuality is attacked and degraded as they become part of a homogeneous group that carries out daily tasks and functions as part of a timetabled mass.

The loss of personality and sense of self begins on admission to a mental hospital when the patient embarks on what Goffman terms a 'moral career' (see Figure 13.1). The first stage is the removal of the patient's sense of identity, which he terms the 'mortification of self'; this is followed by the 'reorganisation of self', which sees the institution replacing what it has taken away. This process may be carried out deliberately, for example in prisons, where the prisoner has his belongings and personal clothes removed and replaced by a standard prison uniform. Or it may be less deliberate, such as a mentally ill patient being provided with clothing from a hospital communal clothes store. This nevertheless has a similar effect to the prison uniform, for it is the removal and denial of clothing as self-expression and its replacement with clothing that suits the needs of the institution rather than the person. Goffman describes quite elegantly how the patient responds to this reorganisation of self. Goffman allows for the patient to respond in a variety of ways rather than becoming automatically institutionalised. He noted that patients can adopt various strategies for dealing with life in an institution and can develop different ways of surviving in the 'underlife' of institutions. There are five broad responses that a patient can make to life in an institution:

- *Colonisation.* The patient adapts unenthusiastically to their new situation.
- *Conversion.* The patient accepts what has happened and becomes institutionalised.
- *Withdrawal.* As far as possible all contact is minimised.
- *Intransigence.* The patient resists attempts to convert their behaviour. This resistance can be quite aggressive.
- *Playing it cool.* This adaptation maximises the chances of surviving the institution with much sense of self and identity intact. It involves minimising visibility and staying out of trouble.

The 1973 film *Papillon* (French for butterfly, with its connotations of freedom) provides an example of how people respond to life in an institution. Starring Steve McQueen and Dustin Hoffman, the film deals with the lives of two prisoners in the French penal colony of Devil's Island. Throughout the movie the harsh authoritarian regime seeks to force all inmates to become compliant to its authority. In the final scene McQueen displays his opposition and *intransigence* by making a daring escape bid, while Hoffman displays his *conversion* by declining to escape, content with life in the prison. Other cinematic representations of institutionalised life can be found in *The Shawshank Redemption* and, of course, *One Flew over the Cuckoo's Nest*.

Links

See Chapter 14 for more information on community care and changes in health and social policy.

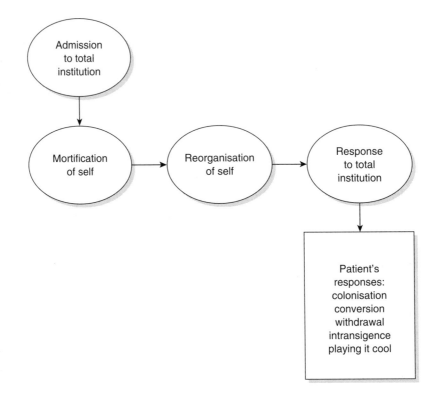

FIGURE 13.1 Institutionalisation

The community

The preceding section highlighted many of the problems that can arise from institutional care: dependency of clients on the institution, iatrogenic effects of care, difficulties in returning people to life outside the institution. This may imply that life and care in the community, on the other hand, is problem-free and inherently good. Unfortunately, much research has indicated that this is not the case. As with institutional care, there exist many problems with life in the community. GP David Widgery (1991) described returning people to the community as the 'sociological equivalent of Siberia' – the idea that people could disappear without trace and adequate support. In addition to the problems of finance and service provision there are problems of trying to understand what the term 'community' means.

What is a community?

Many British readers of this textbook may have an idea of a community as something similar to the depiction of life in popular soaps such as *EastEnders* or *Coronation Street*, where mainly working-class people live interdependent lives in a self-contained area. Occasionally the characters in these dramas may fall out, have arguments or even shoot one another, but essentially there is some form of social cohesion underpinning all interactions. If this were the case, then care in the community would make sense, as people could be returned to an area that was rich in mutual aid and neighbourly goodwill and support. This form of community was depicted in the classic research of Young and Willmott (1961) into an 'urban village' in the working-class East End of London. In the brick-built, back-to-back streets they found strong examples of mutual aid and a community that cared for its members. Dense social networks were maintained by a 'mother–daughter link' and, around this fulcrum, support for family members and neighbours was organised.

Such examples are, however, increasingly rare at the beginning of the twenty-first century. High unemployment, drug-related issues and social disintegration now blight many communities. The fabric of many areas has been altered by changes in social planning and post-war redevelopment. The chances of being part of a protective, supporting community are greatly reduced. Other trends, such as the trio of globalisation, individualisation and detraditionalisation, have been identified by Crow et al. (2002) as being inimical to the continuation of neighbourliness and community. In the US, the highly influential work of Putnam has identified that increasingly Americans are becoming detached from civic society and are less community oriented. Putnam provides a useful metaphor to illustrate this decline in the title of his book *Bowling Alone* (2000). In the 1950s and 1960s in America many Americans belonged to bowling leagues and regularly played and socialised as part of bowling teams. Participation in such leagues and teams has dramatically declined since then and, as Putnam argues, Americans are no longer bowling together but bowling alone.

Questions

Do you think other countries are also becoming less community oriented, with people concentrating on their own lives as opposed to participating in community events?

An initial problem is trying to offer a definition of **community**. There have been many attempts to provide one, but the main problem is that the term covers a heterogeneous collection of interactions, situations and forms. If we look at the following shortlist of what are referred to as communities, we can see some problems:

- student community
- gay community
- business community
- black community
- Protestant community.

Questions

What community or communities do you feel you belong to? What do you share in common with other people in those or communities?

Recently, the multinational coffee chain Starbucks has been marketing its cafés as a form of community–home environment, a move that received a strong rebuke from anti-capitalist Naomi Klein: 'Starbucks pretends to sell us community, but they're selling coffee. This is a betrayal. Community is a strong and powerful idea, and I don't want it stolen from me' (BBC News 2001). What all this demonstrates is that the notion, concept and ownership of 'community' are highly complex and contested. On the above list we can find groups of people who claim to be part of a community but their reasons for claiming membership are varied. In some cases the claim is based on characteristics such as race, in others it is lifestyle, while religion or occupation may be the underlying reasons for others. In some cases these terms will reflect a distinct geographical area (for example, the 'Protestant community' may refer to people of a Protestant background living in the Shankill Road in Belfast). In other cases it may not refer to a distinct location. The business community will draw membership from people living and working in a variety of settings. At other times a claim to belong to a community is made because of a choice (people choose to study at university, therefore their membership of the student community is voluntary). For some, membership is based on an ascribed characteristic (because of skin colour, for example, someone may find themselves 'automatically' belonging to a particular community).

We should consider global influences on community as well. Modern lives are increasingly infused with influences from beyond their immediate location and this too affects how people see those in their immediate surroundings. Savage et al.'s (2005) work on globalisation and belonging points to how the local is infused with global imaginings and meanings. Even though one may live in a particular locality, the liquidity of global flows of information and goods, the symbolic resources that globalisation provides, overlay and enrich the experiences of the spatially situated practices of that local landscape. This can, for example, mean communicating with people on the internet, or the influences on what clothes one wears or the food one eats.

Questions

What examples of globalisation do you encounter in your daily life? Discuss whether or not globalisation is reordering and changing local communities and environments.

In an attempt to overcome these definitional problems we can look at some useful older work by Bell and Newby (1976). They identified three ways in which the concept of community is used:

- as a topographical (geographical) expression
- as a local social system with interconnections between local people and social institutions
- as a human association with no logical connection with places or local social systems.

This may sound interesting in terms of trying to crack an academic problem, but when one turns to applying the conclusions to the real world, to people living in the community, then a few opposite points can be raised:

- What community do they belong to?
- Will someone care for ill or disabled members of the community?
- Will that community take care of people in need?
- Who else belongs to that community?
- Who represents that community?

After considering these issues, another question arises: does caring for people in the community necessarily improve health and avoid the potential problems inherent in institutions? Work by Prior (1993) indicated that in many ways the problems that arise inside institutions are present in communities too. The thrust of his argument arising out of research into community care in Northern Ireland was that even though the location of care had shifted from institutions to the community, the actual substance of patients' daily lives had altered only slightly:

> For when all was said and done, they attended the same day centres as previously, they saw the same social workers, spoke to the same nurses (albeit wearing everyday clothes rather than uniforms), and usually lived with exactly the same individuals as they had done in hospital. For most people it was only the dwellings that were different. (1993: 192)

For many ex-patients, the places they were relocated to still retained many of the features of an institution, with, for example, locked doors or upper-storey windows that could only be partially opened. However, it was more than just the design features of the buildings that echoed the institutions they had come from. The daily routine and the staff they saw also mimicked their experiences in an institution. Life was still lived according to timetables and they saw the same array of mental health workers. Even social events took place in the same locations as they had when the patients were in institutional care.

Questions

How did you react to the preceding paragraph? What do you think of group homes: are they a break from the institution or just the institution in another format? What does this say about attempts to provide better care for those that require it?

One underlying point noted by Prior is that even though changes in discourse and treatment philosophies may change practices in treating mental illness, these changes do not necessarily entail any dramatic shift in the overall circumstances of the patient. It was hoped that the movement away from care in institutions to care in the community would herald a new era of tailored, dignified treatment that broke down barriers and allowed people with mental health problems to become part of the community once more. As Prior notes, however, all that happened for many patients was a change of dwelling. This move might also be into an area that does not regard former mental health care patients as part of their particular community, or welcome them into it.

Care and carers

As mentioned earlier, the NHS and Community Care Act 1990 introduced a variety of changes to the organisation of health and social care. One aspect of this policy was to increase the emphasis on care taking place in a non-institutional context, and to 'firm up' arrangements for informal care. The Conservative government had a variety of reasons for introducing this particular piece of legislation, ranging from efforts to rein in public spending, and a belief in the family as a unit of care, to – as part of their general ideology – an attempt to reduce state provision and to increase individual and family responsibility.

Informal care is a combination of service and affection, provided on the basis of kinship or friendship. It is also mainly unpaid.

Links

The case study of an older person at the end of Chapter 12 provides a useful example of informal care.

The previous paragraph illustrates one of the many ways in which the concept of care is used. Here it is in the context of policy, whereby a particular piece of policy lays out regulations or intentions about how care and caring for people should be carried out. But for most of us the talk of care, especially in an informal context, evokes images of emotions and feelings. However, for those engaged in care work, caring is not just a state of emotionality; it involves onerous work and great physical exertion. Sometimes, caregiving informs ideas about gender roles, especially women's roles. The many facets of care and the way in which the concept of caring is used can make defining care difficult. That is not to say that it has not been attempted. Graham (1983) provides a useful definition of **informal care**. She sees care as being a combination of service and affection. *Service* relates to the 'doing' part of caring, including all the physical aspects such as lifting and handling, washing and bathing, collecting messages and preparing meals. *Affection* relates to the 'feeling' part of caring; this includes love and compassion.

For most people informal care is provided and received on the basis of kinship or family ties (Qureshi and Walker 1989). As care can often involve intimate or physical contact, most people would like care to be provided by a family member, in this order of preference:

- spouse
- relative in lifelong joint household
- daughter
- daughter-in-law
- son
- other relative
- non-relative.

Reciprocity is another factor involved in kinship care: kin have either cared for or will care for other kin.

Gender, class and caregiving

Much of the literature on care indicates that women are the prime caregivers within the family and society as a whole (Lee 1998; Malin et al. 1999). Summarising research, Twigg and Atkin (1994) point to how women are expected to care and how gender makes a difference when it comes to receiving additional support. Men find it easier to access services and are in some ways expected to put up with less than female carers. Morris (1989, cited in Parker 1993) observed that men are less able to take on the caring role. However, one must be careful to avoid the simplistic assumption that all men and all women have uniform experiences. Drawing on the 1985 General Household Survey, and following points made by Graham (1991) that class and race need to be taken into account, Arber and Ginn (1992) indicate that care is multidimensional, with many criss-crossing structural factors. They found quantitative and qualitative differences between men and women according to their class location. The level of physical impairment was only one factor that affected the care experience of households from different class backgrounds; other factors were their ability to access and use different material, financial and cultural resources. Middle-class households had more money available to 'lighten the load' of care. This could be, for example, by building a 'granny flat', or buying aids and adaptations. There was also evidence that middle-class households utilised social services more and were better at obtaining desired outcomes than the working-class households in this study. There was also a class and gender difference. Working-class men were much more likely to be involved in care, looking after someone at home, than were their middle-class counterparts. Looking after someone at home was seen as more demanding, as it restricted employment and leisure opportunities.

Links

Chapter 11 discusses disability in more detail.

Experiences o]f care

The experience of care can vary from being fulfilling and satisfying to being draining and restrictive. As mentioned earlier, affection and feelings of compassion are major reasons for people taking on care work. By demonstrating affection and compassion the carer can realise a sense of purpose and achievement. For many carers, however, there are multiple problems, often to do with restriction of activity, time and money.

Tozer (1999) noted in her research on families with two or more disabled children that the parental carers reported that family life was restricted and they were sometimes left feeling isolated. Dearden and Becker (2000) identified similar findings for young carers, when they reported that for young people involved in care educational opportunities were restricted. Feelings of restriction are commonly noted in research findings. Summarising research, Twigg and Atkin (1994) observed that the problem was not so much restriction caused by carrying out care tasks, though that was important, but generalised feelings of anxiety at leaving the person being cared for on their own. Worries were expressed about safety, or about an unforeseen circumstance arising.

One of the commonest problems facing carers and the people they care for is poverty and financial hardship.

The experience of care: the home and the body

Care brings about many changes and challenges and can unsettle assumptions about two important areas of our lives: how we relate to our home and how we relate to our body. What we shall see in the following discussion is how care leads to a reordering of what home means and how carers interact with the bodies of their loved ones when they are caring for them.

First of all, let us consider and think about what is meant by 'home' as a concept, because 'home' is not just simply a building (a house, in other words) or a place where someone lives, but also an important symbolic and emotional resource. In reviewing the literature from a variety of disciplines on the concept of home, Mallett (2004) draws our attention to how 'home' offers multiple meanings:

- *Memory*. Home is a place where memories reside, though not necessarily tied to a strict chronology or personal narrative. One obvious example of this is the placing of photographs around the home. Photographs in the home capture more than an image of someone; they also capture a particular historical moment or significant person in someone's life. The further one moves in time away from when the image was taken, the more it becomes a memory of that moment or person, and part of the personal narrative.
- *Family*. Traditionally home and family went hand in hand, as the family home and the family house were the same thing. Currently, though, given changes in family structures and the increases in living alone this is not always the case. Especially following divorce and separation, we may have several homes.
- *Haven*. Home is somewhere private that is apart from public life, for example the pressures of work. However, this is increasingly being challenged by the rise of home working.
- *Gender*. Often home is seen as being a female place (though critically one where male authority is ultimately paramount), where women enact their required social roles of home-making and nurturing, with certain spaces in the home being gendered: for example the kitchen as a feminine space and the garage as a masculine space.
- *Identity*. Homes act as a projection or idea of self and who we think we are. In choosing types of decoration, ornaments and furniture we are, in many ways, externalising and putting into objects our sense of self.

Questions

Discuss the importance of place to identity. What trends, if any, can you observe in society that emphasise homes and houses as an important aspect of self?

We must, therefore, be aware that 'home' is a very complex concept and that when care comes into the equation many of the above ideas of what home is can lead to challenges and potential problems. A useful example of this can be found in the research of Angus et al. (2005). They found that the various practices and activities associated with caring could transform and disrupt a household, especially the emotional and symbolic characteristics of a home. This arises (unintentionally) out of the actions of health and social care professionals who are required to make the home more functional (for instance, to make it easier for the person who is being cared for to move about or to use the kitchen) so as to allow the cared-for person to remain in their own home. To do this often means moving furniture or putting in new pieces of equipment. Consequently, this can change how the home is perceived as the various symbolic aspects are disrupted and rearranged. In effect, the home can become a different place, which is no longer the physical and material representation of identity and self. These changes in the home may mirror the changes in the person, with the loss of self that is brought about by illness being visible in the loss of self represented by the rearrangement of the home.

Another aspect of being cared for in the home comes with the involvement of health professionals from the formal care sector. Though health professionals bring valuable skills and experiences to the person who is being cared for, their presence signals another change for the home in a very important way: it becomes a place of work. The changes in how health and social care are organised, with ever more focus on the community, mean that for health professionals the boundaries of their place of work have become increasingly fluid. They are no longer tied to a single location but instead move between multiple locations such as hospitals, community support offices, GP surgeries and people's homes. Again, this is disruptive of the symbolic qualities of home. Normally when someone calls on someone else in their home it is for socialising, or is part of being friends, but when a health or social care professional arrives at someone's house they are not there for informal social interaction but to do their job.

Case study

Mrs Robertson, aged 86, has recently returned home after an operation on a herniated disc that had been causing her some back pain for a considerable time. The operation was very successful, but it will take a few weeks for the discomfort to subside and for her to regain full mobility as she has to use a walking stick. To make life easier, her son has rearranged her living room so that she has more room to walk about and has purchased a high-backed chair to help support her back. In the kitchen, because Mrs Robertson finds it hard to bend down or stretch up to find cooking equipment or packs and cans of food, her son has placed many of these items on the kitchen work surfaces. In many respects, the actions of her son have made life considerably easier for her on a physical functional level. On an emotional level, however, these changes are causing Mrs Robertson distress and anxiety. The neat ordered home with the furniture arranged in particular ways has taken her years to achieve and acts as a strong source of personal identity for her. But with everything in the living room pushed to the walls, it looks, to her, a complete mess and she finds it very embarrassing when friends and neighbours call round for a visit. The kitchen too was often a source of pride but now it just looks messy, with many objects that should be in cupboards now out in the open. All in all, she finds the changes in her home as much a problem as the problems with her back, but worst of all, seeing her home this way makes her feel old, something she does not like.

Much of the physical act of caring for someone involves close physical contact and interacting with someone's body, and research by Twigg (2006) notes that this can lead to many challenges. Often care is quite intimate in what it can involve: for example, it can mean helping someone cut their toenails or assisting them in using a toilet, or washing and dressing them. These activities may seem quite functional, in that they are necessary to maintain the hygiene and the general well-being of someone requiring care. For the person (often a partner or a close family member) who performs the care these activities, however, come with an emotional cost. In Chapter 11 on the body we saw how the body is not just a biological entity but is also important to our sense of self and to how we relate to others. Part of this involves strong social and personal norms concerning which parts of our body we permit others to see and touch. Allowing someone to touch intimate places, such as the genitals, is a very special and symbolic act denoting that we see that individual in a particular way. Thus, the touching becomes part of how we relate to someone on an emotional level, the act of touching being a bodily manifestation of the inner emotions of affection and love, for example. This relationship between emotions and the body is disrupted when the act of touching no longer takes place to demonstrate affection but to maintain the functionality of the body. Many carers report that they begin to see and relate to the body of the person they are caring for, particularly if is their partner, in a different way. The affection intimacy may be replaced with a functional intimacy. This can have an impact on the relationship between the carer and the person they are caring for, as they may no longer see that person as a sexualised human being or the person they relate to in that way.

Questions

What taboos and norms surround the body in contemporary society, especially when it comes to touching and looking at the body? Is there a contradiction between the functional needs of care and the emotional needs of a relationship?

Conclusion

Providing a place to care for people who require assistance, support and someone to look after them has been, and no doubt always will be, a challenging issue for society. What we have reviewed here are various attempts to provide that care, and the often unintentional problems that consequently arise.

Sociological perspectives on the rise of the asylum are mainly critical, on various grounds. This can range from seeing asylums as a 'bricks-and-mortar' manifestation of the power of certain groups in society, to viewing them as a dumping ground for those surplus to capitalism's requirements. Sometimes it is the institutional requirements – needing to organise large groups of people to ensure that they are fed and clothed for example – which lead to an established identity being degraded and transformed into an identity that is compliant and easy to manage for an institution.

Shifts in government policy within the UK have seen an increasing focus on care in the community. This can be viewed as an appealing alternative to some of the issues noted above. In reality, however, community care brings fresh challenges. The actual existence of community, in the sense of a definable entity which will offer care and support for those requiring assistance, is questionable. Various impulses and processes, such as greater emphasis on individualism, are causing a move away from civic involvement and being 'community minded'. This brings into relief who will be doing the care work. Often, in reality, this will mean care being provided by friends and families. Though this brings its own rewards, carers can experience financial difficulties as well as disturbances in their relationship with the person for whom they are providing care.

How all these problems are to be resolved is still open to question. What this chapter clearly draws our attention to is that looking after someone and providing appropriate care is highly complex and multidimensional, in both the physical and financial resourcing of care and the demanding emotional work that accompanies informal care.

Summary points

- Various theories attempt to understand organisations. Weber stresses rationality and bureaucracy; Foucault emphasises surveillance and physical space; Blau notes the existence of informal routines.
- Institutional care has been strongly criticised on the grounds that institutions act as a method of social control or a 'dumping ground' for so-called undesirables.
- Goffman critiques institutions for causing institutionalisation – an assault on self and identity.
- Defining community can be hard, with definitions including places or shared characteristics such as ethnicity or class.
- Care in the community may create further problems and may not necessarily avoid the problems of institutional care.

- Providing care in the home can alter the symbolic and emotional elements of a home.
- The close contact of physical care provided by an informal carer can impinge on their affective relationship with a loved one.

Case study

Bill was admitted to Culliere Hospital 25 years ago diagnosed with a psychotic condition. Initially he was quite ill and had phases of believing that he could hear the thoughts of other people and that they were saying unpleasant things about him. After years of treatment and care the symptoms became manageable and their frequency declined, to the point that he no longer seems very ill any more. Over the years his role within the hospital has changed. He quite often assists with some of the group therapy sessions and has some responsibility for maintaining and tidying the art room. Bill was given that duty as he enjoys painting and is quite an accomplished watercolourist. Some of his work is hung in hospitals throughout the region. On Wednesdays and Sundays he even takes classes with some of the day patients, teaching them the basics of using watercolours. His skilled painting and control over the art room has sometimes led new members of staff to think that he is a part-time member of staff, perhaps a retired art teacher who wants to help in the hospital.

In many ways Bill feels happy and fulfilled in what he does and has expressed no desire to return to his family. However, recently the local health trust has been attempting to reduce the number of long-term patients in the hospital, with an eye to possibly closing the facility down altogether. To this end it has been decided by the hospital and social services that Bill is well enough to live in the community. This has made him feel highly anxious. He does not want to lose his art room or the chance to take classes. On three occasions now he has been taken to a halfway house to see if he would like it there. His initial impressions were all negative. There was no art room and the neighbours in the street did not look particularly friendly, some actually appearing quite hostile. To settle him in he was told that he would still see the same occupational therapist as he had in the hospital, and that it would be possible for him to continue to hold his art classes in the hospital. This reassured him slightly, but ultimately Bill really wanted to stay at Culliere. After all, for him it was home.

1 How has the stay in Culliere Hospital affected Bill?
2 Do you think moving him would help his mental health?
3 Why might the local community not welcome the siting of a halfway home in their area?
4 Where do you think people are best treated or cared for?

Taking your studies further

This chapter will have helped you understand many of the key terms, concepts, theories and debates relating to institutions and community care. Listed below are journal articles and books that will provide deeper and more detailed discussions of the points raised in this chapter. You will also find what is available on the companion website. This offers downloads of relevant material, plus links to useful websites in addition to podcasts and other features.

Recommended reading

Angus, J., Kontos, P., Dyck, I., McKeever, P. and Poland, B. (2005) 'The personal significance of home: habitus and the experience of receiving long-term care', *Sociology of Health and Illness*, 27 (2): 161–87.

Goffman, E. (1975) *Asylums: Essays on the Social Situation of Mental Patients and Other Inmates*. Harmondsworth: Penguin.

Prior, L. (1993) *The Social Organization of Mental Illness*. London: Sage.

Twigg, J. (2006) *The Body in Health and Social Care*. Houndmills: Palgrave Macmillan.

On the companion website

Little, M., Paul, K., Jordens, C.F.C. and Sayers, E.-J. (2000) 'Vulnerability in the narratives of patients and their carers: studies of colorectal cancer', *Health*, 10 (4): 495–510.

14

Health care in context

With Clare Swan and Pedro Morago

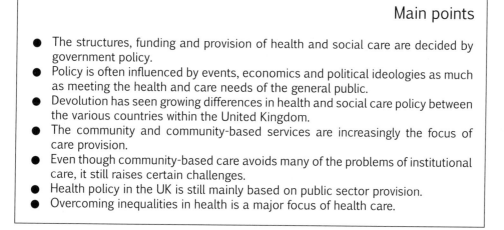

Main points

- The structures, funding and provision of health and social care are decided by government policy.
- Policy is often influenced by events, economics and political ideologies as much as meeting the health and care needs of the general public.
- Devolution has seen growing differences in health and social care policy between the various countries within the United Kingdom.
- The community and community-based services are increasingly the focus of care provision.
- Even though community-based care avoids many of the problems of institutional care, it still raises certain challenges.
- Health policy in the UK is still mainly based on public sector provision.
- Overcoming inequalities in health is a major focus of health care.

Key concepts

Health ● community ● policy ● devolution ● carers ● private ● public ● institutionalisation.

Introduction

The previous chapter discussed various issues and challenges that have arisen in connection with care provided in institutions and in the community. Lately, within the UK as a whole there has been a discernible shift towards community services, as opposed to everything being provided in, let us say, a hospital or other centralised location. This shift has been driven by government policy, and it is both useful and important to have an overview of how changes in government policy have led to changes 'on the ground' which affect the experiences of both those who provide care and those who receive care.

In this chapter, the focus will be on some of the issues and influences that have helped shape government policy on both community and hospital services. What should become evident is that the policy that governments enact is not always entirely made in response to the health and care needs of the population. Often, we see how events, social issues, economics and political ideologies exert a powerful effect on the shape and scope of government policy.

There are two 'complications' in discussing hospital and community care policies in the UK today. Prior to the 1990s wide-sweeping policy changes were quite rare, and developments in the organisation of health and social care services proceeded incrementally and uniformly across all the various regions and nations of the UK. Since 1990 there has been a sea change in health and social care policy. First, policy changes are much more rapid than they used to be. New legislation is brought forth on a very regular basis, often in response to crises, such as concern over waiting times and the cleanliness of hospitals. Therefore, the emphasis is on themes more than on the actual details and mechanics of policy and legislation. Second, the actual political structure of the UK has changed, with Scotland, Wales and, given the hopeful progress of the peace process, Northern Ireland being devolved to greater or lesser extent from central control by Westminster. Scotland exercises the greatest devolved powers and has exclusive control over its health and social care policy. Admittedly at first the differences between Scottish and English policy were fairly minimal, but as devolution cements itself as a political structure the differences are becoming more noticeable, albeit still based on common themes. So one must be very careful in distinguishing between health and social care policies throughout the UK: the most noticeable differences exist between Scotland and England.

In this policy context, some useful definitions are as follows:

- *Public provision or public sector*. Health and social care is organised and provided by the state through a network of different services at national and local level. Funding usually comes from taxation or some form of national or social insurance. This approach is common in European countries.
- *Private provision or private sector*. Individuals are responsible for organising and purchasing their own health and social care. This is achieved by taking out insurance and other policies with private for-profit companies. The extent and level of coverage are decided by what the individual can and wishes to spend. This approach is common in the United States.

- *Market system.* Maximum efficiency, economy and performance are supposedly achieved by having either individuals or organisations competing against each other for customers or clients. The act of competition should increase responsiveness to customer needs. Margaret Thatcher's Conservative administration applied this approach to the UK NHS during the 1980s.
- *Third Way.* A political ideology associated with the British Labour Party that stresses cooperation between private and public provision, by combining the best practices of both.

Community care

The term **community care** is used to cover the range of policies, procedures and legislation that are concerned with the planning, funding and delivery of services for older people, people with learning and physical difficulties and illness, people with mental health problems, people with HIV/AIDS, drug or alcohol problems and other progressive illnesses, and disabled children. Any discussion of community care policies must, by necessity, encompass the policy developments in a number of fields.

There is a need to be selective when identifying the key policies; the sheer volume and range make this an enormous subject area. This chapter will aim to look at where community care policies come from, including a brief historical account of the move away from institutionalisation; the key policy milestones, particularly over the last twenty years; the aims of these policies; and some of the realities for service users and their families.

Links

See Chapter 13 for more sociological perspectives on community, carers and institutionalisation.

It is important when looking at current policies to have some understanding of the nature of institutionalisation and the reasons for the move away from this pattern of service provision. In recent historical terms, any discussion of institutional care begins with the building of large institutions or hospitals during the late nineteenth century. Many were built as a means of providing care and treatment for people with mental health problems and learning disabilities or for people who were seen as being in moral danger.

We now know that people who lived in these large hospitals became institutionalised. By this we mean that all day-to-day activities were organised to cater for the needs of large numbers of people and not for the needs of individuals. Daily routines were set and people had little or no choice about the food they ate, the clothes they wore, the activities they took part in, or the people they socialised with. There was a very clear hierarchy within these institutions, with patients firmly at the bottom. Doors were often locked and people's freedom was restricted, particularly in terms of not being allowed to leave the hospital. The fact that many of these hospitals were located in the countryside added to the sense of isolation and dislocation from mainstream society (Means et al. 2003: 26–32).

The effect that this type of regime had on people who had been patients for a long period, of which there were many, was that they became dependent on the routines of the hospital. They lost the ability to make everyday decisions about their lives and became heavily dependent on the perceived safety and protection of the hospital. Many people found it difficult to form what would be seen as healthy attachments and relationships with other people, and some went on to display more extreme forms of institutionalised behaviour characterised by repetitive movements or patterns of speech.

Questions

What theory have we discussed that provides sociological insights into institutionalisation?

The post-war years saw the first major policy development in the fields of health and social care following the publication of the Beveridge Report in 1942. This report signalled the beginning of a rapid expansion in the provision of health and social services. Lord Beveridge acknowledged that 'the community' had to take on a greater responsibility for the care of the more vulnerable members of society. Another key milestone in the organisation and provision of health and social care was the Royal Commission on Mental Illness and Mental Deficiency in 1957. Its report was the first official document to make mention of the term 'community care'. This document stated that the time had come for a shift to community care. This move away from hospital-based care was continued with the introduction of the Mental Health Act 1959. Increased momentum was gained as a result of a number of high-profile inquiries into the care and treatment provided within state-run hospitals, for example the Ely Hospital Inquiry 1969. This inquiry found that people living in large institutions not only were adversely affected by being institutionalised, but also, in some instances, were treated badly and abused by the people employed to care for them.

It was not until the 1970s and early 1980s that there was significant policy development in relation to the care of older people. The Social Services Act of 1970 placed increasing emphasis on improving the structure of local authorities in order to facilitate the changes in service delivery that were envisaged. The aim was to keep older people out of residential care and to develop community and domiciliary supports such as day centres and home helps. In addition, there was a clear decision to enable people to enter private residential homes. This policy essentially channelled **public sector** funds into the private institutional sector while leaving the domiciliary sector chronically under-resourced. Private residential homes increased in number and, in the absence of the necessary community services, older people had little choice other than the decision about which institution they might enter in the residential **private sector** (Adams et al. 1998: 54).

The Conservative government of the day proposed that a competitive market, which included the private and voluntary sectors, would inevitably provide better, cheaper services than a protected and overly bureaucratic public sector. Margaret Thatcher brought to the forefront of the community care debate the government's concern about the cost of hospital and nursing-based care. She felt that the state should take a back seat in the provision of care for the elderly and those with mental illnesses and learning difficulties (Clarke 1994: 76–82). The *Growing Older* White Paper (1981) was very much in line with Thatcherite policies. It identified the primary source of support for older people in the community as being informal and voluntary, relying heavily on family, friends and neighbours. This kind of informal support was viewed as irreplaceable. Therefore care *in* the community was seen as being care *by* the community (Tinker 1996: 199–207).

Questions

Do you think there should be competition between various parts of the NHS, as the Conservative government in the 1990s attempted to introduce?

There was considerable opposition to this new direction of policy development, as it was seen as being motivated by financial constraints and a desire to curb public spending. One of the main concerns was that care by the community effectively meant care by women, and the benefit payments that existed in no way compensated for the loss of earnings that necessarily occurred when a woman took on extra caring responsibilities. Other concerns, which continue to this day, were that community-based care was seen as a cheaper option, whereas in fact many would argue that for community care to be effective and of a high quality, it can be as expensive, if not more so, than looking after people in large institutions.

The Audit Commission Report *Making a Reality of Community Care* (1986) was critically important in the developments that were to follow. The report stood as an objective and non-political discourse on the state of community care arrangements. Following on from this report, the government commissioned Sir Roy Griffiths to look at the organisation of and funding for community care services. He produced a report called *Community Care: An Agenda for Action* (Griffiths, 1988). This identified three main objectives underpinning the new community care policy. These focused on the individual user and carer in terms of meeting need, improving choice and promoting self-determination.

The Griffiths Report was an important milestone in that it strongly influenced the White Paper *Caring for People: Community Care in the Next Decade and Beyond* (DHSS 1989). This accepted some of the Griffiths proposals and held as centrally important the aims of increasing user choice, promoting non-institutional services and targeting services to those that needed them. In short, though local authorities were to retain responsibility for community care, they were to work far more closely with the private and voluntary sectors. It was also proposed that local authorities would be less involved in the direct provision of services and more involved in the assessment of people's needs and managing the care that was provided. In essence it was planned that they would take on more of a coordinating role. The White Paper was essentially the blueprint for what we recognise today as 'care management' (Means et al. 2003: 43–71).

It was envisaged that the process of these organisational changes would be extremely complex. When the National Health Service and Community Care Act was enacted in June 1990, the Conservative government announced that implementation would be phased in between April 1991 and April 1993.

The way in which this piece of legislation has been implemented has evolved over the last 15 years. In the early 1990s, those involved in the front line of assessing need (care managers and social workers) were encouraged to be innovative and to make use of formal and informal support services in the community. Many who were employed as care managers in 1993 will remember the days when therapies such as aromatherapy and reflexology were included in packages of care. However, the harsh reality of limited budgets soon impacted, and all but essential services were deemed 'wants' and not 'needs'. An essential part of the process of care management is the assessment of people's needs. Policy clearly instructs local authorities and practitioners to focus on individual need and not on the resources available. This remains the cornerstone of good practice, but it is perhaps unavoidable that knowledge of the limited availability of local resources may have some impact on the assessments carried out (McDonald 1999: 15–16).

Since the introduction of the National Health Service and Community Care Act 1990, a range of additional legislation has been introduced, not to replace the 1990 Act but to supplement it. The first two pieces of legislation to be introduced were the Carers (Recognition and Services) Act 1995 and the Community Care Direct Payments Act 1996.

All of the legislation and policy discussed so far have applied to all parts of the UK. However, part of the manifesto of the incoming Labour government of 1997 was a commitment to devolution. Following the referendums in Scotland and Wales in 1997, the new Scottish Parliament and Welsh Assembly met for the first time in 1999. Likewise in Northern Ireland, following the Good Friday Agreement (1998), the Northern Ireland Assembly and Executive was introduced in 1999. The consequence of this is that since 1997 different parts of the UK have developed different legislation and policy through their devolved powers, and this has led to different patterns of service provision across the UK (Sharkey 2007: 1–23).

Questions

Do you think that devolution will or could bring about improvements in health and social care policy?

In Scotland, the Regulation of Care (Scotland) Act 2001 and the Community Care and Health (Scotland) Act 2002 are the two major pieces of legislation introduced since devolution. These developments in legislation are underpinned by policies drawn up and implemented by the Scottish Executive. Community care policy change in Scotland is driven by the Joint Future Agenda. Joint Future is the lead policy on joint working between local authorities and the National Health Service in community care. Its main aim, as stated by the Executive, 'is to provide faster access to better and more joined up services, through improved joint working' (Scottish Government 2010).

In England, the most recent developments in community care legislation include the Community Care (Residential Accommodation) Act 1998, the Carers and Disabled Children Act 2000, the Care Standards Act 2000 and the Carers (Equal Opportunities) Act 2004. All have introduced key developments that have had a direct impact on service users, carers, service providers and regulatory and inspection bodies. More recent developments in policy have come from the Green Paper *Independence, Well-being and Choice* (Department of Health 2005b). This summed up the key themes in the way that the government saw the future of community care, and plans were set out for service users to be able to choose and buy the care they needed. These ideas were incorporated into a joint health and social care White Paper published in early 1996, *Our Health, Our Care, Our Say: A New Direction for Community Services* (Department of Health 2006). This White Paper emphasised the need for joint working between health and social care services. The main policy developments in England, as implemented by the Department of Health, come from the National Service Frameworks, which are designed to bring together health professionals, service users and carers, health service managers, partner agencies and other advocates (for example the *Framework for Mental Health*: Department of Health 2011).

Underpinning the policy and legislative developments discussed above are certain aims and assumptions. Though on the surface they are widely held and adhered to, it is useful to look at them in a little more detail and to acknowledge some of the realities of community care as experienced by service users, carers and social care workers.

First is the belief that people would rather be cared for in their own homes. On the face of it, this is a fairly uncontroversial statement. Most people, when asked, would state that should they need assistance when they are older or if they became unwell or disabled, they would far rather receive this care from people coming to their house than have to move into residential care. Indeed, social workers and care managers are often in the position of supporting families who are struggling with the reality of no longer being able to care for a relative that they promised not to 'put in a home'. The reality, however, can be rather different. The picture provided by the case study on Bella (at the end of this chapter) is not one normally associated with the ideal of caring for people in their own home in accordance with their and their families' wishes. This is in no way an argument against the provision of community care through domiciliary services, but hopefully illustrates some of the complexities involved in caring for people in their own homes. One of the key challenges then is to ensure that domiciliary services are fit for purpose and can adequately meet the needs of the most vulnerable people (Fink 2004: 30–2).

Links

See Chapter 13 for more discussion on issues arising out of caring for people in their own home.

Another common statement made when discussing care in the community is that, given the choice, people would always want to move out of an institution and back to their own home. The pitfalls of institutional living have been well documented and were looked at briefly at the beginning of this chapter. Again, though, the reality can be rather more complex. People who have lived most of their lives in an institution can find the transition to living in smaller community-based accommodation, or even independently in their own homes, daunting and overwhelming. Their whole identity may be tied up in the fabric of the institution that they are leaving. They may have firmly established friendships and social networks and even jobs such as working in the garden or the laundry. They may feel a real sense of belonging and purpose that is hard to replace.

What is also often overlooked is the sense of safety and protection that people may experience when living in an institution. During discussions between a patient group from the local psychiatric hospital and a senior executive of the health board in the north-east of Scotland, it emerged that the proposed removal of the stone wall that separated the hospital from the city was viewed with horror by some patients. They saw this wall as something that offered them protection, not a symbol of segregation as had been assumed by the powers that be.

The case study on Derek, Joe and Ivan (at the end of this chapter) illustrates these conflicting considerations. Again this is in no way an argument against the ideals of community care that say that people should be enabled to live in smaller home-like establishments that are thoroughly integrated in the community. It does highlight though the need to approach the subject with sensitivity and to avoid making simplistic assumptions. A great deal of planning and support is needed to enable service users to move towards a more independent lifestyle with greater contact with the wider community.

Alongside the aims and objectives contained in community care legislation and policy, one of the key factors in the development and delivery of services is the availability of finance to fund and develop the necessary resources. The experiences of all those in receipt of community care services and those involved in its implementation are inevitably affected by the level of funding available. Community care is one of the highest areas of revenue spending for most local authorities. Policy and legislation state that assessments should be *needs led* and not *resource led*, but the reality is that there are insufficient resources or finances to meet the needs of all those assessed as requiring a service. Allocation criteria have been devised and employed to distribute the resources as fairly as possible. This inevitably leads to concerns about the system being overly bureaucratic, with a danger of different client groups competing against each other for their share of the pot. The challenge today for each local authority is to ensure that these limited resources are targeted at the most vulnerable members of society.

The concepts of health, health care and health care policy

The best-known definition of health is that established by the World Health Organisation (WHO) in 1946. Health was then defined as 'a state of complete physical, mental and social well-being and not merely the absence of disease or infirmity' (World Health Organisation 1992). Such a wide definition of health has been criticised as idealistic and impractical (Doll 1992) as well as for describing a state which seems to correspond more to happiness than to health (Saracci 1997). Furthermore, different commentators have urged the WHO, in recent years, to provide a more realistic definition of health that allows the measurement and comparison of states of health and disease as well as the objective evaluation of the effectiveness of health programmes wherever these are implemented (Bok 2004; Saracci 1997; Üstün and Jakob 2005). Nonetheless, the WHO definition had the merit of laying the foundations – more than half a century ago – for an integral approach to health care which takes into consideration the different dimensions of the human being. Largely as a result of such a holistic approach, health care is now widely regarded as the delivery of services aimed at (1) preventing and treating illness, (2) promoting, preserving and restoring mental and physical health, and (3) tackling socio-economic factors that may have a negative impact upon the individual's health. Health care policy, therefore, refers to the set of governmental strategies and initiatives related to the financing and provision of services whose scope falls within any of these three broad areas. The rest of this section provides an overview of how health care is organised in the UK as well as of the structure of the National Health Service in Scotland.

Questions

The paragraph above discussed how health should be defined as more than an absence of disease and should instead be holistic and encompassing social aspects. Reflect on this definition in light of what we have discussed throughout this book.

Health care in the UK: provision, funding and levels of expenditure

The UK health care market is dominated by the public sector, with the National Health Service (NHS) providing around 74 per cent of all health care services. **Private provision** constitutes almost 20 per cent of the UK health care system, while the rest of the market is served by the voluntary sector. However, since some private and voluntary services are funded with public money, it is estimated that more than 81 per cent of the total health care provided in the UK is publicly funded (Ham 2004; Laing and Buisson 2003). The vast majority of public expenditure on health is paid for by general taxation, while the rest of the money is provided by sources such as National Insurance contributions, charges, land and property sales and tobacco duty.

Overall, levels of health care expenditure in the UK are below those of France, Germany and the Scandinavian countries. However, publicly funded health care spending is higher in Scotland than in England. For example, in 2003 Scotland had a total NHS expenditure of £1262 per capita compared to £1085 spent in England in the same period (Alvarez-Rosete et al. 2005). Whether this results in Scotland having better health outcomes and services than England still remains uncertain (Irvine and Ginsberg 2004).

Questions

Should spending on health be increased in the UK? If so, what political issues could arise in raising taxation to fund such a rise?

Although not formally integrated within the health care market, the informal sector deserves a special mention. In fact, a considerable amount of health work is carried out every day by carers who do not form part of the health care market, like women caring for and giving support to relatives who are ill or frail (Allsop 2003). The contribution of this unpaid labour in the community to the functioning of the whole health care system is so important that the Scottish Parliament has formally acknowledged the needs of unpaid carers and promoted strategies for their support in the Community Care and Health (Scotland) Act 2002.

The NHS

Despite the importance of other sectors, the vast majority of health care in the UK is provided, as stated above, by the NHS. Before 1948, health care was provided through different sources such as private services, insurance schemes, and charities and voluntary hospitals. However, these services did not cover the health needs of large sectors of the population, such as those who were not insured workers and chronic patients who could not afford to pay for their health care, the care of whom was often left to overcrowded and poorly resourced infirmaries. In addition, hospital care was not included within insurance-based schemes, so that only primary care was provided to insured workers in return for their contributions.

The above situation was addressed in 1948 with the creation of the NHS, which was founded upon the following principles:

- *Universality and equity.* This means that all members of the UK population have the right to equitable access to NHS services regardless of income, socio-demographic background and health status. Therefore, with the implementation of the NHS health care was enshrined in practice as a fundamental human right to which everyone, without exception or distinction, is entitled.
- *Comprehensiveness of the services provided.* As noted above, before the creation of the NHS, insured workers had only access to primary care services in return for their contributions. However, the situation changed with the creation of the NHS, which is intended to cover all the health needs of the population through a variety of services such as primary care, hospital care and community health services.
- *Free health care at the point of delivery, financed from general taxation.* No longer should anybody be excluded from access to health care services due to their lack of financial resources.

Questions

Discuss what you think about the founding principles of the NHS. Do you think they are still relevant in contemporary Britain?

While the NHS has remained a cornerstone of British society since 1948, the above principles have been somewhat eroded over the last decades by the introduction of charges for some services – e.g. prescriptions, some dental treatment and spectacles – and the prioritising and rationing of resources. Besides, the NHS underwent a major reform with the implementation of the NHS and Community Care Act 1990. This introduced a process of decentralisation in the organisation and provision of health care whereby responsibilities traditionally considered the role of the Department of Health were transferred to lower-level authorities (Allsop 2003). The 1990 Act also created a split between budget holders or purchasers of services and health care trusts – independent organisations which provide hospital services and care in the community. The changes brought by the 1990 Act encouraged the application, to a certain extent, of market principles – like competition between providers – which were expected to result in higher-quality, transparent and accountable services offered at competitive costs.

The NHS reforms initiated by the Conservative governments have generally been consolidated by their Labour successors, which published the 2000 *NHS Plan* (Department of Health 2000), an ambitious programme to transform the NHS over the following 10 years. Perhaps the most significant change in relation to previous policies is that, although maintaining the purchaser/provider split within a quasi-market context, the 2000 *NHS Plan* shifts the emphasis from competition between providers to a more collaborative, longer-term approach between purchasers and providers of health care services. It also continues to strengthen the role of management within health care settings, a factor which, coupled with the rise of consumerism and public expectations, has led to a relative decline of medical dominance within the NHS (Allsop 2003).

The NHS in Scotland

In 1999 responsibility for health was devolved to the Scottish political institutions. The Scottish Parliament now has the power to pass laws in the area of health, and the Minister for Health and Community Care within the Scottish Executive is responsible for the overall running of the health and community care services in Scotland. In 2000, the Scottish Executive Health Department – the government department designed to set health care policies as well as to manage the NHS – published *Our National Health: A Plan for Action, a Plan for Change* (Scottish Executive 2000), the Scottish national health strategy. This document contains the Scottish Executive's plans to reform the NHS according to the principles of standard setting, public involvement and health improvement – with special emphasis on coronary heart disease, cancer, mental health, and the health of children and older people (Pullen 2002).

In Scotland, the NHS provides the following services or levels of care:

- *Primary care.* This includes general practice, dentistry, optics, pharmacy and community nursing. These services are mostly delivered by community health partnerships which, although formally integrated within NHS boards, manage their own budget and have relatively high decision-making levels.

- *Secondary or hospital care.* This is provided by the NHS boards – which own hospitals and are managed by their own boards of governors – and several special health boards.
- *Tertiary care.* This consists of highly specialised services for unusual or complex clinical problems.
- *Community care.* Community care for older people, individuals with mental health problems and individuals with a learning disability is also provided by NHS boards in partnership with local authorities.
- *Public health.* This involves major initiatives aimed at disease prevention as well as health promotion among the general population of Scotland. These areas are the responsibility of public health departments integrated into each NHS board.

Health inequalities in the UK

Despite the NHS principles of comprehensiveness of care and equitable access to NHS services for all sections of the UK population, some groups appear to be significantly healthier than others. While health inequalities can be somehow associated with factors such as geography, age, gender, ethnicity, mental health status and disability, a considerable body of evidence – which will be examined below – suggests that socio-economic inequalities are the main contributor to the health divide. The first major study to investigate health differentials between social classes in the UK was commissioned by the Labour government in 1976. The study – known as the Black Report (Black et al. 1980) – showed an overall poorer health experience amongst lower occupational groups: for example, mortality levels for unskilled manual workers were 2.5 times higher than for professional workers. The findings of the Black Report were confirmed and expanded by 'The health divide' (Whitehead 1987) and the *Independent Inquiry into Inequalities in Health* (Acheson et al. 1998). This inquiry, also known as the Acheson Report, found that the health gap in the UK had been widening since the 1970s. By the early 1990s mortality amongst unskilled workers was three times higher than for those in professional occupations. Another example is the increase in life expectancy between the late 1970s and the late 1980s, which was higher for individuals in the highest occupational groups – two years for men and women – than for those in the lowest classes – 1.4 years for men and one year for women (Hattersly 1997).

The problem of health disparities is particularly serious in Scotland. First of all, comparative studies show that health and life expectancy in Scotland – particularly among women – are poor compared to the rest of the UK and most Northern and Western European countries (Hanlon et al. 2001; Leon et al. 2001). In addition, health inequalities between socio-economic groups in Scotland have increased over the last decades (Shaw et al. 1999). A major study commissioned by the Health Promotion Policy Unit in partnership with the Public Health Institute of Scotland (Blamey et al. 2002) has reviewed the evidence in this area, providing – amongst others – the following examples of health differentials within Scotland:

- The differential in premature death rates between the 'best health' and the 'worst health' areas of Scotland increased over the 1990s (Rahman et al. 2000).
- Individuals living in the most deprived areas of Scotland are between two and three times more likely to experience lung cancer than those living in the least deprived areas (Scottish Executive 2001; Sharp and Brewster 1999).
- The risk of dying from coronary heart disease is 2.5 times greater amongst individuals living in the most deprived areas of Scotland than those living in the least deprived areas (Scottish Executive 2001).
- Since 1995, consumption of fresh fruit increased more in the least deprived areas of Scotland than in the most deprived areas (Shaw et al. 2000).

A more recent study produced by the New Policy Institute for the Joseph Rowntree Foundation shows similar findings. For example, individuals aged 35–59 living in social housing are three times more likely to have a limiting long-standing illness than owner-occupiers within the same age range; and the proportion of babies born with a low birth weight is twice as high in the most deprived areas as in areas with below-average deprivation rates (Palmer et al. 2005). The above and other examples demonstrate that, despite certain progress in Scotland's overall health profile, substantial health inequalities still remain between different socio-economic groups.

Links

See Chapter 6 for more information on class and health inequalities, including the Black Report.

Policy developments and strategies

Initiatives in this area during the 1980s and early 1990s put considerable emphasis on the role of health-related behaviours (Fulop et al. 1998). However, the evidence presented in the *Independent Inquiry into Inequalities in Health* (Acheson et al. 1998) showed the major impact of socio-economic factors on health inequalities. Shortly after the publication of the Acheson Report the British government published the public health White Paper *Saving Lives: Our Healthier Nation* (Department of Health 1999a). Besides broad priority areas and new targets for health improvement, the White Paper expressed the government's commitment to reducing health inequalities. This area was expanded in *Reducing Health Inequalities: An Action Report* (Department of Health 1999b), *The NHS Plan* (Department of Health 2000) and *Tackling Health Inequalities: A Programme for*

Action (Department of Health 2003), which set out the national strategy to tackle health inequalities in England over the following three years. A new White Paper was released in 2004; in *Choosing Health: Making Healthy Choices Easier* (Department of Health 2004) the government focuses on reducing and preventing unhealthy lifestyles and also outlines the increasingly important role of primary care trusts – particularly those serving deprived areas – in tackling health inequalities. In addition, it reiterates the targets and commitments contained in *Tackling Health Inequalities.* Progress towards those targets has been reviewed in *Tackling Health Inequalities: Status Report on the Programme for Action* (Department of Health 2005a). The report notes significant developments in child poverty reduction since 1997 as well as improvements in housing quality for lower socio-economic groups. Death rates from circulatory disease and cancer are other areas in which the health gap seems to be narrowing. However, although the indicators reported are promising in the long term, it is not clear whether they will be sufficient in order to meet the targets set for 2010.

Tackling health inequalities is also a major goal of the Scottish Executive's health policies. The White Paper *Towards a Healthier Scotland* (Scottish Office Department of Health 1999) set targets in relation to coronary heart disease, cancer, smoking, alcohol abuse, unwanted teenage pregnancy and dental health to reduce health inequalities between socio-economic groups by 2010. Narrowing the health gap also appears as one of the main themes of the publications *Improving Health in Scotland: The Challenge* (Scottish Executive 2003) and *Building a Better Scotland* (Scottish Executive 2004a). These major initiatives have been complemented by:

- the Scottish Executive's anti-poverty strategy *Closing the Opportunity Gap* (Scottish Executive 2004b) which, focusing on deprived communities, includes action in the areas of education, housing, employment and health
- *Fair to All, Personal to Each: The Next Step for the NHS Scotland* (Scottish Executive 2004c), a policy paper on NHS targets and performances which also includes tackling health inequalities as one of its priorities
- *Delivering for Health 2005* (Scottish Executive 2005), a programme which – among other objectives – seeks to strengthen and enhance primary care services to achieve better health outcomes in the most deprived areas as well as to reduce health inequalities.

Questions

What policies do you think are required to reduce health inequalities in society?

Conclusion

Despite the principles of free and equitable access to NHS services for all members of the population and comprehensiveness of the services provided, health inequality remains a major public health problem in the UK. In past decades, the debate around such a challenging phenomenon has often been characterised by the advocacy of simple explanations (West 1998). However, a large body of evidence from research studies suggests that a combination of mutually reinforcing socio-economic factors is the driving force behind the health divide. Consequently, reducing health inequalities requires a strategic, multidimensional response which addresses the underlying determinants of such inequalities, such as poverty and social exclusion, unequal distribution of wealth and life chances, and adverse living and working conditions. Although recent policies in the UK seem to adopt a holistic approach to tackling health inequalities, it is still too early to know whether such initiatives will be sufficient to achieve higher levels of social justice and a better distribution of wealth, resources and opportunities (Bywaters 1999).

Summary points

- The organisation and delivery of care are shaped by government policy.
- Policy is often influenced by political ideology, events and economics.
- Over the last 10 years or so there has been a substantial increase in the frequency and volume of new health and social care policies being introduced.
- Devolution within the UK has seen increasingly different policy initiatives being pursued by England and Scotland, though many commonalities still remain.
- Community care policy sought to provide care tailored to the needs of the individual and to avoid the problems of institutional care.
- The reality of community care is often different from its intentions. Finance is a major constraint in deciding the level of care and support.
- The NHS was founded to provide free and equal access to hospital care.
- Health policy across the UK currently focuses on the reduction of health inequalities.

Case study: Bella

Bella lived on her own in a two-bedroomed council flat. Her only daughter lived about 200 miles away and visited once a year. Bella had always been determined that should she need assistance as she grew older, this should be provided in her own home. Her daughter was determined to uphold Bella's wishes with regard to this and was reluctant to discuss the possibility that her mother might at some point need to be cared for in a residential setting.

Bella was diagnosed with severe dementia and was disoriented with regard to time, space and people. Carers came to her house to help her to get up in the morning and dress her; to administer her medication; to prepare her food and supervise her while she ate it; to do her shopping and collect her pension; and to help her to wash and get into bed at the end of the day.

The reality of providing this level of support is that a number of agencies (private, voluntary and local authority) needed to be involved. This necessitated a high number of staff providing care and support. There was the occasional, perhaps inevitable, breakdown in communication if a carer was off sick or rotas had been changed. This meant that sometimes Bella could sit waiting for one of her meals, or need help getting in and out of bed, and no one would turn up to assist her.

Even when services did run smoothly, Bella was confused by the number of people, often unfamiliar due to high staff turnover, who came to her house. She became frightened and suspicious and often refused to let people in. When this happened staff spent an increasing amount time trying to negotiate their way into the flat and therefore had little time to spend with Bella. This resulted in support being provided in a very functional way with little time for social interaction.

1 Why might Bella's daughter be unwilling to see Bella being cared for in a residential setting?
2 Discuss in what ways health and social care workers can disrupt or change the symbolic and emotional aspects of someone's home as outlined in Chapter 13.

Case study: Derek, Joe and Ivan

Derek, Joe and Ivan had lived together in the same psychiatric hospital for approximately 30 years. They each had a long-standing diagnosis of schizophrenia, but no longer experienced any of the positive symptoms of the illness. Prior to them moving out of the hospital, it was recognised that their main support needs were the result of long-term institutionalisation rather than the illnesses that had originally caused them to be admitted to hospital.

They moved into supported accommodation in the community in 1990. Support was provided by a local supported housing project which was run by a voluntary organisation. Though keen to move into their new flat, all three experienced feelings of loss once they had moved. For a number of years after they had moved away from the hospital they continued to attend the hospital workshop five days a week, sticking to the same timetable that they had had for many years in the hospital. Through choice they continued to receive their medication from the hospital rather than the local GP. They quickly established a weekly routine of shopping, washing and collecting their benefits. In many ways, their day-to-day lives had changed little, other than perhaps through the gaining of a sense of pride that they now felt in being able to live in their own flat. They clearly still viewed the hospital as a place of safety and security and tried to replicate the familiar routines as far as possible in their new accommodation.

1 Why do you think that the three men in the case still feel attached to their former hospital?
2 What sociological perspectives may be useful in understanding some of the processes identified above?

Taking your studies further

This chapter will have helped you understand many of the key terms, concepts, theories and debates relating to health and social care policy. Listed below are books that will provide deeper and more detailed discussions of the points raised in this chapter. You will also find what is available on the companion website. This offers downloads of relevant material, plus links to useful websites in addition to podcasts and other features.

Recommended reading

Adams, R. (2002) *Social Policy for Social Work*. Basingstoke: Palgrave Macmillan.

Allsop, J. (2003) 'Health care', in P. Alcock, A. Erskine and M. May (eds), *The Student's Companion to Social Policy*, 2nd edn. Oxford: Blackwell.

Graham, H. (2000) 'The challenge of health inequalities', in H. Graham (ed.), *Understanding Health Inequalities*. Buckingham: Open University Press.

Ham, C. (2004) *Health Policy in Britain*, 5th edn. Basingstoke: Palgrave Macmillan.

Pascal, G. (2007) 'Health and health policy', in J. Baldock, N. Manning and S. Vickerstaff (eds), *Social Policy*, 3rd edn. Oxford: Oxford University Press.

Phillips, J., Ray, M. and Marshall, M. (2006) *Social Work with Older People*, 4th edn. Basingstoke: Palgrave Macmillan.

On the companion website

Bradshaw, P. and Bradshaw, G. (2004) *Health Policy for Health Care Professionals*. London: Sage. Chapter 1.

15

A brief social history of health and healing

Main points

- Humans have throughout history and pre-history sought to be healthy and to heal the sick.
- The causes of disease emerge out of how humans interact with others and change the environment around them.
- Ideas about health and healing relate to society, whether it 'allows' or enables people to think in a certain way.
- Mortality from infectious disease in Britain was greatly reduced not through bio-medicine but by changes to society.
- Despite the many innovations and advances that have made a difference to health, ill health and early mortality remain prevalent in high-income countries.

Key concepts

Health   healing   medicine   society   humours   Islam   the Enlightenment   biomedicine.

Introduction

One way of better understanding the present is to explore the past in order to work out how and why we arrived at the place we have. Doing so raises many interesting questions, paradoxes and points on which to reflect. That is the task of this chapter: to take stock not just of how medicine as we encounter and understand it today came into being but also of the wider social and historical influences that frame, inhibit or enable certain developments to take place. One key lesson to highlight here in the introduction is that when we look through time at the rise of medicine, what we find is that the broader social and cultural context is much more important in many respects than the activities and endeavours of a few individuals making discoveries or formulating new drugs. In fact, medicine as a distinct profession based on a particular understanding of the human body is actually a historical late arrival on the health and healing scene. That particular point alone actually begs the question of why humans (in high-income nations at least) were becoming much healthier and living longer before the arrival of the various drugs, therapies and proce-dures that biomedicine makes claims about in order to privilege its place in society. So any history of health and healing has to range more widely than simply cataloguing who did what and when; by just focusing on the 'Great Men' of medicine we may ignore the much richer and more interesting circumstances that gave humans their understanding of the body, illness and disease and what it is to be healthy. That is why this chapter is called 'a history of health and healing' as opposed to 'a history of medicine', in order to capture those wider dynamics.

Trying to include all of the history of health and healing in a single chapter would be almost impossible. It is such a varied and complex topic. We focus instead on a few impor-tant points in time that illustrate either how diseases and illnesses came into being or how humans went about understanding disease and developing methods of healing. So what we find is that many of the diseases that have affected humans over time arise out of how they shape the world around them, whether this is to switch to farming and settled living or to found vast cities that, for example, allow diseases to jump species or create conditions that make it easy for bacteria to spread. We also find that the development of ideas on health and healing requires societies that permit and provide certain stable and accepting social conditions that allow individuals to think, to experiment and to write about health, the body and healing. Finally, we also find that many of the great leaps forward in improving human health are not down to the innovations of biomedicine but are the results of changes to the social and environmental conditions in which we live.

The McKeown thesis

McKeown (1976) is widely credited with pointing out that the reason for the health advan-tage (albeit one riddled with inequality) that people in high-income western countries can expect is not the brilliance of medical science but much more the increases in living standards. McKeown contended that between the 1750s and 1914 the advances made by medical science had an almost negligible influence on the general health of the population. Changes to and improvements in diet and housing in particular and other broader social and economic changes instead ensured that the life expectancy of the British population increased. The decline of tuberculosis (TB) provides the classic example that is indicative of his overall approach. He charts how the death rate attributable to the disease went from 4000 per million in the 1830s to almost zero in the 1960s. What is notable about TB is that by the time the main treatments and inoculations had been developed in the 1940s and 1950s the disease was almost over.

As a thesis this exerted a considerable influence when it was published in the 1970s and helped to shake up thinking on what it is that makes people ill and what contributes to health. Various other commentators have challenged the detail of what McKeown put forward and queried him on methodological grounds, ranging from a less than critical acceptance of older and more modern approaches to categorising and classifying disease, to not appreciating the sizeable contribution of public health officials in the late 1800s in combating infectious disease, and to attaching too much importance to wider social and economic changes (Colgrove 2002; Szreter 1988; 2002). The fact that his thesis has been critiqued does not mean that the general assumption of widening our search for the causes and cures of disease beyond the domain of biomedicine is incorrect; as Harris (2004) has argued, the broad lesson of McKeown's work, that health is enmeshed in social and economic change, is clearly defensible. It is in this spirit of charting the wider influences that society exerts on health and healing that the rest of this chapter proceeds.

Health and healing in deep history

Humans have always sought to keep themselves healthy and to heal the members of their community who fall ill. The roots of medicine and the healing arts are commonly associated with antiquity and the ancient civilisations of Greece and Rome (approximately 3000 years ago) and the writings of Galen and Hippocrates (both of whom are covered in the next section), but we can extend the historical narrative further back in time. The archaeological record speaks of many interesting instances where humans in the *Neolithic* (or the New Stone Age, approximately 5000 years ago) attempted to practise various forms of healing crafts and even surgical procedures. The most obvious (and perhaps dramatic) ancient form of healing was trepanation or trepanning; this procedure involved using a sharp flint tool to bore a hole in the skull in order to remove bone. Though trepanning may have evolved as part of some ritual, to release a malignant spirit trapped in the skull, for example, it definitely also exhibited medical uses. As primitive as trepanning may appear to the modern mind – using a piece of stone with none of the technology and the facilities

The Neolithic period began roughly 9500 BC, and refers to a time that witnessed a sudden increase in human technology using natural materials such as stone and flint.

The Neolithic Revolution refers to the transition away from hunting to farming and a settled way of life that allowed for early villages and towns to emerge. It began around 9500 BC in the Middle East and reached Britain around 5000 BC.

we would associate with contemporary cranial surgery – a reasonable number of people apparently did survive the procedure.

There is also recent archaeological evidence that the necessary surgical skills required to amputate limbs were present in the Neolithic period. An excavation in 2005 found the grave of a young male whose left forearm bones were missing (Buquet-Marcon et al. 2009). No other explanation for why those particular bones were missing could be identified, and close examination of the upper arm strongly suggested that an operation had taken place; this had proven successful, as fresh bone growth on the amputated bone indicated that the man possibly lived a number of years following the removal of his lower arm. Not only does this example imply that our Neolithic ancestors could exercise surgical skills, it also suggests that they possessed knowledge concerning the skills of pain management and infection control to complement and make the removal of a limb successful.

What is possibly of more interest in exploring health and healing in the Neolithic is that many of the various diseases that have affected human health for thousands of years have their origin in this deeper history. The Neolithic period witnessed an important historical transition for human beings: the ending of a nomadic hunter-gatherer lifestyle and the adoption of a settled agricultural lifestyle. This development is known as the *Neolithic Revolution*. So instead of the main source of food being what was made available through hunting big game, scavenging the carcasses of dead animals and foraging for wild fruits, nuts and berries, there was a switch to what could be produced by domesticating wild animals

Zoonosis or zoonotic disease refers to diseases that are prevalent in one species and transfer to another, where often the new host has very little resistance to the new disease.

and wild plants in a process we now call agriculture. Where this process began is hard to formally identify, and it is probable that the shift to a settled lifestyle occurred reasonably simultaneously across different regions and for different and unique regional reasons. However, an area known as the Fertile Crescent in the Middle East, spanning the northern regions of present-day Egypt, Palestine, Israel, Iraq and Iran, can credibly claim to demonstrate the first instances of a move away from the old nomadic hunter-gatherer lifestyle to the new fixed and settled farming culture.

Endemic refers to a disease that is constantly present in a particular community but at a low frequency, while epidemic refers to the outbreak of a disease that is new to a particular community.

The taking up of a fixed-place lifestyle carried substantial implications for health. By domesticating wild animals (the ancestors of cattle, pigs, chickens and sheep in particular), human beings came into contact with animals on a regular basis, often in close proximity in living and sleeping quarters. That high level of contact alongside the build-up of animal waste products near domestic settlements created the opportunity for diseases to transfer from one species to another. Thus an influenza that was originally only found in pigs, for example, could be picked up by humans in a process known as *zoonosis*, coming from the Greek *zoo* meaning animal and *nosis* meaning ailment. Being infected by such a virus was bad news for the new human hosts as they had very limited immunity to the new viruses.

Another change in people's health was that sufficient populations existed in the new settlements for disease to become *endemic*. Bands of hunter-gatherers had comprised too few individuals to constitute a viable and stable population for certain viruses to exist and proliferate. Quite simply, the virus itself would die out as its hosts died out, and being nomadic such small groups would rarely come into contact with other groups of humans to allow the virus to spread to a new group of hosts. By living in larger numbers and in greater concentration with others, humans created the ideal conditions for viruses and new diseases both to spread and to become endemic within a population. Measles is an example of such an endemic disease and first appears in the historical record as the Antonine Plague in AD 165–180.

What is emerging here is that there is something about the way that humans go about being social and creating new social forms and societies that leads to disease and illness. Even at a bacterial level there is a strong social aspect in the emergence of those pathogens that are harmful to human health.

Questions

The history of zoonotic disease stretches deep into time. Can you identify more recent examples of zoonosis? Also, think of the social reasons that have created the conditions for a disease to jump between animals and humans.

Ancient Greece: physicians and philosophy

No history of health and healing can ignore the developments in Ancient Greek medicine attributed to Hippocrates (*c.* 460 to *c.* 370 BC) and the body of work later developed by Galen (AD 129–216). Hippocrates is an interesting figure in the history of healing as he is popularly credited with being the first great physician, and he was responsible for penning the more than 60 texts gathered together in what is known as the *Hippocratic Corpus*. Today we often think of Hippocrates in relation to the Hippocratic Oath, even though very few doctors actually take this oath. Doctors in the UK instead agree to uphold a set of ethical principles defined by the General Medical Council.

Ancient Greece or Classical Greece refers to Greek society from the eighth century BC to 146 BC (the Roman conquest). This period in Greece is characterised by the building of the Parthenon in Athens and the rich philosophical traditions of Plato, Aristotle and Sophocles.

There is one slight problem with Hippocrates as a living breathing historical man: there is very little evidence that he actually existed. Textually the same author does not write the works that are attached to his name, and close reading of the texts indicates that they are collections of material by a variety of authors, taken from different sources and covering quite a diverse subject range. In effect, the Corpus is akin to a wiki document, which is multiply and anonymously authored, like an entry in Wikipedia, except over a much longer period! Differences and contradictions exist within the Corpus too: the most notable is that not all the texts agree on exactly what substances constitute the various fluids or humours (more of which soon) that are responsible for health and illness and which form the basis of Ancient Greek medicine.

Regardless of the exact historical details, what emerged out of Greece in the ancient period was one of the world's first recognisable systematic approaches to health and healing. It was a system that basically shaped not only how the Ancient Greek world understood medicine but also the medieval world, and it still resonates today, though more likely in alternative therapies rather than in mainstream medicine. The system of medicine that the Ancient Greeks formulated was centred on the four **humours**, as outlined in the Hippocratic text *On the Nature of Man* (likely to have been written by the physician Polybus, *fl. c.* 400 BC). These four humours were vital life-giving substances *internal* to the body but they were additionally and importantly associated with other *external* characteristics. This internal/external relationship meant that the humoral system was essentially holistic, perceiving health as being an outcome of different forces, of processes directly connected both with the person and with the world in which they lived. The various relationships between the humours, the person and the world needed to be in balance for a person to be healthy. Should the humours become unbalanced then illness would follow.

The four humours consisted of blood, phlegm, yellow bile and black bile. The first two humours (blood and phlegm) are fairly easy to identify, with the blood obviously being the blood that flows through the body and phlegm being mucus. The two biles, on the other hand, are a little more complex and it is harder to find a modern-day equivalent. Yellow bile is foam associated with the formation of blood, while black bile is a darker heavier substance also produced during the formation of blood and most likely to be found in the dark matter of excrement. Both biles are present in blood and flow in the blood around the body. One of the reasons for the inclusion of the two biles is that by having four humours it was easier to produce a symmetrically neat philosophical system that could be related to other qualities that were already established in Ancient Greek thought. Each humour was therefore in turn connected to a primary quality of hot, cold, dry or wet; to a type of behaviour of sanguine (extroverted and 'red blooded'), phlegmatic (calm and on an 'even keel'), choleric (ambitious and 'go getting') or melancholic (introverted and kind); and to a season of spring, summer, autumn or winter. The easiest way to understand the relationships between the humours and their various other attributes is diagrammatically, and this can be found in Figure 15.1.

The restoration of balance was the critical element in the practice of Ancient Greek medicine. It relied upon the physician making careful observations of the patient, not just of their signs and symptoms, but of how those signs and symptoms related to the life of the patient,

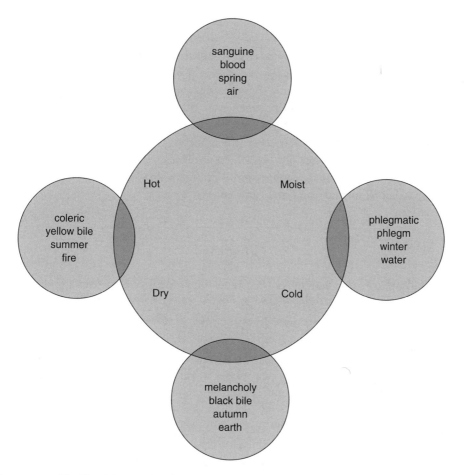

FIGURE 15.1   The Greek humoral system

the context in which they lived, the part of town in which they resided and so on – basically, as full a determination of all aspects of the patient's life as possible. There was also no division between the mind and the body in Ancient Greek medicine; the two were regarded as being intrinsically related to each other, and therefore separating out a physical malady from a mental malady simply did not make any sense for the Ancient Greek physician. So after a prolonged period of gathering observations the physician would have to decide, based upon his judgement, intuition and reference to the Hippocratic texts, which humour was out of balance and what course of action was required to bring that humour back into line. So, for example, if someone was judged to be too hot, then this related to excess blood and too much exercise. To restore balance, blood might be let and drained from the body while a period of rest and little activity would be also be recommended, as would foods that were thought to be cooling. Diet was an important part of Greek medicine and much of the physician's advice given to a patient would have been dietary, as foods were also ascribed humoral properties.

Some of these 'cures' may appear today to be a little bizarre, offering very little chance of actually healing anyone, and this low probability of success raises the question: why did ordinary people go along with them? Any success of the humoral system was possibly due to the very personal basis of treatment, whereby an ill person received lengthy one-to-one attention from a well-read and respected member of the community, and so could feel better as a result of some form of 'placebo' effect. The humoral system was also relatively easy to understand and appealed to common-sense notions of balance that most people would find intuitively believable. Finally, in the short term at least, the blood-letting could provide relief from high blood temperature and could also assist with sleep.

Questions

What advantages do you think Ancient Greek medicine may have over current bio-medicine in terms of the relationship between physicians and patients?

What is important about Ancient Greek medicine is that it is very much a product of the society from which it came. The Ancient Greek world was a highly philosophical society, with philosophy pervading every aspect of thought, producing such philosophers as Plato and Aristotle, whose philosophy forms the bedrock of much contemporary western thought. Ancient Greek medicine was part of that philosophical culture and tradition. It was bound up in the philosophical quest to find the basic elements from which all life arose and to advance a complete and integrated model of how everything worked. The four humours fitted this bill, with the substances of the four humours being the building blocks of life, while the overall neatness of the humoral system meets the Ancient Greek quest for a system of philosophy that can explain everything.

Health and healing in early medieval Islam: preservation and innovation

The Ancient Greek system of medicine was to become a highly pervasive body of thought, defining and informing discourses and practices of health and healing for centuries to come. It was not until the 1700s that it finally began to fall out of favour, to be replaced by germ theory as developed in the 1800s. Even today the presence of the four humours is still very much evident in alternative and complementary medicine. In addition to the influence of the humours in

systems of healing, another reason for their continued longevity was their absorption historically into everyday culture. Shakespeare in his plays, for example, often wrote the main characters to reflect a particular humour, such as the sanguine Falstaff or the melancholy Hamlet.

The dominance of humoral medicine over such a long period
did not mean that the system did not go without any further
development. It was in the early medieval period (*c.* AD 500–1000)
and in the Islamic world that most of the enriching and progressing
of Greek medicine occurred, and this is what is considered next.

Particular features of Islamic society at this time are crucial in
understanding why ideas of health and healing advanced among
the Islamic countries and not in Northern and Western Europe.
In the early Middle Ages the Islamic and Arabic countries
were, in so many respects, leading global civilisation, exhibiting innovative developments in architecture, technology, math-
ematics (algebra, for example, is derived from the Arabic word
Al-jabr, reflecting its origin in Islamic science), art, philosophy
and medicine. Western Europe was living through what until

> Early medieval Islam (or
> the Golden Age of Islam)
> was broadly speaking a
> period between CE 750 and
> 1250, when Islamic coun-
> tries across the Middle East,
> North Africa and Spain made
> advances and innovations
> in art, philosophy, literature,
> engineering, mathematics
> and medicine.

recently was commonly referred to as the 'Dark Ages', a violent episode of Viking raids and
Anglo-Saxon invasions that followed the collapse of Classical Roman and Greek civilisation.
Any traditions of formal medicine in Europe were in a critical state. Instead of being widely
used and part-and-parcel of everyday life, any of the Ancient Greek texts to have survived
into this period were safely locked away in monasteries, out of sight and out of mind of the
general populace. Even when life became a little more peaceful the power of the Church and
the centrality of Christian religion tended to restrain and inhibit any substantial advances in
healing. Christianity did not completely forbid the practice of medicine, since much of what
took place as healing activity was overseen by the Church, but they preferred and privileged
their divine mission to save souls over any mundane matters of health. Medical historian
Roy Porter neatly captures this mindset as follows: 'Thus in the case of the dying, it was
more important that they should be blessed by a priest than bled by a doctor' (1999: 110).
The Church and religion held further control over matters of health and healing by ensuring
that hospitals were in the hands of monks and that healing shrines dedicated to saints who
were associated with some divine act of healing were the main port of call for most ill people.
Porter also notes the continued role of superstition and folk medicines among lay notions of
healing. The cure for epilepsy, for example, was for the sufferer to be in contact with the herb
oak-mistletoe.

In comparison the Islamic countries to the south were more peaceful, but it was not just
the absence of war and violence that made a difference. The geographic reach of Islam was
sizeable, encompassing not just the Middle East, which we most often associate with Islam
today, but also North Africa, India and Spain. It was this vast reach around southern Europe,
the southern Mediterranean and India, and the connections with China, that allowed Islamic

FIGURE 15.2   Details from the medieval Spanish city of Toledo. Left to right: an Islamic arch, a Christian cross and a street sign for a Jewish synagogue, indicating something of the cosmopolitan history of religious and ethnic coexistence in the city, whether under Islamic or Christian rule, in the early and high Middle Ages

scholars to preserve, gather and translate the various works and books of Ancient Greek medicine that had survived the decline of the ancient period around the fourth century.

Islamic society also exhibited openness to other cultures, which provided another social reason as to why medicine in the Islamic world flourished. Given the historical period, Islamic societies were *relatively* tolerant of other cultures, allowing Christians and Jews to practise their religious beliefs and to practise as physicians too. This tolerance also promoted the sharing of ideas, and the multicultural towns of the Arab world, like Toledo in central Spain, became places of vibrant creativity and innovation, with Northern Europe by comparison being nowhere near as dynamic (Figure 15.2). It was not until the Renaissance of the twelfth century that the arts, science, medicine and philosophy in European society were to flourish.

Although, drawing extensively on the Greek traditions of the four humours, the Islamic scholars held onto and retained the knowledge generated by the Greeks, they also added and considerably developed that knowledge. Most Arabic scholars began by translating the Greek originals, but in doing so they began to adapt and augment them by including material from their own Arabic traditions and, more importantly, their own discoveries. Ophthalmology (anatomy, physiology and diseases of the eye) provides a useful example of the process just mentioned. Whilst this practice was based on Greek originals, the Islamic scholars identified new diseases and developed new treatments, some of which were surgical. For example, in the *Memorandum Book for Oculists* 130 eye diseases are detailed, and in Khalīfah's *The Sufficient Book on Ophthalmology* various intricate instruments for eye surgery are identified and guidance is given on their use. Other examples of Islamic innovation include the work of Ibn Sīnā (*c.* 980–1037), or Avicenna as he is more commonly referred to in the west. He compiled and wrote the formidable *Canon of Medicine*, a pinnacle document of Islamic medicine. This work is a highly structured summary and synthesis of the philosophy of medicine. Other works by the likes of al-Kaskarī in his *Compendium* recorded case histories and examples of the practice of medicine (Pormann and Savage-Smith 2007).

Many of these texts were to find their way into Western European culture around the 1100s and onwards as the 'Golden Age ' of medieval Islam came to an end. The main route for these texts into Western Europe was through translation into Latin, with the Latin versions being warmly received in the nascent university systems of Europe. As Pormann and Savage-Smith (2007) relate, the rigour of the Islamic texts was highly appreciated and Ibn Sīnā's *Canon* was still used by European universities during the 1500s.

What we can gather from Islamic ideas on health and healing is that for ideas to develop and to grow, the social circumstances have to be right. In this case a reasonably open society where ideas and thoughts could be exchanged and debated was vital for both the retention of older healing systems and their subsequent development. This brief survey of Islamic medicine also indicates that medicine as we understand it today is not purely the invention of the west and that its genesis is much more global, drawing on a variety of cultures and traditions.

The 1700s: the Enlightenment and revolutions

The 1700s saw the beginnings of modern medicine. Before discussing ideas of health and healing in this period, it is useful to summarise what was happening in the 1700s. This was the beginning of a new historic epoch, one that was markedly different from the feudal period preceding it. Much of the understanding of life was tied into religion, and all explanations of both the natural and the social worlds related to God, religion and the monarchy in some way. We encountered some of the limitations that religion in Western Europe placed upon medicine in the previous section. For example, even up to the early 1700s it was still widely believed that the King or Queen was in a divine relationship with God, and with that relationship came supernatural powers to cure the sick just by his or her touch. An illustration of the extent to which religion dominated everyday life was the trial and execution in Edinburgh of 18-year-old Scottish theology student Thomas Aikenhead in 1697. His crime was to question the existence of God and the truth of the Bible. In such an intolerant society it was difficult to envisage any form of thinking that broke with religious conformity, let alone developed new ideas about medicine. But within a few years of his death and in the same city, all sorts of new ideas were coming to the fore that fundamentally changed how people think. What occurred in the 1700s (though some trends had begun in the 1600s) was a period of social change and substantial transformation (Figure 15.3). This period of change was prompted by three interweaving historical events: the Enlightenment, the Industrial Revolution and the French Revolution. The three events swept aside the old society which was religious and monarchic and replaced it with one that was scientific and

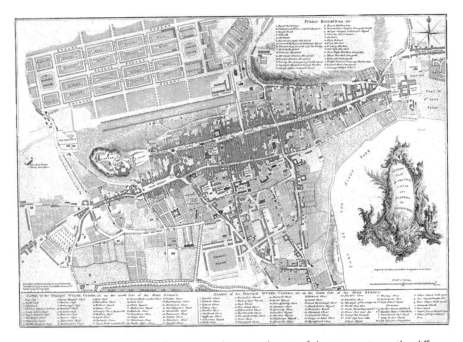

FIGURE 15.3   A map of Edinburgh from 1773. The street layout of the city captures the differences between the old feudal society and the modern society brought in by the Enlightenment. The New Town, near the top of the map, is formal, rational and scientifically laid out in accordance with Enlightenment principles, while the Old Town towards the bottom of the map consists of rambling unplanned streets, with the two main sources of power, the Monarchy and the Church, dominating the high ground in the middle of the map

Source: Faden, William, Jefferys and Thomas (1773) 'General Plan of the City Castle and Suburbs of Edinburgh'. London. Available at: www.rsgs.org/ifa/gems/mapped1773.html

modern, and one where people could develop new ideas without fear of the hangman's rope, the fate of Aikenhead, being the reward for thinking differently.

The Enlightenment: thinking scientifically

The Enlightenment was a historic period that changed how humans interpreted and understood the natural world in which they lived and the social worlds that they created. This change in human thinking was led by various Scottish and French philosophers in the 1700s, people such as David Hume (1711–76), Adam Smith (1723–90), Lord Kames (1696–1782) and Adam Ferguson (1723--1816) (in Edinburgh and Glasgow) and Jean-Jacques Rousseau, Voltaire and Montesquieu (in France), though German philosophers such as Immanuel Kant also figure prominently. The Enlightenment was also a period of intense optimism: that human beings could not only understand the world on their own terms but were now capable of changing the world for the better, and were in a position to sweep aside all the barriers that had restrained previous generations. One of those barriers was disease, and the new scientific methods of understanding that allowed the human body to be understood in a depth and a detail never known before held the promise of allowing humans to free themselves from the fear of disease and pain.

The work of David Hume is significant both within the story of the Enlightenment and for how he helped pave the way for the experimental science with which we are familiar today. As a philosopher he developed the empiricist ideas of the English philosopher John Locke. The main contribution of Hume's work as laid out in *An Enquiry Concerning Human Understanding* was to develop a method or process whereby events that occurred in the natural world could be scientifically understood. He emphasised the importance of repeated observation of whatever was under study as a method of grounding an understanding of that object of study in scientific terms. His influence is evident in how people went about understanding the body and disease. Observation (or sense impressions as he called them) and experimentation were the keys to unlocking the secrets of the body, as was a dismissing of religious and supernatural interpretations of what one found.

Albrecht von Haller (1707–77) provides a useful example of how medicine progressed during the Enlightenment in line with the 'new' scientific methods advocated by the likes of Hume. He was a prodigious if not precocious scholar, publishing numerous volumes. His most important works include the *Primae lineae physiologiae* (1747) and all eight volumes of the *Elementa physiologiae corporis humani* (1757–66). These two works would be very recognisable to anyone who studies physiology and anatomy today; they are filled with detailed and rigorous depictions and annotated illustrations of the inner workings and composition of the human body (Figure 15.4).

Recording the human body in a series of two-dimensional illustrations, such as von Haller and others had done, changed how the body is perceived. Instead of it being a rounded, integrated living entity, the various body parts were just that: a series of parts, similar to what may be found in any other machine. Though not intended, the mapping of the human body in this way resulted in a separation of the mind from the body, and the person from their social context. Such a move led to healing being markedly less holistic than in previous times; the whole person was gone, to be replaced with an unfeeling machine but made of flesh instead of metal.

This tendency within the Enlightenment to strip away all the wonder of being, as some saw it, and replace it with a mechanistic account of what it is to be human, was not, however, accepted by all. In Germany, for example, the Romantic movement, consisting of artists, writers and the exponents of *Glaubensphilosophie* or *Gefühlsphilosophie* (philosophers of faith or feeling) such as Schiller and Goethe, sought in their works to bring back the wholeness if not the magic and enchantment of life (Banning 2010). Some medical people of the time were also influenced by this Romantic backlash against the over-rationalism of the Enlightenment; they attempted to create a form of medicine that kept the insights into the human body gained by the new scientific approaches but did not lose sight of the whole person. The influence of the German Romantic philosophers was evident, for example, in the work of German physiologist Johannes Müller (1801–58). He was very much imbued, at

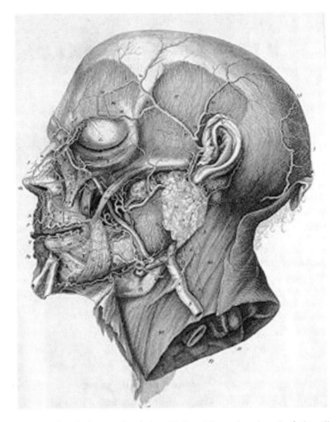

FIGURE 15.4 An example of the work of von Haller. Note the detail of this illustration of the muscles and veins beneath the skin of the human head

least as a younger man, with the Romantic philosophical ideals of unity and meaning. Such ideas led to a rejection of the fragmenting tendencies of French and English rationalist science which disconnected one part of the body from another and, in the process of separating the person into her constituent parts, lost all sense of the total human being. Instead, Müller wanted to fuse together his studies of physiology with his knowledge of philosophy so that physiology was not just the examination of isolated and separate systems within the human body but the study of the complete person (Shyrock 1979: 197). Had this approach as advanced by Müller become more popular and not been eclipsed by more materialist and fragmentary approaches to body, then contemporary medicine *might* have become more holistic and less reductionist than it is – a tantalising thought!

The Industrial Revolution: preventing disease on an industrial scale

If the Enlightenment fundamentally affected what people think, then the Industrial Revolution fundamentally changed what people do. Prior to the Industrial Revolution the bulk of the production of household goods, for example, was on a small-scale craft basis, involving skilled workers labouring on an object from beginning to end, often based in their own home or in a local workshop. Whatever was made, be it a table, an iron pot or a piece of cloth, was also a one-off, and likely to be unique in many respects. What the Industrial Revolution did was to sweep this form of craft industry aside and replace it with large-scale homogenised factory production, resulting in the manufacturing of vast volumes of goods on a scale never known before in human history. The Industrial Revolution also reshaped society in two other important ways that had a profound influence on health.

The first is, in many ways, obvious: the massive expansion of urbanism (living in cities) that occurred from the late 1700s and into the late 1800s. The new urban centres, such as Manchester in England and Glasgow in Scotland, which had been relatively small market towns or quiet coastal towns, experienced considerable growth in a very short period. People abandoned rural life for a variety of reasons, such as poverty, shifts towards less labour-intensive agricultural production or the collapse of traditional feudal ways of life, and headed towards the newly expanding industrial cities. On arrival they would seek work in the new factories but they would also live in conditions of absolute squalor created by the pollution of the smoke-belching factories in which they worked and the overcrowded insanitary housing that was their only choice (Figure 15.5). Urban historian Tristram Hunt (2005) claims that it is hard to overemphasise just how bad early Victorian city life really was. In addition to the smoke, soot, noise and dirt that were byproducts of industrialisation, people kept domestic livestock (pigs, sheep and cows, plus their faeces, were common in cities); sewage was frequently dumped into rivers; and, as the main means of transporting both people and goods about the new cities was horse-drawn carriages, the streets were filled with horse manure. This was squalor on a grand scale.

It is little surprise to find that life expectancy was low and early death commonplace. In the great cities of Manchester, Liverpool and Glasgow, average life expectancy in the 1840s for most people was somewhere in their middle twenties. All the filth, pollution and cramped living conditions ensured frequent outbreaks of cholera, typhoid and typhus. The young Friedrich Engels (2009: 67–8), future associate of Karl Marx, provides a contemporary account of the effects of this urban privation on the health of working-class people in Manchester:

> These courts were built in this way from the beginning, and communicate with the streets by means of covered passages. If the totally planless construction is injurious to the health of the workers by preventing ventilation, this method of shutting them up in courts surrounded on all sides by buildings is far more so. The air simply cannot escape; the chimneys of the houses are the sole drains for the imprisoned atmosphere of the courts, and they serve the purpose only so long as fire is kept burning. Moreover, the houses surrounding such courts are usually built back to back, having the rear wall in common; and this alone suffices to prevent any sufficient through ventilation. And, as the police charged with care of the streets does not trouble itself about the condition of these courts, as everything quietly lies where it is thrown, there is no cause for wonder at the filth and heaps of ashes and offal to be found here. I have been in courts, in Millers Street, at least half a foot below the level of the thoroughfare, and without the slightest drainage for the water that accumulates in them in rainy weather!

FIGURE 15.5 *Manchester from Kersal Moor,* William Wylde (1857). The stark difference between the rural countryside and the polluted smoke-filled city is evident in this mid-nineteenth-century painting

Again, the causes of ill health and early death outlined above are to be found in how human beings have interacted with their environment and each other. Essentially, it is all down to human activity. Yes, there are naturally occurring bacteria at work in the form of *Vibrio cholerae* (cholera), *Rickettsia* (typhus) and *Salmonella enterica enterica* (typhoid), but there is no intrinsic capability within the bacteria by which they can spread themselves unassisted. The devastating death tolls required humans to shape the world around them in a particular way (unhealthy, in this instance) that allowed the bacteria to infect so many people.

What is caused by human action can also be undone by human action. It was not the intervention of biomedicine that came to the rescue of people dying from communicable diseases in the Victorian city, but rather people intentionally deciding to reshape their environments and social interactions in ways that dealt with the conditions that allowed cholera, typhus and typhoid to spread.

The reshaping of cities took place from the mid 1800s onwards in Victorian Britain. New sewage systems were constructed, clean water supplies were introduced, and attempts were made to clear away the worst of the living conditions in many of the major cities across Britain. It was these innovations in city life that were responsible for the increases in the health and life expectancy of people living in cities. There are many figures, not connected with the medical profession or medical establishment, who greatly contributed to the health of British cities but whose contribution is not fully appreciated. One example is the civil engineer Joseph Bazalgette (1819–91). In 1858 an event that was known as the Great Stink overwhelmed London, when the fetid smell of raw human waste that had been discharged into the Thames became utterly unbearable. The stench was so profound that the Houses of Parliament were almost shut down for four weeks as MPs could not work in the smell. Bazalgette was charged to overhaul London's sewage system in order to tackle the stench and to deal with the ever-increasing volumes of human waste. The hundreds of miles of sewers, the pumping houses and the sizeable alterations to the Thames riverbank which he designed, and whose construction he oversaw, all dealt with the sewage and saw off the stink. However, as the sewage and waste were directed out of the city, the drinking water supply became free from contamination; outbreaks of cholera, like the Broad Street episode in 1854 that claimed over 600 lives, were to be consigned to history. Thousands of lives were potentially saved not by an innovation of medical science but by an act of civil engineering (Barnett 2008).

The work of Florence Nightingale on hospital wards provides the second useful example of how changes in social organisation can lead to better health. Her approach to hygiene and cleanliness may appear to be obvious and commonsensical, but at the time it was highly innovative, saving many lives by avoiding unnecessary infection. Perhaps more effective, however, in treating the ill than her work as popular 'lady of the lamp' and ministering angel in the wards, as her image holds her to be, was her powerful grasp of statistics (Figure 15.6). Through innovative and in many respects groundbreaking use of statistics she was able to demonstrate the links between good sanitation and good health, a relationship not readily accepted by male medical doctors of the time. Her work was additionally powerful in contesting male domination of health, by establishing a professional vocation for women that offered social status within both the hospital and wider society.

We have seen great advances in health and in understanding of the body emerging from the 1700s into the 1800s. It is, once more, to the wider social perspectives that we must turn to explain these developments. Had the Enlightenment not occurred then the social conditions for people to think about health and healing in a more secular and scientific manner might not have come into existence; and even when people did formulate more scientific approaches to health, these alone were not as effective as changes made to the fabrics of cities or the organisation of hospital wards, for example.

The final comment to be made here is that it was in 1858 with the Medical Registration Act that the medical profession became the legally dominant group in society in relation to health and healing. Many of the breakthrough techniques to cure and help ill people also came along at that time too, with the formulation of germ theory by Louis Pasteur in the 1860s and Robert Koch in 1890. The medical profession as we understand it today arguably arrived late in the day after much of the main causes of illness and death had been dealt with.

Bringing it up to date

The last few pages have covered a great deal of historical time. In the course of moving through that time we have noted that many of the diseases that have faced humans over the centuries have resulted, in some way, from human impact on the environment,

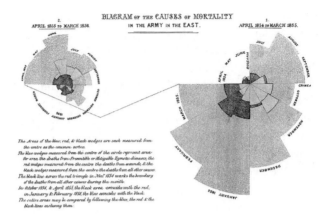

FIGURE 15.6   Florence Nightingale's 'Diagram of the Causes of Mortality in the Army in the East'

whether switching to farming or building waste-filled cities; and we have seen that the means of curing or preventing those diseases relate to broader and wider social developments.

When we arrive at the beginning of the twentieth century, what we find is that the main killers of the preceding centuries such as TB, cholera and typhus were pretty much over in high-income countries like Britain. Infectious disease generally, with the notable exception of the Spanish flu outbreak following the First World War, was no longer a major source of mortality. There is a 'however' coming into play here. Despite the many advances in discovery and development such as germ theory, penicillin and various diagnostic procedures, and in public health measures like the National Health Service in the United Kingdom or private health care in the United States, people still experience pain, distress and illness and ultimately die.

So in some respects things have not really changed that much. A great many of the illnesses that humans encounter are created by their actions and how they arrange their societies. In the Neolithic it was the shift to farming and living with animals that was responsible for many historically new health problems; in the Victorian city it was the filth of society; and in the twenty-first century it is the complexity and inequalities of modern life (Wilkinson and Pickett 2009). As discussed in Chapter 6, inequalities do not have to exist, at least to the extent that they do; there are particular political and social reasons why so many experience sizeable differences, not just in their health and well-being but in many other aspects of their lives. So it is not cholera that kills people in the twenty-first century but cancer, stroke and heart disease – conditions that emerge out of artificial social inequality. The actual type of disease may have changed but the deep causes remain embedded in human society, and it is at that level that we need to focus in order to understand the deeper meanings of health and well-being.

Summary points

- Humans have exhibited for long periods of time a desire to heal ill and sick fellow humans.
- The best way of understanding the history of health and healing is to explore the wider dynamics of the society you are studying. Doing so reveals why certain health issues exist in the first place and why certain forms of healing come into being.
- Modern scientific medicine is very effective at curing people, but (a) this capability has existed only comparatively recently in human history and (b) the major gains in human health have been made by how humans organize and reorganize the societies in which they live.
- The development of modern medicine, for example, required not just people to perform experiments but for deeper changes to be made in society that allowed people to develop scientific approaches.

Case study

Kallinos has been feeling unwell for some time. His temperature is very high, it is a hot summer and regardless whether he sits on his rooftop where he can catch some of the cooling breeze coming across the plain from the sea, or in the shade of his house. His wife, Althaia, has sent for the physician, who lives in a nearby village, to come and visit to see if he can practice his arts, skills and judgement in order, the Gods willing, to cure the malady that is affecting Kallinos. She is worried that he may die – she had lost her brother last year at this time, and the burden of so much grief would be too great for her to bear.

The physician arrives, and Althaia welcomes him in to her house. She is glad to see him and his presence is very reassuring, he has deep wise eyes and asks after her, how she is coping with her husband's illness. He then sits with Kallinos. He is there for a long time. Althaia listens and notes that the physician does not simply ask about the illness but enquires into so many aspects of Kallinos's life, how often he exercises, what he eats, how often he lies down with his wife, how angry he gets when something does not go the way he wants, and what he thinks about life in general. By the end of the consultation, Kallinos appears to be slightly better, he is laughing and smiling for the first time in several weeks. Thinking deeply, and rubbing his head as if he is turning the pages of a book, the physician decides that Kallinos is not too ill, he has just been eating too many rich foods, so for a cure he must eat as simple, plain food as possible with each meal containing lettuce with a little coriander to finish, as this will help Kallinos sleep. It would also be good to keep him cool as possible but on this occasion he thinks bleeding Kallinos would not be for the best, something he would normally prescribe given that heat and blood are so closely aligned. The change in Kallinos's diet maybe sufficient to help.

Questions

The above case study is set in Ancient Greece. Which knowledge base is the physician drawing upon in order to heal his patient? Outline its basic concepts and approaches.

How does this knowledge base relate to wider aspects of ancient Greek society?

In what ways is the Ancient Greek system different from contemporary approaches to health and healing? Is there anything in the Ancient Greek approach to healing that could potentially be superior to contemporary medicine?

Why did this particular system survive as a healing discourse for so long in history and why is it now making a comeback in certain forms of alternative therapies or complementary therapies?

Taking your studies further

This chapter will have helped you understand many of the key terms, concepts, theories and debates relating to the history of health and healing. Listed below are books that will provide deeper and more detailed discussions of the points raised in this chapter. You will also find what is available on the companion website. This offers downloads of relevant material, plus links to useful websites in addition to podcasts and other features.

Recommended reading

Barnett, R. (2008) *Sick City: Two Thousand Years of Life and Death in London*. London: Strange Attractor.

Pormann, P.E. and Savage-Smith, E. (2007) *Medieval Islamic Medicine*. Edinburgh: Edinburgh University Press.

Porter, R. (1999) *The Greatest Benefit to Mankind: A Medical History of Humanity from Antiquity to the Present*. Hammersmith: Fontana.

On the companion website

Bos, J. (2009) 'The rise and decline of character: humoral psychology in ancient and early modern medical theory', *History of the Human Sciences*, 22 (3): 29-50.

Laws, J. (2011) 'Crackpots and basket-cases: a history of therapeutic work and occupation', *History of the Human Sciences*, 24 (2): 65-81.

16

Sport, health, exercise and the body

Main points

- Sport and exercise are not separate from social influences and social processes.
- Sport and exercise as part of the overarching concept of leisure are complex to define and more than just forms of physical activity.
- Social inequalities such as class, gender and ethnicity exert strong influences on why people elect to become involved in particular forms of sport and exercise.
- Sport assists in the channelling of violence and similar emotions.
- Some sports, such as football, emerge as forms of social control and an expression of class identity.
- Society plays a strong role in shaping men's and women's bodies for particular forms of sport.
- Racism and discrimination influence the participation and experiences of black and ethnic minority people in sport and exercise.

Key concepts

Sport • health • exercise • class • gender • ethnicity • social control • civilising process.

Introduction

The iconic image in Figure 16.1 is from the 1968 Mexico City Olympics. In it, African-American athletes Tommie Smith and John Carlos, after receiving their winners' medals

Figure 16.1 Black power salute at the 1968 Olympics: an example of where sport and wider social issues were not separate entities

© Time Life Pictures. Source: www.timelifepictures.com

and while the American national anthem is playing, raise their fists in a Black Power salute. They took this dramatic course of action in order to protest against racism in the United States. White Australian athlete Peter Norman, also on the podium, displays solidarity with their cause by wearing the badge of the Olympic Project for Human Rights. America at that time was experiencing the shocks of various civil rights movements that sought to end the discrimination faced by a number of minority groups. Black civil rights was one of those social movements. Led by people such as the powerful orator Martin Luther King and the more radical and militant Malcolm X, the movement aimed to realise racial equality and to end the second-class status of African-American people, which ranged from segregation on public transport, in schools and in restaurants to denial of the freedom to exercise constitutional and political rights.

The point being made here is that sport is far more than simply an activity concerning individuals and teams competing against each other. Sport and exercise and their potentially health-giving outcomes are very much locked into society, and are subject to its norms, values, cultures, structures and inequalities.

Sport, exercise and health?

Sport and exercise are widely accepted as being important for health. There appears to be ample evidence that engaging in some form of physical activity or even purposeful leisure pursuits is associated with good health. So, for example, in reviewing a wider range of research on sport, exercise and health, Collins and Kay (2003: 28) summarise a great number of benefits. These stretch from the *personal* level (for example, individual fitness, positive mental attitude, meaning and purpose) to the *social* level (community building, bridging with minority groups), to the *economic* level (cheap but effective health promotion, a fitter workforce), and to the *environmental* and *national* levels (improved environmental health, national pride, among others). This picture of people jogging or exercising or even, as Iso-Ahola has noted, just participating in some form of purposeful and active leisure (as opposed to passively watching the television, for example), ties in with common-sense perceptions of what it is to be healthy (Blaxter 1990).

There is a very strong sociological 'however' to be entered into the discussion at this point. Physical exercise and activity are good for health but they are *far* from being the defining criteria for good health. As we have explored in the rest of this book so far, health is multifaceted and often social and structural mechanisms are more important for health than biological factors or risk behaviours (smoking, diet and exercise). So, staying with the exercise theme of this chapter, what makes healthy people healthy is not that they are all enthusiastic sports people or fitness fanatics, but rather their social location. This often predicts how much control they have in organising their working and home lives and in gaining a sense of reward in relation to their efforts at work – or alternatively, as Wilkinson and Pickett (2009) would highlight, the levels of inequality within a society and the psycho-social impacts of that inequality. If you would like some figures to illustrate that point, Marmot (2004: 44) suggests that around a *third* of health inequality is explicable by risk factors such as smoking, bad diet and no exercise. The rest is down to society.

Questions

How does the point above, that sport and exercise may not be the most successful approach to reduce health inequalities, challenge common perceptions of the causes of ill health?

So, giving everyone in the UK a free gym pass, for example, would help reduce *some* of the burden of health inequality. A substantial level of health inequality would, however, still remain. To reduce that burden in any substantial amount would require deeper causes of health inequality (such as economic inequality, poverty and the negative effects of social structures) to be tackled. Indeed, it is those social structures that often prevent people from participating in sports and exercise in any meaningful way – a point considered in greater depth throughout this chapter.

The rest of this chapter focuses on the themes outlined above. It explores the interesting interrelationships between the three main social structures of class, gender and ethnicity, taking account of how those structures shape and influence people's approaches to sport and interpretations of sport. Before proceeding any further, however, and as we have done throughout this book, it is important to try and define the topic of discussion. It is on a definition of sport and exercise that attention falls next.

Definitions and concepts

Sport and exercise are commonly perceived as being activities that occur in free time, the time after or between work, and therefore an area of life separate from work. To some extent that is true. We can, as Dumazedier (1967) has done in his classic work on the subject of leisure, define leisure activities (including sport and exercise) as being a separate sphere or area of human life, where the individual can exert more control over what they do and pursue pleasurable activities, albeit activities that are contextualised by the type of culture and society in which they live.

Substantial problems do exist, however, with the preceding definition and with considering work and leisure to be discrete and separate entities. Let us begin with the notion that leisure and work activities exist in separate domains and have nothing to do with each other.

It does not take much to raise questions about whether such a clean and neat divide is actually sustainable. A recent piece of research by the hotel group Premier Inn found that for most people the weekend did not begin till 12.38 p.m. on Saturday and it was effectively over by 3.55 p.m. on Sunday, due to recovering from work in the first instance and beginning to become stressed and anxious about work in the second. The time between is not necessarily filled with relaxation and leisure, however. Smartphones and the option of having work e-mails 'pushed' through to us mean that work can colonise time outside the traditional nine-to-five and also outside the physical boundaries of the workplace; this tilting of the work–life balance in favour of work can have quite damaging health effects (Bryson et al. 2007). Lefebvre (2008) has also challenged the separate-domain perspective on work and leisure. He argues that leisure is freedom from work but only up to a point: the reason we need leisure is to recover from work, and people at leisure are in effect recharging themselves for work; therefore leisure should be seen not as existing separately from work but rather as an *extension* of work.

Sport is also a reflection of the prevailing culture, norms and values of a society as opposed to a self-contained separate entity within society – a point we discuss in greater detail in the next section. The types of sport played in a society do not just rise spontaneously from nowhere; rather they emerge from the fabric of a society and *inform* us about that society. One useful example (but perhaps dramatic!) of sport being the product of society can be found in Ancient Mayan society, which existed in Central America from *c.* 2000 BC to the arrival of the Spanish Conquistadores in the early 1500s. Their main sport was similar to a fast and furious fusion of volleyball and basketball, where teams would attempt to score points by hitting a large rubber ball through a vertical hoop inside a walled courtyard by rebounding the ball off the walls using their thighs and hips. The game itself reflected the wider tradition in Mayan society of highly ritualised human sacrifice. After the close of each game, which was attended by the high priesthood of the community, a sacrifice of prisoners, and possibly at certain times the losing team, would take place. This ritualised killing of people was as much a part of the game as the action on the court.

There also exists the further complication that sport and exercise, like so much in a capitalist society, is subject to commoditisation and is part of some very big business indeed, where any health-giving properties and the sheer embodied pleasure of sport and exercise are lost in the cash nexus and pursuit of profit. When one, therefore, engages in sport or exercise, one is generally bound into the commercial concerns of a company and market forces. Cashmore (2005), for example, discusses the extent to which global multinationals such as Nike and business people like Rupert Murdoch can exert considerable influence and control over a wide range of sports (such as football) in terms of broadcasting rights, sponsorship, sports clothing and in some cases even outright ownership of a sporting club. Featherstone (1991) ably summarises the intrusion of commercialism into what should be the spontaneity of exercise as follows:

The notion of running for running's sake, purposiveness without purpose, a sensuous experience in harmony with embodied and physical nature, is completely submerged amidst the welter of benefits called up by market and health experts.

However, Moor (2007) cautions us with the interesting point that just because sport is being increasingly colonised and taken over by commercial concerns, that does not necessarily diminish the emotions and feelings of people who choose to engage in sporting practices as athletes or those of the followers of sports.

Questions

How would you define sport and leisure? Do you agree or disagree with the comments made above as to why sport and leisure are problematic to define? Try to identify other examples of where the boundaries between work and leisure are blurry and hard to define.

Trying to capture all of the above in a simple definitional schema is challenging. What we have reviewed here is that understandings of sport and exercise, or their grouping together as leisure, are open to many interpretations. The one point that is hopefully clear is that sport and leisure are elements of social life that are not separate from the fabric of the wider society of which they constitute a part. The following sociological formulation by Giulianotti (2005) goes some way to provide a definition of sport that captures both the *internal* dimensions of defining sport as it is played and something of sport's *external* relations with wider society. According to Giulianotti (2005: xii), sport is:

1 *structured* by rules and codes of conflict, spatial and temporal frameworks (playing fields and time limits on games), and instruments of government
2 *goal-oriented*, aimed at particular objectives, e.g. scoring goals, winning contests, increasing averages, and thus winners and losers are identifiable
3 *competitive* – rivals are defeated, records are broken
4 *ludic*, enabling playful experiences, generating excitement
5 *culturally situated*, in that items 1–4 correspond closely to the value systems and power relations within the relevant sport's host society.

The next section on Elias and sport further underpins how sport is tied into the deeper weave of society and culture, again demonstrating the deep interconnection between society and sport.

Elias and the sociology of sport

Many sociological theories and perspectives seek to explain sport and investigate its role, place and purpose in the wider arc of society, but the work of Norbert Elias is, in some ways, more commonly consulted than others. What his particular writings on sport indicate is that sport is on one level about fun and excitement but more importantly it is tied into the deeper 'building blocks' of a society; sport is more about providing a level of control and order within society, but one expressed in the control that people exert over their own aggressive and violent emotions.

The focus of the work of Elias and his colleagues on sport is therefore to provide an explanation of how society becomes less violent *internally* but yet can remain violent *externally*. What this means is that whilst a society can 'legitimately' engage in warfare and violence with other nation-states outside its borders (for example, the current conflicts in Iraq and Afghanistan), inside those borders violence is conversely tightly controlled. This may be through coercive means, such as the police force, but much more frequently is through symbolic and ritual means (such as sport) that act by disciplining the bodily actions of people and creating a 'civilised' society within a much broader and historical **civilising process**.

This relationship between violence and civilisation is the basis of Elias' wider sociological perspective as laid out in his main theoretical framework of the civilising process. He claims that as societies develop there is an increasing and parallel emphasis and expansion on individual discipline and self-control (the rationalisation of one's body) away from external constraints in order to maintain the smooth running and ordering of society. This civilising effect operates on two different but related levels. There is a social level whereby there is an expectation that one behaves publicly in an appropriate manner, and a psychological level whereby our internal thoughts and ideas are reorganised to respond to the social level. Elias (1982) charts some interesting historical examples by way of illustrating his general overall thesis in his classic work on social manners, appropriately entitled *The History of Manners*. If we take one example from that work, that of breaking wind in public, it was not a problem to do this in the Middle Ages; an individual who broke wind at the table or in the company of others would not have been singled out as rude, and they themselves would not have felt embarrassed or ashamed. Over time, as society develops, so too do taboos and limitations on what one can do publicly with one's body. Now the breaking of wind in public is met with disapproval and the person who has broken wind experiences shame and embarrassment. What is evident here is that as society becomes more rule bound, this socially created framework of restraints translates into the inner psychology of the people within that society.

> The concept of the civilising process within the work of Norbert Elias refers to the long-term tendency of the behaviour of people to become less violent and uninhibited so as to allow society to operate successfully. As a result, expressions of emotion and use of the body become increasingly controlled and refined over time, with emotions such as shame regulating social situations and violence being confined to sports as opposed to being prevalent in everyday life.

One note of caution is required before progressing with the discussion of Elias and sport. He uses the term 'civilising' throughout his work. He is categorically *not* referring to western civilisation as being the ultimate expression of human life, and is not suggesting that current society is somehow the height of civilisation and that civilisation has reached its end point. On the contrary, people in contemporary society may appear to be utterly barbaric and uncouth to future generations, in the same way that our medieval ancestors appear to us now. Part of the reason for being cautious is that in the original German-language publications of Elias, he uses the word *Zivilisation* which, though sounding like 'civilisation' in English, actually carries a slightly different meaning. It refers more to manners, etiquette and self-control rather than to notions of being superior in terms of possessing better technology, art, education and so forth.

The role of sport for Elias then is to also act as a method whereby the violent tensions and impulses that could otherwise destabilise and disrupt the smooth order of society are contained and controlled. Such a dynamic is evident when sport is considered historically. Over time the various activities that could be classed as being sport have become more civilised, moving away from violent contact sports that could easily result in death to sports where violence is still present but is contained and controlled by tight frameworks, rules and regulations. So, for example, in the ancient period sports were highly violent, the obvious example being Ancient Roman gladiatorial events. Though not always a fight to the death, as popularly portrayed in films, the sport could quite easily lead to the death of the combatants. The Ancient Greeks, with whom we may associate the civilised Olympic sports of running, discus and javelin, also practised highly violent sports. Boxing at this time was not restricted to the use of fists; all parts of the body could be used to strike the opponent, with gouging and biting being deemed quite permissible. In the medieval period, sport also lacked the rules and restraints we associate with modern sport. Games that bear an affinity with modern-day football, in that they involved a ball of some description and had a designated place to bring the ball in order to score, were common in most villages and towns in this period. These versions of 'folk football' would involve the men of entire communities playing in teams of indeterminate numbers and guided by very few rules other than that the first team to score was the winner. Injury, sometimes death, was commonplace, with participants punching and kicking each other regardless of who was actually in possession of the ball. One of the closest surviving examples of folk football is the Kirkwall Ba' Game played in Orkney. Here two opposing teams of players, called the Uppies and the Doonies, attempt to score a single goal in order to win, with the Doonies aiming to submerge the ball in the harbour and the Uppies trying to reach the junction of Main Street with new Scapa Road. The game is played over several hours and the teams vary in size.

The transition from unbounded violence to bounded violence in sport took place in parallel with the increasing civilising and stabilising of society as a whole. In the ancient world both Rome and Athens were highly militaristic societies with civil disputes being resolved through violence rather than through law. As society and the civilising process progressed, the requirement to internally pacify societies resulted in sports becoming considerably more rule bound; the traditional folk games, such as the Kirkwall Ba' Game, become increasingly subject to regulation and control, a process Elias terms *sportisation*.

So, if we consider contemporary societies we can identify the increasing rationalisation and control of the body taking place alongside the increasing regulation of games as society itself becomes more civilised. Rugby, for example, is one of the most aggressive games that are popular on a global scale in contemporary society. The playing of the game requires players to engage each other in highly aggressive physical contact in scrums, rucks and mauls, the appearance of which can seem

Sportisation is another concept within the work of Elias. It is similar to the civilising process as it refers to how comparatively unregulated, chaotic and rule-free folk games become rule-bound sport. Again, this long-term process absorbs violence out of general society and places it into the safer and controllable confines of sport.

quite chaotic to the untrained eye. It is, however, far different from the folk football games that preceded it; they were violent too but with almost no form of rules. Although rugby is still a physical and brutal pursuit it is a highly *regulated* one; it has none of the outright violence of games of previous eras, and players are required to restrain their use of violence as opposed to acting how they would like. Certain forms of violent contact such as the infamous 'spear tackle', which involves inverting a player, turning him upside down and effectively crashing him headfirst onto the pitch, and which can result in serious neck and spinal injuries, are forbidden, even though such tactics would be very effective for neutralising an opponent. What rugby and other games in effect achieve for Elias is to remove the violence that could disrupt and destroy society and then to channel that violence into a ritualised format where it is contained and thereby social order is maintained.

Questions

Reflect on Elias' ideas on sport and society. Do they alter your perceptions of sport? Do you agree with him that sports are not simply 'games' but play an important role in maintaining social control? Which sports do you think exhibit the most controlled forms of violence?

Social structure and the conditions of choice

As Donnelly (2005) notes, there is often an assumption that people have the agency and the free will to choose to engage or otherwise in sport and exercise. The sociological position and research on sport and exercise, he continues, strongly suggest the opposite. Why people as social agents choose to engage with certain forms of pastimes is strongly mediated by their class, ethnic and gender location in society. A useful example of how the social structures just mentioned influence and shape the way people approach sport and exercise is indicated in recent research by Steinbach et al. (2011), who investigated the reasons why people take up cycling in London. Their research suggested that the decision to take up cycling and become what they term a 'cycling body-machine' (2011: 1129) was not accountable in terms of people wishing to exercise and be healthy, having access to resources or becoming proficient enough to cycle in such a demanding environment as London. Class, gender and ethnicity intervened as strong mediating factors; so, the people most likely to take up the 'active transport' of cycling were predominantly white middle-class men. As a group, cycling was an extension of both their lifestyles and their gender. They could adopt cycling as a green or an aesthetic (wearing cycling gear, for instance) lifestyle choice, while the adrenalin rush of cycling in quite aggressive circumstances appealed to their sense of masculinity. For women the aggression of cycling could be a disincentive; in addition the social norms of femininity (hair, make-up and clothes) constricted their choices as cycling made it difficult to perform those feminine expectations. There were also issues of childcare, with women possibly having to make longer trips to collect or drop off their children at childcare. Finally, for people from ethnic minority groups, the results from this research were less clear, but again social processes held sway. Black women could feel at odds with the white male-dominated world of London cycling, while ideas on an efficient cycling body were tied closely into white discourses of an ideal body shape that did not always culturally resonate with Asian women.

The ways these social structures intersect with sport, and how they shape individual social agents' approaches to sport and exercise, are expanded on in greater depth below. The main lesson is that there is more to sport and exercise than physical exertion alone.

Questions

Do you think everyone enjoys equal opportunities to participate in sport? How subtle are the barriers to participation mentioned in the example above?

Class and sport

Sport and class are firmly and inescapably associated with each other. Different sports appear to appeal to different social classes. In Britain, for example, and generally speaking, the working class is the mainstay of football (or soccer as it is known in the US), rugby by-and-large maintains middle-class support, while sports such as polo are favoured by the super-rich elite. Again deeper currents are at play: sport throughout history has acted as a means of maintaining social control, training people for their class position, and generating differences or distinction between social classes.

First of all, let us investigate how sport has been a method by which to maintain social control, taking football as a useful example. Although football is often cast as possessing a long deep history, the twentieth-century origins of many British football teams lie not with the pursuit of a pastime, or with individuals combining together for the love of kicking a ball about, but with an attempt to control and discipline working-class people in their free time, when they were away from the workplace. This concern with the moral welfare of the working class needs to be situated within the fixation in wider Victorian society on the morals and behaviours of the 'lower classes'. The sudden expansion of urbanisation throughout Britain during the 1800s had destabilised and challenged traditional conventions concerning respect and 'people knowing their place'. The newly enlarged urban environments were much freer places where people could form identities much more on their terms, free from the old restrictions (Hunt 2005). As a consequence it was feared that the social order as a whole could collapse. Binding people, especially young men, into some form of institution and association was perceived as an effective way to prevent the further decay of society.

There was also another benefit for employers in having their employees commit their spare time to sport. This was that fit and healthy workers would make better workers, plus football acted as a mechanism to keep people out of the pubs. Manchester United FC emerged out of the Newton Heath LYR (Lancashire and Yorkshire Rail) Football Club in 1878, based, as the name so obviously suggests, on a section of workers within that rail company. The most obvious example of a football team's relationship with a workplace is probably Arsenal FC, formed out of the workforce of The Royal Arsenal, an armaments manufacturer for the British Army. The connection with the workplace is also the reason why football matches have traditionally kicked off at 3 p.m. on a Saturday afternoon, which was the start of the weekend for working-class men in Victorian and Edwardian Britain. An interest in sport to maintain the well-being of the workforce could also make the average worker fitter and more productive.

In Scotland, football also acted as a mechanism for social control, but this time based not so much on the workplace but on religion, with particular connection to the Catholic Church. Irish migration in the late 1800s had brought thousands of people from all parts of Ireland. Many of those Irish migrants were Catholic, and football was seen by the Catholic clergy and priesthood as one method whereby they could keep an eye on their flocks, so that they did not become tempted to convert to Protestantism or, even worse, become part of the increasing mass of non-religious city dwellers. The most widely known example of the relationship between football and Irish immigrant Catholics in Scotland is Glasgow Celtic, founded in 1877 by Brother Wilfred of the Marist Catholic religious order. This trend of football teams comprising Catholic Irish immigrants was also evident in Edinburgh with Hibernian, founded by Irish immigrants in 1875 (two years before their more famous Glaswegian counterparts), and in Dundee, with Dundee Hibernian (who were to change their name to the present Dundee United in 1923) founded in 1903.

Sport has functioned for the upper classes too, but as a form of moral and physical discipline; the Duke of Wellington was supposed to have remarked at Waterloo in 1815 that the British victory over Napoleon and the French was 'won on the playing fields of Eton'. Sport provided a means of assisting the sons of the ruling classes to develop the relevant mental attitudes and prerequisite physical robustness to run the empire, display leadership, and play for the team and not one's own personal interests. The lyrical poem *Vitaï Lampada* by Henry Newbolt (1892) – a fine example of British imperial literature – captures something of this empire-building spirit. A comparison is drawn between a schoolboy on the fields of a public school giving his all at the behest and encouragement of his captain, not for personal glory but for the greater good of the team during a cricket match (though it could be any sport played at an English public school), and the same boy as a soldier, this time fighting on a foreign field:

> There's a breathless hush in the Close to-night
> Ten to make and the match to win
> A bumping pitch and a blinding light,
> An hour to play, and the last man in.
> And it's not for the sake of a ribboned coat.
> Or the selfish hope of a season's fame,
> But his captain's hand on his shoulder smote
> 'Play up! Play up! And play the game!'
>
> The sand of the desert is sodden red –
> Red with the wreck of a square that broke
> The Gatling's jammed and the colonel dead,
> And the regiment blind with dust and smoke.
> The river of death has brimmed its banks,
> And England's far, and Honour a name,
> But the voice of a schoolboy rallies the ranks –
> 'Play up! Play up! And play the game!'

The discussion of sport so far has been historical, but it is a history that informs the present day. Football still remains a working-class activity, while the legacy of Irish immigration echoes very strongly in many local derby fixtures in Scottish football. Relationships between class and sport are perhaps a little more subtle in contemporary society but, nevertheless, are still present. The work of French sociologist Bourdieu (1984) is useful here. His sociology concentrates on how in capitalist society the distinctions between social classes are produced and reproduced using a variety of symbolic strategies and signs to denote boundaries and differences between people and their social classes. So, for example, if one considers newspapers, a different status is attached to having a copy of *The Times* tucked under one's arm rather than having *The Sun*. Buying a particular newspaper (whether the heavyweight *Times* or the tabloid *Sun*) is not purely based on what one likes to read but also sends out a signal of social class, with certain cultural symbols indicating to which social class one belongs.

What guides social agents to particular sports is explainable by reference to what Bourdieu terms *habitus*, a concept best understood by reference to his wider sociology. Bourdieu sought to explain why people from certain class backgrounds acted in they way they did. What he identified was that bound up into social class were sets of practices, ways of being and doing, tastes and dispositions that guided people to behave in certain ways. These sets of practices and so forth are also learned through socialisation as we grow and mature in a particular class background, with people often carrying them out unknowingly or as if that were the 'natural thing' to do. It is these guiding practices, which we are often unaware we are following, that constitute and make up the habitus.

In the work of Pierre Bourdieu, habitus refers to a variety of tastes, dispositions, preferences and ways of being that emerge out of the society in which we live, shaping how we act and think. The habitus often operates at a subconscious level and we do not necessarily realise that we are behaving in a way that is influenced and structured by society, as it seems a natural and normal way to be.

Earlier, when discussing cycling, we encountered an example of habitus in action. For the middle-class white men, their class habitus guided them to cycling as it was consistent with certain middle-class ideas of leisure and environmentalism. Widening the perspective, the habitus and sport can be seen in evidence on a variety of fronts. Broadly speaking, for Bourdieu the habitus sets the scene in which people engage with a particular sport.

Questions

Identify other examples where habitus influences the choice of sport and leisure. Do you agree with Bourdieu that society subtly and without our direct knowledge directs our choices in sport and leisure?

Gender, body and sport

Sport is also a highly gendered landscape, where men and women traditionally play different forms of sport and exercise (see Figure 16.2). So, for example, men dominate physical contact sports such as football and rugby, and women dominate sports such as netball and field hockey which are less physically aggressive. On a very general level this separation of sport into gender-specific activities is not wholly explicable as an accident or as a consequence of physiology. In a physiological explanation, the differences would all be seen as the result of men being naturally more muscular and therefore attracted to sports requiring a robust and strong body, while physically more diminutive women would be drawn to less demanding sports. The problem with this line of reasoning is that it runs the risk of essentialising the

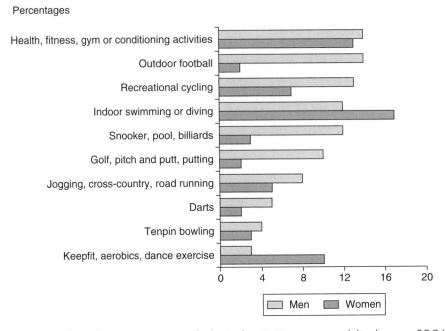

FIGURE 16.2   Selected sports, games and physical activities among adults, by sex, 2006-7, England

differences between men and women, whereby it is assumed that all differences between men and women can be understood by reference to biology alone. In such a perspective there is a rerun of the stereotypical (and sexist) notion of women being naturally and inescapably passive and men being naturally active.

An alternative, sociological interpretation of the gendered body and sport would emphasise that the relationship between body and society is, in fact, the other way around. The actual physical dispositions of men and women, in terms of how they use their bodies and how their bodies develop a distinctive body shape (or otherwise), can be explained by how society prioritises different forms of physical being as desirable and appropriate for men and women. Socialisation and social expectation exert a strong influence in this process. Boys and girls are brought up in specific ways that help to develop their bodies in similarly specific ways. So they are directed to different types of activity, which develop their bodies in different ways. One social norm emphasises femininity, and appearing less muscular than men, a situation we touched on in the London cycling example above. In terms of a girl's social and physical development, young girls are therefore guided to less physically demanding sports and are encouraged to express their femininity by being physically less competent than boys. This sequence, which ultimately leads women to physically limit both their physical bodies and their expectations of what they capable of, is neatly summarised by Fredrickson and Harrison:

Believing in their own frailty can in turn create a self-fulfilling prophecy as girls' and women's erroneous beliefs lead them to limit the effort they put into physical tasks and take the resulting handicapped performance as evidence of their low ability. (2005: 93)

Feminist Iris Marion Young advances the above argument further in her classic essay 'Throwing like a girl', where she discusses how society is not open and equal for men and women and how women's bodies are negatively shaped by sexist and patriarchal agendas:

Women in sexist society are physically handicapped. Insofar as we learn to live out our existence in accordance with the definition that patriarchal culture assigns to us, we are physically inhibited, confined, positioned, and objectified. As lived bodies we are not open and unambiguous transcendences that move out to master a world that belongs to us, a world constituted by our own intentions and projections. (1980: 42–3)

Sport also provides men with the means and place to perform their masculinity and to assert their male social identities (Woodward 2007). As we have discussed elsewhere in this book, masculinity and what it is to be a man are not at all monolithic. Connell (2005) usefully conceptualises masculinity as a hierarchy ranging from hegemonic masculinity, which extols physical prowess, heterosexual sexual success, aggression and being the alpha male; to complicit masculinity, where men may lack the resources to claim to be 'top dog' but are still heavily influenced by the ideas of hegemonic masculinity; and finally to subordinate masculinity, a form for men who are gay, effeminate, bookish, or physically weak. Chimot and Louveau (2010), for example, identify the problems encountered by adolescent boys who transgress and go against notions of masculinity by taking up rhythmic gymnastics, thereby placing them into a subordinate masculine role. Many of the boys experience some form of stigma for participating in what is perceived as a women's sport. As they report of two boys who had decided to give up rhythmic gymnastics:

When we interviewed them, they had stopped this sport to play a sport considered 'more masculine' like football or rugby. When they were performing rhythmic gymnastics they were not encouraged by the men of the family and were stigmatized by other boys. This 'feminine' practice became too costly for them within the framework of the construction of their gender identity at adolescence. (2010: 454)

Links

See Chapter 8 on gender and health for more detail on Connell's theory of hegemonic masculinity.

One further example of the influence of hegemonic masculinity in sport can be found in the paucity of openly gay professional football players. There is currently only *one* professional football player who has come out publicly as being gay. Twenty-year-old Anton Hysén, who plays in the fourth tier of Swedish football, came out as gay in March 2011. His decision to come out has received mixed responses. His team-mates have been supportive while some sections of his club's supporters have been hostile. Considering how much homophobia as a negative undercurrent and form of discrimination in society has been challenged and its prominence reduced in European society since the 1960s, it is surprising that such a development nearly 50 years later has taken so long to emerge. The continuing presence of homophobia is also surprising considering that one of football's main celebrities, David Beckham, is also a gay icon and often presents a very feminine dress sense (the sarong episode in 1998, for example) (Cashmore 2002). Even though one can point to figures like David Beckham within football and broader developments against homophobia, the continuing suppression of openly gay footballers perhaps indicates just how deeply the dominant forms of masculinity are entrenched within football.

In addition to marginalising the participation of gay men and women in sport, prevailing norms of gender hierarchy also carry 'health risks'. As Fogel (2011) notes, dominant forms of masculinity encourage professional sportsmen to endure high levels of injury and pain for fear of being castigated as weak or letting the side down. Among the Canadian football (American gridiron football, this time) players he interviewed, he found that some injuries were considered to be more 'manly' than others. If there was blood or broken bones, then that was considered an acceptable and legitimate injury to receive. If the injury lacked those more dramatic physical signs of pain then the injury lacked legitimacy. This situation was especially relevant for concussion injuries, where players stayed on the field of play after being concussed because of the hidden nature of the injury, leaving them open to the accusation of faking it or being soft.

Questions

In Chapter 8 on gender, we discussed how hegemonic masculinity could actually work against the health of men. Reflect on why this may also be the case with sport. In what ways does performing traditional ideas of masculinity actually harm your health?

Ethnicity and sport

Chapter 7, on ethnicity and race, outlined the various modalities and routes by which stereotypes and out-and-out racism negatively affect the health of black and other ethnic minority people. Those same processes shape black and ethnic minority experiences of sport and exercise. One obvious example of how racism affects sport is evident in the over-representation of black people in various sports at a field level, but the under-representation of black people at higher governing levels of sport. English football provides a useful example. Approximately one in five players have a black Caribbean heritage, yet only 3 per cent of the English population are from that ethnic group (Cashmore 2005). If we examine the other end of football and look at the number of officials, managers and executives, the overall picture becomes almost exclusively white. In the 2010–11 season there were no black managers in the English Premier league, and only two black managers in the top four divisions of English football (Paul Ince at Notts County and Chris Powell at Charlton Athletic). Given the numbers of English black players that came into English football in the 1980s, there should be a much higher number of English black managers in all four divisions. At the executive level of English football, the Football Association (FA), none of the main board of the FA are black (and none are women). A similar situation exists in the USA, where African-American players are over-represented on the field in sports such as American football and basketball (Cashmore 2005).

Questions

Can you identify certain sports where there is an over-representation of a particular ethnic group? Think about the reasons as to why that may be the case in the sports you have considered.

Very clear patterns of variance in ethnic levels of participation on the field and exclusion from powerful positions across different sports do exist, but the interesting point is to try and explain why these patterns exist in the first place. Various reasons are put forward to explain why this should be so (Giulianotti 2005; Sailes 1998). Some, for example, focus on supposed physical reasons, such as that the physiology of black people provides them with an edge at sport. Others focus on cultural reasons, such as that the high rate of absent fathers prompts young black men to seek a father figure in sports coaches. There is no convincing evidence to support either of these explanations. In addition, reasons put forward for black sporting superiority may lapse into racist stereotypes which recall older forms of racism, such as that black people are physical superior but intellectually inferior, or that they create cultures with unstable families and welfare dependency.

It is therefore to how racism plays out in society that we must turn in order to provide the most convincing explanations. The main reason – historically at least – is that sport was one of the few social milieux where black people were allowed to be successful. Entrance to high office in either the public realm or the corporate boardroom was always difficult, but access to the sporting arena was much easier, especially in overtly physical and muscular sports such as boxing or football (both soccer and American gridiron), but less so in the more 'genteel' sports such as tennis and golf.

This interpretation of black sporting success as being a product of racism may seem hard to sustain now, given the high number of black athletes and sportsmen and sportswomen competing globally – and often very successfully. As Carrington (2010) argues, however, perhaps black sports have left the downtown ghetto but only to have entered what he terms the 'Golden Ghetto'. In this new ghetto black sportsmen and sportswomen have the opportunities to become successful and very rich, but the wealth and success do not fundamentally challenge existing (white) power structures. Cashmore (2008) discusses the emergence of golfer Tiger Woods, who has managed to breach the barriers around ethnic minority participation in golf, but whose individual success has not translated into wider changes for ethnic minority people in that sport or across wider society.

This point takes us back to where we started in this section on ethnicity sport (and indeed to the opening image from the 1968 Olympics) and helps to explain why British football may have many black players but very few black managers. Black people and people from other ethnic minorities have the ability to lead but are prevented from doing so by a range of often quite subtle mechanisms that exclude them from reaching positions of leadership.

Conclusion

In this chapter we have sought to explore sport and exercise in relation to health. What we identified was that sport and leisure are not simply separate entities in society that exist on their own terms. Accepting such an interpretation of sport and exercise in turn leads us to question the 'neutrality' of sport and exercise and their existence as pure forms of physical and mental healthy exertion. They are, instead, bound into broader society, reflecting the various social structures, inequalities and cultures of that society. There is also a more fundamental lesson: that while sport and exercise definitely do make a difference to individual health, at a population level they are not enough to reverse the various health inequalities that we have explored in previous chapters.

Summary points

- Sport is not simply about health and exercise, and particular sports can only be understood by reference to the society in which they are played.

- For sociologist Elias, sport plays a significant role in bringing about greater degrees of social control in society as violence is displaced from everyday life and into the 'safer' arena of sports, where it can be regulated and confined.
- Sport is highly gendered, in that it acts as a way for people to perform their gender identities, but also acts in shaping those gender identities by influencing the physical development of men's and women's bodies.
- Sport also displays other social inequalities in relation to ethnicity and class.
- In relation to ethnicity sport can be a contradictory place where people from ethnic minority groups can tackle and overcome the barriers of racism, while simultaneously being a place where racism is experienced.
- In relation to class, sport acts as symbol of distinction between different class groups and can assist in reproducing wider class identities and inequalities.

Case study

Richie's has been suffering pain, in his leg for several weeks now. He can walk fine and jog no problem, but it is when he picks up the pace a little more, approaching a run, that the problems really begin. The pain starts in his knee and then quickly spreads down his leg towards his calf muscle. If he focuses hard he can ignore the pain for a while but after perhaps twenty minutes or so the pain saps his energy and focus. The cause of the pain in his knee is easy enough for him to identify, a big crushing tackle in that away game where he found himself upended into the air before being brought down heavily to the ground, his knee being the principal point of contact between him and the pitch. He had been so close, just two more metres and that would have been an excellent try, one to remember. The ball had broken loose after a botched pass back from a maul, the opposing team's scrum half somehow fumbling a relatively simple catch. Richie was first to react, breaking forward and scooping up the loose ball, before stepping inside their fullback (who really should have nailed him then and there as he was still picking up speed) and then opening up his pace as he sprinted towards the line. Big mistake, 'white line fever' as the coach calls it, all you see is the glory of a score and not the massive wing-forward coming at you with the simple task of stopping you at all costs. It wasn't till about five minutes after his moment of glory had terminated into a messy heap of bodies, with him dropping the ball forwards that Richie realized he was in agony. He kept playing, though, as he couldn't see any real injury, it was just intensely sore, but no blood, swelling or anything obviously broken.

He really should tell someone about it, he's sure the coach would like to know or the team physio, after all he could be making things worse for himself, but somehow he just can't bring himself to do it. Perhaps if he keeps playing and training the pain will just simply go away...

(Continued)

(Continued)

Before exploring the more health orientated questions below, discuss the role of physical sports, such as rugby featured in the case study above, in society. You should to discuss your answer in relation to:

a) class (in what ways does rugby differ from other physical sports such as football, for instance?)
b) and with reference to Elias' theory of the 'civilizing process'.

Identify and discuss the wider discourses of gender that may be influencing Richie in not seeking help for his injured knee.

How could you change the culture in a sports team that would make it easier for injured players to seek assistance for their injuries? Can such a change be achieved solely in one team, or do you think that it may require changes on a larger societal scale?

Taking your studies further

This chapter will have helped you understand many of the key terms, concepts, theories and debates relating to sport, exercise and the body. Listed below are books that will provide deeper and more detailed discussions of the points raised in this chapter. You will also find what is available on the companion website. This offers downloads of relevant material, plus links to useful websites in addition to podcasts and other features.

Recommended reading

Carrington, B. (2010) *Race, Sport and Politics: The Sporting Black Diaspora*. London: Sage.
Collins, M.F. (2003) *Sport and Social Exclusion*. London: Routledge.
Giulianotti, R. (2005) *Sport: A Critical Sociology*. Cambridge: Polity.

On the companion website

Keane, H. (2005) 'Diagnosing the male steroid user: drug use, body image and disordered masculinity', *Health*, 9 (2): 189-208.

17

Death and dying

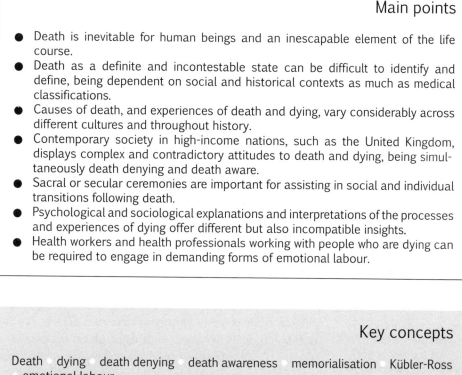

Main points

- Death is inevitable for human beings and an inescapable element of the life course.
- Death as a definite and incontestable state can be difficult to identify and define, being dependent on social and historical contexts as much as medical classifications.
- Causes of death, and experiences of death and dying, vary considerably across different cultures and throughout history.
- Contemporary society in high-income nations, such as the United Kingdom, displays complex and contradictory attitudes to death and dying, being simultaneously death denying and death aware.
- Sacral or secular ceremonies are important for assisting in social and individual transitions following death.
- Psychological and sociological explanations and interpretations of the processes and experiences of dying offer different but also incompatible insights.
- Health workers and health professionals working with people who are dying can be required to engage in demanding forms of emotional labour.

Key concepts

Death • dying • death denying • death awareness • memorialisation • Kübler-Ross • emotional labour.

Introduction

Quite simply, death is unavoidable and an inevitable feature of human existence. As corporeal biological and embodied beings, humans are locked into an inescapable sequence of birth, life and death: cells wear out, core vital organs shut down, and the biological body ceases to function. Regardless of all humanity's achievements in altering and controlling for its own benefit many of the challenges posed by nature, death still remains as a place and part of existence beyond our complete control. Humans can definitely alter and condition the cultural practices surrounding dying and the causes of death, but the actuality of death occurring cannot be transcended. A wider study of death and dying, and the rituals and representations that surround death, reveals the impulses and motivations behind many human activities and cultural practices involving death, whether in commemorating the passing of loved ones, or in dealing with the existential anxiety of one's own demise. In the British Isles, for example, many of the significant structures that mark the rural landscape or punctuate the urban skyline involve, to some extent, death. The oldest surviving structures, megaliths (more commonly referred to as standing stones) and chambered tombs from the Neolithic period, involve some form of engagement with death, dying and the cycles of life; while even in the increasingly busy and high-rise profile of many urban environments it is still spires and steeples that rise above the rooftops, again structures whose rationale was in part to engage with the dramas of life and death.

The main lesson to be found in this chapter is that for all that death may be regarded as the ultimate 'victory' of biology and nature over all the abilities of humanity, the process of dying and the moment of death are as profoundly social as they are natural – and it is that theme that is explored in greater depth in the four main sections below. First, as in keeping with practice throughout this book, we scrutinise the actual concept of death, in order to open up and query basic assumptions of what constitutes death and how it can be defined. What is important here is that defining death is far from easy and without dispute, and is strongly bound into social and cultural norms and traditions. Attention then moves to discussing how the causes of death vary between nations and within nations. What becomes evident here is that what leads to one's death depends on the society in which one lives.

Secularisation refers to the process whereby society becomes increasingly less religious. Secular refers to a non-religious society or non-religious ways of understanding society. Sacral refers to religion and religious understandings of the world.

Dying of natural causes after a long-lived life, for instance, may be the preserve of a select section of relatively wealthy people living in high-income nations like the United Kingdom, whereas other poorer members of that same society can die much younger. When we open a wider global perspective it becomes obvious that causes of death and the age of dying are once more heavily dependent on the society in which one lives. The third section considers a topic of considerable debate in sociological assessments of death: whether or not contemporary western society has become increasingly death denying, in that death as the inevitable end of human life is a taboo topic. The final two sections focus on the parallel experiences of those who are dying, and those health workers and health professionals who work with the dying and the dead.

What is 'death'? Conceptualising and defining the end of life

One important function of the sociological imagination is not to accept any social phenomena at face or surface value. What people encounter on a daily basis is always open to further question and deeper investigation; that is the purpose and promise of the sociological imagination. As has been explored in relation to class, gender and ethnicity, new insights into what we are studying can be gained by questioning what the concepts of, for instance, class, gender and ethnicity actually mean and how they relate to events and patterns in wider society. So, when discussing death (and we shall return to defining dying later), what do we mean by death? A review of the main debates and arguments reveals that it is more complex than first inspection would indicate.

French poststructuralist philosopher Derrida (1993), in his deconstruction of popular and scholarly ideas, has questioned the existence of a tight and clear delineation and border between life and death. Instead, he draws attention to how mutable and fluid ideas of death are bound into different cultures and are variable and changing across time and history. Death is also, he notes, a state of being that is neither fully social nor fully biological but exists in the fusion and interrelationship of the two. This highlighting of issues relating to defining and conceptualising death and dying is highly useful as it guides us to thinking of death not just as a simple state of 'non-life' or the non-functioning of core bodily processes and no brain activity, but rather as a process which exists in the midst of other processes, bound into culture, society, history and biology.

Let us focus a little more on the biological aspects of death briefly mentioned above. In many popular hospital-based dramas the iconic image of a heart monitor flatlining while emitting a high-pitched monotone is used to signal the death of a patient. Such an image informs lay perceptions concerning the finality of death, that death is an unambiguous and definite state: the person alive is now dead, and the two are very clear and distinct separate states. A great many complications exist, however, that question and challenge this straightforward understanding of death. Philosophically, it can be asked: what is death? Such a question raises thorny issues about the relationship between mind, body and self-identity, or more broadly put: what is it to be alive? This question is very difficult to answer succinctly. Is life purely a biological function? Is life the ability to interact with other human beings? Is it a combination of both? And, if so, is one more powerful than the other?

Kellehear (2008) has identified how the criteria used to pronounce death have changed over historical time. In the Middle Ages, the signs that were sought out to establish death were *external*; the body was examined for stiffness of the muscles, discoloration of the skin, or putrefaction and decay. In modernity the focus has become increasingly *internal*, with an emphasis on cardiovascular and brain activity. The change as to what constitutes death parallels, in certain regards, the wider historical trend of the increasing rationalisation and advance of technological scientific perspectives, in that designating someone as being dead is made in the context of what a piece of technology (what Latour (1992) would term a 'non-human actor' in a wider network of activity and decision making) records as being patterns of a particular electrical or neural activity that are interpreted as being significant of a change in status, in this case, from being alive to being dead. As has been raised in Chapter 2 in a discussion on medical technology and the wider medical model, just because a particular event or interaction between people is mediated by scientific principles does not necessarily entail that scientific medicine provides any definitive answers. There are cases, as Kellehear (2008) notes, where people who may be classifiable as 'brain dead' and therefore technically dead, kept going only with the support of technology, are still capable of conceiving or giving birth – two qualities that for many people would signify life not death.

The inverse of the above may also be true, because the body may remain clinically alive in that the heart beats and the various biological organs function perfectly well, but that does not necessarily entail that the person is alive. After all, sociologically speaking, being an active human agent usually implies some form of interaction with others. So the body can be alive, but what makes the individual a particular person is no longer present. Such a state can be evident in cases of dementia and allied conditions that affect the memory of an individual, where what is termed a 'social death' can occur. The body is physically present but the person who was known by their friends and family has, to all intents and purposes, passed away. Defining death is made even more complex with current technological developments. Stem-cell technology and the ability of science to operate on a molecular level open up a range of debates as to what is alive and what is dead, given that the lifetime of human cells can be prolonged almost indefinitely, which again raises the question: when is someone truly dead?

Mortality and the global causes of death

Seale (2000) has mapped out the main coordinates of death in contemporary global society, and what his work reveals is that death is far from a unitary phenomenon and experience across all societies. Death rates, trajectories of dying, causes of death and age of death (see Figure 17.1) vary markedly from country to country. What passes as being a 'normal' way to die in a high-income western nation is notably different from what is normal in a low-income sub-Saharan nation. Comparing deaths due to HIV/AIDS and cancers provides a useful illustration of these differences between global regions (see Figure 17.2 for other selected causes of death). According to the WHO (2011: 74) the mortality rate for HIV/AIDS in 2009 in the Africa region was 117 per 100,000 in comparison to 19 per 100,000 in the Europe region, a rate that is just over

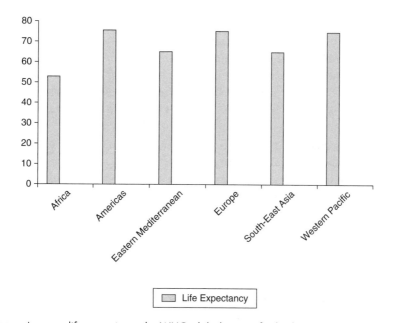

FIGURE 17.1 Average life expectancy by WHO global region for both sexes, in 2008

Source: WHO (2010) *World Health Statistics*. Geneva: World Health Organization.

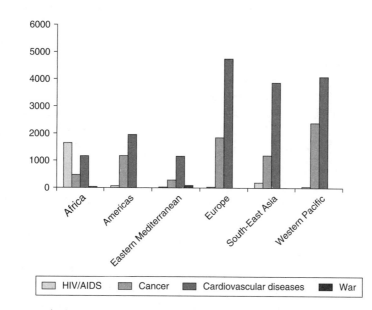

FIGURE 17.2 Deaths (000s) in WHO regions, estimates for 2004

Source: WHO (2008) *Global Burden of Disease: 2004 Update*. Geneva: World Health Organization.

six times higher. In comparing cancer (or malignant neoplasms) the differences in mortality between regions are less stark, but they are still quite pronounced. It is the Europe region this time that exhibits the higher number of deaths with a mortality ratio of c.350 per 100,000 in comparison to a mortality ratio of c.160 per 100,000 in the Africa region (WHO 2010: 14). These statistics reveal a number of interesting insights into just how experiences and contexts differ globally. First, the leading causes of death are quite different: HIV/AIDS in Africa and cancer in Europe, with each cause of death accounting for quite high numbers of people. However, one should take care not to lapse into some form of equivalence – into thinking that the two causes of death are essentially similar in that they are both likely to lead to illness with the strong possibility of death. How those causes of death are socially situated, and what the contexts are in which death occurs, are decidedly and critically different.

HIV/AIDS in the Africa region is more likely to kill younger people in their teens and twenties, thus reducing the numbers of economically active people, and also creating a crisis with the number of children who are orphaned after their parents die of AIDS. There may also be a lack of medication and appropriate hospital services, which means that the process of dying (of which more later) is marked by higher levels of discomfort and pain, plus a reduction in the time left available in which to live out an already shorter life. Cancer deaths typically (though not in every instance) generally affect older people who have been economically active, but more importantly the European person dying of cancer will have led a longer life, with the advantages of being able to achieve life goals and engage in the various activities that are important and meaningful to someone across their life course.

Considerable and substantial differences are also present *within* countries just as much as *between* countries. Section 2 of this book focuses on health inequalities that emerge out of wider social inequalities, and these wider social inequalities also apply to death. What is evident is that death is not due to random chance, an unlucky roll of destiny's dice, but is found in one's class, ethnic and gender location. So, a person from a working-class background will live on average seven years less than someone from a middle-class background; and in some cases, as was discussed in relation to areas in Glasgow, the mortality difference can be up to 30 years. In terms of gender, even though the gap is closing, women still outlive men by five or so years; and in regard to ethnicity, people from ethnic minority backgrounds will on average die earlier than those from ethnic majority backgrounds. Remember that these inequalities often run together, and people who are at the intersection of inequalities will experience increased chances of early mortality. Death, as with so much in life, is therefore to do with social structures rather than chance, biology or individual agency.

War as a cause of death is included in Figure 17.2 among the more expected 'medical' conditions. It is included to highlight that when seeking to understand death it is important to situate death in its fullest context, and that considerable numbers of people die of a cause that is purely the outcome of human intervention in the form of particular (and failed) social and political processes. Medical sociology as a subdiscipline has, as Williams (2004) notes, been silent on the issue of war and health, which is surprising given that war is fundamentally concerned with the negation of human life and bringing harm to embodied human beings. The actual numbers of people killed in the recent wars in the Middle East, for example, are hard to identify; estimates of deaths attributable to war-related violence in Iraq have ranged from 151,000 in a survey for the World Health Organisation (Alkhuzai et al. 2008) to 607,207 in a survey published by *The Lancet* journal (Burnham et al. 2006). Regardless of the exact numbers of civilians who have died lately as a direct and indirect consequence of conflict, the point here is that death for many is the result not of ill health but of violent human action.

Modern society: 'death denying' or 'death aware'?

Since the publication in English of the highly influential and stimulating work of Philippe Ariès on death in *The Hour of our Death* (1982) and *Western Attitudes toward Death: From the Middle Ages to the Present* (1974), modern European society has been characterised as being *death denying*. This particular concept implies that modern society silences discussion of death, forbids the topic of death and dying in everyday conversation, and excludes and isolates the dead and dying to the physical and symbolic outer regions and limits of society. In effect a taboo surrounds death and modern society denies its existence, to a similar degree that sex was a taboo in Victorian society. Ariès' thesis is based upon his empirical study of cultural, literary and artistic representations of death and dying. From his study he contends that practices and rituals surrounding death have changed and altered over time in parallel with how society understands and creates death. He offers a periodisation (Small 1997) of death in which it moves from being seen as an inevitable experience towards being an experience that can be tamed, where the dying person can focus on sorting out their affairs with the full involvement of their family and friends so as to lead to a good death. In the eighteenth century, death was romanticised as being almost a beautiful experience but one bathed in pathos and ideas of personal tragedy. The one main arc of historical change he notes is the move away from public recognition – if not very public display – of the dead and the dying to a privatised and hidden death, where death becomes dirty and an event to be shunned and relegated to the margins of conversation.

> Death denying implies that a society and individuals who are part of that society attempt to ignore the subject of death in conversation and generally behave as if death did not exist. Death aware is the reverse of death denying, where death is acknowledged and accepted but not necessarily in a way that is consistent and without contradictions.

FIGURE 17.3   The Danse Macabre

Source: Wolgemut (1493) 'Dance of Death'. Available at en.wikipedia.org/wiki/File:Holbein-death.png

It is useful to briefly consult the historical record here again in order to indicate just how much has changed in terms of our relationships with both death and the dead. At other points in history death was all-pervasive, experienced by having dead family members in the household, seeing the dead in the streets and observing the dead represented in art forms. The Black Death that raged across Europe in the middle 1300s claimed the lives of somewhere in the region of 375 million people, one of the most devastating pandemics in human history. The sheer scale of the disease challenged and reshaped society on a myriad of levels. The power and social role of the Church for one was questioned, but one of the more visual manifestations of death in this period was the frequent use of death images in art. This tradition was most evident in the various *Danse Macabre* images of the medieval period (Figure 17.3), where skeletons engaged in a wild dance with each other, or mischievously taunted the living that their own death could happen without warning at any moment.

The possible reasons for the movement from an open and accepting culture of death to a denial of death can be traced to distinct social developments within the twentieth century. Walter (1994: Chapter 1) advances the following reasons for why contemporary society can be perceived to be death denying, a state in which the often interrelated processes inherent in modernity lead to the depersonalisation of death and the repression of emotion and grief. The end result of all these processes acting on and shaping societal and individual beliefs is that death becomes a taboo subject, an off-limits area of conversation, blanked out as an issue in personal reflection on one's life and its future:

- *Rationalisation.* Like so much of modern life, death has become the object of the various forces and processes of rationalisation, where the very intimate moments of death become subject to timetables, bureaucracy and categorisation. Death is not just the ending of someone's life, but an element of the great paper trail of modernity, where every aspect of life is recorded and filed. The end result is that death becomes disconnected from private emotional reference points, grief in particular, and attached to the cold emotionless framework of the public office and public official. The death certificate is an example. As a document the death certificate records very objective information such as date of birth, the cause of death and the name of the recording officer. Subjective and affective information, such as the emotions of the surviving relatives, go unrecorded. This is all very useful for the running of a large bureaucratic state, which requires information on its citizens but is not very effective at dealing with the issues of loss and grieving.
- *Medicalisation.* Discussed earlier in this book, medicalisation involves the colonisation (the 'taking over') of an increasing number of areas of life that were once regarded as existing outside the medical gaze. The same applies to death and dying. Death for most of human history was explicable in religious terms; it was God's Will that people should die, and therefore religion was the only source of insights into and understandings of death. As medical technology has developed, however, death has become framed less as a moment defined by the divine and increasingly as a medical event, with death resulting out of a distinct sequence of biological stages. Walter also notes one further way in which death has become medicalised: the change in the location of dying. In western high-income countries the place of death is now more likely to be in the hospital under the auspices of the medical profession than in the home supported by friends and family.
- *Secularisation.* Allied to the above, one other development within modernity is the decline of sacral or religious belief. Modern society has become increasingly secular, which means that people do not interpret their lives within the symbolic framework of religion. Previously, in a Judeo-Christian context at least, images of death, resurrection and redemption informed the minds and actions of people. Without the presence of such imagery, death becomes less a feature of life. Walter (1994) points to the First World War as a turning point in religious belief in Western Europe, where the idea of a loving God became increasingly untenable given the mass death and suffering of the conflict. However, as both Hunt (2005) and Bruce and Glendinning (2010) maintain, secularisation begins much earlier in the eighteenth century, when the new urbanisation brought

The following terms are used in Walter's discussion of death denying:

Rationalisation, where society becomes more controlled, governed and ordered but at the expense of spontaneity and human emotion.

Medicalisation, where the medical profession increasingly colonises more aspects of everyday life, and what were once regarded as normal social problems (shyness, for instance) are recast as medical problems.

Secularisation, where society becomes less religious and more inclined to humanistic or scientific understandings of social and natural events.

Individualisation, where people focus less on the wider community and more on themselves, with their actions being self rather than other directed.

about by the Industrial Revolution removed ordinary people from the control and teachings of the church.

- *Individualisation.* One debated trend within contemporary society is the move away from community to a life based more on individualism. Such a trend may sound appealing in that we now possess the potential to make more of our lives as and how we wish, unbidden by pressures from the wider community. Walter notes, however, that one rather demanding cost of being individual is that one lacks the ties to other people who could provide emotional support in times of crisis, such as when facing death. The upshot is that it is better to ignore rather than embrace death.

Walter does not include *consumerism* in his summary of why today's society might be death denying, but the various characteristics of consumer culture could also contribute to a death denying culture, extolling as it does the perfect, young but crucially *living* body. The number of facial cosmetics and the ease of access to cosmetic surgery could be cited as further evidence of death denial, since the purpose of such products (and here surgery is as much a product as an anti-ageing cream) is to deny the passing of time and ageing, let alone the very real finality of death.

Questions

How are the processes that have arguably led to a denying of death unique to modernity as a historical epoch? Identify further examples of how each process could influence how we approach and understand issues of death and dying.

This perception of modern society being death denying has been challenged by a number of sociologists (such as Seale 2000), and the work of Ariès and others who have advanced the death-denying thesis has been critiqued. One of the main objections to Ariès' analysis of death, for example, parallels that of critiques of his work on childhood: that by drawing ostensibly on artistic and literary sources for his empirical data, he does not allow for those sources to be contextualised as idealised versions of death and dying at a particular point in history rather than as how death and dying was actually experienced and understood at that time. What Ariès presents in effect is an overly romanticised view of death and dying that is nostalgic for a past that never was, as opposed to an accurate recreation of the place of death and dying in the past and over time.

The main thrust of the counter-argument is that contemporary society is not death denying but is just as **death aware** as in previous times, only in a way that is more fluid, complex and contradictory. On the one hand, unlike Victorian society, contemporary society denies death; it is a topic shunned in conversation, and issues of dying, such as the ageing process, have become almost a taboo subject. On the other hand, death is frequently depicted in many mainstream cultural products, where the subject of death and what it is to be dead form the basis of plotlines in films and television serials. Death and what the dead are like are very distinct and idiosyncratic in such media. In many contemporary films and TV shows, such as the *Twilight* trilogy or *Buffy the Vampire Slayer*, to be dead is to be reborn in the afterlife as an emotionally complex but still very sexy American teenager, where death is not about bodily decay or the end of self but instead is a continuation of self at the peak of one's young powers. One could claim, as Gorer (1965) did back in the 1960s, that this form of death awareness is 'pornography' and does not really deal with death; yet these depictions of the dead and death are often more nuanced and subtle than the traditional blood-'n'-gore movies of that period.

Throughout popular culture there is other ample evidence of engagement with death. In addition to the new wave of vampire movies, one could point to *The Time Traveller's Wife* (both the novel and the film), which focuses on memory of a loved one and dealing with loss, as does *The Finkler Question*, and to the various geographic variations of the American crime series *CSI*, where death and the dead are treated and portrayed in computer-generated high detail. In popular music there is the subgenre of death metal, where fast and furious bass-heavy songs in doom-laden minor keys celebrate motifs of death and dying, and where bands refer to death in their names, such as Korpse, Entombed and (the not so subtle) Death. There is also, of course, the Goth subculture (Hodkinson 2002) in which adherents also, albeit probably more playfully and elegantly than in death metal, adopt imagery and symbols associated with death.

It is, overall, difficult to sustain a perspective that claims that modern society is exclusively death denying. A quick survey of popular culture, as revealed above, finds plenty of evidence to the contrary. Seymour (2001), though, cautions against such a simplistic 'either/or' dichotomy of society being either death denying or death aware; the actuality, she argues, is much more complex, but then again so is the phase of modernity. As Kellehear (2007) maintains, the practices and understandings of death and dying parallel the norms and cultures of a given society; so as society becomes much more complex, an equally complex approach to death and dying develops. Walter (1994) characterises this complexity towards death and dying as being consistent with postmodern trends in society. As with other postmodern trends there is a rejection of a simple 'one-size-fits-all' approach, with its implication of everyone acting uniformly, and instead an acceptance that everyone follows a path that is much more of their own making, drawing on whichever elements of social culture and social symbols they choose. Seale (2000) notes something similar: that in late modernity a greater reflexivity exists in how people approach various aspects of their life course, in that they are frequently engaged in working out how they make *their* lives meaningful, in a context that is most appropriate to them. So, what we can see today is not one mass society-wide approach to death but a myriad of individual approaches. However, one must be careful to acknowledge that these choices are not open to all. As Kellehear (2004) reminds us, not everyone possesses the power to choose exactly how they live and how they die, depending on class, gender and ethnic differences.

Rites, rituals and ceremonies: dealing with death

Regardless of how a society defines death, when it does occur it can lead to a traumatic and significantly upsetting period both in the lives of friends and relatives and also in wider society. The various bonds that link a person to others and to wider society are, for a time at least, broken and damaged; a phase of uncertainty and change follows, where people need time to make adjustments and hopefully re-establish their own personal and social narratives. That is why so many rites and rituals surround death, the purpose of which is to repair and heal those social and individual bonds so as to allow for the return of some form of 'normal' functioning.

Religious narratives and symbols were the traditional discourse that people deployed to deal with and assist in either their own dying or the death of a loved one. All religions, whether historic or contemporary, offer a core set of symbolic beliefs concerning death and dying. Historically, for example, in Neolithic (Stone Age) and Iron Age Britain the dead were not separate from the living. As archaeologist Francis Prior (2004) has discerned about Neolithic society and its religious affirmations, death and life were firmly enmeshed together both physically and symbolically. It was common in that period for burials, for example, to be close to human habitation. In some instances, the dead were buried beneath the floors of roundhouses to indicate a connection with their ancestors and the great cycles of life and death, the moon and the sun; while the landscape itself would be altered to symbolically record the dead with burial mounds and standing stone circles marking the horizon (see Figure 17.4). Neolithic social ceremonies also involved a close physical and symbolic relationship with the dead. The placement of human remains found in chambered tombs, such as the West Kennet Long Barrow near Silbury Hill in Wiltshire, strongly suggests that the disarticulated bones of deceased relatives of ancestors were regularly moved around, taken out from the tomb and used in ceremonies that were important and significant for the people of that time.

FIGURE 17.4 The central recumbent stones, c. 5000 years old, East Aquhorthies Neolithic standing stone circle, near Inverurie in Scotland

In western Judeo-Christianity the central symbolic narrative and mythology concern resurrection: that by believing in God, not committing sin and acting in a compassionate and caring manner, your soul will be saved and you will be granted eternal life in paradise. Other religious faiths and belief systems offer different interpretations as to what happens after death. Hinduism and Sikhism, for instance, have reincarnation as their understanding, while Buddhism reveals rebirth, in some respects similar to reincarnation. There may be some quite different ideas as to what happens after death throughout the world's religions, but the fact that they all deal with issues of death is what is important. The world's religions also provide various ceremonies and rituals to structure and provide focus for those who have lost someone. As Durkheim highlighted in his functionalist sociology, humans require and develop rituals and ceremonies to mark all the important transitions in their lives, and death is no exception. The traditional Christian funeral in western high-income nations involves either a burial or a cremation, preceded by a ceremony that focuses on how the departed individual is now in a better place, involving prayers and hymns and reference to God and an afterlife. The ceremony also allows relatives and friends an acceptable place and appropriate occasion in which to grieve; though as Elias has argued, grieving is not always a spontaneous outburst of emotion, and the various civilising processes present set parameters, especially for men, as to what is appropriate or dignified.

One current social trend, however, is the increasing secularisation of society, principally within the UK and other European states, where belief in organised Christian religion is in considerable decline. This development does pose a question: how do non-religious societies deal with death? If Durkheim is correct in claiming that humans require ritual to mark and make sense of important stages in the life course, then what ceremonies do secular societies provide to endure the challenges posed by death? In fact, there has been a proliferation of different forms of funerary practice. Humanist funerals have become increasingly popular. As a ceremony they may resemble conventional Christian funerals in so far as there will be a burial or a cremation, with the ceremony led by a specially designated individual, accompanied by songs and readings. There are crucial differences, however. The focus of the ceremony is not on an afterlife or a supernatural being (or God) but entirely on the deceased, celebrating their life and recording their favourite experiences and music. One of the more colourful practices that can be used in secular funerals is the balloon release. Here mourners gather together each holding a balloon; once they have reflected on the life of the deceased and they feel at some form of peace, they release the balloons, symbolising a letting go of grief.

In addition to the secular ceremonies and belief structures discussed above, Lee (2008) notes that various developments concerning New Age religion and beliefs offer a re-enchantment of society. He makes this point in reference to Weber's key criticism of capitalist society: that it robs the world of enchantment and the 'magic' of life and replaces all that is special and unique, in a process of disenchantment that leads to modern life being similar to living in an 'iron cage'. Finally, one other recent trend in memorialisation of those who have died is evident in the increase in roadside memorials, usually in the form of flowers, but also including poems, stuffed toys, football shirts, or other objects that were meaningful for the deceased. So, even if the traditional forms of funeral and memorialisation are on the wane, new forms are beginning to appear that could become how future societies celebrate the life of a deceased friend or family member.

Dying and the anticipation of death

It is useful once more to highlight that death and dying are not solely biological events, but are crucially bound and interwoven into social relationships and the culture of a particular society. What counts as being dead, and the experience and process of dying, are defined and set by the context and society in which someone lives (and of course dies!). In this section on dying, about the anticipation of death and how both the individual and society make adjustments to the end of life, it is vital to bear in mind that dying here is not limited exclusively to the biological experience of dying. What is under discussion is how that biological (or embodied) element of the process is prefigured and contextualised into an array of social relationships that vary by society and by historical period.

Before any further discussion it would be helpful to tie down what is meant by dying, as was carried out earlier in this chapter when defining death. As Kellehear (2007) notes, death is a very particular biological point when nerves and tissue irreversibly cease to function; but as humans are emotional beings, their experience of dying is not just limited to the biological horizon but is, instead, tied into existential reflection, social norms and personal relationships. Kellehear also usefully defines the process and anticipation of dying in the following more sociologically nuanced manner, where emphasis is placed on wider social relationships, and dying is seen as a social process but one which is also animated by individual desire and agency:

> I speak here of dying as a self-conscious anticipation of impending death and the social alterations in one's lifestyle prompted by ourselves and others that are based upon that awareness. This is the conscious living part of dying rather than the dying we observe as the final collapsing of a failing biological machine. (2007: 2)

For people living in contemporary high-income nations the idea of dying, or the anticipation of dying and their own death, exists in the distance of time, a process to be encountered and endured towards the end of up to eight or more decades of life, probably following a lengthy debilitating illness or the slow natural demise of the body. During the intervening years the focus is on life and living rather than on dying. This distancing of dying is a comparatively recent development in experiencing the life course brought about by the extension of life expectancy through the twentieth century. In previous epochs, the distinction between life, dying and death would not have been so marked. There would have been greater awareness of the inescapable fact that life is short and death could happen much sooner than one would wish. Indeed, given how rapid death could be in other historical times (due to an accident or aggressive infectious disease), dying as both a social activity and a social relationship may have been quite different from how dying is thought of today. In the Neolithic era death was, for example, a very sudden event, and there simply would not have been an extended period for the dying person to reflect on their life and the big change that was happening to them. Instead, the process of dying would begin well *within* life, but essentially as a *symbolic* activity, with people making preparations for their death by making sure that their journey through the afterlife was well stocked with appropriate weapons for a man, or food supplies for a woman. These preparations could have involved planting a certain type of tree that was symbolically rich for the tribe, for example, or by storing an axe to be collected in the afterlife. Once someone had died, let us say, of an accident whilst out hunting or gathering food, it was the surrounding members of the tribe who would 'do' the dying, engaging in ceremonies that would ease the journey from this world into the other world for the recently deceased member of their tribe and community (Kellehear 2007).

As human society develops and changes over time so does the process of dying and how people go about the business of dying. One advantage that humans gained from establishing settled farming communities is that they could begin to develop the basics (steady food supply, shelter and safety) that would allow them to live longer. By living longer, time for dying and a space for personal reflection was created, as death would become less of a random, swift and unexpected event. Again, how people approach dying alters across time as society develops.

The best-known interpretation of what a dying person undergoes is provided by Elisabeth Kübler-Ross. Her work emerges out of her reaction against what she perceived to be the increasingly inhuman and cold treatment of dying people in modern society. In her landmark and highly influential work *On Death and Dying* (1969) she presents a stage model consisting of what Walter (1994: 70) terms the 'famous five' stages that dying people pass through as they die and move from denying to accepting that they are dying:

- *Denial.* This is a phase of the person not believing what they have been told by the doctor or specialist, that the terrible news they have been given must be the result of an incorrect test, that someone has made a mistake in the lab, and that if the results were to be rechecked then all would be well and they would not be dying. The related reaction of *isolation* can also occur here, where the dying person withdraws from the world about them, seeking their own company and avoiding the company of others.
- *Anger.* Denial may be impossible to maintain and the initial feelings of rejecting what they have been told transmute into anger and rage. The target of this anger can range from people they know who have engaged in much less healthy lifestyles than they have, but more likely the anger will be funnelled towards the medical staff and health professionals around them.
- *Bargaining.* Here the dying person attempts to gain more time in which to live. Bargaining can be with God or the medical staff, running on the lines of, 'If you give me more time, then I'll do something for you in return.'
- *Depression.* As the realisation sinks in that bargaining leads nowhere, due to ongoing and increasingly debilitating medical and surgical procedures, for example, the dying patient can experience loss of role and an awareness that the end is near, though they can remain in this stage for quite some time.
- *Acceptance.* This is the last stop on the journey of dying and accepting that death is now inevitable.

This five-stage model may read quite neatly and provide a nice and ordered approach to the no doubt highly traumatic and difficult experience of dying, but it is not without its shortcomings, which throw into question the actual usefulness and accuracy of its basic precepts. Walter (1994) provides a useful summary of the problems that have been identified with the Kübler-Ross model of dying, and the key ones are as follows:

- Doctors and health professionals may misinterpret the patient's actions and behaviours, incorrectly assigning them to the denial or anger stage. Doing so can give rise to miscommunication and misunderstandings, resulting in negative impact on the patient's health and care in the ward.
- Very little empirical research has been carried out on the five-stage approach in order to assess how accurate it is. This lack of rigour has potentially allowed the stage model of dying to gain a credibility that is perhaps questionable.
- It is *too* neat and tidy. The concept of such a linear approach to death is not necessarily reflective of reality; approaches, adjustments and interpretations of death and dying (as discussed in the previous section) are more fluid.
- The whole model is very American in its orientation, reflecting American cultural values of individualism, with the emphasis being on the person and not the wider social context in which they live.
- Finally, Kübler-Ross' work is perhaps less an academic thesis and more a personal vision of how dying could and should be.

Questions

Assess the disadvantages and advantages of the Kübler-Ross approach to dying. Do you agree or disagree with the criticisms listed above? Provide reasons for your answers.

The emotional labour of working with the dead and dying

As indicated earlier in this chapter, the majority of people in contemporary high-income nations such as Britain die in a hospital. In such locations a whole array of health professionals and health workers will obviously be found, and part of their daily labour and practice will involve working with people who are dying and with those who have died. One subtheme of this chapter has been that death involves a certain emotional cost for those who are connected in some way with the dying and the dead. If that is the case – that emotions, and here the more 'negative' and troubling emotions of grief, are the focus – how are those workers and professionals affected?

Emotional labour refers to the performance, suppression or drawing upon of emotions as required of an individual person by an institution (usually the workplace). As a form of work emotional labour, using one's emotions to work, is increasing in the modern workplace, replacing older manual skills. Emotional labour can exert a cost on the worker as they may feel emotionally burned out or that they are emotional fakes.

The theory of *emotional labour* as developed by Arlie Hochschild (1983) provides a useful starting point in exploring and answering the question just set. Her theory centres on one particular development in the field of work in late modernity: the shift away from work requiring a set of skills to do with the physical movement of the body (such as being able to turn a lathe or operate machinery) to work involving the emotions of the body, where as part of the working day (or night) enacting and performing appropriate emotional displays are the core requirement of the job (hence *emotional* labour). Emotional labour can therefore require the suppression of how one is really feeling and the simultaneous performance of emotions that one is not really experiencing. So, for example, when working with a client, the health professional may have to hide and not display feelings of boredom and frustration with that client and instead perform or enact an outward display of care and interest.

The original focus of Hochschild's research fell on female airline stewardesses, who as part of their job were obliged by the organisation they worked for to create a certain emotional environment for the airline passengers, involving making the passengers feel welcome. The creation of a relaxed and welcoming ambience relied on the ability of the stewardesses to act enthusiastically in response to the passengers' needs and demands. On first inspection, having a job that involves only flashing a few smiles and being 'nice' to people may appear to be relatively undemanding and perhaps even enjoyable. Hochschild's (1983) findings pointed, however, to a quite different reality. The stewardesses reported that they were alienated from their emotions, they felt that their smiles were no longer their own, their emotional display and feeling were somehow 'false' and synthetic, and they had an overall feeling of being 'burnt out'. The reason for the stewardesses reporting emotional exhaustion and damage to their emotional self was that the surface acting of emotions (that is, smiling to welcome a passenger) can require the manufacture of emotion and also a drawing upon real, deep and core emotions, which were not an infinite resource and whose reserves could be depleted over time – in effect, using up all their emotions.

A parallel situation can be seen to exist for health workers and health professionals in working with the dying and the dead. Contemporary health care requires a combination of professional, instrumental skills and, just as importantly, the emotional skills necessary to engage with the emotional aspects of care and the patient experience. There are distinct occasions in health care where emotional skills play an important role in assuring both patient dignity and the success of care and treatment. Nurses working in intensive care, for example, may engage in emotion work in order to provide a more human environment for patients who are dying in a place that is cold and filled with cold technology, and to assist in the development of good relations between the patient, clinical staff and family members (Seymour 2001).Emotional labour, as Hochschild strongly suggests, often comes with a cost, as indicated in the discussion above concerning airline stewardesses. A variety of research has identified that the emotional labour costs associated with the care of dying people are multiple, and include burnout, feelings of aggression, alcohol or substance (mis)use, and suicidal ideation.As Sorensen and Iedema (2009) argue, the problem with the stresses and anxieties that emerge from emotional labour in a hospital or health care setting is that they are less well understood than the normal stresses and anxieties (such as the number of hours worked and the amount of task-centred labour) associated with organisational and institutional demands. They are less obvious and therefore harder to identify and quantify, which makes taking any ameliorative action quite problematic; the negative consequences of emotional labour therefore remain unchallenged, creating further and deeper issues of well-being for health workers and health professionals.

Questions

Reflect on the concept of emotional labour in relation to your own experiences of work (this does not necessarily have to be in the health field). Identify how important certain emotional performances are in the modern working environment and what effect they could have on the person doing the performing.

Conclusion

Death will unfortunately come to us all; that is an inescapable part of being human. However, our experiences of dying and our understandings of death will differ greatly by social class, gender and ethnicity on the one hand, and by wider social, global and historical developments on the other. So, we all may die but that final stage of existence is also cut across by the various inequalities that structured and conditioned the life we had before our death. By also discussing those social differences, another point is made about death and dying: as moments in our life they are not solely explicable in biological terms. Biology is a very important element in relation to the terminal changes that occur in the body, but these biological events are woven into the wider social and cultural contexts that can be both the cause of death and the provider of the symbols and rituals that help to make sense of death and dying.

So, once again, we can see how sociology and the sociological imagination provide insights into a very intimate and difficult part of our life and our health, and how essential an appreciation of social processes is in order to gain a fuller and deeper understanding of death and dying.

Summary points

- Human beings have always sought to deal and cope with death and dying.
- Death is not necessarily an unambiguous state, and what counts as being dead changes across time and across cultures.
- The reasons why people die are again highly variable and depend on which part of the world you live in.
- There is a debate as to how much contemporary western societies deny death. There may not be the same direct openness about the existence of death that existed in Victorian times, for example, but perhaps a more subtle and nuanced acceptance of death has developed which does not necessarily rely upon public display.
- New forms of funerary rites are beginning to emerge that are replacing older and traditional religious approaches as society becomes increasingly secular.
- Health professionals require a certain level of emotional labour when working with people who are dying.

Case study

What some people noticed at Jamie's funeral, especially the older people who had a little more acquaintance with death and what must be done when someone passes away, was that even though it was in the city crematorium it wasn't a minister or a priest that conducted the service. Instead, there was a man who in very dignified tones informed the packed room that he was a humanist celebrant and would be leading not a funeral service but instead a celebration of Jamie's life. Jamie was nineteen when he died, a silly and pointless accident where a second's inattention had made the difference. Out camping with friends he had walked to some nearby cliffs. The long coastal grass had over grown the cliff top giving a false impression that the edge was a little further away than it actually was. He had stepped forward not realising where the true edge was. Both he and his family were not religious and it just seemed inappropriate to involve someone from the church – plus the last thing Jamie would have wanted was for his farewell to be anything but a big joyous party! So, no one was to wear anything associated with mourning, and the music that was played between the various speeches made by friends and family was his favourite songs and some of the demo tracks he had recorded with his band.

Questions

The above case study may seem to portray a very modern way of managing death and conducting a ritual for someone who has died, but try to detect and identify any themes that could be found in any other historical time or even in any other society. Jamie's funeral was a humanist service – how does this choice of ceremony reflect wider changes in society in relation to organised religion?

Why do you think humans needs to mark key moments across the life course (think of other events as well as death) – try to relate you discussion to sociological theories and concepts.

Taking your studies further

This chapter will have helped you understand many of the key terms, concepts, theories and debates relating to death and dying. Listed below are books that will provide deeper and more detailed discussions of the points raised in this chapter. You will also find what is available on the companion website. This offers downloads of relevant material, plus links to useful websites in addition to podcasts and other features.

Recommended reading

Kellehear, A. (2007) *A Social History of Dying*. Cambridge: Cambridge University Press.

Seale, C. (1998) *Constructing Death: The Sociology of Dying and Bereavement*. Cambridge: Cambridge University Press.

Walter, T. (2004) *The Revival of Death*. London: Routledge.

On the companion website

Hadders, H. (2009) 'Enacting death in the intensive care unit: medical technology and the multiple ontologies of death', *Health*, 13 (6): 571-87.

Glossary

A

Absolute poverty: having such restricted access to food, shelter and clothing that it is life threatening.

Ageism: a combination of a set of beliefs originating in biological variation related to the ageing process and the actions of corporate bodies and their agents, and the resulting views of ordinary people.

Agency: *see* **Structure**.

Alternative medicine: any medical practice that falls outside the boundaries of conventional medicine. Some commentators use the term 'complementary medicine' to imply that non-conventional medicine can be used in conjunction with western biomedicine rather than as a radical alternative.

Analysis: making sense of data and deriving conclusions that inform a research question.

B

Biographical disruption: the destabilisation, questioning and reorganisation of identity after the onset of chronic illness.

C

Civilised body: a concept developed by Norbert Elias to denote a historical and cultural shift whereby the body is subject to increasing restraints that appear to limit the 'natural' body. The development of rules around eating manners is an example of how the body has become 'civilised'.

Class: a complex stratification of society based on access to and control of power, status and economic resources.

Clinical autonomy: the freedom of clinicians to make decisions on the basis of their professional judgement and specialist knowledge. This definition implies the downgrading of other assessments of the same situation.

Clinical gaze: belongs to a specific discourse on the body in which the body is perceived as a physical object capable of being observed, measured and treated with little or no reference to the person.

Clinical method: the process that begins with diagnosis and continues with prognosis and subsequent treatment.

Community: a contested concept in sociology that basically refers to a group of people who possess, or create, a common identity.

Community care: the range of policies, procedures and legislation that is concerned with the planning, funding and delivery of services for older people, people with learning and physical difficulties and illness, people with mental health problems, people with HIV/AIDS, drug or alcohol problems and other progressive illnesses, and disabled children.

D

Dependency theory: this claims that older people's lives are restricted by poverty and by being unable to access social and cultural resources.

Discourse: a specific way of thinking about and conceptualising a particular subject. The essence of a discourse is the language used to express thoughts. Science is an example of a discourse that rules out some kinds of explanation (for example spiritual) and only allows for others (for example, rational and evidenced 'facts').

Discrimination: acting in a way that treats people from another race or ethnic group unequally.

Disengagement theory: the theory that older people relinquish their roles in society so as to minimise social disruption as they approach their final years.

Dissemination: making the results and conclusions of research known to a wider audience.

E

Embodiment: the experience of living through and with the physical body. Our experiences are essentially embodied. For example, we experience pleasure and pain through the body. Feelings of happiness and sadness are as physical as they are emotional.

Enlightenment, The: a body of thought developed in the eighteenth century, which challenged explanations of the world based on religious or superstitious explanations. Enlightenment thought, by contrast, was based on a commitment to rational, secular and scientific explanations.

Ethics: guiding principles and considerations concerning the conduct of the researcher in ensuring that no harm is done to the physical and emotional well-being of those who participate in their research.

Ethnicity: the cultural heritage and identity of a group of people.

F

Feminism: a broad concept that explains social structures as fundamentally based on inequalities between women and men. In general, feminist sociologists have challenged the traditional preoccupation of the discipline with the effects of industrialisation and the world of paid work and institutional politics. Such an approach, it is argued, has ignored the significant elements of society such as the family and gender relationships.

Functionalism: a theory of human society as a collection of interrelated substructures, the purpose of which is to sustain the overarching structure of society. As such, functionalism provides a 'consensual' representation of society based on, first, an agreement to sustain society as it is and, second, shared norms and beliefs.

G
Gender: the social, cultural and psychological differences between men and women.

H
Hegemonic masculinity: the dominant form of masculinity in society. Currently, this refers to men who are healthy, wealthy, white and powerful and act in a 'macho' manner. Very few men live up to this expectation but it exerts a strong influence over both men and women.

Hysteria: a 'disease' once thought to be caused by the movement of the womb around the body but later described as a disease of the nervous system. The symptoms of hysteria have been described as weeping, fainting and a general malaise (James 1994).

I
Iatrogenesis: harm caused by doctors. In its most literal sense it refers to the harmful consequences of medical intervention. Illich also uses the concept to draw attention to our cultural dependence on medicine and medical practitioners, such that we do not seek alternative explanations or alternative remedies for ill health.

Informal care: a combination of service and affection provided on the basis of kinship or friendship. It is mainly unpaid.

Institutional racism: the intentional or unintentional actions of a public or private body that result in people from ethnic minority backgrounds being discriminated against.

L
Life course: a way of conceptualising the passage of life that better recognises the increasing fluidity and fragmentation of contemporary society, and the interaction of individual agency and social structure.

Life cycle: a concept borrowed from natural science, implying a series of set rigid stages that humans move through in their lives.

Literature review: a systematic analysis of all published material that is of interest or relevant to the research.

M
Macro: the larger, structural aspects of society. In terms of criminal activities, this might refer to an analysis of the economic circumstances of criminals, and an analysis of law making and law enforcement, as well as of the role of the state in regulating such behaviour.

Market system: a system where maximum efficiency, economy and performance are supposedly achieved by having either individuals or organisations competing against each other for customers or clients. The act of competition is thought to increase responsiveness to customer needs. Margaret Thatcher's Conservative administration applied this approach to the UK NHS during the 1980s.

Marxism: a theory that explains social phenomena as primarily determined by the economic structure of society. Social change, it argues, is the product of changes in economic relationships. In the context of the modern period the advent of capitalism and industrialisation are seen as producing social divisions based on the ownership or non-ownership of property.

Matriarchy: *see* **Patriarchy**.

Medical model of disability: a model that places a strong emphasis on seeing disability as an individual tragedy where, by a quirk of fate, either genetic or accidental, someone becomes disabled and their life is in many ways ruined.

Medical model of health: a specific way of thinking about and explaining disease based on biological factors.

Medicalisation: a concept used to describe a tendency to explain behaviour and experiences in medical terms.

Method: the way in which actual data are gathered.

Micro: the small-scale aspects of human behaviour, for example why individuals embark on criminal activities.

N

Neo-material perspectives: these offer explanations of class and health inequality that emphasise the unequal distribution of resources such as housing, income and access to education.

P

Paradigm: a systematic way of thinking.

Passing: attempts to conceal a potential stigma and prevent its disclosure.

Patriarchy: male domination in society, expressed both privately and publicly in culture, economics and politics and through physical violence. Matriarchy refers to a society that is female dominated.

Postmodernist theories: these veer away from all-embracing theories that attempt to explain all social phenomena. Instead, the emphasis is on the impossibility of uncovering the 'truth' about society. Postmodernism draws our attention to how our knowledge of the social world is constructed, and offers a critical and questioning approach to understanding the world around us. Also *see* **Discourse**.

Power: a subject of much debate within sociology. In the context of this discussion, the concept refers to (a) the ability to ensure that a particular point of view prevails in a disputed situation, (b) the capacity to ensure that someone acts in a certain way, and (c) the ability to stifle opposition to a particular perspective.

Prejudice: a negative attitude towards someone from another race or ethnic group.

Private provision or private sector: the situation when individuals are responsible for organising and purchasing their own health and social care. This is achieved by taking out insurance and other policies with private for-profit companies. The extent and level of coverage are decided by what the individual can and wishes to spend. This approach is common in the United States.

Psycho-social perspectives: explanations of class and health inequality that emphasise the negative emotional experiences of living in an unequal society, particularly feelings of stress, shame and powerlessness.

Public provision or public sector: the situation when health and social care is organised and provided by the state through a network of different services at national and local level. Funding usually comes from taxation or some form of national or social insurance. This approach is common in European countries.

Q

Qualitative research: mainly interview-based research that seeks to find out the meanings that people attach to their experiences and actions.

Quantitative research: mainly statistics-based research that is useful for answering research questions that focus on measuring the extent and range of particular phenomena.

R

Race: biological differences between people based on skin colour and other physical features, though the genetic differences between races are extremely small.

Racism: the belief that one race is superior to another.

Relative poverty: having the minimum requirements of a particular society *in relation to other people in that society.*

Reproductive technology: a range of medical interventions (pharmaceutical and invasive), the purpose of which is either to promote or to prevent pregnancy.

Research question: the aspect of the social world that is to be investigated.

S

Secularisation: the acceptance of non-religious explanations of the world.

Sex: the biological differences between men and women.

Sick role: a functionalist theory that outlines the privileges and expectations associated with being legitimately sick in contemporary society.

Social constructionism: a theory that emphasises the extent to which 'society' is actively and creatively produced by human beings.

Social model of disability: the argument that prejudicial attitudes, disabling environments and cultural barriers socially create disability.

Social model of health: the view that health is multidimensional with social factors, such as class, gender and ethnicity, influencing and patterning health and illness.

Social policy: how governments organise the meeting of the health and social needs of their population.

Socialisation: the process whereby we become aware of the values and beliefs of society.

Society: a range of external factors that influence our beliefs and behaviours.

Sociological imagination: a concept developed by C. Wright Mills, referring to a specific way of thinking about the world, characterised by a willingness to think beyond our own experiences and to challenge common-sense or obvious explanations of human society and human behaviour.

Sociology: the study of the interaction between groups and individuals in human society.

Stigma: an attribute that 'discredits', or prevents, someone's full acceptance in a particular situation.

Structure: a similar term to 'society' in so far as it draws our attention to those factors that help determine our experiences through the establishment of expected ways of behaving. The contrasting concept of agency means that individuals do not simply act out predetermined roles but 'interpret' those roles in a way unique to them.

Surveillance: a form of scrutiny and observation that does not necessarily depend directly on the physical proximity of the watcher and the watched. Subtle forms of surveillance are said to characterise modern society, as typified by the tendency of individuals to act in ways that they think they 'ought' to.

Symbolic interactionism: a theory of social phenomena from the perspective of its participants. An essential element of this theoretical perspective is the unique nature of the social world as made up of the actions of participants motivated by human consciousness. The meaning of human action cannot, therefore, be observed or assumed, but is 'interpreted' by studying the meanings that people attach to their behaviour.

T

Theory: within sociology, this refers to attempts to provide systematic and consistent explanations of social phenomena.

Third Age theory: the theory that old age is a 'golden age' where enriching and rewarding experiences are available due to freedom from family and work commitments made possible by a consumerist society.

Third Way: a political ideology associated with the British Labour Party that stresses cooperation between private and public provision, by combining the best practices of both.

References

Aakster, C.W. (1993) 'Concepts in alternative medicine', in A. Beattie, M. Gott, L. Jones and M. Sidell (eds), *Health and Well-being: A Reader*. London: Macmillan/ Open University.

ACE (Age Concern England) (2002a) *Issues Facing Older Lesbians, Gay Men and Bisexuals*. Policy Position Paper 15. London.

ACE (Age Concern England) (2002b) *Ageism*. Policy Position Paper. London.

Acheson, D. (1998) *Independent Inquiry into Inequalities in Health*. London: Stationery Office.

Acheson, D., Barker, D., Chambers, J., Marmot, H. and Whitehead, M. (1998) *Independent Inquiry into Inequalities in Health: Report to the Secretary of State for Health*. London: Stationery Office.

Adams, R., Dominelli, L. and Payne, M. (eds) (1998) *Social Work: Themes, Issues and Critical Debates*. Basingstoke: Palgrave.

Age UK (2010) *Lesbian, Gay or Bisexual: Planning for Later Life*. London.

Ahmad, W.I.U. (2000) *Ethnicity, Disability and Chronic Illness*. Buckingham: Open University Press.

Alkhuzai, A.H., Ahmad, I.J., Hweel, M.J., Ismail, T.W., et al. (2008) 'Violence-related mortality in Iraq from 2002 to 2006', *The New England Journal of Medicine*, 358 (2): 484–93.

Allsop, J. (2003) 'Health care', in P. Alcock, A. Erskine and M. May (eds), *The Student's Companion to Social Policy*, 2nd edn. Oxford: Blackwell.

Alvarez-Rosete, A., Bevan, G., Mays, N. and Dixon, J. (2005) 'Effect of diverging policy across the NHS', *British Medical Journal*, 331: 946–50.

Angermeyer, M.C. and Matschinger, H. (1999) 'Lay beliefs about mental disorders: a comparison between the western and the eastern parts of Germany', *Social Psychiatry and Psychiatric Epidemiology*, 34 (5): 275–81.

Angus, J., Kontos, P., Dyck, I., McKeever, P. and Poland, B. (2005) 'The personal significance of home: habitus and the experience of receiving long-term home care', *Sociology of Health and Illness*, 27 (2): 161–87.

Annandale, H. and Hunt, K. (eds) (2000) *Gender Inequalities in Health*. Buckingham: Open University Press.

Arber, S.L. and Ginn, J. (1992) 'Class and caring: a neglected dimension', *Sociology*, 26 (4): 619–34.

Archibald, B. (2011) 'Police report massive rise in Scottish gay hate crime', *Scotland on Sunday*, 6 February.

Ariès, P. (1974) *Western Attitudes toward Death: From the Middle Ages to the Present.* Baltimore, MA: The Johns Hopkins University.

Ariès, P. (1982) *The Hour of our Death.* London: Vintage.

Atkin, K., Ahmad, W.I.U. and Jones, L. (2002) 'Young South Asian deaf people and their families: negotiating relationships and identities', *Sociology of Health and Illness*, 24 (1): 21–45.

Audit Commission (1986) *Making a Reality of Community Care.* London: Stationery Office.

Baker, S. and MacPherson, J. (2000) *Counting the Cost: Mental Health in the Media.* London: MIND.

Banks, I. (2001) 'No man's land: men, illness, and the NHS', *British Medical Journal*, 323: 1058–60.

Banning, T. (2010) *The Romantic Revolution.* London: W&N.

Barnes, C., Mercer, G. and Shakespeare, T. (1999) *Exploring Disability: A Sociological Introduction.* Cambridge: Polity.

Barnett, R. (2008) *Sick City: Two Thousand Years of Life and Death in London.* London: Strange Attractor.

Bartley, M. (2003) *Health Inequality: An Introduction to Concepts, Theories and Methods.* Cambridge: Polity.

Bauman, Z. (1990) *Thinking Sociologically.* Oxford: Basil Blackwell.

BBC (2000) 'Washing up bowls 'a health hazard'. http://news.bbc.co.uk/1/hi/health/1056364.stm

BBC News (2001) 'Naomi Klein: "Know logo"'. http://news.bbc.co.uk/hi/english/health/newsid_1312000/1312479.stm

BBC News (2002) 'Britain "a racist society" – poll'. http://news.bbc.co.uk/1/hi/uk/1993597.stm

Bebbington, P. (1996) 'The origins of sex differences in depressive disorder: bridging the gap', *International Review of Psychiatry*, 8: 295–332.

Beck, U. (2002) 'The cosmopolitan society and its enemies', *Theory Culture and Society*, 19: 17–44.

Becker, H. (1974) 'Labelling theory reconsidered', in P. Rock and M. McIntosh (eds), *Deviance and Social Control.* London: Tavistock.

Bell, C. and Newby, H. (1976) 'Communion, communalism, class and community action: the sources of the new urban politics', in D. Herbert and R. Johnston (eds), *Social Areas in Cities*, vol. 2. Chichester: Wiley.

Bellina, J. and Wilson, J. (1986) *The Fertility Handbook: A Positive and Practical Guide.* Harmondsworth: Penguin.

Bendelow, G., Birke, L. and Williams, S.J. (eds) (2003) *Debating Biology: Sociological Reflections on Health, Medicine and Society.* London: Routledge.

Benson, S. (1997) 'The body, health and eating disorders', in K. Woodward (ed.), *Identity and Difference*. London: Sage.

Bernal, M. (1991) *Black Athena. Afro-Asiatic Roots of Classical Civilization: The Fabrication of Ancient Greece, 1785–1985*, vol. 1. London: Vintage.

Bernal, M. (2001) *Black Athena Writes Back: Martin Bernal Responds to His Critics*. Durham, NC: Duke University Press.

Berney, L., Blane, D., Smith, G.D., Gunnell, D.J., Holland, P. and Montgomery, S.M. (2000) 'Socioeconomic measures in early old age as indicators of previous lifetime exposure to environmental health hazards', *Sociology of Health and Illness*, 22 (4): 415–30.

Bilton, T., Bonett, K., Jones, P., Lawson, T., Skinner, D., Stansworth, M. and Webster, A. (1996) *Introductory Sociology*, 3rd edn. London: Macmillan.

Birke, L. (1992) 'Transforming human biology', in H. Crowley and S. Himmelweit (eds), *Knowing Women: Feminism and Knowledge*. Cambridge: Polity/Open University.

Black, D., Morris, J., Smith, C. and Townsend, P. (1980) *Inequalities in Health: Report of a Research Working Group*. London: Department of Health and Social Security.

Blackburn, R. (1998) *The Making of New World Slavery: From the Baroque to the Modern, 1492–1800*. London: Verso.

Blamey, A., Hanlon, P., Judge, K. and Muirie, J. (eds) (2002) *Health Inequalities in the New Scotland*. Glasgow: Public Health Institute of Scotland.

Blane, D., Higgs, P., Hyde, M. and Wiggins, R.D. (2004) 'Life course influences on quality of life in early old age', *Social Science and Medicine*, 58 (11): 2171–9.

Blau, P.M. (1963) *The Dynamics of Bureaucracy*, 2nd edn. Chicago: University of Chicago Press.

Blaxter, M. (1990) *Health and Life Styles*. London: Routledge.

BMA (British Medical Association) (1993) *Complementary Medicine: New Approaches to Good Practice*. Oxford: Oxford University Press.

BMA (British Medical Association) (2000) *Eating Disorders, Body Image and the Media*. London: BMJ Books.

Boeije, H., Duijnstee, M.S.H., Grypdonck, M.H.F. and Pool, A. (2002) 'Encountering the downward phase: biographical work in people with multiple sclerosis living at home', *Social Science and Medicine*, 55: 881–93.

Bok, S. (2004) *Rethinking the WHO Definition of Health*. Working Paper Series, vol. 14, no. 7. Cambridge, MA: Harvard Center for Population and Development Studies.

Bond, J., Coleman, P. and Peace, S. (eds) (1993) *Ageing and Society: An Introduction to Social Gerontology*, 2nd edn. London: Sage.

Bond, R. and Rosie, M. (2002) 'National identities in post-devolution Scotland'. www.institute-of-governance.org/onlinepub/bondrosie.html.

Booth, C. (1902) *Life and Labour of the People in London. Final Volume. Notes on Social Influences and Conclusions*. London: Macmillan.

Bordo, S. (1990) 'Reading the slender body', in M. Jacobs, E.F. Keller and S. Shuttleworth (eds), *Body/Politics: Women and the Discourse of Science*. New York: Routledge.

Bourdieu, P. (1984) *Distinction: A Social Critique of the Judgement of Taste*. London: Routledge and Kegan Paul.

Bradby, H. (1995) 'Ethnicity: not a black and white issue. A research note', *Sociology of Health and Illness*, 17 (3): 405–17.

Breast Cancer Care (2011) *Lesbian and Bisexual Women and Breast Cancer: A Policy Briefing*. London.

Brown, G.W. and Harris, T. (1978) *Social Origins of Depression: A Study of Psychiatric Disorder in Women*. Cambridge: Cambridge University Press.

Bruce, S. (1999) *Sociology: A Very Short Introduction*. Oxford: Oxford University Press.

Bruce, S. and Glendinning, T. (2010) 'When was secularization? Dating the decline of the British churches and locating its cause', *The British Journal of Sociology*, 61: 107–26.

Bryson, L., Warner-Smith, P., Brown, P. and Fray, L. (2007) 'Managing the work–life roller-coaster: private stress or public health issue', *Social Science and Medicine*, 65 (6): 1142–53.

Buquet-Marcon, C., Charlier, P. and Samzun, A. (2009) 'A possible Early Neolithic amputation at Buthiers-Boulancourt (Seine-et-Marne), France', *Antiquity*, 83 (322).

Burawoy, M. (2004) '2004 presidential address: for public sociology', *American Sociological Review*, 70 (Feb.): 4–28.

Burnham, G., Lafta, R., Doocy, D. and Roberts, L. (2006) 'Mortality after the 2003 invasion of Iraq: across-sectional cluster sample survey', *Lancet*, 368: 1421–8.

Bury, M. (1991) 'The sociology of chronic illness: a review of research and prospects', *Sociology of Health and Illness*, 13 (4): 451–68.

Bury, M. (1997) *Health and Illness in a Changing Society*. London: Routledge.

Bury, M. (2000) 'Health, ageing and the lifecourse', in S.J. Williams, J. Gabe and M. Calnan (eds), *Health, Medicine and Society: Key Theories, Future Agendas*. London: Routledge.

Busfield, J. (2000) 'Introduction: rethinking the sociology of mental health', *Sociology of Mental Health and Illness*, 22: 543–88.

Bytheway, B. (1995) *Ageism*. Buckingham: Open University Press.

Bytheway, B. and Johnson, J. (1990) 'On defining ageism', *Critical Social Policy*, 27: 27–39.

Bywaters, P. (1999) 'Social work and health inequalities', *British Journal of Social Work*, 29: 811–16.

Carpenter, M. (2000) 'Reinforcing the pillars: rethinking gender', in H. Annandale and K. Hunt (eds), *Gender Inequalities in Health*. Buckingham: Open University Press.

Carricaburu, D. and Pierret, J. (1995) 'From biographical disruption to biographical reinforcement: the case of HIV-positive men', *Sociology of Health and Illness*, 17 (1): 65–88.

Carrington, B. (2010) *Race, Sport and Politics: The Sporting Black Diaspora*. London: Sage.

Cashmore, E. (2002) *Beckham*. Cambridge: Polity.

Cashmore, E. (2005) *Making Sense of Sport*, 4th edn. London: Routledge.

Cashmore, E. (2008) 'Tiger Woods and the new racial order', *Current Sociology*, 56: 621–34.

Castells, M. (1997) *The Power of Identity*. Oxford: Blackwell.

Chahal, K. (2004) *Experiencing Ethnicity: Discrimination and Service Provision*. York: York Publication Services.

Chahal, K. and Julienne, L. (1999) *'We Can't All Be White!' Racist Victimisation in the UK*. York: York Publication Services.

Chakraborty, A., McManus, S., Brugha, T. and Bebbington, P. (2011) 'Mental health of the non-heterosexual population of England', *The British Journal of Psychiatry*, 198: 143–8.

Charmaz, K. (1983) 'Loss of self: a fundamental form of suffering in the chronically ill', *Sociology of Health and Illness*, 5 (2): 168–95.

Chimot, C. and Louveau, C. (2010) 'Becoming a man while playing a female sport: the construction of masculine identity in boys doing rhythmic gymnastics', *International Review for the Sociology of Sport*, 45 (4): 436–56.

Clarke, J. (ed.) (1994) *A Crisis in Care? Challenges to Social Work*. London: Sage.

Cochrane, K. (2011) 'Miriam O'Reilly: "Standing up to the BBC was the right thing to do"', *The Guardian*, 11 February.

Coker, N. (ed.) (2001) *Racism in Medicine: An Agenda for Change*. London: King's Fund.

Colgrove, J. (2002) 'The McKeown thesis: a historical controversy and its enduring influence', *American Journal of Public Health*, 92 (5): 725–9.

Collins, M.F. and Kay, T. (2003) *Sport and Social Exclusion*. London: Routledge.

Colman, P. (1995) *Rosie the Riveter: Women Workers on the Home Front in World War II*. New York: Crown.

Connell, R. (2002) *Gender*. Cambridge: Polity.

Connell, R.W. (2005) *Masculinities*. Cambridge: Polity.

Coward, R. (1993) 'The myth of alternative health', in A. Beattie, M. Gott, L. Jones and M. Sidell (eds), *Health and Well-being: A Reader*. London: Macmillan/Open University.

Craib, I. (1997) *Classical Social Theory*. Cambridge: Polity.

Crang, M. and Cook, I. (2007) *Doing Ethnographies*. London: Sage.

Crinson, I. and Yuill, C. (2008) 'What can alienation theory contribute to an understanding of social inequalities in health?', *International Journal of Health Services*, 38 (3): 455–70.

Crow, G., Allan, G. and Summers, M. (2002) 'Neither busybodies nor nobodies: managing proximity and distance in neighbourly relations', *Sociology*, 36 (2): 127–45.

CSDH (Commission on Social Determinants of Health) (2008) *Closing the Gap in a Generation: Health Equity through Action on the Social Determinants of Health*. Final Report of the Commission on Social Determinants of Health. Geneva: World Health Organisation.

Cumming, E. and Henry, W. (1961) *Growing Old: The Process of Disengagement*. New York: Basic.

Cunningham, A. (1994) 'Blood', in C. Seale and S. Pattison (eds), *Medical Knowledge: Doubt and Certainty*. Buckingham: Open University Press.

Dearden, C. and Becker, S. (2000) *Young Carers' Transitions into Adulthood*. York: Joseph Rowntree Foundation.

Department of Health (1989) *Working for Patients*. London: HMSO.

Department of Health (1999a) *Saving Lives: Our Healthier Nation*. Cm 4386. London: Stationery Office.

Department of Health (1999b) *Reducing Health Inequalities: An Action Report*. London: Stationery Office.

Department of Health (2000) *The NHS Plan: A Plan for Investment, a Plan for Reform*. London: Stationery Office.

Department of Health (2001) *Valuing People: A New Strategy for Learning Disability for the 21st Century*. London: HMSO.

Department of Health (2003) *Tackling Health Inequalities: A Programme for Action*. London.

Department of Health (2004) *Choosing Health: Making Healthier Choices Easier*. London.

Department of Health (2005a) *Tackling Health Inequalities: Status Report on the Programme for Action*. London.

Department of Health (2005b) *Independence, Well-being and Choice*. Green Paper on Adult Social Care. London.

Department of Health (2006) *Our Health, Our Care, Our Say: A New Direction for Community Services*. London.

Department of Health (2011) *National Service Framework for Mental Health*. http://www.dh.gov.uk/en/Publicationsandstatistics/Publications/PublicationsPolicyAndGuidance/DH_4009598.

Derrida, J. (1993) *Aporias*. Stanford, CA: Stanford University Press.

DHSS (Department of Health and Social Security) (1989) *Caring for People: Community Care in the Next Decade and Beyond*. London: Stationery Office.

Doll, R. (1992) 'Health and the environment in the 1990s', *American Journal of Public Health*, 82: 933–41.

Donnelly, P. (2005) 'Sport and social theory', in B. Houlihan, *Sport and Society* (2nd edn). London: Sage.

Dorling, D., Mitchell, R., Shaw, M., Orford, S. and Smith, G.D. (2000) 'The ghost of Christmas past: health effects of poverty in London in 1896 and 1991', *British Medical Journal*, 321: 1547–51.

Douglas, J.D. (1967) *The Social Meanings of Suicide*. Princeton, NJ: Princeton University Press.

Doyal, L. (1979) *The Political Economy of Health*. London: Pluto.

Doyal, L. (1994) *What Makes Women Sick? The Political Economy of Health*. London: Macmillan.

Doyal, L. (2001) 'Sex, gender and health: the need for a new approach', *British Medical Journal*, 323: 1061–3.

Drabble, L., Midanik, L.T. and Trocki, K. (2005) 'Reports of alcohol consumption and alcohol-related problems among homosexual, bisexual and heterosexual respondents: Results from the 2000 National Alcohol Survey', *Journal of Studies on Alcohol*, 66: 111–20.

Dumazedier, J. (1967) *Towards a Society of Leisure*. New York: Free.

Durkheim, E. (1970) *Suicide: A Study in Sociology* (1897). London: Routledge and Kegan Paul.

Elias, N. (1982) *The Civilising Process. Vol. 1: A History of Manners*. Oxford: Blackwell.

Emslie, C., Ridge, D., Ziebland, S. and Hunt, K. (2006) 'Men's account of depression: reconstructing or resisting hegemonic masculinity?', *Social Science and Medicine*, 62: 2246–57.

Engels, F. (2009) *The Condition of the Working Class in England*. Oxford: Oxford University Press.

Faircloth, C.A., Boylstein, C., Rittman, M., Young, M.E. and Gubrium, J. (2004) 'Sudden illness and biographical flow in narratives of stroke recovery', *Sociology of Health and Illness*, 26 (2): 242–61.

Fairhurst, E. (1998) '"Growing old gracefully" as opposed to "mutton dressed as lamb": the social construction of recognising older women', in S. Nettleton and J. Watson (eds), *The Body in Everyday Life*. London: Routledge.

Faris, R. and Dunham, H. (1939) *Mental Disorders in Urban Areas: An Ecological Study of Schizophrenia and Other Psychoses*. Chicago: University of Chicago Press.

Featherstone, M. (1991) *Consumer Culture and Postmodernism*. London: Sage.

Featherstone, M. and Hepworth, M. (1993) 'Images of ageing', in J. Bond, P. Coleman and S. Peace (eds), *Ageing and Society: An Introduction to Social Gerontology*, 2nd edn. London: Sage.

Fenton, A. and Charsley, K. (2000) 'Epidemiology and sociology as incommensurate games: accounts from the study of health and ethnicity', *Health*, 4 (4): 403–25.

Fenton, S. and Sadiq-Sangster, A. (1996) 'Culture, relativism and the experience of mental distress: South Asian women in Britain', *Sociology of Health and Illness*, 18 (1): 66–85.

Festinger, A., Riecken, H.W. and Schachter, S. (1956) *When Prophecy Fails*. New York: Harper & Row.

Field, D. (1992) 'Contemporary issues in relation to the elderly', in M. O'Donnell (ed.), *New Introductory Reader in Sociology*. Walton-on-Thames: Nelson.

Fink, J. (2004) *Care: Personal Lives and Social Policy*. Milton Keynes: Open University Press.

Fish, J. (2010) *Coming Out about Breast Cancer: Lesbian and Bisexual Women's Experiences of Breast Cancer*. National Cancer Action Team and De Montfort University.

Fogel, C. (2011) 'Sporting masculinity on the gridiron: construction, characteristics and consequences', *Canadian Social Science*, 7 (2) 1–14.

Foster, P. (1995) *Women and the Health Care Industry: An Unhealthy Relationship?* Buckingham: Open University Press.

Foucault, M. (1967) *Madness and Civilisation: A History of Insanity in the Age of Reason*. London: Tavistock.

Foucault, M. (1970) *The Order of Things: An Archaeology of the Human Sciences*. London: Tavistock.

Foucault, M. (1973) *The Birth of the Clinic: An Archaeology of Medical Perception*. London: Tavistock.

Foucault, M. (1979a) *Discipline and Punish: The Birth of the Prison*. Harmondsworth: Penguin.

Foucault, M. (1979b) *The Will to Knowledge. The History of Sexuality, Vol. I*. London: Allen Lane.

Frank, A.W. (1995) *The Wounded Storyteller: Body, Illness and Ethics.* Chicago: University of Chicago Press.

Franklin, S. (1997) *Embodied Progress: A Cultural Account of Assisted Conception.* London: Routledge.

Fredrickson, B.L. and Harrison, K. (2005) 'Throwing like a girl: self-objectification predicts adolescent girls' motor performance', *Journal of Sport and Social Issues*, 29: 79–101.

Fulop, N., Elston, J., Hensher, M., McKee, M. and Walters, R. (1998) 'Evaluation of the implementation of *The Health of the Nation*', in Department of Health (ed.), *The Health of the Nation: A Policy Assessed.* London: Stationery Office.

Giddens, A. (1986) *Sociology: A Brief but Critical Introduction.* London: Macmillan.

Giddens, A. (1991) *Modernity and Self-Identity: Self and Society in the Late Modern Age.* Cambridge: Polity.

Giddens, A. (1994) *Sociology.* Cambridge: Polity.

Giddens, A. (1997) *Introductory Readings.* Cambridge: Polity.

Giddens, A. (ed.) (2001) *Sociology: Introductory Readings.* Cambridge: Polity.

Ginn, J. and Arber, S. (1995) '"Only Connect": Gender Relations and Ageing', in S. Arber and J. Ginn (eds), *Connecting Gender and Ageing: A Sociological Approach.* Buckingham: Open University Press.

Giulianotti, R. (2005) *Sport: A Critical Sociology.* Cambridge: Polity.

Goffman, E. (1961) *Asylums: Essays on the Social Situation of Mental Patients and Other Inmates.* Harmondsworth: Penguin.

Goffman, E. (1968) *Stigma: Notes on the Management of a Spoiled Identity.* Harmondsworth: Penguin.

Goodley, D. (2001) '"Learning Difficulties", the social model of disability and impairment: challenging epistemologies', *Disability & Society*, 16 (2): 207–31.

Gorer, G. (1965) *Death, Grief and Mourning.* London: Cresset.

Gott, M. (2005) *Sexuality, Sexual Health and Ageing.* Maidenhead: Open University Press.

Gould, S.J. (1980) *The Panda's Thumb.* New York: W. W. Norton.

Gove, W.R. (1984) 'Gender differences in mental and physical illness: the effects of fixed roles and nurturant roles', *Social Science and Medicine*, 19 (2): 77–91.

Graham, H. (1983) 'Caring: a labour of love', in J. Finch and D. Groves (eds), *A Labour of Love: Women, Work and Caring.* London: Routledge & Kegan Paul.

Graham, H. (1991) 'The concept of caring in feminist research: the case of domestic service', *Sociology*, 25 (1): 61–78.

Graham, H. (1993) *Hardship and Health in Women's Lives.* New York: Wheatsheaf.

Green, J. and Thorogood, N. (2004) *Qualitative Methods for Health Research.* London: Sage.

Griffiths, R. (1988) *Community Care: An Agenda for Action.* London: Stationery Office.

Gupta, S., de Belder, A. and O'Hughes, L. (1995) 'Avoiding premature coronary deaths in Asians in Britain: spend now on prevention or pay later for treatment', *British Medical Journal*, 311: 1035–6.

Hall, P., Brockington, I.F., Levings, J. and Murphy, C. (1993) 'A comparison of responses to the mentally ill in two communities', *British Journal of Psychiatry*, 162: 99–108.

Hall, S. (2003) 'Women still on 72% of men's pay', *The Guardian*, 17 October.

Ham, C. (2004) *Health Policy in Britain*, 5th edn. Basingstoke: Palgrave Macmillan.

Hanlon, P., Walsh, D., Buchanan, D., Redpath, A., Bain, M., Brewster, D., Chalmers, J., Muir, R., Smalls, M., Willis, J. and Wood, R. (2001) *Chasing the Scottish Effect. Why Scotland Needs a Step-Change in Health If It Is To Catch Up with the Rest of Europe*. Glasgow: Public Health Institute of Scotland.

Hardey, M. (2002) '"The story of my illness": personal accounts of illness on the internet', *Health*, 6 (1): 31–46.

Hardley, M. (1998) *The Social Context of Health*. Buckingham: Open University Press.

Harris, B. (2004) 'Public health, nutrition and the decline of mortality: the McKeown thesis revisited', *Social History of Medicine*, 17 (3): 379–407.

Harris, R., Tobias, M., Jeffreys, M., Waldegrave, K., Karlsen, S. and Nazroo, J. (2006) 'Racism and health: the relationship between experience of racial discrimination and health in New Zealand', *Social Science and Medicine*, 63: 1428–41.

Harvey, J. (1997) 'The technological regulation of death: with reference to the technological regulation of birth', *Sociology*, 31 (4): 719–35.

Hattersly, L. (1997) 'Expectation of life by social class', in F. Drever and M. Whitehead (eds), *Health Inequalities: Decennial Supplement*. London: Stationery Office.

Hawkes, G. (1996) *A Sociology of Sex and Sexuality*. Buckingham: Open University Press.

Heaphy, B., Yip, A. and Thompson D. (2004) 'Ageing in a non-heterosexual context', *Ageing and Society*, 24: 881–902.

Hewitt, P. and Warren, J. (1997) 'A self-made man', in A. Giddens (ed.), *Sociology: Introductory Readings*. Cambridge: Polity.

Hibbard, J.H. and Pope, C.R. (1986) 'Another look at sex differences in the use of medical care: illness orientation and the types of morbidities for which services are used', *Women and Health*, 11 (2): 21–36.

Higginbottom, G.M.A. (2006) '"Pressure of life": ethnicity as a mediating factor in mid-life and older people's experiences of high blood pressure', *Sociology of Health and Illness*, 28 (5): 583–610.

Hines, S. and Sanger, T. (eds) (2010) *Transgender Identities: Towards a Social Analysis of Gender Diversity*. London: Routledge.

Hochschild, A. (1983) *The Managed Heart: Commercialization of Human Feeling*. Berkeley, CA: University of California Press.

Hockey, J. and James, A. (2003) *Social Identities across the Life Course*. Basingstoke: Palgrave Macmillan.

Hodkinson, P. (2002) *Goth: Identity, Style and Subculture*. Oxford: Berg.

Holland, S. (2004) *Alternative Femininities: Body, Age and Identity*. Oxford: Berg.

Hollingshead, A. and Redlich, F. (1953) 'Social stratification and psychiatric disorders', *American Sociological Review*, 18 (2): 163–9.

Hughes T.L. and Jacobson, K.M. (2003) 'Sexual orientation and women's smoking', *Current Women's Health Reports*, 3: 254–61.

Hunt, R. and Fish, J. (2008) *Prescription for Change: Lesbian and Bisexual Women's Health Check*. London: Stonewall.

Hunt, R., Cowan, K. and Chamberlain, B. (2007) *Being the Gay One: Experiences of Lesbian, Gay and Bisexual People Working in the Health and Social Care Sector*. London: Stonewall.

Hunt, T. (2005) *Building Jerusalem: The Rise and Fall of the Victorian City*. London: Phoenix.

Hunter, D.J. (1994) 'From tribalism to corporatism: the managerial challenge to medical dominance', in J. Gabe, D. Kelleher and G. Williams (eds), *Challenging Medicine*. London: Routledge.

Hunter, M. (2001) 'Medical research under threat after Alder Hey scandal', *British Medical Journal*, 322 (24 February): 448.

Illich, I. (1976) *Limits to Medicine*. Harmondsworth: Penguin.

Illich, I. (1993) 'The epidemics of modern medicine', in N. Black, D. Boswell, A. Gray, S. Murphy and J. Popay (eds), *Health and Disease: A Reader*. Milton Keynes: Open University Press.

Institute for Fiscal Studies (2011) *Poverty and Inequality in the UK: 2011*. London: The Institute for Fiscal Studies.

Iphofen, R. (1996) 'Coping with a "perforated life": a close study in managing the stigma of petit mal epilepsy', *Sociology*, 24 (3): 447–63.

Irvine, B. and Ginsberg, I. (2004) *England versus Scotland: Does More Money Mean Better Health?* London: Civitas.

James, M. (1994) 'Hysteria', in C. Seale and S. Pattison (eds), *Medical Knowledge: Doubt and Certainty*. Milton Keynes: Open University Press.

James, O. (1998) *Britain on the Couch. Why We're Unhappier Compared with 1950, Despite Being Richer: A Treatment for the Low-Serotonin Society*. London: Arrow.

Jenkins, R. (2004) *Social Identity*, 2nd edn. London: Routledge.

Jewson, N.D. (1976) 'The disappearance of the sick-man from medical cosmology, 1770–1870', *Sociology*, 10(2): 225–44.

Jorm, J.F. (2000) 'Mental health literacy: public knowledge and beliefs about mental disorder', *British Journal of Psychiatry*, 177: 396–401.

Kandrack, M., Grant, K. and Segall, A. (1991) 'Gender differences in health-related behaviour: some unanswered questions', *Social Science and Medicine*, 32 (5): 579–90.

Kangas, I. (2001) 'Making sense of depression: perceptions of melancholia in lay narratives', *Health*, 5 (1): 76–92.

Karasz, A. (2005) 'Cultural differences in conceptual models of depression', *Social Science Medicine*, 60 (7): 1625–35.

Karlsen, S. and Nazroo, J.Y. (2002a) 'Agency and structure: the impact of ethnic identity and racism on the health of ethnic minority people', *Sociology of Health and Illness*, 24 (1): 1–20.

Karlsen, S. and Nazroo, J.Y. (2002b) 'The relationship between racial discrimination, social class and health among ethnic minority groups', *American Journal of Public Health*, 92 (4): 624–31.

Karlsen, S. and Nazroo, J. (2004) 'Fear of racism and health', *Journal of Epidemiology and Community Health*, 58: 1017–18.

Karlsen, S., Nazroo, J.Y. and Stephenson, R. (2002) 'Ethnicity, environment and health: putting ethnic inequalities in health in their place', *Social Science and Medicine*, 55 (9): 155–69.

Kellehear, A. (2007) *A Social History of Dying*. Cambridge: Cambridge University Press.

Kellehear, A. (2008) 'Dying as a social relationship: a sociological review of debates on the determination of death', *Social Science and Medicine*, 66 (7): 1533–44.

Kelly, L. (1988) *Surviving Sexual Violence*. Cambridge: Polity.

King, M. and McKeowan, E. (2003) *Mental Health and Social Wellbeing of Gay Men, Lesbians and Bisexuals in England and Wales*. London: MIND.

Kirby, M., Kidd, W., Koubel, F., Barter, J., Hope, T., Kirton, A., Madry, N., Manning, P. and Triggs, K. (2000) *Sociology in Perspective*. Oxford: Heinemann.

Krieger, N., Chen, J.T., Waterman, P.D., Rehkopf, D.H. and Subramanian, S.V. (2005) 'Painting a truer picture of US socioeconomic and racial/ethnic health inequalities: the Public Health Disparities Geocoding Project', *American Journal of Public Health*, 95: 312–23.

Kübler-Ross, E. (1969) *On Death and Dying*. London: Routledge.

Laing, W. and Buisson, E. (2003) *Laing's Healthcare Market Review 2003–2004*. London.

Langdon, S.A., Eagle, A. and Warner, J. (2007) 'Making sense of dementia in the social world: a qualitative study', *Social Science and Medicine*, 64 (4): 989–1000.

Laslett, P. (1987) 'The emergence of the third age', *Ageing and Society*, 7 (2): 133–60.

Laslett, P. (1989) *Fresh Map of Life: Emergence of the Third Age*. London: Weidenfeld and Nicholson.

Laslett, P. (1996) *A Fresh Map of Life: The Emergence of the Third Age*. London: Macmillan.

Latour, B. (1992) 'Where Are the Missing Masses? The Sociology of a Few Mundane Artifacts', in W.E. Bijker and John Law (eds), *Shaping Technology/Building Society: Studies in Sociotechnical Change*. Cambridge, MA: MIT Press. pp. 225–58.

Lawler, J. (1991) *Behind the Screens: Nursing, Somatology and the Body*. London: Churchill Livingstone.

Lawson, T. (1997) *Economics and Reality*. London: Routledge.

Lee, C. (1998) *Women's Health: Psychological and Social Perspectives*. London: Sage.

Lee, R. (2008) 'Modernity, mortality and re-enchantment: the death taboo revisited', *Sociology*, 42 (4): 745–75.

Lefebvre, H. (2008) *Critique of Everyday Life*. London: Verso.

Leon, D.A., Walt, G. and Gilson, L. (2001) 'Recent advances: international perspectives on health inequalities and policy', *British Medical Journal*, 322 (7286): 591–4.

Levinson, R. (1998) 'Issues at the interface of medical sociology and public health', in G. Scambler and P. Higgs (eds) *Modernity, Medicine and Health*. London: Routledge.

LSE (London School of Economics) (2006) *The Depression Report: A New Deal for Depression and Anxiety Disorders*. London: LSE.

Lupton, D. (1994) *Medicine as Culture: Illness, Disease and the Body in Western Societies.* London: Sage.

Lupton, D. (1996) *The Imperative of Health: Public Health and the Regulated Body.* London: Sage.

Lutfey, K. (2005) 'On practices of "good doctoring": reconsidering the relationship between provider roles and patient adherence', *Sociology of Health and Illness*, 27 (4): 421–47.

Lynch, J., Davey-Smith, G., Kaplan, G. and House, J. (2000) 'Income inequality and mortality: importance to health of individual income, psychosocial environment, or material conditions', *British Medical Journal*, 320: 1200–4.

MacDonald, L. (1988) 'The experience of stigma: living with rectal cancer', in R. Anderson and M. Bury (eds), *Living with Chronic Illness: The Experience of Patients and their Families.* London: Unwin Hyman.

Macintyre, S. (1997) 'The Black Report and beyond: what are the issues?', *Social Science and Medicine*, 44:723–46.

Macintyre, S., Ford, G. and Hunt, K. (1999) 'Do women "over-report" morbidity? Men's and women's responses to structured prompting on a standard question on long-standing illness', *Social Science and Medicine*, 48: 89–98.

Macintyre, S., Hunt, K. and Sweeting, H. (1996) 'Gender differences in health: are things as simple as they seem?', *Social Science and Medicine*, 42: 617–24.

MacPherson, W. (1999) *The Stephen Lawrence Inquiry: Report of an Inquiry by Sir William MacPherson of Cluny.* London: Stationery Office.

Malin, N., Manthorpe, J., Race, D. and Wilmot, S. (1999) *Community Care for Nurses and the Caring Professions.* Buckingham: Open University Press.

Mallett, S. (2004) 'Understanding home: a critical review of the literature', *Sociological Review*, 52 (1): 62–89.

Marmot, M. (2004) *Status Syndrome: How Your Social Standing Directly Affects Your Health and Life Expectancy.* London: Bloomsbury.

Marshall, G. (1998) *Oxford Dictionary of Sociology.* Oxford: Oxford University Press.

Marsland, D. (1996) *Welfare or Welfare State: Contradictions and Dilemmas in Social Policy.* Basingstoke: Macmillan.

Mayall, B. (1996) *Children, Health and the Social Order.* Buckingham: Open University Press.

McDonald, A. (1999) *Understanding Community Care: A Guide for Social Workers.* Basingstoke: Macmillan.

McEwen, B.S. (2000) 'Allostasis and allostatic load: implications for neuropsychopharmacology', *Neuropsychopharmacology*, 22 (2): 108–24.

McKeown, T. (1976) *The Modern Rise of Population.* New York: Academic.

McKie, L. (1995) 'The art of surveillance or reasonable prevention? The case of cervical screening', *Sociology of Health and Illness*, 17 (4): 441–57.

McLaren, L. and Johnson, M. (2004) 'Understanding the rising tide of anti-immigrant sentiment', in A. Park, J. Curtice, K. Thomson, C. Bromley and M. Phillips (eds), *British Social Attitudes. The 21st Report.* London: Sage. pp. 169–200.

McPherson, S. and Armstrong, D. (2006) 'Social determinants of diagnostic labels in depression', *Social Science and Medicine*, 62: 50–8.

McQuaide, M.M. (2005) 'The rise of alternative health care: a sociological account', *Social Theory and Health*, 3: 286–301.

Mead, M. (1930) *Growing Up in New Guinea*. New York: Harper and Collins.

Means, R., Richards, S. and Smith, R. (2003) *Community Care Policy and Practice*, 3rd edn. Basingstoke: Palgrave Macmillan.

Mills, C. Wright (1970) *The Sociological Imagination*. Harmondsworth: Penguin.

MIND (1999) *Suicide*. London.

MIND (2000a) *Mental Health Statistics 1: How Common Is Mental Distress?* London.

MIND (2000b) *The Mental Health of Irish-Born People in Britain*. London.

Minton, A. (2009) *Ground Control: Fear and Happiness in the Twenty-First-Century City*. London: Penguin.

Mitchell, R., Shaw, M. and Dorling, D. (2000) *Inequalities in Life and Death: What If Britain Were More Equal?* Bristol: Policy.

Moon, G. and Gillespie, R. (1995) *Society and Health: An Introduction to Social Science for Health Professionals*. London: Routledge.

Moor, L. (2007) 'Sport and commodification: a reflection on key concepts', *Journal of Sport and Social Issues*, 31 (2): 128–42.

Morgan, M., Calnan, M. and Manning, N. (1985) *Sociological Approaches to Health and Medicine*. London: Croom Helm.

Morris, J. (ed.) (1989) *Able Lives: Women's Experience of Paralysis*. London: Women's Press.

Muntaner, C. (2004) 'Commentary: social capital, social class, and the slow progress of psychosocial epidemiology', *International Journal of Epidemiology*, 33: 674–80.

Musingarimi, P. (2008) *Health Issues Affecting Older Gay, Lesbian and Bisexual People in the UK: A Policy Brief*. London: ILC-UK.

Navarro, V. (1976) *Medicine under Capitalism*. New York: Prodist.

Navarro, V. (ed.) (2002) *The Political Economy of Social Inequalities: Consequences for Health and Quality of Life*. Amityville, NY: Baywood.

Nazroo, J.Y. (1997) *The Health of Britain's Ethnic Minorities: Findings from a National Survey*. London: Policy Studies Institute.

Nazroo, J.Y. (1998) 'Genetic, cultural or socio-economic vulnerability? Explaining ethnic inequalities in health', *Sociology of Health and Illness*, 20: 710–30.

Nazroo, J.Y. (2001) *Ethnicity, Class and Health*. London: Policy Studies Institute.

Nazroo, J.Y. (ed.) (2006) *Health and Social Research in Multiethnic Societies*. London: Routledge.

Nazroo, J., Edwards, A. and Brown, G.W. (1998) 'Gender differences in the prevalence of depression: artefact, alternative disorders, biology or roles?', *Sociology of Health and Illness*, 20 (3): 312–30.

Nettleton, S. (1995) *The Sociology of Health and Illness*. Cambridge: Polity.

Nettleton, S. and Watson, J. (1998) *The Body in Everyday Life*. London: Routledge.

Netto, G., Gaag, S., Thanki, M., Bondi, L. and Munro, M. (2001) *A Suitable Space: Improving Counselling Services for Asian People.* York: Joseph Rowntree Foundation and Policy.

Noon, M. (1993) 'Racial discrimination in speculative applications: evidence from the UK's top 100 firms', *Human Resource Management Journal*, 3 (4): 35–47.

Oakley, A. (1984) *The Captured Womb: A History of the Medical Care of Pregnant Women.* Oxford: Blackwell.

Oakley, A. (1987) 'From walking wombs to test-tube babies', in M. Stanworth (ed.), *Reproductive Technologies: Gender, Motherhood and Medicine.* Cambridge: Polity.

O'Brien, R., Hunt, K. and Hart, G. (2005) 'It's caveman stuff, but that is to a certain extent how guys still operate', *Social Science and Medicine*, 61 (3): 503–16.

O'Keeffe, M., Hills, A., Doyle, M., McCreadie, C., Scholes, S., Constantine, R., Tinker, A., Manthorpe, J., Biggs, S. and Erens, B. (2007) *UK Study of Abuse and Neglect of Older People: Prevalence Survey Report.* London: NatCen.

Oliver, M. (1990) *The Politics of Disablement.* London: Macmillan.

Oliver, M. (1993) 'Redefining disability: a challenge to the research', in J. Swain, V. Finkelstein, S. French and M. Oliver (eds), *Disabling Barriers: Enabling Environments.* London: Sage.

ONS (Office for National Statistics) *Census 2001.* London: Stationery Office.

ONS (Office for National Statistics) (2003) *Health Statistics Quarterly no. 20: Winter 2003.* London: Stationery Office.

ONS (Office for National Statistics) (2004) *Focus on Social Inequalities.* London: Stationery Office.

ONS (Office for National Statistics) (2005a) *Focus on Older People.* London: Stationery Office.

ONS (Office for National Statistics) (2005b) *Focus on Ethnicity and Identity.* London: Stationery Office.

ONS (Office for National Statistics) (2006a) *Focus on Gender.* London: Stationery Office.

ONS (Office for National Statistics) (2006b) *Focus on Health.* London: Stationery Office.

Palmer, G., Carr, J. and Kenway, P. (2005) *Monitoring Poverty and Social Exclusion in Scotland 2005.* York: New Policy Institute and Joseph Rowntree Foundation.

Parker, G. (1993) *With This Body: Caring and Disability in Marriage.* Buckingham: Open University Press.

Parks, A., Curtice, J., Clery, E. and Bryson, C. (2010) *British Social Attitudes. The 27th Report.* London: Sage.

Peterson, A. (1997) 'Risk, governance and the new public health', in A. Peterson and R. Bunton (eds), *Foucault: Health and Medicine.* London: Routledge.

Phillips, T. and Phillips, M. (1999) *Windrush: The Irresistible Rise of Multi-racial Britain.* London: HarperCollins.

Philo, G. (ed.) (1996) *Media and Mental Distress.* London: Longman.

Picardie, R. (1993) *Before I Say Goodbye.* London: Penguin.

Pilgrim, D. and Rogers, A. (1993) *A Sociology of Mental Health and Illness.* Buckingham: Open University Press.

Pilgrim, D. and Rogers, A. (1994) 'Something old, something new … sociology and the organisation of psychiatry', *Sociology*, 28 (2): 521–38.

Plummer, K. (1981) *The Making of the Modern Homosexual.* New Jersey: Barnes and Noble.

Porter, M. (1990) 'Professional–client relationships and women's reproductive health care', in S. Cunningham-Burley and N. McKeganey (eds), *Readings in Medical Sociology.* London: Tavistock.

Porter, R. (1999) *The Greatest Benefit to Mankind: A Medical History of Humanity from Antiquity to the Present.* Hammersmith: Fontana.

Porter, R. and Porter, D. (1985) 'Sickness and health in pre-modern England', in R. Porter and D. Porter (eds), *In Sickness and in Health: The British Experience 1650–1850.* London: Fourth Estate.

Pormann, P.E. and Savage-Smith, E. (2007) *Medieval Islamic Medicine.* Edinburgh: Edinburgh University Press.

Pound, P., Britten, N., Morgan, M., Yardley, L., Pope, C., Daker-White, G. and Campbell, R. (2005) 'Resisting medicines: a synthesis of qualitative studies of medicine taking', *Social Science and Medicine*, 61: 133–55.

Pound, P., Gompertz, P. and Ebrahim, S. (1998) 'Illness in the context of older age: the case of stroke', *Sociology of Health and Illness*, 20 (4): 489–506.

Prior, F. (2004) *Britain BC: Life in Britain and Ireland Before the Romans.* London: Harper Perennial.

Prior, L. (1993) *The Social Organization of Mental Illness.* London: Sage.

Pugh, S. (2005) 'Assessing the Cultural Needs of Older Lesbians and Gay Men: Implications for Practice', *Practice: A Journal of the British Association of Social Workers*, 17 (3): 207–18.

Pullen, I. (2002) 'The Scottish scene', *Psychiatric Bulletin*, 26: 86–7.

Putnam, R. (2000) *Bowling Alone: The Collapse and Revival of American Community.* New York: Simon & Schuster.

Qureshi, H. and Walker, A. (1989) *The Caring Relationship: Elderly People and Their Families.* Basingstoke: Macmillan.

Race, D. (2002) 'The historical context', in D. Race (ed.), *Learning Disability: A Social Approach.* London: Routledge.

Radia, K. (1996) *Ignored, Silenced, Neglected: Housing and Mental Health Care Needs of Asian People.* York: York Publication Services for Joseph Rowntree Foundation.

Rahman, M., Palmer, G., Kenway, P. and Howarth, C. (2000) *Monitoring Poverty and Social Exclusion.* London: New Policy Institute.

Ramazanaglu, C. (1989) *Feminism and the Contradictions of Oppression.* London: Routledge.

Reissman, L. (1992) 'Women and medicalisation: a new perspective', in L. McDowell and R. Pringle (eds), *Defining Women: Social Institutions and Gender Divisions.* Cambridge: Polity/Open University.

Rich, A. (1980) 'Compulsory heterosexuality and lesbian existence', *Signs*, 5 (4): 630–60.

Ristock, J. (2002) *No More Secrets: Violence in Lesbian Relationships*. London: Routledge.

Robinson, I. (1988) *Multiple Sclerosis*. London: Routledge.

Rooney, S. (2002) 'Social inclusion and people with profound and multiple disabilities: reality or myth?', in D.Race (ed.) *Learning Disability: A Social Approach*. London: Routledge.

Rose, S. (2005) *Lifelines: Life beyond the Gene*. London: Vintage.

Rose, S. (2006) *The 21st-Century Brain*. London: Vintage.

Rosenhan, D.L. (1973) 'On being sane in insane places', *Science*, 179: 250–8.

Roughead, W. (2000) 'The body snatchers' (1921), in B.D. Osborne and R. Armstrong (eds), *Wicked Men and Fools: A Scottish Crime Anthology*. Edinburgh: Birlinn.

Sabat, S.R. (2001) *The Experience of Alzheimer's Disease*. Oxford: Blackwell.

Sailes, G.A. (1998) 'The African-American athlete', in G.A. Sailes (ed.), *African-Americans in Sport*. New Brunswick, NJ: Transaction.

Saks, M. (ed.) (1992) *Alternative Medicine in Britain*. Oxford: Clarendon.

Saks, M. (1994) 'The alternatives to medicine', in J. Gabe, D. Kelleher and G. Williams (eds), *Challenging Medicine*. London: Routledge.

Saks, M. (1998) 'Medicine and complementary medicine', in G. Scambler and P. Higgs (eds), *Modernity, Medicine and Health: Medical Sociology towards 2000*. London: Routledge.

Samson, C. (1995) 'Madness and psychiatry', in B. Turner with C. Samson, *Medical Power and Social Knowledge*. London: Sage.

Sanders, C., Donovan, J. and Dieppe, P. (2002) 'The significance and consequences of having painful and disabled joints in older age: co-existing accounts of normal and disrupted biographies', *Sociology of Health and Illness*, 24 (2): 227–53.

Sapolsky, R.M. (1992) *Stress: Aging Brain and the Mechanisms of Neuron Death*. Michigan: MIT Press.

Saracci, R. (1997) 'The World Health Organisation needs to reconsider its definition of health', *British Medical Journal*, 314: 1409.

Savage, M., Bagnall, G. and Longhurst, B. (2005) *Globalisation and Belonging*. London: Sage.

Scambler, G. (2001) 'Critical realism, sociology and health inequalities: social class as a generative mechanism and its media of enactment', *Journal of Critical Realism*, 4: 35–42.

Scheff, T. (1966) *Being Mentally Ill: A Sociology Theory*. Chicago: Aldine.

Schnittker, J. (2005) 'Chronic illness and depressive symptoms', *Social Science and Medicine*, 60: 13–23.

Scottish Executive (2000) *Our National Health: A Plan for Action, a Plan for Change*. Edinburgh.

Scottish Executive (2001) *Health in Scotland 2000*. Report of the Chief Medical Officer for Scotland. Edinburgh: Stationery Office.

Scottish Executive (2003) *Improving Health in Scotland: The Challenge*. Edinburgh: Stationery Office.

Scottish Executive (2004a) *Building a Better Scotland. Spending Proposals 2005–2008: Enterprise, Opportunity, Fairness. Technical Notes*. Edinburgh.

Scottish Executive (2004b) *Closing the Opportunity Gap*. Edinburgh.

Scottish Executive (2004c) *Fair To All, Personal To Each: The Next Step for the NHS Scotland*. Edinburgh.

Scottish Executive (2005) *Delivering for Health 2005*. Edinburgh.

Scottish Government (2010) www.scotland.gov.uk/Topics/Health/care/JointFuture.

Scottish Office Department of Health (1999) *Towards a Healthier Scotland: A White Paper on Health*. Edinburgh: Stationery Office.

Scull, A. (1979) *Museums of Madness: The Social Organization of Insanity in Nineteenth Century England*. London: Allen Lane.

Seale C. (1998) *Constructing Death: The Sociology of Dying and Bereavement*. Cambridge: Cambridge University Press.

Seale, C. (1998) 'Normal/pathological', in C. Jenks (ed.), *Core Sociological Dichotomies*. London: Sage.

Seale, C.F. (2000) 'Changing patterns of death and dying', *Social Science and Medicine*, 51: 917–30.

Seale, C. (2005) 'New directions for critical internet health studies: representing cancer experiences on the web', *Sociology of Health and Illness*, 27 (4): 515–40.

Seale, C. and Pattison, S. (1994) *Medical Knowledge: Doubt and Certainty*. Milton Keynes: Open University Press.

Seymour, J.E. (2001) *Critical Moments: Death and Dying in Intensive Care*. Buckingham: Open University Press.

Shakespeare, T. (2006) *Disability Rights and Wrongs*. London: Routledge.

Sharkey, P. (2007) *The Essentials of Community Care*. Basingstoke: Palgrave Macmillan.

Sharma, U. (1992) *Complementary Medicine Today: Practitioners and Patients*. London: Routledge.

Sharp, L. and Brewster, D. (1999) 'The epidemiology of lung cancer in Scotland: a review of trends in incidence, survival and mortality and prospects for prevention', *Health Bulletin*, 57 (5): 318–31.

Shaw, A., McMunn, A. and Field, J. (eds) (2000) *The Scottish Health Survey 1998. A Survey Carried Out on Behalf of the Scottish Executive Health Department*. Edinburgh: Scottish Executive.

Shaw, M., Dorling, D., Gordon D. and Davey-Smith, G. (1999) *The Widening Gap: Health Inequalities and Policy in Britain*. Bristol: Policy.

Shryock, R.H. (1979) *The Development of Modern Medicine: An Interpretation of the Social and Scientific Factors Involved*. Wisconsin: The Wisconsin University Press.

Singer, E. (1974) 'Premature social ageing: the social psychological consequences of a chronic illness', *Social Science and Medicine*, 8: 143–51.

Smaje C. (1995) *Health, 'Race' and Ethnicity: Making Sense of the Evidence*. London: King's Fund Institute.

Smaje, C. (1996) 'The ethnic patterning of health: new directions for theory and research', *Sociology of Health and Illness*, 18 (2): 139–71.

Small, N. (1997) 'Death and difference', in D. Field, J. Hockey and N. Small (eds), *Death, Gender and Ethnicity*. London: Routledge. pp. 202–21.

Smart, C. (1996) 'Deconstructing motherhood', in E. Bortolaia Silva (ed.), *Good Enough Mothering? Feminist Perspectives on Lone Motherhood*. London: Routledge.

Smith, G., Shaw, M., Mitchell, R., Dorling, D. and Gordon, D. (2000) 'Inequalities in health continue to grow despite government's pledges', *British Medical Journal*, 320: 582.

Sorensen, R. and Iedema, R. (2009) 'Emotional labour: clinicians' attitudes to death and dying', *Journal of Health Organization and Management*, 23 (1): 5–22.

SPIU (Scottish Poverty Information Unit) (1997) *Defining Poverty*. Glasgow: Glasgow Caledonian University. http://spiu.gcal.ac.uk/briefing1.html.

SPIU (Scottish Poverty Information Unit) (2002) *Poverty in Scotland*. Glasgow: Glasgow Caledonian University.

Stacey, M. (1988) *The Sociology of Health and Healing*. London: Routledge.

Star, S. (1955) 'The public's idea about mental illness'. Paper presented at the National Association for Mental Health Meeting, Chicago, November.

Steinbach, R., Green, J., Datta, J. and Edwards, P. (2011) 'Cycling and the city: a case study of how gendered, ethnic and class identities can shape healthy transport choices', *Social Science and Medicine*, 72 (7): 1123–30.

Strauss, A.L. (1987) *Qualitative Analysis for Social Scientists*. Cambridge: Cambridge University Press.

Stryker, S. and Whittle, S. (2006) *The Transgender Studies Reader*. London: Routledge.

Sweeting, H. and Gilhooly, M. (1997) 'Dementia and the phenomenon of social death', *Sociology of Health and Illness*, 19 (1): 93–117.

Szreter, S. (1988) 'The importance of social intervention in Britain's mortality decline *c.* 1850–1914: a reinterpretation of the role of public health', *Social History of Medicine*, 1: 1–38.

Szreter, S. (2002) 'Rethinking McKeown: the relationship between public health and social change', *American Journal of Public Health*, 92 (5): 722–5.

Taylor, S. (1989) *Suicide*. London: Longman.

Taylor, S. (1990) 'Beyond Durkheim: sociology and suicide', *Social Studies Review*, 6 (2): 70–4.

Thomas, B., Pritchard, J., Ballas, D., Vickers , D. and Dorling, D. (2009) *A Tale of Two Cities: The Sheffield Project*. Sheffield: The University of Sheffield.

Tinker, A. (1996) *Older People in Modern Society*. Harlow: Longman.

Tozer, R. (1999) *Supporting Families with Two or More Severely Disabled Children*. York: Joseph Rowntree Foundation.

Turner, B.S. (1994) *Medical Power and Social Knowledge*. London: Sage.

Turner, B. with Samson, C. (1995) *Medical Power and Social Knowledge*. London: Sage.

Twigg, J. (2006) *The Body in Health and Social Care*. Basingstoke: Palgrave Macmillan.

Twigg, J. (2007) 'Clothing, age and the body: a critical review', *Ageing and Society*, 27: 285–305.

Twigg, J. and Atkin, K. (1994) *Carers Perceived: Policy and Practice in Informal Care.* Buckingham: Open University Press.

United Nations (2005) *Demographic Year Book 2002.* New York: United Nations.

Üstün, B. and Jakob, R. (2005) 'Calling a spade a spade: meaningful definitions of health conditions', *Bulletin of the World Health Organisation*, 83: 802.

Vargo, M. (2002) *Scandal: Infamous Gay Controversies of the Twentieth Century.* London: Routledge.

Wade, D.T. (2001) 'Ethical issues in the diagnosis of permanent vegetative state', *British Medical Journal*, 322 (10 February): 352–4.

Walby, S. (1989) 'Theorising patriarchy', *Sociology*, 23 (2): 213–34.

Walby, S. and Allen, J. (2004) *Domestic Violence, Sexual Assault and Stalking: Findings from the British Crime Survey.* Home Office Research no. 276. London: Home Office. www. homeoffice.gov.uk/rds/violencewomen.html, accessed 13 May 2011.

Walter, T. (1994) *The Revival of Death.* London: Routledge.

Warnock, M. (1985) *A Question of Life.* Oxford: Blackwell.

Watney, S. (2000) *Imagine Hope: AIDS and Gay Identity.* London: Routledge.

Watson, J. (2000) *Male Bodies: Health, Culture, and Identity.* London: Taylor & Francis.

Weber, M. (1997) *Theory of Social and Economic Organization.* London: Free.

Weber, M. (2001) *The Protestant Work Ethic and the Spirit of Capitalism.* London: Routledge.

Weeks, J. (2003) *Sexuality.* London: Routledge.

West, P. (1998) *Perspectives on Health Inequalities: The Need for a Lifecourse Approach.* Glasgow: Medical Research Council Social and Public Health Sciences Unit, University of Glasgow.

West, R. (1993) 'Alternative medicine: prospects and speculation', in N. Black, D. Boswell, A. Gray, S. Murphy and J. Popay (eds), *Health and Disease: A Reader.* Milton Keynes: Open University Press.

Whitehead, S.M. (1987) 'The health divide', in P. Townsend, M. Whitehead and N. Davidson (eds), *Inequalities in Health: The Black Report and the Health Divide.* London: Penguin.

Whitehead, S.M. (2002) *Men and Masculinities: Key Themes and New Directions.* Cambridge: Polity.

Widgery, D. (1991) *Some Lives! A GP's East End.* London: Simon & Schuster.

Wiles, R., Ashburn, A., Payne, S. and Murphy, C. (2004) 'Discharge from physiotherapy following stroke: the management of disappointment', *Social Science and Medicine*, 59: 1263–73.

Wilkinson, R. (1996) *Unhealthy Societies: The Afflictions of Inequality.* London: Routledge.

Wilkinson, R.G. (2002) 'Income inequality, social cohesion, and health: clarifying the theory: A reply to Muntaner and Lynch', in V. Navarro, *The Political Economy of Social Inequalities: Consequences for Health and Quality of Life.* Amityville: New York. pp. 347–65.

Wilkinson, R. (2005) *The Impact of Inequality: How to Make Sick Societies Healthier.* London: Routledge.

Wilkinson, R.G. and Pickett, K. (2009) *The Spirit Level: Why Equality Is Better for Everyone.* London: Penguin.

Williams, S.J. (1999) 'Is anybody there? Critical realism, chronic illness and the disability debate', *Sociology of Health and Illness*, 21 (6): 797–819.

Williams, S.J. (2000) 'Chronic illness as biographical disruption or biographical disruption as chronic illness? Reflections on a core concept', *Sociology of Health and Illness*, 22 (1): 40–67.

Williams, S.J. (2003) *Medicine and the Body*. London: Sage.

Williams, S.J. (2004) 'Bio-attack or panic attack? Critical reflections on the ill-logic of bio-terrorism and biowarfare in late/postmodernity', *Social Theory and Health*, 2: 67–93.

Wilton, T. (2000) *Sexualities in Health and Social Care: A Textbook*. Basingstoke: Open University Press.

Witz, A. (1992) *Professions and Patriarchy*. London: Routledge.

Wogan, P. (2004) 'Deep hanging out: reflections on fieldwork and multisided Andean ethnography', *Identities: Global Studies in Culture and Power*, 11: 129–39.

Woodward, K. (2007) *Boxing, Masculinity and Identity: The 'I' of the Tiger*. London: Routledge.

World Health Organisation (WHO) (1992) *Basic Documents*, 39th edn. Geneva.

World Health Organization (WHO) (2010) *Global Status Report on Noncommunicable Diseases*. Geneva: World Health Organization.

World Health Organization (WHO) (2011) *World Health Statistics*. Geneva: World Health Organization.

Young, I.M. (1980) 'Throwing like a girl: a phenomenology of feminine body comportment motility and spatiality', *Human Studies*, 3 (1).

Young, M. and Willmott, P. (1961) *Family and Kinship in East London*. Harmondsworth: Penguin.

Yuill, C. (2005) 'Marx: capitalism, alienation and health', *Social Theory and Health*, (3): 126–43.

Yuill, C. (2007) 'The body as weapon: Bobby Sands and the Republican hunger strikes', *Sociological Research Online*, 12 (2). www.socresonline.org.uk/12/2/yuill.html.

Yuill, C. (2010) '"The Spirit Level", health inequalities and economic democracy', *International Journal of Management Concepts and Philosophy*, 4(2): 177–93.

Zsembik, B.A. and Fennell, D. (2005) 'Ethnic variation in health and the determinants of health among Latinos', *Social Science and Medicine*, 61 (11): 53–63.

Index

Page numbers in *italics* indicate figures and tables